John James Given

The Truth of Scripture

In Connection with Revelation, Inspiration, and the Canon

John James Given

The Truth of Scripture
In Connection with Revelation, Inspiration, and the Canon

ISBN/EAN: 9783337183417

Printed in Europe, USA, Canada, Australia, Japan

Cover: Foto ©Lupo / pixelio.de

More available books at **www.hansebooks.com**

THE TRUTH OF SCRIPTURE

IN CONNECTION WITH

REVELATION, INSPIRATION, AND THE CANON.

BY

JOHN JAMES GIVEN, Ph.D.,

PROFESSOR OF HEBREW AND HERMENEUTICS IN MAGEE COLLEGE, LONDONDERRY.

EDINBURGH:
T. & T. CLARK, 38 GEORGE STREET.
1881.

PREFACE.

THE present is an age of inquiry. In every department of science and art, of philosophy and theology, of criticism and interpretation, we are required to give a reason for the truths believed and the courses pursued. This within proper limits cannot reasonably be objected to; it is both sensible and scriptural. Sometimes, however, matters are carried to an extreme, and the demand becomes too exacting: but even to the froward we may not show ourselves froward; while we are required to be "ready always to give an answer to every man that asketh us a reason of the hope that is in us, with meekness and fear."

Some of the signs of the times are not a little ominous. In this fast age in which we live, when knowledge is increasing so amazingly and men running to and fro so rapidly, there is an impatience of old beliefs. The brilliant achievements of physical science, not a few of which make themselves palpable by contributing in so many ways to the conveniences and comforts of daily life, naturally create a longing for a similar advance—something of a like striking and startling nature in other departments. It is quite possible, too, that even multiplied ecclesiastical machinery may co-exist with much spiritual leanness. At all events, from many causes, be they what they may, scepticism is unusually rife—it is in the air. That there is a tendency in many quarters to shift the old moorings, or to remove the old landmarks, cannot be denied. What with the unbelief of some openly avowing infidel sentiments, the misbelief of others greedily embracing erroneous views if they only present the aspect of novelty, and the disbelief of many turning aside from the faith of former times, the humble believer is tempted to relax his own firm grasp of truth, and is far too apt to harbour gloomy forebodings about the future. But, fully convinced of the power and prevalence of truth in general, and having firm confidence in the truth of Scripture in particular, we have no just ground for present apprehension or alarm, and nothing whatever to fear for the ultimate result.

Our first duty is to determine our own individual position in relation to the truth of God. We are enjoined to "prove all things, but to hold fast that which is good." Now, as, according to the old saying, life is short and art is long, we must deprecate the idea of always learning and never coming to a knowledge of the truth—of always proving and never actually possessing—of always trying but not yet tenaciously holding what has been already tried. Life is too short for this sort of seesawing. It is our duty as well as privilege to examine the matter thoroughly, searchingly, honestly; but let it be done once for all. What the apostle advises in a particular case, admits a more extended application when he says: "I speak unto wise men, judge ye what I say." When, then, we have duly exercised our judgment in the matter, when we have used all available means for that purpose, and when, under the guidance of God's good Spirit, we have come to a legitimate conclusion on the subject of divine truth itself and of our personal relation to it,—a subject of greatest importance and most vital concern, involving as it does our welfare for time and eternity,—then let us in God's great name and by His grace fearlessly abide the issue.

It then remains to look to the interests of the truth of God in the Church and in the world. The truth of Scripture has been tried and tested thousands of times in the past. In the early ages of Christianity Celsus tried it, Porphyry tried it, Julian tried it; the English infidels in the beginning and middle of the 18th century tried it—Chubb, and Collins, and Tyndal, and Toland, and the rest of them; the French Encyclopedists tried it; the German Illuminati tried it; the infidelity of the 19th century is now trying it—the transcendental philosopher, the scientist, the critic, all try it in turn. It has been often put upon its trial, it has stood many a test, it has passed through many an ordeal; but as it was in the past so it is in the present and ever shall be; again and yet again the enemy comes in like a flood, but the Spirit of the

Lord lifts up a standard against him. Nay, the more the truth of Scripture is searched and sifted the purer it is found, the brighter and clearer it becomes: "The words of the Lord are pure words; as silver tried in a furnace of earth, purified seven times."

We need not wonder when the truth of Scripture is once more attacked anew. Revelation, Inspiration, and the Canon have been assailed, sometimes singly, again collectively. But these fresh assaults are not a whit more formidable than those of former times, nor likely to prove in the least more successful. Now the object of the present treatise is to furnish some weapons of defence, and to indicate the source of many more; it is purely defensive, not aggressive. Where subjects of recent or present discussion are touched on in it, they are dealt with apologetically, not controversially. Reasons for adhering to traditional beliefs are assigned, but no railing accusation is brought against the opponents of those beliefs; for "the wrath of man worketh not the righteousness of God." Besides, this treatise is meant to be merely suggestive and in no sense exhaustive. To treat such subjects as Revelation, Inspiration, or the Canon fully, or, perhaps I should say, satisfactorily, would require a treatise as large or larger than the present for each of them separately. To plain persons, however, who are earnestly seeking truth, I venture to think that this succinct and synoptical treatment, as I may call it, of the subjects indicated, may be of some service, to others it may help to popularise certain topics involving critical difficulties, while to junior students at least it may point out the right way to further and fuller investigation.

On the subject of Revelation several publications of varying excellence are well known and easily accessible; on Inspiration, Lee and Bannerman are standard authorities; while on the Canon of the New Testament, Lardner and Kirchofer and Westcott, with Stuart and Alexander on that of the Old Testament, may be consulted with advantage. From all these the author has derived benefit; while obligations incurred in other quarters will be found duly acknowledged in their proper place.

The great and ultimate end which the author has endeavoured steadily to keep before him is the promotion of a justly appreciative sense of the divine original of Scripture, with a view to the attainment of a sound and enlightened acquaintance with its saving truths, and a cordially sympathetic acceptance thereof; so that he that writes and they who read may be enabled to entertain a good hope by grace, as also to render a right reason for the ground of that hope.

Head and heart must go together here; the affections and intellect must be enlisted at the same time; else the right result is not attained. A man may, like the great Orientalist Gesenius, who did so much for Hebrew learning, be possessed of advanced scholarship and truly critical judgment; and yet, like the same great man, he may be the victim of a cold rationalism, and presume to treat the everlasting verities with a smile or even a sarcasm. You pass, let us suppose, through a lovely district after the shades of evening have fallen on the earth, when the busy world has sunk to rest, and while silence reigns around. The full-orbed moon sheds down her silvery light on field and flood and forest, on hill and valley, on tower and town. The scene is beautiful, but the stillness is death-like; the landscape is charming, but a chilly coldness pervades it; the moonbeams are bright, but there is no warmth nor animation. You pass through the same district in the light of day at the busy hour of noon, when the warm radiance of the summer's sun is beaming on all, brightening all, and beautifying all, and at the same time diffusing warmth throughout the district, quickening the pulses of daily life, and animating the labour of the industrious. What a change! You will say, What an improvement! That landscape seen by the moonbeams may represent divine truth as seen in the clear cold light of rationalistic criticism; but that landscape seen amid the sunshine, is the same truth as it is exhibited by the sanctified criticism of the scholar whose heart has been warmed by the rays of the Sun of righteousness, and whose understanding has been enlightened by the Spirit of the Lord.

J. J. G.

32 CLARENDON STREET, LONDONDERRY,
December 2, 1880.

CONTENTS.

PART I.—REVELATION.

CHAPTER I.

REVELATION AND MIRACLES.

Importance of Revelation—Necessity for Revelation—Possibility of Revelation—Miraculous element in Revelation—Definitions of Miracle—Law of Nature—Scripture names of Miracles—Probability of Miracle—Credibility of Miracles—Tests of Miracle—False Miracles—Character and competency of the witnesses, ... **9**

CHAPTER II.

FULFILMENT OF PROPHECY.

Conditions necessary—Alleged predictions in Secular History—Prophecies relating to Nineveh—Predictions of Nahum—Prophecies concerning the Jews—Prophecies relating to Egypt—Predictions by Ezekiel—Predictions by Jeremiah, ... **43**

CHAPTER III.

ST. JOHN AND THE SYNOPTISTS.

Naturalistic method of Paulus—Mythical method of Strauss—Legendary method of Renan—Two main objections to the genuineness of John's Gospel—Course of events in our Lord's life—Character of His discourses—Difference between John's Gospel and Revelation urged as another objection—External evidence for the genuineness of John's Gospel—Objections answered—Tendency theory of Baur, . . **57**

CHAPTER IV.

RELATION OF THE LINES OF EVIDENCE.

The objective standard—The subjective standard—The requisite subjective element, ... **81**

CHAPTER V.

THE MORALITY OF THE BIBLE.

Moral system of Plato—Moral system of Aristotle—Moral system of the Stoics—Moral system of Epicurus—Moral system of the Bible—Comparison of Ethical systems with Scripture—The principle and practice of each—Experimental evidence, ... 85

PART II.—INSPIRATION.

CHAPTER VI.

NATURE AND PROOF OF PLENARY INSPIRATION.

Statements of Scripture on Inspiration—The Saviour's promised power and presence—Testimony of the Synoptic Gospels—Proofs from the Johannean Gospel—Testimony of the Spirit—Inspiration not Omniscience—The sacred penmen claim Inspiration—Inspiration involved in the use of single terms—Inspiration belongs to both Testaments—Inspiration affirmed of each part of Scripture—Inspiration extends to the less important matters—Quotations in New Testament consistent with Inspiration—Scripture not contradicted by Science, . . 104

CHAPTER VII.

OBJECTIONS EXAMINED.

Supposed contradictions—Diversity differs from discrepancy—Apparent not real discrepancies—Several examples considered—Biblical and classical subjects compared—Difficulties removed—Attacks on inspired truth never successful, ... 137

CHAPTER VIII.

CONFIRMATIONS OF INSPIRED SCRIPTURE.

Section I.—Direct Confirmations.

A peculiar distribution—Inscriptions—Fall of Babylon—Sinaitic peninsula.

Section II.—Indirect Confirmations.

A remarkable adjustment—Starvation a species of combustion—Circulation and vitality of the blood—Striking coincidences in the narrative of St. Paul's voyage, ... 161

CHAPTER IX.

SOLOMONIC AUTHORSHIP OF ECCLESIASTES.

The name of the Book—Certain statements the ground of objection—Account of Solomon's reign in 1 Kings compared with Ecclesiastes—

CONTENTS.

Exceptions taken to the style of language—Statements by the author himself—Hebrew and Christian tradition—Relation of Ecclesiastes to Job and Proverbs—Practical remarks in closing Part II., . . 184

PART III.—THE CANON.

CHAPTER X.

WHAT CONSTITUTES CANONICITY.

Principal theories of canonicity—Genuineness and authenticity—Integrity and credibility, ... 203

CHAPTER XI.

THE NEW TESTAMENT CANON.

Section I.—*Formation of the Canon.*

New Testament writings originated in special circumstances—Connection of Paul and Luke—Connection of Peter and Mark.

Section II.—*The Writers claim Divine Direction.*

Luke's own account of his Gospel history—Ground on which the inspired writers rest their claim.

Section III.—*Evidence of Divine Help.*

The divine sanction of the New Testament writings.

Section IV.—*Authentication and Diffusion of the Inspired Writings.*

Two erroneous allegations refuted—Effect of reading the Epistles in the public assemblies—Apparently exceptional cases.

Section V.—*A more detailed Account of certain Books of New Testament Canon.*

Earliest account of the Gospels by Papias—Renan's account and admissions—The Pauline Epistles—Hebrews—Arguments for and against the Pauline authorship of Hebrews—Conclusion of Hug—Canonicity of 2 Peter—Canonicity of James and Jude.

Section VI.—*Inspiration of New Testament Penmen acknowledged by their Contemporaries.*

Testimony of the sub-apostolic writers—Testimony of Clemens Romanus—Testimony of Polycarp—Testimony of Ignatius—General observations on this part of the subject—Testimony of the Apologists—Testimony of Justin Martyr—Testimony of the opponents of heresies—Testimony of Irenæus—Testimony of Tertullian—Testimony of the Philosophic School of Alexandria—Testimony of Clemens Alexandrinus—Testimony of Origen, ... 213

CHAPTER XII.

OLD TESTAMENT CANON.

Section I.—Fact of Recognition of the Old Testament in the New.

Manner of New Testament quotation—Conclusions therefrom with respect to the fact of recognition.

Section II.—Character of this Recognition.

Section III.—The Means and Method of Identification.

Important statement of Josephus—The same threefold division mentioned by Sirachides—The same threefold division mentioned by Philo—Confirmation from Septuagint—Confirmation from Old Syriac—Confirmation from Melito—Confirmation from Jerome.

Section IV.—The Exclusion of the Apocrypha.

The reasons of that exclusion.

Section V.—The Principle on which Canon formed, and Period of its Close.

Inspiration comprehends two agencies—Various circumstances point to the time of closing the Canon—Ezra's connection with the Canon—Belief of the early Christian Church on Ezra's relation to the Canon—Nehemiah's connection with the Canon—Time of closing the Canon inferred from Sirachides—Time of closing the Canon according to Josephus—Confirmation of same from Pirke Avoth—The same confirmed by Babylonian Gemara, ... 279

CHAPTER XIII.

A SUMMARY OF THE DEUTERONOMIC DISCUSSION.

Analysis of the Book of Deuteronomy—Distinction of Priest and Levite recognised in Deuteronomy—Various arguments in proof thereof—Difference of expressions relating to priestly and Levitical service—Certain conclusions arrived at—Chapter x. 8 of Deuteronomy examined—Rebellion of Korah differed in its object from that of Dathan and Abiram—Implied reference in Deuteronomy xxxiii. 8–10 to different orders among the Levites—The law of the kingdom as stated in Deuteronomy involves reproof—The law of the kingdom acknowledged by Samuel and alluded to by Abimelech—The law of one national sanctuary, with its exceptions—The operation of this law—Abnormal condition of things in Samuel's time—The altar built by Joshua on

CONTENTS.

	PAGE
Mount Ebal—The Deuteronomic law acknowledged in Joshua's time, as inferred from the altar of witness—Supposed discrepancies in minor details,	312
CONCLUSION OF THE WHOLE,	344–346

APPENDIX A.—Probability in favour of Resurrection, . . . 347

APPENDIX B.—The LXX. version of Isaiah liii. compared with the original, ... 349

APPENDIX C.—The Ignatian Epistles, ... 350

APPENDIX D.—Early diffusion of Canonical Scriptures according to several authorities, ... 359

APPENDIX E.—The Epistle of Barnabas, 362

PART I.

REVELATION.

CHAPTER I.

REVELATION AND MIRACLES.

THE importance of the subject of Revelation cannot be readily over-estimated. Issues of the most momentous kind depend upon it. In the absence of the teachings of revelation, or, what amounts to the same thing, in the ignorance or disbelief of those teachings, we are deprived, or voluntarily deprive ourselves, of the only true solution of the great problems of human existence. The only key that promises to unlock the mysteries of our being is flung away or lost. Conjecture is substituted in the stead of certainty; dim anticipation takes the place of well-founded faith, and gloomy foreboding that of Christian hope. Apart from the truth of revelation, we have no reliable information as to man's origin, present position, and future prospects; while to such questions as, What in reality is man? why is he? whence is he? and whither is he going? we are left without any satisfactory answer. Has man a soul distinct from his material organization; and does that soul merely co-exist with the body, or is it capable of a separate existence? Does this present life exhaust the term of his being, and is death an everlasting sleep? Or is there a life beyond, that shall continue while æons lapse and ages roll away? Shall that life, moreover, be one of happiness or misery; and will that state of weal or woe be connected with or dependent on man's course and conduct in the present world? Have the great and good, that benefited their race and were eminently useful in their day and generation, passed hence to heaven; or have they, sad and melancholy thought! faded for ever into "the infinite azure of the past"? What about the beloved dead, endeared to us by every tender tie, lovely in life, and even in death leaving us the fragrance of their memory behind? When in deep distress from sore bereavement—

>"We sigh for the touch of the vanish'd hand,
>And long for the voice that is still,"

is there no hopeful prospect of reunion? Now to these and kindred questions certain analogies may indicate a reply, but in revelation alone is the decided and unfaltering answer found.

The *necessity* of revelation is, I am aware, denied by some who would substitute reason for revelation, shoving the latter out of the way, or setting it in opposition to the former. But against the existence of this supposed antagonism, we feel bound at the very outset strongly to protest. Revelation does not supersede reason, it does not supplant reason, it only supplements reason. If reason be the eye of the mind, then revelation is the telescope that extends immensely its field of vision; if reason be the human arm, then revelation is the heavenly leverage that multiplies its power more than a thousandfold; if reason be the common method of managing quantity and number, then revelation is the higher calculus that grapples with those problems to which the former is inadequate.

We admit to the fullest extent the power of conscience, the light of nature, and the important province of reason, but we affirm their utter incompetence to expound fully man's destiny and duty. We refuse to credit the natural reason of man with power to offer any satisfactory solution of the engima of our being, or to shed light on the nature and character of the Author of that being, setting clearly before our eyes our relationship to Him, and the obligations which that relationship involves. We deny that it can rectify what is abnormal in the latter, or remove the consequences of neglecting the former. And where is the individual with any right insight into the workings of his own spirit, and any proper understanding of his own real wants, who will confidently affirm that reason can fully meet all the needs of his spiritual nature?

Scant and stinted as is man's knowledge of God by nature, it is ever prone to diminish in quantity and deteriorate in quality. What was known of God by natural reason, with its two spheres of operation,—creation without and conscience within,—though sufficient to leave man without excuse, was partial in its nature and unpractical in its effect; for when they knew God, they glorified Him not as God. Their worship and their works alike were worse than even the scantiness of their knowledge would warrant one to expect. There was a reciprocal action between head and heart; faults in the life bred errors in the brain, while errors in the brain reacted by producing faults in the life. After indulging "the lusts of their own hearts," they "changed the truth of God into a lie;" and conversely, when they ceased "to retain God in their knowledge," they commenced "to do those things which are not convenient." Peruse the brightest page in the history of heathendom. Go to Greece at the period when speculation was rifest, when philosophy was most cultivated, and when the mightiest minds were busied with its problems, and what do we find? An unqualified acknowledgment of the impotence of man, without the aid of heaven, to master the mysteries of man's spiritual nature. They are feeling after God, if haply they may find Him; they look out with straining eyes towards the remote heavens, and long for some hint from thence. Plato alludes, once and again, and not obscurely, to man's ignorance of divine things, and the consequent need for a revelation from on high, or a heaven-sent instructor. Socrates consults his *daimonion*, not his conscience, not his guardian spirit or special genius, not his conviction of a divine mission, but a sort of vague presentiment taking the place of, and approximating to, an immediate revelation, though of such a sort as to restrain from, not incite to, action—preventing one course of conduct, and only so far forth prompting to the opposite.

But it may be said that, as the world has grown much older, it has become much wiser; that reason, benefited by the experience of the ages, advanced by modern culture, and schooled by revelation, has outgrown revelation, and is now able to "shift for herself," as the phrase has it. Why, to talk of the severance of reason and revelation at this time of day, is nothing better than the merest myth. Such independence is impossible in the nature of things, for, moulded at first by the teachings of revelation, reason can never shake itself entirely loose from its control. Suppose revelation were discarded, still reason and revelation have so long intermingled in human developments, that what is the product of reason, and what the result of revelation, it would now be most difficult, if not altogether impossible, to discriminate. Certain differential equations become comparatively easy once you separate the variables, but it is just that separation of the variables that constitutes the chief part of the problem, and it is only when the separation is effected that the relation of those variables to each other becomes ascertainable. But what power of calculus can separate entirely the direct effect of reason, and the indirect influence of revelation, and so estimate exactly the varying amount of these two potent factors in human advancement?

Man is sunk in sin; he is in the darkness and shadow of death. He is given to idolatry, prone to superstition, while his heart is deceitful above all things, and desperately wicked. He cannot restore himself to the divine favour, or renew himself in the divine image. In his struggle against sin he cannot subdue it, or save himself from it. By nature he is not only morally impotent, but a stranger to holiness. Thus the light is dim and the power weak. Again, the all but universal acknowledgment of sin, and the many diverse expedients resorted to in all the lands of heathendom, while they bear witness to the existence of conscience, do at the same time prove its variations and errors, and consequent need of something higher and better to rectify its aberrations, remove its erroneous judgments, and purify the stream at the very fountainhead. The mirror is there, but the silvering is so impaired that the reflections are always inexact and often most defective. While thus the intellect is darkened by error and the conscience dimmed by sin, while nature gives some notion of God's goodness but speaks nothing of His grace, and while reason and philosophy can raise no effectual barrier against the power as well as ruinous effects of iniquity, the only resource is revelation making known the great redemption—God's remedy for sin.

Wherever sin precedes, misery follows; God has so wedded them that man cannot divorce them, and where is there any redress for the misery of man? Human reason, when brought to the highest acme of perfection under the tuition of philosophy, has proved perfectly powerless. The most it can do is to opiate the sense or petrify the feelings; or, when this fails, the wretched sufferer plunges headlong into the whirlpool of dissipation, that he may forget for a while his misery, or in some sort mitigate his woe. Again we are driven back to revelation as setting before us the only refuge from all the ruin that sin has wrought.

But what of death? Even the wisest of the ancient sages and the father of several of the old philosophies, in the close of his address to his judges, and in the near prospect of his dissolution, is reported to have said: "It is now time to depart,—for me to die, for you to live. But which of us is going to a better state is unknown to every one but God." The most eminent of those sages speak of and try to argue for the immortality of the soul, but they evince a lurking misgiving about the matter, while there is a lingering hesitancy in most of their utterances on the subject. They represent it as an old tradition, and qualify it by such expressions as "according as we are told," or "if the things told us be true." But instead of calmly and certainly reposing in it, they resort to the alternative of an utter extinction of being, or a state of entire insensibility. Even Cicero, who reflects so largely the sentiments of the most enlightened among the Greek philosophers, and who in the first book of his Tusculan Questions enumerates various considerations in favour of the soul's immortality, yet scarce ventures to decide whether the soul dies with the body or survives it; or, in case of its survival, he cannot determine whether that survival be temporary or perpetual, not advancing beyond a conjecture, and concluding the whole with the most undisguised avowal of extreme uncertainty, when he says in one place: "Which of these opinions is true some god must determine; it is an important question for us which has the most appearance of truth;"

and again in his peroration, at the close: "For if that last day does not occasion an entire extinction, but a change of abode only, what can be more desirable? and if it, on the other hand, destroys and absolutely puts an end to us, what can be preferable to the having a deep sleep fall on us in the midst of the fatigues of life, and being thus overtaken, to sleep to eternity?"

But we may put this part of our subject into a few sentences, which may serve as a summary of the whole.

By all that irrepressible yearning of the human spirit after God, for man must have a God, whether true or false; by all that is incorrect and uncertain in human imaginings about the nature and being of God; by all those unsatisfied cravings of man's soul for communion with God, and by all those unauthorized and often unhallowed modes of worship, and more than questionable means of man's devising for securing such communion; by all that confirmation which the teachings of natural reason required, and by all that enlargement which those teachings, even if things had remained as at the beginning, would make probable,—by all these weighty considerations, the conviction must force itself on any unprejudiced mind, that revelation is an undeniable necessity. Then, when we reflect on the sad departure and alienation from God brought about by the introduction of evil, while the existence of evil is something that cannot be gainsaid, and that man cannot by the flickering light and feeble power of reason recover himself from that state of degradation; that all the while he cannot feel at ease within, unless some means of expiation or some method of satisfaction be resorted to; that, moreover, he finds in his own moral consciousness a strange dualism, so that, notwithstanding all his love and longings for the right, he is utterly unable to resist a tyrant power of wrongdoing that so often dominates and brings him into thraldom; that defective as is his knowledge, his practice is yet in arrear of that knowledge, and that, through this discord of his daily life, guilt is accumulating, while, worst of all, he lacks the right way of atoning for the past, and the proper power of elevating himself above his evil tendencies for the future; in other words, that he is as little able to regenerate as to redeem himself,—by such reflections as these the conviction of the needfulness of revelation is immensely strengthened. Add to this, that, just as in the incertitudes of his condition there is nothing that can give him assurance or inspire him with well-grounded confidence, so amid the miseries of his state there is nothing to bring him that consolation and comfort of which he stands so sorely in need; and that, above all, when with the instinctive love of life he has to face dissolution and blank despair, or if he carries forward his view beyond the precincts of the tomb, there is the dread of something after death rather than any element of hope or prospect of happiness. Put all these together, and the greatest opponent of revelation must have the persuasion, though he may be slow to make the admission, that above and beyond his natural reason man needs some communication from a higher and better world, some radiance shed from heaven on our mortal life and strife, something to encourage us by making known deliverance from sin here, and something to cheer us by the hope of life and immortality hereafter.

Let us now consider the *possibility* of a revelation, for this has been denied. Can that God, who is absolute and infinite, make communication of Himself to finite and limited humanity? Or can man, who is so limited and finite, comprehend it? If a complete communication of the infinite to the finite were the question, we might hesitate about the answer; but here and now we only know in part, and see through a glass darkly. And while the Infinite One, still infinite and supramundane, is pleased to reveal Himself, there is on His part a self-limitation to which He condescends, whether it be through angelic medium, or human form, or physical phenomenon, to such an extent that His back parts only are discernible, for He has expressly declared: "My face shall not be seen." On the other and human side, though man cannot comprehend, yet he may apprehend Him who is unapproachable and invisible. Nor yet is the unchangeableness of the Eternal in any way compromised by such communication, for in His plan and purpose from eternity He had perfect foreknowledge of all, and made proper and previous arrangement for all, so that, owing to that prearranged harmony, no alterations that man's defection might make necessary could possibly interfere with Him who is ever the same, and whose very name of *I am that I am* bespeaks His nature to be the same yesterday, to-day, and for ever. And so, while in one aspect He is the self-communicating One, in another He is still the unchangeable, as He is the incomprehensible One. But could those that received such a communication be certain that it was an objective communication from without that they received, and not a subjective suggestion from within? Here we encounter the difficulty of Kant and Fichte. It might be enough to say that surely God, when He made the communication at all, could make it readily recognisable, and certify it to the recipients. But the external miraculous event that usually accompanied the communication, sometimes filling them with awe, sometimes prostrating them to the earth, left no room to doubt about its objectivity; while predictions stretching away into the far distant future, and revelations unfathomable even by the recipients, could not possibly be the product of their own mental powers.

But now that we are face to face with miracle, we proceed to consider the objections urged against the miraculous element in revelation. In recent times the objections urged against the Bible as containing, or more correctly, as being a revelation from God, come from two distinct quarters. The objectors of the present day resemble two detachments of the same army, coming from two distant points and attacking different portions of the outworks, yet concentrating their chief and combined assault on the citadel. The great aim of scepticism now-a-days, whether the scepticism of certain philosophers or that of some biblical critics, is to eliminate the *supernatural* from Scripture; and if they succeed in eliminating the supernatural, they unquestionably eviscerate the whole.

Now the objection which the opponents of a revelation from God, such as we believe the Bible to be, seem to consider the strongest and urge with greatest force, is the *miraculous* element embodied in, and if really existing, establishing such revelation. But as the term miracle has been very variously defined, sometimes with more and sometimes with less accuracy, it may not be amiss to glance at some of those definitions. The well-known statement of Thomas Aquinas, that miracles are wrought "præter naturam, supra naturam, et contra naturam," is still maintained by many, though not a few omit or lay less stress on the *contra*. Some take high ground, and speak of a miracle as a violation, or suspension, or even transgression, of a law of nature; others call it a deviation from the established order of the material world. "A miracle," says Butler, "is relative to a course of nature, and implies somewhat different from it considered as being so." Again, there are those who regard it as an exercise of superhuman power; as commonly understood, it is a sensible event produced by the direct volition of God; while a recent acute and able writer has hazarded a definition new and original, at least in expression, to the effect that it is "an immediate transition from a volition to an external result." Though we strongly suspect that none of these definitions would satisfy the logical laws of definition, yet, since we shall have occasion to notice some of these as we proceed, we may be satisfied with a description, if not a definition, of miracle amply sufficient for our purpose. It is a Scriptural one, and from the lips of a Jewish ruler, namely, "works which no man can do except God be with him." There may be wonders in nature which form exceptions to ordinary experience, there may be marvels in art which startle by their exceeding strangeness, there may be interpositions of Providence seemingly special and very singular; but none of all these, however remarkable, can be considered miraculous. In miracle proper there is something that impresses the senses of man while it obviously bespeaks the power of God; there is a work of power, and a prophetic word to notify it; there is a command and a consequence without any apparent intermediate agency to link them together; and all in furtherance of a divine purpose or in proof of a divine mission. When Augustine defines a miracle in the words, "miraculum voco quidquid arduum aut insolitum supra spem vel facultatem mirantis apparet," and when he gives the following explanation of the miracle at Cana: "ipse fecit vinum in nuptiis qui omni anno hoc facit in vitibus; illud autem non miramur quia omni anno fit, assiduitate amisit admirationem," he certainly diminishes the improbability of miracle, but just in the same proportion he weakens its distinctive element. If miracle be only an acceleration of natural processes or a more rapid movement among secondary causes, what is gained in probability is lost in power, while the disturbing force still remains to be accounted for.

But it is argued that a miracle is impossible, or improbable, or incredible, or all combined. Any one who has marked the tendency of modern thought must have observed, that while the argument against such miraculous interposition as a revelation implies has been shifted off the old line, still it keeps alongside of that line with more or less closeness of proximity. The sceptical argument of philosophy has advanced in substance little if anything beyond the point at which Hume left it. That argument of Hume, more celebrated than sound, and more specious than solid, whether in its original form or with subsequent modifications, requires to be dealt with in detail. We need not quote his words, so well known, and forming, as they do, a sort of infidel apostles' creed on the subject of miracle. The gist of them is, that universal experience vouches for the constancy of the laws of nature, but a miracle is a violation of those laws, and so contrary to such experience. But this argument, whether as advanced by Hume or adduced with modern variations, has never, we conceive, been so presented as to be free from fallacy. When it is asserted that a miracle is contrary to universal experience, there is surely more than a legitimate postulate; for if experience against the miraculous be universal, that experience thus presumed to be universal admits no exception, and so denies at the very onset, before argument and without proof, the past or possible existence of the miraculous. If this be not a plain *petitio principii*, or sheer begging of the question, it were difficult to find an instance of that species of sophism. But there is an implicit and undue assumption in the word *contrary* itself, for what is the real import of a miracle being contrary to experience? Why, for example, if one individual out of the many usually present when our Lord performed His miracles came forward and solemnly averred that, though present at the time when and in the place where an alleged miracle was wrought, and though in the full exercise of all his faculties and with every means of observation, he had witnessed no such miraculous occurrence, the miracle would no doubt be contrary to his experience; but no such case is once hinted at even by the bitterest enemies of Christ. One and all they acknowledged the fact of the miracle, however erroneously they might attempt to account for it. Further, a miracle is not contrary to even your experience or mine; for unless we had been circumstanced as in the case just supposed, and unless we had been actually present at the performance of an alleged miracle, and, with every capacity for examining and facility for testing it, had failed to observe or realize its existence, then and only then would it be truly contrary to our experience. Surely this *want* of experience on our part is no contradiction of or contrariety to the experience of others; it is no counter-experience, neither can the negative evidence of persons distant both in time and space from the scene of a miracle ever overthrow the positive testimony of persons who were present on the spot.

Again, it is alleged that a miracle is a *violation* of the laws of nature. But such language is loose, unguarded, and highly objectionable. If the same cause, operating under the self-same conditions, produced in succession or at intervals two different and contrary effects, there would in such a case be a violation of a law of nature and the occurrence of something unnatural. If, for example, the law of chemical decomposition, instead of causing the putrefaction of a corpse, actually produced the opposite effect of preventing it, there would be a violation, that is, a reversal of an ordinary law. A milder way of putting it is, that a miracle is a *suspension* of a law of nature, but it does not even amount to that; and this statement of the matter is little less chargeable with error than the preceding. Instead, however, of a suspension of the law of cause and effect, there is a *superadded* factor in the case, or what Brown calls the introduction of a new force. Mill admits and so far agrees with Brown. "A miracle," says the former, "is no contradiction to the law of cause and effect; it is a new effect; it is a new effect supposed to be produced by the introduction of a new cause." No doubt he neutralizes that admission when he denies the probability of the existence of such a cause, but of this anon. When, then, a new force supervenes, it controls, or checks, or counteracts the force or forces previously operating, so that the resultant takes a new and different direction. In such a case there is no violation of a law of nature; it is only a physical force that is overcome by the introduction of one more powerful.

But the great question, after all, is not how this new force acts, but how comes it to act at all? By whom is it introduced? Here we at once admit that its introduction must be referred to the direct interposition of the divine will. In the forces that everywhere operate around us there is a well-known gradation. Statical equilibrium is overborne by dynamical force; chemical action controls mechanical forces, whether dynamical or statical; vital force, again, checks chemical action; the brain issues a mandate along some efferent motor nerve, and muscular motion ensues. Not only does the human will thus originate muscular action, but that muscular action interferes with physical forces, so that the stone, which by the force of gravity lay quiescent on the ground, is hurled by the hand through the air, and still the law of gravity is not thereby nullified, for the otherwise onward direction of the stone is changed by it into a parabolic curve. And we all know how frequently moral force counteracts and overcomes physical. Thus the higher realm ever rules over the lower. In like manner the divine will, as it is most natural to expect, dominates over all; and so it either supplies or becomes itself the superadded factor in the case of miraculous operation. When the "waters were a wall" to Israel in their passage through the sea, we do not need to suppose that the atmospheric pressure was either lessened or entirely lifted off the surface of the waters, neither are we to understand that the law of gravity was even suspended; we have only to conceive that the force of gravity which tends to spread out waters laterally was held in abeyance by an equivalent to the force of cohesion which keeps a wall of stone stable and erect; but that equivalence must ultimately resolve itself into the will or word of the Almighty.

Whatever notion, then, we form of a cause, whether we

understand it to be an immediate and invariable antecedent, as Brown does, though he seems to include something more when he admits the *aptitude* of a cause to precede; or whether we agree with Mill, who makes it an invariable and unconditional antecedent; or whether we take it to import invariableness of sequence without any notion of efficiency or force, events being conjoined, not *connected*, as Hume does; or understand, with Hamilton, the concurrence of at least two causes to every effect; or affirm, with a living metaphysician of the Scotch school, that " in a cause there is a substance acting according to its powers and properties," while " in every effect there is a change or a new object,"—we have in miracle not an effect without a cause, nor an effect without an adequate cause, nor an effect for which we can assign a natural cause; but an effect of which the cause is supernatural, or more correctly, superhuman, and so traceable to the direct agency or immediate will of God.

Again, the expression *law of nature* is used in a very vague and wide sense. A law of nature is the order of sequences as observed by us, or the method in which phenomena succeed one another; but a law of nature does not tell us who established that particular order, nor explain to us what arranged the mode of this phenomenal succession and made it what it is. Much less has a law of nature any power of this kind itself. And yet we invest it with a motive power, and thus lose sight of the agent in the law according to which he acts. Behind these laws of nature, then, there is a power that makes the phenomena what they are—that has arranged these series of sequences, appointing the system of causes and effects, which sequences men observe and classify, and then call *laws* —in a word, that originates these second causes, Himself the *causa causarum* or great First Cause of all. If this be acknowledged, and acknowledged it must be, except by that Atheism which outrages common sense, stultifies human reason, insults high heaven, and fearfully frustrates the uplooking soul of man, then the possibility of miracles cannot be consistently denied. Once admit the existence of a personal God, and the possibility of a miracle is undeniable, for you thereby acknowledge the existence of a being who has the power, if He possess the will or have a reason to work it,—who, if the occasion be great enough, the circumstances urgent enough, and the end high enough, has, beyond a peradventure, the ability to perform it. Once admit that those regular recurrences in nature, which men name laws, were in the beginning ordained by God,—that the course of nature, as we have it, was constituted in conformity to His will from the first,—and we do not see how you can reasonably deny the possibility of divine intervention at any subsequent stage; for you thus admit the existence of a power above nature and independent of nature, and consequently capable of exercising control over nature, so as to add to or take from, or otherwise modify at pleasure His own workmanship. Otherwise you involve yourself in the contradiction of admitting omnipotence, and then setting limits to the exercise of omnipotent power, and so circumscribing the sphere of its operation as to confine it within certain bounds. Or you concede to Him power to create, but not to change anything He has created,—to command into existence, but not to control the objects made to exist. What is this but to own the existence of an omnipotent workman, and at the same time to deny Him the power or debar Him from the privilege of ever after interfering with His own work?

Further, men speak of the uniformity of physical laws as something rigidly fixed and absolutely unyielding, and seem to regard them as rules that allow no exception. But is it really so that these laws admit no relaxation, and that these rules know no deviation? Is it reasonable to suppose that the Creator, whose will is law to all the universe, subjected His freedom to natural law, or laid such restraint on His own operations as to preclude the possibility of relaxing any law or modifying any rule, even in view of some great moral end, or in order to effect some most beneficent and salutary purpose? Such a supposition is, we think, at variance not only with reason, but with facts. It is a well-known principle that *cold contracts and heat expands;* but this law, general as it is, has its limitation; and to this principle, well established as it is, there is a most salutary exception. As water cools down it contracts till it reaches 4° centigrade. But once this point of maximum density is reached the law is just reversed, and expansion sets in and increases rapidly as the freezing-point is approached; and while the freezing process goes on the expansion proceeds at the rate of 10 per cent. Why is this? Is it a mere freak of nature, or a chance change of natural law? Or is this reversion of the ordinary series of occurrences due to the government of God? Few will hesitate to assign it to the beneficent action of the latter, which retains the ice on the surface in consequence of its being lighter and keeps it from sinking down layer after layer, and so preserves the whole from being frozen, and thus prevents our lakes and rivers in winter from becoming solid masses of ice and our climate completely Arctic. Need it be thought strange, then, if for purposes of still higher beneficence the Creator should interject exceptional effects among the ordinary sequences of nature?

But this leads us to consider the *probability* of miracle. Is a miracle probable? Granting it to be possible, is its occurrence probable? In the divine government there are two departments, the material and the moral; but the moral is decidedly superior to the material, as moral agents occupy a higher sphere than material forces, and moral ends take precedence of material effects. Surely, then, it is at least supposable that the lower should serve the higher, and that the material should be made subservient to the moral. When the Framer of this universe established that uniformity to which we are accustomed, and which is so advantageous, He was not likely to overlook the mighty magnitude of moral ends, and so He comprehended both in His original scheme, while, with that wonderful economy of energy which characterizes all His operations, He appointed certain departures from the former as beneficial to the furtherance of the latter. The presumption would thus be for rather than against such miraculous intervention. Indeed, the probability of miracle falls little, if at all, short of the highest point to which probability can reach. It rests on the surest grounds, and combines many elements of strength; so that whatever be the presumption against miracles from the general uniformity of nature, or from the supposed presence of the same identical forces in nature to the exclusion of all supernatural interference, that presumption is entirely overborne by the probabilities of the case when some great moral end is to be attained, and when that end is not only most easily and effectually attainable by miracle, but cannot be attained at all without miracle.

If all the efforts of philosophy had failed to make man what he ought to be, what he feels he is capable of being, and what the instincts of his own moral nature tell him he was designed to become; if the world of man was to be kept from becoming a total wreck and a terrible failure; if truths, which unaided human reason could never reach, were to be made known to humankind; if, in short, man was to be redeemed, regenerated, and made for ever free as well as finally happy,—a supernatural communication was indispensable, while at the same time a revelation of this kind required, as foremost among its evidences, the unmistakable certificate of supernatural signs. And though we do not leave out of sight the special and subordinate purposes served by miracles as specimens of the Saviour's exercise of sympathy towards the distressed and compassionate relief of the suffering, as symbols of spiritual benefits, and as forestalments of the future restitution of all things, still we recognise their great and primary purpose to be this evidential use. In it we find the true point of contact between miracle and revelation, and the real relation in which they stand to each other.

A teacher sent from God required divine credentials to certify the authority with which He was invested, and to prove the commission which He professed to bear; miraculous interpositions were needed to authenticate His mission, and vouch for the superhuman nature of His message to man. The divine mission thus authenticated, and the divine authority of the teacher once guaranteed, the truth of the doctrines followed as a necessary and inevitable corollary. Accordingly, the possibility and the probability of miracle being once established, the miracles not only recorded in, but interwoven with, the contents of the Bible throughout, stamp divinity on its teachings, and become a most material witness to it as the truth of God. It was from a similar standpoint, and in a similar light, that the Jewish ruler Nicodemus viewed miracle when he said, "Rabbi, *we* know that Thou art a teacher come from God: for no man can do these miracles that Thou doest, except God be with him." Nor was it an expression of mere individual opinion on his part, it was a statement of the common belief in the validity of authentication by miracle; neither was that belief without foundation in fact, for the Saviour's own positive declaration was on this wise: "The works which the Father hath given me to finish, the same works that I do, bear witness of me that the Father hath sent me." His definite answer, and conclusive proof of Messiahship, was to the same effect: "If Thou be the Christ, tell us plainly. Jesus answered them, 'I told you, and ye believed not; the works that I do in my Father's name, they bear witness of me.'" Here, then, we perceive that miracle is appealed to as evidence of a divine commission in general —as setting the seal of divinity on the Saviour's mission as a whole. But this is not all. Miracle is also employed to attest a particular fact asserted or a single truth communicated. Thus our Lord, after saying to the Jews: "But that ye may know that the Son of man hath power on earth to forgive sins," proceeds in proof of this particular statement to perform a miraculous cure, saying to the paralytic: "Rise, take up thy bed and walk." A miracle was thus not merely a פֶּלֶא separated by its very singularity from all ordinary and occurrent events; and a τέρας producing wonder in its subjective effect on the mind and arresting attention; it was objectively a δύναμις, a manifestation of power resulting from the forthputting of superhuman energy and of divine interposition, either immediately without or mediately through the agency of man; while it was ever a σημεῖον, a sign of a higher power—a token of the finger of God, and so a pledge to faith of a heaven-bestowed commission and of a divinely authenticated ambassador. Here, then, from the terms applied to miracle, we learn the essence of a miracle, its exceptional nature, its effect, and its end. Its essence is superhuman power (δύναμις); its exceptional nature consists in its being singled out and separated from all ordinary events (פֶּלֶא); its effect on the minds of men is wonderment (τέρας); its end is to serve as a sign (σημεῖον) of divine power attesting a divine commission, and giving it the sanction of divine authority. Hence we might frame a definition of miracle similar in substance to that above noted as commonly given.

But some will still be inclined to ask, Is it likely that God, departing from His general manifestations in nature, would thus specially interpose? Would it not argue a defect in the system of nature, or an afterthought in the arrangements of the Deity? Or what, after all, is so vastly important in the interests of man as to warrant such exceptional interference on the part of the Almighty? What is the *dignus vindice nodus?* To an honest deist—a consistent believer in theism—these questions are capable of a tolerably easy answer. Such an one, professing as he does faith in a personal God, and disbelieving the eternity of matter, cannot fail to perceive and acknowledge that such interposition has actually occurred. The existence of the world is a palpable proof of it; for at whatever period creation took place, it was an instance of such interposition, originating in a fiat of the Creator's will; or rather, it was a series of such interpositions, for every creative act, by which a distinct type of being was called into existence, must be regarded as proceeding therefrom. The extinct tribes and races of which geology informs us are examples of the same, for whensoever they existed, it was by a miracle of creation calling them into being at the first.

Omnipotence, moreover, is not the sole attribute of Deity; He is omniscient as well as omnipotent; while He possesses *moral* attributes beside. Knowing, then, the end from the beginning, He foresaw the crisis at which such special miraculous interferences or exercises of personal divine power would be needful, and provided for it accordingly; He knew the exact spot where they would fit in, and arranged it. It was no slack afterthought, but a prudent and provident forethought. It was only a part of the general plan, and contemplated in the original purpose, so that, whatever deviation from the order of the material world might occur, it was in strict conformity with and regular promotion of the law of the moral universe. It was no readjusting of a machine which by reason of its own imperfection had been thrown out of gear—it was no mending of an original flaw in the physical universe, nor remedying of an inherent defect in the system of nature. The object was not physical, but spiritual. True, the entrance of evil created confusion, where all had been not merely good, but very good before; man's sin disturbed the good order that had prevailed at the beginning. Hence it was that the direct interposition of the Creator became needful to remove the disorder which the wrongdoing of the creature had occasioned, and to rectify the consequently abnormal state of things. Thus it came to pass that the supernatural was an expedient rendered necessary to correct and counteract the unnatural. By man left to the freedom of his will came sin, by sin came death; hence arose the necessity for divine intervention, not to repair any physical deficiency, but to redeem from or visit with retribution moral delinquency. And who will pretend to affirm that the Creator, after completing the work of creation, was bound to tie up His hands and isolate Himself from His works? Nay, we are so busied about the works themselves and their method, that we frequently fail to recognise the worker; is there not then a plausibility, to say the least, in the conception that He should deem it needful to vindicate His authority over His own workmanship, assert His supremacy over natural law, and manifest in a manner unmistakable His almighty sovereignty? And if so, would not miracle be the most obvious way of making the supremacy of His power recognisable by man? Again, who will deny His competency to introduce a parenthetic clause into the records of divine procedure, or to interpose certain exceptional circumstances at the time and place at once of prevision and provision? The will of man can interfere to mould and modify material forces, as also the action or direction of these forces; much more can the will of God. If the revelation of the divine will be an object of paramount importance to our race; if the benefits thence resulting be enormous in amount and everlasting in duration; if the Christian religion be a boon of unspeakable value to mankind; if that religion be an embodiment of the doctrines taught and of the duties enjoined in the Bible, and if the doctrines and duties which that blessed book inculcates could not be established without the evidence and attestation of miracle; if the soul of man be capable of infinite pleasure or incalculable pain, and if that state of pain or pleasure be connected with knowledge of and obedience to the divine will; if, in a word, the human soul be the most priceless jewel in all creation,—then surely there is an object well worthy of and fully warranting divine miraculous intervention in order to make known the means of that soul's salvation. Neither can it be deemed derogatory even to the dignity of Deity—with reverence be it spoken—to interpose, not mediately but immediately, not by proxy but in person, not through the intervention of second causes but by direct efficiency or divine causality, for such a grand and glorious consummation. Would a general be chargeable with fickleness or otherwise censurable, if, in a great emergency, instead of sending messages or issuing orders through subordinates as usual, he went from regiment to regiment reconnoitring the field, and delivered his commands in person, changing at the same time where necessary the disposition of his troops? Neither is that householder chargeable with fickleness, who takes his journey into a far country, leaving a trusty caretaker to look after his concerns and to superintend the domestics; but, on ascertaining that all things are not as they should be, returns of a sudden, supersedes that officer, and for a time assumes his functions, discharging the duties himself.

But though *possible* and *probable*, are miracles *credible?* Here there is a balancing of opposite improbabilities—the improbability of the occurrence of the miracle on the one hand, and the improbability of the falsehood of the testimony on the other. In dealing with this part of the subject, Hume is guilty of a double unfairness. He vastly over-estimates the improbability of miracles by keeping out of view the almighty power of the Creator, the greatness of His interest in the creatures He has made, and the supreme importance of the purpose to be served. On the other hand, he greatly under-estimates the probability of the falsehood of the testimony, by stating that we are under no necessity whatever to account for the existence of the testimony or of the history so attested. And yet necessity is surely laid on those, who deny the ground commonly assigned and currently believed for that testimony or that history, to suggest a substitute, and one, too, in full accordance with the recognised principles of human action and human conduct. With the antecedent unlikelihood we have already dealt, and now proceed to inquire whether and to what extent the strength of the evidence is sufficient to overcome the resistance to belief, which the uncommonness of a miraculous event presents. That there is no *a priori* impossibility, and that it is a question of evidence, even Mill admits, when he says: " That divine interference with nature could be proved, if we had the same sort of evidence for it which we have for human interferences." In passing we need not do more than advert to the general value of testimony, the absence of which would leave the past a blank, expunging the facts of history; while it would put an effectual stop to the transactions of the present, by destroying the ground on which the commerce and communion of man with man are based.

Here, again, we are confronted by another statement of Hume, namely, that no testimony can prove a miracle; for, while there is unvarying experience for the constancy of nature, there is no unvarying experience for the truth of testimony. Campbell's refutation of this part of that philosopher's reasoning has been pretty generally acquiesced in; still one cannot help thinking, that at the commencement of that refutation he reasons somewhat loosely and dwells too long on a matter of secondary importance, so that the strictures of Chalmers were not quite uncalled for. Yet a careful examination will be most likely to lead us to the opinion that those strictures themselves are also and equally faulty, though in a different way. You may go a certain length with both, without fully agreeing with either. This much, at all events, can scarcely be denied, that while, in opposition to Hume, belief in testimony does not originate in experience, yet experience corrects that belief and calls forth the exercise of discrimination, producing in one direction *diffidence*, according to Campbell, and in the opposite direction *confidence*, according to Chalmers—that is to say, diffidence in one class of testimony, and confidence in another and different class,

When the constancy of nature is set over against the truth of testimony, these, as it appears to us, are heterogeneous, and, like quantities that have no common measure, remain incommensurable. But it is alleged that unvarying experience established the one, while there is no such experience to support the other. Here is a fallacy of ambiguity in the use of the term experience; for if the experience meant be *personal*, experience in that sense is so restricted in time and space, that it would be absurd to speak of it as meeting the case; if *universal* experience be intended, we have already seen that the argument labours under the fatal defect of making the conclusion simply synonymous with or a mere reassertion of one of the premisses, and so amounts only to denial instead of disproof. This universal experience, moreover, combines at once a preposterous presumption and a positive misstatement of fact—a presumption that the evidence of experience has been completely exhausted, that all the causes in the whole series have been ascertained to the exclusion of every other, either possible or assignable, that there has been a perfect induction; while the misstatement consists in quietly ignoring or boldly pushing aside the unimpeachable and unfaltering testimony of the most trustworthy witnesses on the other side. There remains yet another supposition about the nature of the experience meant—it may be the *general*, not universal experience of mankind. But how is this general experience itself ascertained? Only by the testimony of people who have lived at different periods and in different parts of the world. Such experience is nothing more or less than testimony put upon record, and so it is virtually a balancing not of experience against testimony, nor yet of testimony, in the sense of contradictory, against testimony, but of testimony for one series of events against testimony for other events imagined to be incompatible or at variance with the former.

But, after all, how do we come by this notion of nature's uniformity, about which we hear so much? This, in our opinion, we are not entitled to identify, as some do, with the universality of the law of causation. It is well known that the causal judgment, or the belief that every effect has a cause, has been variously accounted for. You may regard it as experiential or intuitional in its origin. You may treat it as a result of experience, or as a condition of intelligence. You may, according to one school, make it a product of induction, or explain it by custom. Or you may view it, in accordance with the other, as an original and necessary principle, or even as contingent, leaving out the idea of necessity, with Brown; or you may analyze it into sheer mental impotency to conceive absolute commencement, as Hamilton does. With Kant, you may regard the causal judgment to be one of the forms of the understanding—one of the conditions under which one must think; or you may look upon the notion as a particular property acquired by facts from their peculiar connection. You may even take sides with Comte, the founder of the Positive Philosophy, and confine yourself to the classification of phenomena, rejecting altogether the search after causes as vain. Still nature will reassert herself, "*Naturam expellas furca tamen usque recurret*," and you will, consciously or unconsciously, voluntarily or involuntarily, act in accordance with that law of mind which in reviewing phenomena makes one a cause and another an effect. And here it may be observed that Mozley admits a serious flaw into his defence of miracles, when making common cause with the positivist he adopts his principle, to the effect that "we see no causes in nature—that the whole chain of physical succession is a rope of sand." It is to be regretted that by this admission instead of strengthening he weakens his argument. On the other hand, when Tyndall affirms that "nature has never been crossed by spontaneous action," and that it is bound in "the bonds of fate," his assertion is a contradiction of fact. It is refuted by the proportion between the surface and the progressive population of our globe, by the geological changes under the crust of the earth, and by the connection of our planet with the great centre of the solar system. But it matters not which system you follow, or what theory of causation you adopt, as far as belief in the uniformity of nature is concerned, for it must rest on other ground. We cannot help believing in the universality of causation, but our belief in the uniformity of nature does not rise above an expectation, for I cannot tell whether the same causes, and under the same circumstances, that exist to-day, will continue in existence to-morrow. Though I believe in the universality of causation, I cannot infer from that the recurrence of to-morrow's light, because I cannot be sure of the continuance of the self-same cause, and under the self-same conditions. My confidence in the uniformity of nature is a kind of mechanical reflecting of the future in the mirror of the past, it is a sort of natural impulse, it is an instinctive expectation that the future will resemble the past—the known the unknown; in any case, it is more akin to instinct than to reason. But when we have the record of trustworthy witnesses to past occurrences, the appeal is to our reason; the language of that appeal is tantamount to "I speak unto wise men, judge ye what I say." Which then, in the balancing of probabilities, deserves greater consideration—the instinct or the reason, the impulse or the evidence? Surely in such a case, if the appeal of testimony to reason be sufficiently strong, the unreason must give way to reason, the impression to rational belief.

But the very author who hazards the assertion that miracle is incapable of proof from testimony, by a strange inconsistency not only recedes from that position, but makes an admission of the very opposite. He supposes a case of miraculous darkness of eight days' duration, so supported by testimony that "philosophers, instead of doubting of that fact, ought to receive it for certain." So it happens not unfrequently that men tear to pieces with their own hand the flimsy spider-like web they had woven, whether it is that in their better moments the intellectual vision becomes clearer, or that conscience proves more potent than their creed.

But the matter may be disposed of in another way, and the whole argument, so to speak, put into a nutshell as follows:—

Two courses lay open to Hume. One was to show on *a priori* grounds the impossibility of miracle. But instead of pursuing this method, he takes the contrary course, and admits, as we have just seen, the possibility of miracle. The other was to prove by *a posteriori* evidence the non-occurrence of miracle; but this he does not attempt. Instead of *a posteriori* argument of this kind he employs two assumptions, and these assumptions are made to do double duty. They are meant to set aside his admission of the *a priori* possibility of miracle, and so the concession is only verbal and then virtually revoked; and to serve at the same time as a substitute for the *a posteriori* argument.

At the first blush of the thing the admission looks generous and fair, but it is soon seen to resemble a gift offered with one hand, while the other prevents acceptance. It is thus, if not actually withdrawn, at least practically nullified. The argument *a posteriori* is quietly presumed to be needless and superfluous. The two assumptions deemed so potent by Hume are, (1) that uniform experience is a full disproof of miracle; but this uniformity or universality of experience is just the matter in dispute, namely, Is the experience of every one, without any exception, opposed to miracle? Besides, this uniformity of experience includes the aggregate of all individual experiences, comprehending all the events of human history, embracing all the phenomena that have taken place on earth, for a single exception would vitiate the whole—in fact, an exhaustive induction of all particulars. The question of important exceptions is thus shirked or shelved. Now, that there have been exceptions, is alleged as the experience of a respectable minority of men; and it must not be forgotten that there can only be a minority in the case, for the experience of the majority would transfer an event out of the list of miracle altogether into that of ordinary occurrences. The (2) assumption is, that a miracle has never been observed in any age or country. But this is the very point to be proved, and mere assertion, however positive, can never take the place of proof. Both these assumptions, moreover, take for granted the thing to be proved, and both of them, instead of sifting the testimony or examining witnesses, deny the existence of either. Thus the only means of testing the truth is ignored, the testimony by which historical events are established is rejected, the witnesses by which matters of fact are discovered refused a hearing, and testimony, the falsehood of which would be more miraculous than miracle, is demanded, while by that very demand the possibility of the thing demanded is denied. Then there is the extraordinary statement that without uniform experience against a miracle, it would not be a miracle at all,—a proposition which, if it be not self-contradictory, is much the same as if one said, a comet has never been observed in any age or country, or, if it has been observed, it could not be a comet.

Again, objections have been drawn from the false miracles of heathenism, or those of mediæval and later times. In reality, however, such objections rather tell in favour of than against true miracles; just as bad money is sure proof that there has been good currency, and counterfeits owe their very existence to the fact that there has been genuine coinage. The answer which Butler has given to such objections is concise, and to an unbiassed mind convincing. He asks, "What would such a conclusion really amount to but this, that evidence confuted by contrary evidence, or any way overbalanced, destroys the credibility of other evidence, neither confuted nor overbalanced;" and he further illustrates the case as follows: "This is the same as to argue, that if two men of equally good reputation had given evidence in different cases no way connected, and one of them had been convicted of perjury, this confuted the testimony of the other." Such is the illustrative example by which the author of the *Analogy* disposes of the unreasonableness of denying the reality of miracles on the ground that certain evidence has been pretended in support of false miracles. But this necessitates our looking more closely at the miracles of Scripture. When we do so, we find them occupying a platform unspeakably higher than the alleged miracles of heathenism, or Judaism, or even pseudo-Christianity; and that, whether we take into account the character of the miracles themselves, or the conduct of the persons who wrought them, or the object for which they were wrought, or the evidence by which they are attested. As to their *character*, they were truly *sui generis* and perfectly unique. If we confine ourselves to those of New Testament times, we find as the normal type restoration to life, and resurrection from the dead. True there were cures, but not doubtful ones; visions, but well authenticated; demoniac expulsions rendered palpable by the results, and altogether different from pretended exorcisms. There is nothing in these or any of the Christian miracles that bears even a remote resemblance to the clever manipulations of men of superior scientific knowledge among a people of an ignorant, barbarous, and credulous age. Neither was the miracle-working power diffused among a multitude, so that if some failed, others might chance to succeed. It was lodged in one central head, and in those to whom He delegated the privilege. And here we may note as not improbable the common opinion which makes the miracles of the ancient Church cease with the last surviving disciples, to whom such power had been transferred from apostolic hands, about the middle of the second century, by which time Christianity had secured for itself a firm footing throughout the Roman Empire, and miraculous gifts were no longer needed. The gradual withdrawal of miraculous powers from the Church accounts, according to Kaye, for the uncertainty that prevailed about the time of their cessation. "The power of working miracles," he concludes, "was not extended beyond the disciples upon whom the apostles conferred it by the imposition of their hands. As the number of those disciples gradually diminished, the instances of the exercise of miraculous powers became continually less frequent, and ceased entirely at the death of the last individual on whom the hands of the apostles had been laid. That event would in the natural course of things take place before the middle of the second century." Think again of their *object*. They are wrought on the most momentous occasions, and for the highest moral ends—not to excite mere wonderment or surprise by a vain display of power, or gratify a prurient curiosity, or foster superstition, or promote a purposeless prying into the sphere of the spiritual. Add to all this the unparalleled *weight of evidence* by which they are supported. They were wrought in the broad light of open day, before the eyes of friends and foes, under the scrutiny of other senses beside that of sight, amid circumstances of greatest publicity, and after a fashion that enabled the learned and the unlearned alike to put them to the proof; while that evidence has come down to us from eye-witnesses and contemporaries, and has been transmitted to us by men of heavenly aspirations and holy impulses, by men in circumstances calculated to kindle the highest enthusiasm, yet confining their enthusiasm within the bounds of good sense, practical in their purpose and grave in their testimony; and never was testimony so tested as in the person of these men, who passed through ordeals the most stern and sufferings the most severe.

But the moral world has its laws as well as the natural; and testimony may furnish guarantees of its truthfulness so strong, that the supposed falsehood of such testimony would be as great a miracle in the moral, as any miraculous occurrence could possibly be in the physical world. Besides, it may be set down as axiomatic that there are only two possible ways in which testimony can be set aside, namely, proof of the incompetency of the witnesses, or proof of their being subject to some sinister influence in giving their testimony. Further, to impeach the testimony of witnesses, all whose qualities and all whose circumstances prove them credible, is to subvert the law of evidence, and to assume a miracle in itself quite as great, and under all the circumstances even greater, than any of the miracles of Scripture; thus the improbability is shifted to the wrong side. For if, in balancing the improbability of miracle with the improbability of the falsehood of testimony, we allow the former to preponderate, we pronounce the laws of evidence deceptive, and calculated to mislead; nay more, we commit ourselves to the absurd and monstrous notion, that there is a greater likelihood of divine power being employed to make men of unimpeachable truthfulness testify untruth, than of the same power being exercised miraculously in attesting the truth that saves. It is nothing short of a moral miracle—a real violation of the laws of thought and action—that ten or twelve, or more, whom there is every reason to believe honest, should combine to falsify. Such falsification in the moral world would be as marvellous as any supernatural event ever recorded in the physical world. That God should make or allow the testimony of upright men to become the vehicle of falsehood, would be a thousand times less probable than the working of a miracle. The miracle then is surely far more likely to occur on the side, on which Scripture represents it, than in the department of testimony where the opponents of the supernatural would place it, ignoring, as they do, the beneficence of the purpose, the excellence of the end, the exigencies of the occasion, and the unspeakable importance of the scheme of mercy to man as well as glory to God, which miracles subserve.

The position that no amount of human testimony *for* can outweigh the uniform experience of mankind *against* a departure from the course of nature, has been subjected to a rigorous mathematical test, first by Babbage, then by Young, with demonstration of the following result: That if thirteen witnesses, whose veracity is such that each of them tells one falsehood in every ten statements, testify without collusion to the truth of a specified miracle, the probability of the truth of their statement is five times the probability for the constancy of nature—that is, the probability for the miracle is five times the greatest possible probability against it.

Passing, however, from this abstract probability to a more practical mode of testing the matter, we are shut up to one or other alternative on the supposition of the falsehood of the miracles; either that the witnesses to them were themselves the victims of *delusion*, or that they were chargeable with *deception*. That so many witnesses, say of our Lord's miracles, should all simultaneously be the victims of delusion—in other words, be so devoid of sagacity to detect fraud, if fraud existed, were a greater miracle than any of those to which they testify. Even Renan, after proceeding for some length with this theory of hallucination, seems forced to give it up and boldly face the alternative of deception. He vacillates from the very difficulty of his position. Completely cornered by the overwhelming evidence for the miraculous, and yet vainly labouring to escape from it, he finds himself compelled to combine enthusiasm and fraud. At this particular point his theory hopelessly breaks down. His conception of the Saviour proves an impossibility, because of his rejection of the miraculous; for, to steer clear of the miraculous, he has to resort to *delusion* or *deception*, or both united; and then what becomes of those sublime qualities, both of head and heart—that incomparable excellence, which Renan attributes to Him whom he, thus with such strange inconsistency, pronounces to be the greatest of the sons of men? The last words of his *Vie de Jésus* to this effect are truly remarkable: "Jésus ne sera surpassé.... Tous les siècles proclameront qui entre les fils des hommes, il n'en est pas né de plus grand que Jésus."

Now Jewish teachers have laid down six tests of miracle, and Rawlinson has stated several canons of historical criticism; the former are too numerous, and the latter perhaps too elaborate. Other tests might be suggested, as, for example, publicity, perceptibility by the senses, performance by power apart from second causes, proper reason assignable for their performance, and permanence of effect. These would serve the purpose very well. Still we prefer the four common tests, with which all are familiar, that have been applied to ascertain the facts of history. To all these the miracles of both Old and New Testament fully answer. Take the miracles of any of the three great epochs of miracle—that is to say, those wrought by Moses, or by Elijah, or by Jesus—and they will be found to stand the tests. (1) They were *sensible*—matters of fact cognizable of the bodily senses; the eyes, the hands, the taste, could all be made available for the purpose. Some of them were so prominent, and of such paramount importance and engrossing interest, as to leave an indelible impression on every faculty and feeling of the human breast; for the passage of the Red Sea, the miracles of healing and of feeding multitudes, the central miracle of our Lord's resurrection, could not possibly be mistaken. (2) They were public—done openly, not in a corner, not in secret; at a period of enlightenment, in the presence of men of intelligence; before the face of persons keen and vigilant to detect any flaw—hostile as well as friendly spectators. (3) Monuments of a public kind, or memorial acts, were instituted to perpetuate the memory of those transactions. (4) These commemorative attestations were commenced at the time the events took place, and have continued ever since, such as the Passover and segregation of the first-born, among the Jews; with the Lord's Supper, the Sabbath, among Christians, not to speak of the institution of the Christian Church itself, with its ordinances and offices. You have only to apply these tests at your leisure, and you must conclude that matters so triable by the senses, so publicly performed, so extensively commemorated,—while that commemoration, commencing contemporaneously, has continued constantly,—could not, according to the first and second tests, by any possibility be mistaken by the first actors and original witnesses; and just as little can they, according to the third and fourth tests, mislead and impose on us.

But what can we gather further about the capability and character of the witnesses themselves—their motives and object? Enough, certainly, to free them from the imputation either of being self-deceived or of attempting to deceive others. They were as trustworthy as intelligent. They wore all the appearance of true men; their honesty was not called in question. They agree substantially, yet there is no symptom of concert. They persisted in their attestation in spite of greatest perils—they persevered through evil report and good report. They cheerfully surrendered their earthly all; they toiled, they suffered, they bled, they died (many of them), in testimony of the truths they taught. And all this, be it observed, in attestation not of *belief* merely, but of *facts*, which we must hold to be a most important distinction. We may confidently ask, therefore, as has been asked before,—

> " Whence but from heaven could men unskilled in arts,
> In different ages born, in different parts,
> Weave such agreeing truths? or how or why
> Should all conspire to cheat us with a lie?
> Unasked their pains, ungrateful their advice,
> Starving their gains, and martyrdom their price."

We conclude, then, that the miracles by which the seal of its divine origin is affixed to revelation are not only possible and probable, but credible. We close with a case somewhat analogous, and which should commend itself to the consideration of scientists. A certain planet pursued its course according to the established laws of planetary motion; but when it reached a certain part of its orbit, perturbations occurred. No one could tell how or why these irregularities took place. Many were the guesses and numerous the theories to account for these irregular movements. But in vain. Some power unseen, and for long unknown, counteracted the ordinary effects of centrifugal and centripetal forces. At length a Frenchman and an Englishman, independently and by marvellously difficult calculations, reached the conclusion that there must be another orb of a certain size and at such a distance in the remote invisible space; and a German turned his telescope to the spot indicated, and sure enough another heavenly body of huge dimensions was discovered. And now it was made clear that that far-off planet—unknown, unseen till then—was exerting the disturbing force. So, in regard to miracle, the course of nature went on year by year and century after century without interruption or alteration; but now and again at certain points that course was interfered with—a perturbation of a particular kind took place. From the first till now, no doubt, many ways of accounting for it have been imagined; but safe reckonings, guided by the word and based on the ways of God, assure us of a power at work beyond, while the telescope of faith discovers, away in the remote heavens, that potent agency which produced the strange but salutary deviation. Thus it ever shall be; the honest seeker after truth, whether in relation to the mechanism of the material heavens or the moral movements of a higher sphere, shall seldom or never have reason to complain that his search has been unrewarded by at least some moderate measure of successful discovery.

It is not our intention to dwell on or draw an argument from the rapid propagation of Christianity. That rapid progress and wide diffusion seem little if anything short of *miraculous*. Turning to the testimony of Tertullian on this subject, and making all due allowance for his rhetorical style, we cannot read without surprise such statements as the following: "Though," he says in his *Apology*, addressed to the Governors of proconsular Africa, "we date our existence only from yesterday, we have filled every part of your empire; we are to be found in your cities, your islands, your camps, your palaces, your forum. . . . . Were we only to withdraw ourselves from you, and to remove by a common consent to some remote corner of the globe, our mere secession would be sufficient to accomplish your destruction and to avenge our cause. You would be left without subjects to govern, and would tremble at the solitude and silence around you—at the awful stillness of a dead world." Again he says in his argument against the Jews: " We witness the accomplishment of the words of the Psalmist, ' Their sound is gone out into all the earth, and their words unto the ends of the world.' For not only the various countries from which worshippers were collected at Jerusalem on the day of Pentecost, but the most distant regions, have received the faith of Christ. He reigns among people whom the Roman arms have never yet subdued, among the different tribes of Getulia and Mauretania,—in the farthest extremities of Spain, and Gaul, and Britain,—among the Sarmatians, Dacians, Germans, and Scythians,—in countries and islands scarcely known to us by name." This wide-spread and wonderfully rapid diffusion of the Christian religion, in itself marvellous, becomes more so when we consider the obstacles that had to be overcome. There was the uncompromising nature of that religion itself; then there was opposition to be encountered on every side—from Jew and heathen. There were the strong prejudices of persons attached to ancient beliefs, the passions of the populace, easily roused against innovators, the selfish motives of mercenary priests and other interested parties, the perils to which the propagators of the new faith were in consequence exposed, and the fierce persecutions which they had to endure. The attempt of Gibbon to minimise the difficulties and dangers in the way of its propagators appears at first sight plausible, but on more careful consideration it proves the opposite of what its author intended. His account of the matter is as follows: " The various modes of worship which prevailed in the Roman world were all considered by the people as equally true, by the philosophers as equally false, and by the magistrates as equally useful." Paley's reply to this, though well known, is so able in itself, and so triumphantly refutes the specious but shallow plea of the historian, that no apology is needed for calling attention to it here. " I would ask," says the archdeacon, " from which of these three classes of men were the Christian missionaries to look for protection or impunity ? Could they expect it from the people, ' whose acknowledged confidence in the public religion ' they subverted from the foundation ? from the philosopher, who, 'considering all religions as equally false,' would of course rank theirs among the number, with the addition of regarding them as busy and troublesome zealots? or from the magistrate, who, satisfied with the utility of the subsisting religion, would not be likely to countenance a spirit of proselytism and innovation—a system which declared war against every other, and which, if it prevailed, must end in a total rupture of public opinion; an upstart religion, in a word, which was not content with its own authority, but must disgrace all the settled religions of the world?"

Mosheim, the Church historian, assigns two chief causes for the rapid propagation of Christianity, namely, apologies composed in its defence, and the translation of the New Testament into different languages. The former may be admitted to have served that purpose to some small extent, but only as a secondary and subordinate means; the latter, as exhibiting the doctrines and duties of Christianity, and their suitability to the wellbeing of society and to the promotion of the best interests of man, would no doubt be a primary means. The good impression made by the teachings of the New Testament, brought by those translations within the reach of all, would be deepened by the apologies. But nothing short of the divine origin of the truths thus taught, and divine power accompanying the teachers, can satisfactorily account for the reception which they met, and the marvellous progress which they made.

CHAPTER II.

FULFILMENT OF PROPHECY.

HAVING examined the leading objections to, and exhibited the force of, miracles in evidence that the Bible is the word of God, we proceed to a kindred kind of proof, namely, the *fulfilment of prophecy*. This naturally follows miracle; prophecy is, in fact, a species of miracle, being a miracle of knowledge. As miracle is the superhuman in power, prophecy is the superhuman in knowledge; and these two combined with the superhuman in excellence, form three main lines of apologetic defence.

Here it must be premised that two conditions are indispensable to invest prophecy with an evidential function in reference to the truth of Scripture. Indeed, the two conditions referred to enter into the very essence of prophecy properly so called. They are the following:—First, that it is clearly provable that the prediction was prior, by an interval less or more, to the event; and secondly, that no supposable foresight, or calculation of probabilities, or power of conjecture, or mystical lore resulting from lengthened experience, could possibly lead to, or account for, the discovery of the far future or more nearly approaching event that forms the subject of prophecy. A third condition is added by some, namely, the palpable and positive fulfilment of the prediction. But this is scarcely necessary as a condition, because it is taken for granted, and is implied in the very nature of the case. Of course without such fulfilment at one time or other, the prediction would consist of so many mere idle words, the prophecy would have no existence, and the very name would be a sheer misnomer, or an entire misapplication of language.

The prophecies of Scripture are very numerous and very various. Many of them have been fulfilled in the most astonishing manner and in the most minute details. Nothing less and nothing short of omniscience could have accurately predicted so many and strange events, many years, often centuries, before their fulfilment. Some of these predictions have been so clear, so distinct, so altogether beyond the reach of human sagacity or probable conjecture, that the unbeliever's chief way of attempting to evade their force, is either to treat them as *vaticinia post eventum*, written after the event; or as the shrewd anticipation of events in the immediate future. But not a few of the prophecies of Scripture are of such a sort that no ingenuity can divest them of their validity as testimonies to the truth of God. These prophecies, moreover, are a perfect contrast to the oracular responses of the heathen, in several most noteworthy respects, such as the *depth* to which they penetrate into the future, while those responses float on the surface; the total *impossibility* of any previous knowledge of the preparatory circumstances, while such formed the groundwork of those guesses by which the heathen pretended to foretell the future; the *absence of all ambiguity* as opposed to the equivocation of heathen oracles, such as the responses to Pyrrhus, " aio te, Æacida, Romanos vincere posse," so equivocal as to foretell the victory of Pyrrhus over the Romans or of the Romans over Pyrrhus, and in neither case to be falsified by the event; or the Delphic response to Crœsus : " That if he should make war on the Persians, he would destroy a mighty empire " (ἢν στρατεύηται ἐπὶ Πέρσας μεγάλην ἀρχήν μιν καταλῦσαι), thus leaving it doubtful whether it would be the Lydian or the Persian Empire that would be destroyed; still more the unswerving independence and unimpeachable disinterestedness and poverty of the Hebrew prophets as compared with the fawning sycophancy and servile venality of, for example, the Delphic prophetess, whom Demosthenes distinctly charged with *Philippizing*.

Certain alleged predictions in secular history have been placed on a par with those of Scripture. Among these, that of Seneca, supposed to foretell the discovery of America, is perhaps the most conspicuous. But instead of being entitled to rank as a prophecy, it is only the poet's expression of belief in an old tradition. If classed as a prediction, it is too vague to be applicable, for it might refer to any land beyond any sea; while the expression "in late years," put in the mouth of a chorus belonging to the fabulous era of Grecian story, must be referred to the times of Seneca himself rather than to those of Columbus, fourteen centuries later. Besides, where it does seem capable of application, it is incorrect, because in contradiction to the so-called prophecy. Thule is still the utmost land in those hyperborean seas. From previous discoveries, particularly of a geographical kind, and from the extreme probability of other lands being discovered in a great ocean unexplored, there could not be much difficulty in forecasting other discoveries, both geographical and physical. It was a conjecture well-founded and most likely to be made by a man of such vivid imagination as Seneca. Whether, therefore, he sings in the *Medea*,—

" Venient annis	Pateat tellus, Tiphysque novas
Sæcula seris, quibus oceanus,	Detegat orbes ; nec sit terris
Vincula rerum laxet, et ingens	Ultima Thule ;"

or whether he says in his *Naturales Questiones:* " Quam multa animalia hoc primum cognovimus sæculo! quam multa negotia ne hoc quidem! Multa venientis ævi populus ignota nobis sciet. Multa sæculis tunc futuris, cum memoria nostra exoleverit, reservantur," he speaks in perfect keeping with the natural force of his own lively fancy, and in entire accordance with the commonest probabilities. Instead, therefore, of a prediction in the proper sense, the expression of Seneca was an obvious and most natural anticipation.

Where predictions are so numerous and marvellous as those of the Bible, the difficulty is to select or particularise. Let us, however, take as samples certain predictions that all must acknowledge to be unequivocal and particular—predictions confessedly beyond the reach of human foresight, admittedly uttered, one of them many centuries, the other one century at least, before the fulfilment began. The one relates to the fate of a city, the other to the fortunes of a people.

The first relates to *Nineveh*. (1) An exceeding great city, one of the mightiest the sun of heaven ever shone on, dating from nearly the time of the flood, occupied, what with palaces, buildings, parks, and vacant spaces, an area stretching five and twenty miles or more in length along the left bank of the

Tigris, and some fifteen in breadth from the river back to the eastern hills. It was protected by its ramparts, forts, frowning embattled towers, and strong encompassing walls. Wealth had poured in from many sources—from the luxuriant pasture lands and the harvests of fertile plains adjoining, from the richly laden craft that crowded her magnificent river, and carried on her commerce with different and distant lands. Occupying the position of a central emporium on the great line of traffic between the Mediterranean Sea and the Indian Ocean, this city had in some measure united east and west. Combining the military with the merchant element in her population (a rare union), she also enriched herself with the spoils of war, and sent out her messengers like Rabshakeh to demand or levy the tribute of subject states. Such was Nineveh; but succumbing to the combined assault of the Medes under Cyaxares and the Babylonians under Nabopolassar, that great city vanished all at once, with a singular abruptness, from the face of the earth. In the time of Herodotus, four centuries before Christ, it had ceased to exist, and had become a thing of the past; for, referring to its site on the river, he says οἴκητο, that is, it had formerly stood. Xenophon, in the retreat of the ten thousand, passed the place, but the very memory of its name was gone. Lucian says: not a trace of it remains, nor can any one tell where it once stood. For two thousand years and more it had disappeared, leaving no trace to tell where once it was. No one knew exactly where its site had been—it was buried, and no one could point out its grave. But the minutest circumstances of its fall, the manner of its destruction, and the fact of its total disappearance, were all foretold by the prophet Nahum, a full century before, and with astonishing particularity. Nearly the whole Book of Nahum, besides some other Scriptures, is occupied with this subject; we can only, therefore, indicate a few of the facts so circumstantially foretold. With besieging foe, flood and fire united to accomplish the ruin of the world-famed city. The king, elated with some insignificant success he had achieved in conflict with the besiegers, was feasting his troops and indulging in mistimed revelry, when, attacked by the enemies, he and his army were defeated, and driven within the walls, just as the prophet has it: "While they be folden together as thorns, and while they are drunken as drunkards." Their activity in preparing against the siege, as recorded by Diodorus, was foretold in the words: "The defence shall be prepared, draw thee waters for the siege, fortify the strongholds."

In the third year of the siege, the river, which had done so much for the city, then turned its strength against it; an extraordinary rise of the river Tigris, swollen by excessive rains, swept away a considerable portion of the walls. This also the prophet had predicted: " The gates of the rivers shall be opened." The monarch in despair, and alarmed by a tradition, distorted perhaps from the very prediction just quoted, fired the palace and perished in the flames, as foretold: "The palace shall be dissolved (molten)." Meantime the besiegers found a ready ingress through the breach already made in the walls by the waters of the river, according to the prophet's words: "The gates of thy land shall be set wide open unto thine enemies." We are aware that by "gates" here some understand the passes leading into the country. Then followed a scene of indiscriminate slaughter and spoliation, in strict agreement with the prediction: "The sword shall cut thee off, it shall eat thee up like the cankerworm;" and again: "Take ye the spoil of silver, take the spoil of gold."

This concluded, the savage conquerors consigned the whole city to the flames; just as had been prophesied: "I will burn her chariots in the smoke;" again: "The fire shall devour thy bars;" and once more: "There shall the fire devour thee."

Thus foe and flood and fire, a very unlikely combination, completed once for all and for ever the destruction of Nineveh, precisely as the prophet had foretold: "He shall make an utter end of the place thereof," or more literally, "He shall make the place thereof a desolation;" that is to say, not only the city itself, but the place it had occupied—its very site was to be made a desolation. Not only so; it is added: "He will make an utter end;" "There is no healing of thy bruise." Other great cities perished gradually, or survived their capture, or rose again from their ruins; but for Nineveh there was to be no resurrection.

It was to be hidden, moreover: "Thou shalt be hid," literally, "Thou shalt be a thing hidden (תְּהִי נַעֲלָמָה)," the substantive verb and passive participle denoting a *continuance*. At length that city, after lying in the grave for twenty centuries, was disinterred and its palaces disentombed, when further confirmations of the prophecies came to light. The action of fire was everywhere apparent among the ruins. "The recent excavations," says Rawlinson, "have shown that fire was a great instrument in the destruction of the Nineveh palaces. Calcined alabaster, masses of charred wood and charcoal, colossal statues split through with heat, are met with in parts of the Ninevite mounds, and attest the veracity of prophecy." The same author also states that "the palaces of Khorsabad and Nimrud show equal traces of fire with Koyunjik."

Hitzig and others, we admit, have attempted to show that certain peculiarities of language evidence a later date than that usually assigned to the prophecy of Nahum; but the attempt is utterly futile, for (*a*) the peculiarities in question are found in the oldest books of Scripture, as, for example, in the Pentateuch. Of these the following specimens may suffice:—

- I. 13, ii. 4. The suffix הו occurs in לְמִינֵהוּ fourteen times in the Pentateuch; though, no doubt, it is most frequently found in words ending with ־ָה.
- II. 11. חלחלה, Pilpel, is a conjugation occurring from Genesis כִּלְכֵּל downwards; besides, חלחלה is met with in Nahum's contemporary, Isa. xxi. 3.
- II. 14. מַלְאָכֵבָה, if written בָּה (as in some copies), is found in the following passages of the Pentateuch: Gen. iii. 9; Ex. xiii. 16, xxix. 35.
- III. 18. נָפֹשׁוּ, Niphal of פּוּשׁ, which is the root of the river called *Pishon*.

But (*b*) the prophecy of Nahum is coincident in point of time with that of Isaiah in the reign of Hezekiah, and is the very counterpart of the condition of things at the second invasion of Sennacherib, and before the miraculous destruction of his host. At no subsequent period did the state of things exactly correspond with that pictured by the prophet, and which is the following:—The Assyrian capital was in the vigour of its strength; her merchantmen were countless as locusts, or as the stars of heaven; her military men were violent as ever, their hands stained with blood and filled with prey; her messengers went forth to demand submission or exact tribute; the order of the day was still mischievous devices against God and His people; the people of Palestine were galled by and groaning under the Assyrian yoke, but there is a promise of its speedy removal; godless invasion was interfering with the feasts of Judah, but that was soon to pass away; the alarms of war were still around them, but these were ere long to give place to the proclamation of peace. Further, (c) some of the predictions of Nahum in relation to Nineveh are fulfilling to the present hour, and are as true now as they were two thousand years ago, and as true then as now; in proof of which we might refer to its charred ruins, long hidden relics, and thorough desolation. If space permitted, we should refer to the inscriptions on the walls of Nineveh's palaces, on bricks, on stone tablets, and cones of clay, that have come forth out of the bowels of the earth, and from under the heaped-up rubbish of Assyrian mounds, to proclaim to an unbelieving age, with an eloquence and emphasis that nothing can gainsay, the everlasting verities of the Bible, and to publish to all lands that it is indeed the word of God.

The second prediction referred to concerns *the Jews*. (2) We hasten to notice briefly a prophecy delivered, as all are obliged to confess, many centuries before its fulfilment began, and of which the fulfilment has continued for many centuries since, nor has it ceased to the present day.

There is scarcely a large town in any country in the world where you will not meet, along its streets, or on its exchange, or in its market-place, certain persons of Eastern visage, and usually with marked Oriental features. They belong to a race peeled and scattered and sifted. They are dispersed among all nations, and their laws are diverse from all people. They are found everywhere, and as a race have a home nowhere. They are literally what the poet terms them: "tribes of the wandering foot and weary breast." They have been in this condition for well-nigh two thousand years. But fifteen hundred years before they were reduced to this condition,

D

in the very infancy of their national existence, it was prophesied concerning them most accurately and truthfully, as the event has proved—and the prophecy still stands recorded in the Bible—as follows: "The Lord shall scatter thee among all people from the one end of the earth even unto the other, and among these nations shalt thou find no ease, neither the sole of thy foot have rest." It was further prophesied: "Lo, the people shall dwell alone, and shall not be reckoned among the nations;" and so it has been. The great peoples and mighty empires of antiquity have passed away—no vestige of them remains—no man can trace his lineage to Assyrian or Babylonian progenitors—no man can affirm that a drop of pure Roman or Grecian blood flows in his veins. Yet here is a nation—a nation *sui generis*—a monumental nation with monumental institutions, and with records contemporaneous with its origin—that can trace its pedigree up to the patriarchal man, who received the honourable appellation of "father of the faithful and friend of God." The most singular circumstance perhaps of all is, that scattered as they have been, through all countries and all climes, they have so kept apart and dwelt alone, not reckoned among, because not amalgamating with, the nations, and that they can thus trace their lineage in one unbroken line up to its very source. Every Jew, then, that you meet is thus a living walking witness to the truth of revelation—the truth of the Bible, proving it to be the word of God.

To the prophecies about a city and a people respectively, may be subjoined one about a country.

(3) Another prophecy which draws attention to it by recent events, and which derives impressiveness from those events, is one relating to the land of Egypt. The prophecy in question is one which, from the very nature of the case, precludes the possibility of guesswork, and excludes generalities. It is precise, minute, and varied. It dates from the days of Ezekiel, nearly six centuries before Christ. The prophet sketches with a few bold and broad strokes an outline history of the country and capital for more than twenty centuries in advance.

The prophecy, so minutely and remarkably fulfilled as we

shall see, is found in Ezekiel, chaps. xxix. and xxx. We shall only cite the portions that are directly to the purpose.

In chap. xxix. 15 we read: "It (Egypt) shall be the *basest* of the *kingdoms;*" that is to say, a base kingdom, the basest of kingdoms, but still a kingdom. But the prophecy proceeds: "Neither shall it exalt itself any more above the nations: for I will diminish them, that they shall no more rule over the nations."

In chap. xxx. 13 it is written: "And there shall be *no more a prince of the land* of Egypt." In the same chapter, at the preceding verse: "I will sell the land into the hand of *the wicked:* and I will make the land waste, and all that is therein, by the hand of *strangers:* I the Lord have spoken it." Again, in the two following verses we read: "I will execute judgments in No . . ., and I will cut off the *multitude of No* . . ., and No shall be *rent asunder.*" Also the unavailing remedial measures are alluded to in the 21st verse: "It shall *not be bound up to be healed,* to put a roller to bind it."

In both chapters we have a prediction about the desolation of the country and its cities in the midst of surrounding desolation—in the 12th verse of the 29th chapter, and also in the 7th verse of the 30th chapter, where the same is repeated in words of like sad and solemn import as follows:—

"I will make the land of Egypt desolate in the midst of the countries that are desolate;" "They (*i.e.* the inhabitants) shall be desolate in the midst of the countries that are desolate, and her cities shall be in the midst of the cities that are wasted."

To these may be added Jeremiah's prediction about Noph in the book of that prophet, chap. xlvi. 19: "Noph shall be waste and desolate without an inhabitant." The remarkable nature of these predictions about Egypt may well entitle them to a more detailed consideration.

It was (*a*) to retain its rank as a *kingdom.* Empires not then in existence rose and fell; kingdoms unheard of for ages after started into being, lived their day, and died; states with government of one form or other came into existence, but long ago disappeared from the map of the world, and have become mere matter of history; yet throughout all those centuries Egypt has remained a kingdom. But, strange to say, (β) during all that time no *native* prince or king has held the reins of government, or sat on an ancestral throne, and that in a country where once not merely successive, but contemporary monarchs reigned. Persian, Greek, Roman, Saracen, and Turk have ruled in succession, and in turn have swayed the sceptre of the Pharaohs. Stranger still, though subjected to the rule or misrule of so many sovereigns of alien race and blood, it still holds a place among the commonwealth of nations. Though exhausted it is not extinct, though downtrodden it is not destroyed; though all along it has been in a condition of gradually progressive decadence, it has not yet reached the point of entire dissolution. True, it is (γ) a *base* kingdom. The descendants of the ancient Egyptians have sadly degenerated. While this deterioration is visible in the *personnel* of the people, it is still more manifest in the want of mental power. This is just what might be expected, for it is a truth old as the days of Homer, that when a man loses his liberty he loses half his worth; and what is thus true of individuals is true of nations. No people has ever groaned under more cruel oppressions, or has been ground down under more harassing exactions of governors and officials. Science and art and literature have left the land, trade dwindles, manufactures languish, commerce has found other channels, industry and thrift are discouraged, enterprise and energy are completely paralyzed; add to all this, taxes enormous, wages quite unremunerative, resources exhausted, ruined industries, besides forced labour levies. If we compare modern with ancient Egypt, or the Egypt of the Khedives with the Egypt of the Pharaohs, we feel the force of the superlative, that it is (δ) the *basest* of kingdoms. A greater contrast could scarcely be imagined. That country which was once the granary of the world, is scarcely able to supply a scanty subsistence to its wretched inhabitants; the cradle of the arts and sciences, which passed thence to Greece, and from Greece to Europe, and onward to the world, is become the home of a stupid and besotted people; the early seat of civilisation is only a short remove from a state semi-barbarous; the land of the pyramids and of other works that challenge the admiration, while they remain the wonder of the world, has sunk into total ignorance or disuse of mechanical skill. The soil possesses its ancient capabilities, and the source of its fertility flows onward as of yore, but the tillage is miserably defective, and its resources undeveloped. In addition to all this, picture a people fearfully oppressed, the country impoverished, the finances exhausted, and the government bankrupt, its rulers at the mercy of foreign powers, and you may form some idea of the complete degradation which justifies the title of *basest* of kingdoms. It is added: "neither shall it exalt itself any more above the nations: for I will diminish them, that they shall no more rule over the nations." Their tyrannous exercise of power over the Jews and neighbouring nations was to come at length to an end; as they had long and often done to others, so was it in turn done to them. Never was Nemesis more perfect and patent.

Nor is even this all. The ruler of Egypt was long appointed by, and subject to, the Sultan of Turkey, or even those military slaves called Mamelukes, while internal disorders not unfrequently called for the interference and control of other foreign powers. And this suggests the next point of this wonderful prediction. The agents that wrought the ruin of the country are (ε) distinctly pointed out, and characterized as being *strangers and wicked;* into the hand of such the Lord threatened to *sell* the land; as if alluding to the fact that Pashas often purchased their power. Now it is notorious that unscrupulously wicked strangers have blackened by their wickedness page after page of Egyptian history. Out of such a long list of strangers chargeable with this sad misgovernment, one needs only single out the tyranny of the Greeks, the persecutions and blighting influences of the Saracens, the untold villanies and brutalities of the Turks, as also the imbecilities and cruelties of Pashas. The heart of humanity aches, and the face of humanity blushes for the crimes of the nefarious strangers that have disgraced and degraded that wretched country. No doubt, attempts have been made from time to time to remedy the ruin referred to, or to rectify this calamitous state of affairs, but *those attempts have been without any permanent success,* or have even made matters worse. This also (η) forms part of the prediction. Passing over former efforts of this sort, and coming down to the present century, we find that Mehemet Ali, a man of strong will and independent spirit, threw off the galling yoke of the Grand Seignior, and made the Pashalik hereditary in his family, introducing at the same time many schemes for the education and general improvement of the country. But all those schemes, instead of benefiting the country, made its ruler a monopolist, and resulted in his personal aggrandizement. So with the late Khedive, his habits and tastes were expensive, the gratification of his own wants and wishes were of primary importance, and his extravagance ended in national insolvency, and an allowance only partly paid. The present viceroy promises fairly, he has issued a programme. His intention appears to be an honest endeavour to remove abuses, remodel matters of finance, and effect necessary retrenchment. He proposes changes of administration that seem salutary, while the Comptrollers-General, that England and France have nominated, may help to stay for a time the entire disorganization, and stave off the utter ruin of this hapless land. At all events, it will be another of the oft-tried but hitherto unavailing remedies which prophecy foretold and history records.

But it remains to say a word of the ancient capital of Egypt and the countries adjacent. The prophet's vision comprised them all. This country has changed its capital almost as often as it has changed its rulers, to wit, Thebes, Memphis, Alexandria, Cairo. The first of these is celebrated by the poet Homer for its might and its magnitude. Its one hundred gates give some notion of the extent of the place; the 200 chariots, and 20,000 men that issued out of each, give us some idea of the population and prowess of the people, even after making all due allowance for a poet's exaggeration. But (θ) populous as No, the Scripture name of Thebes, had been, *the multitude was to be cut off*, its populousness was to cease, judgments were to be executed upon it. After many disasters, it received the finishing blow from the grandfather of Cleopatra, after a three years' siege. Not only that, it was to be *rent asunder*, and so in truth it was, so that a quarter of a century before Christ its ruins were partitioned, according to the testimony of the geographer Strabo, into several villages; while at the present day a few (nine it is said) hamlets occupy its ancient site. Noph, that is Memphis, the capital in succession after Thebes, fared still worse; for of it nought remains but the bare sands that cover its site or perhaps a broken column to tell where the populous city stood. "Noph," says Jeremiah, "shall be waste and desolate without an inhabitant" (Jer. xlvi. 19).

Further, (*i*) the land was to be *desolate in the midst of the countries that are desolate*, and her cities in the midst of cities that are wasted. To the east lay the land of Edom, Palestine, and Syria; it had Ethiopia on the south, with Fezzan and Barca on the west. The fate of these regions is so well known as to need no comment. The district last named may be taken as a specimen of the whole. It once contained five flourishing cities—the Pentapolis of former days—Cyrene, Berenice, Apollonia, Arsinoe, and Ptolemais, with others of less note. Where are those cities now? All gone—they have either altogether vanished like some dissolving view, or their ruins alone remain.

Here, then, there is not one prediction merely, but a whole series fulfilled and yet fulfilling. Where is the eye that foresaw all this, surveying the long perspective of years and centuries? Whose is the wisdom that forecast all this, and foretold it with such precision and particularity? Whose is the power that forced futurity to surrender its secrets? Who but the Allwise, Almighty One Himself could make His servant acquainted with so many distinct events away in the distant future, undreamt of and unexpected by any human being, improbable in their nature, and seemingly impossible of accomplishment? None surely but that God, whose eye sees the end from the beginning, tracing the whole course of events, and whose hand has made itself manifest in all their accomplishment, and whose Spirit endued His servants the prophets with the qualifications needed for the clear vision and unerring record of their wondrously varied details.

CHAPTER III.

ST. JOHN AND THE SYNOPTISTS.

IN order to get rid of the supernatural, Scepticism tries various expedients. Sometimes it employs the discoveries of science, again it resorts to the results of criticism. More especially has it in recent times impressed the latter into its service. Criticism of this sort busies itself in finding out a new author, or in assigning a late date for some book of Scripture. If in either way the book can be discredited, its narratives are falsified, and the miraculous that may be mixed up with them falls as a matter of course to the ground. The difference of style which distinguishes the inspired penmen of the Gospels, especially John from the Synoptists, has been fixed on for this purpose. An argument is based thereon for the later date of the Johannean Gospel, by which it is referred to post-apostolic times. It is still the supernatural that is the main object of attack. This is distinctly avowed. Strauss pronounces a narrative unhistorical when the thing narrated is "irreconcilable with known and elsewhere universally prevailing laws;" in like manner Renan declares the Gospels to be legendary, since they are full of miracles and the supernatural. His words are: "Que les Évangiles soient en partie légendaires, c'est ce qui est évident, puisqu'ils sont pleins de miracles et de surnaturel."

When the naturalistic method of Paulus failed, and when he did not succeed in bringing the miracles of Scripture down to ordinary natural events, and such as fall within the sphere of natural law, Strauss tried the mythical. But *his* failure was equally or even more signal, when he attempted to reduce miracles, not to conscious fabrications indeed, but to the involuntary outgrowths of childlike imagination in a credulous unthinking age, embodying a common faith, or a common fear, or a common hope, as the case might be, and mistaken for facts—in other words, the imaginings of artless enthusiasts, whose unwitting fictions passed for realities. No wonder such a theory could not long maintain itself, for the character of the apostolic days was quite unmythical; it was no rude time of unwritten records, it was far removed from those primitive days, when men of quick fancies and strong feelings personified the objects of nature around them, or deified the ancestors who had gone before them. It was, on the contrary, a period of great intellectual activity and general intelligence—conditions the very opposite of a myth-producing age. Besides, who or where were the men of mythopœic faculty to invent the myths? There was no body of persons to whom they could be ascribed. Further, there was no proper soil in which the myths could grow, neither was there sufficient time between the death of the miracle-worker and the record, oral or written, of the miracles, in which that growth could be developed. Myths, moreover, bear the impress of the people and place where they originate; the Gospel narratives are in spirit as universal as our race. Accordingly, the author of the mythical method had eventually to retrace his steps, or at least re-state his theory. But he continued to cling to the name, even when he felt himself compelled to change the nature of his system, holding that the term myth may have such convenient latitude of meaning as to apply to the intentional invention of a single individual instead of the unconscious fabrications of a whole enthusiastic community. Renan, perceiving the utter weakness of the mythical, proposed the legendary theory. With him the accounts of miracles were acknowledged to have a nucleus of fact. They were actual occurrences, but poeticised and highly coloured. He regarded them rather as the transformation of fact, than the pure invention of pious enthusiasm. He admits that the story of the life of Christ, as told by the evangelists, is real history, only distorted by legends. But though he admits in the main the genuineness of the documents and the reality of the life they record, he takes care to deny that there is anything whatever supernatural in that life. Certain events in the life of our Lord, remarkable enough in themselves, wore the appearance of the miraculous. But how did they assume that aspect? Through the enthusiasm of devoted followers. A strange hallucination truly! But this is not enough to account for the seemingly miraculous in the narrative. Renan himself feels that more is needed—that another element is wanting, and he does not hesitate to supply it. With hallucination he combines pious fraud on the part of the disciples. But even that is not sufficient. The Master Himself must bear His share. If the disciples were the active agents of the fraud, He must have been a consenting party. And yet how inconsistent is this with Renan's own representation of the Saviour! How unworthy of that "wondrously beautiful" character as seen in the portrait of the Christ with which Renan himself presents us! We may well say: "Quantum mutatus ab illo!" We cannot stop to notice the three periods into which he distributes the life of Christ. We need only say of them, that they are a sort of anticlimax from bad to worse, and then to worst. Enough, too, has been said to indicate the inconsistency of his legendary theory. But Baur, at the head of the Tübingen school, also tried his hand at the work of divesting Christianity of any miraculous element. His is known as the tendency theory. He sought to show that the tendency of the Gospels as well as of other early Christian writings was to exalt Petrinism or Paulism, that is to say, Jewish Christianity or Gentile Christianity; or to mediate between and reconcile them. Of the New Testament books which he acknowledged to be genuine, he reckoned the Gospel of John the latest, because of its fully developed Christology. This theory may, we think, from another point of view be termed the chronological theory, as its aim is to bring down to a later period the composition of the books in question. Still, much as these theorists differ from one another, and actually demolish each other's arguments and supplant or supersede each other's systems, there is one rallying point which unites them all, and that is disbelief of the miraculous, and consequent desire to do away with the supernatural. As the raising of Lazarus from the dead in all probability precipitated the hostile action of the Jewish leaders; so the record of that miracle in particular probably tended most to provoke the ire of the sceptics, and to occasion their fierce attack on the Johannean authorship of the fourth Gospel.

The two circumstances mainly seized on by those who try to invalidate the genuineness of this Gospel, are the *course of events* in our Lord's life, and the *character of His discourses*. It is at the latter especially that Renan staggers, though he is far from going the lawless length of the Tübingen critics. The record of John differs manifestly in the two respects referred to from that of the Synoptists. But just here an insuperable obstacle in the way of their theory stares these theorists in the face, and that at the very outset; a stone of stumbling lies in their way at the very commencement, which they can neither step over nor walk round. For if the fourth Gospel had been forged by some one living in the year of our Lord 120, or 140, or 160,—since there is difficulty as also diversity of opinion among them, as there well may be, in regard to the time of the supposed forgery,—the very thing of all others which the author of such a forgery would have been most careful to guard against, if he wished his forgery to become a success and gain acceptance, was every relation that might clash with, or diverge from, or even appear incompatible with, or in any way contradictory to the accounts of the other Gospels so long prior, and so long current, and so favourably received in all the communities, so widely spread even then like a network over Christendom. This very divergence, so plain and palpable, coming so many years after the genuine Gospels, must have proved fatal to the forgery, if forgery it had been. On the present occasion, we can only refer in a few passing observations to the *external* evidence for the genuineness of John's Gospel. Besides the indirect quotations of the apostolic Fathers Ignatius and Barnabas, there is sufficient ground for the belief that Polycarp and Papias were acquainted with this Gospel, and approved of it as the genuine production of the apostle. They had both had intercourse with John, and received instruction from him; they were both familiar with his first Epistle; the former quotes it in his extant Epistle to the Philippians; the latter used testimonies from it, according to Eusebius. It scarcely admits a doubt, therefore, that they both knew and acknowledged the Johannean Gospel. Among other patristic witnesses to the canonicity and authorship of this Gospel, may be reckoned Justin Martyr, Irenæus, Tertullian, Clement of Alexandria, Tatian, who composed his Diatessaron, or Harmony from the Four Canonical Gospels, and Theophilus of Antioch, who first quotes it by name, all in the second century; together with Origen in the third, on to Eusebius and Jerome in the fourth. It is found in the oldest versions of the New Testament—the Old Latin, dating from the middle of the second century, and the Peshito Syriac, still older. The Gospel of John is assigned the fourth place among the four Gospels in the Muratorian Fragment, which contains a list of the books esteemed canonical by the Western Church soon after the middle of the second century. Other sections of the Church, in Syria, Africa, and Alexandria, endorse this judgment. Neither can we do much more than direct attention in passing to some of those *internal* characteristics which constitute the strongest possible presumption in favour of the Johannean authorship of this Gospel. It were instructive as interesting to notice the extreme naturalness and artlessness of manner throughout it, the freshness and versimilitude of the narratives, the many graphic touches, the portraiture of the inward workings of deep human feeling, the variety and number of incidental notices, which none but an eye-witness of the events related could possibly produce, together with the numerous signs of thorough personal knowledge. Among the latter may be mentioned the author's intimate acquaintance with places and persons in Palestine, the manners and customs of the people, their mode of life and various employments, the productions of the country, both animal and vegetable, the prevalent modes of thought and feeling—in fact, with all matters, political and religious, civil and social, down to the smallest details. That any writer in post-apostolic times could write so naturally, so graphically, so minutely, and withal so truthfully, of a state of things that had existed a century before his time, and of events that had taken place without his personal knowledge or presence, far transcends the limits of human belief. Equally incredible it is that any such writer would expose himself to detection at so many points and in so many ways.

(1) The statement that no one but an eye-witness could furnish so many particulars and such minute details of places, persons, seasons, and ceremonies, may be illustrated by the following examples. Among the *places* in and around Jerusalem as well as throughout the Holy Land, he makes mention of the Pool of Siloam, the Wady of the Kidron, the Treasury, Solomon's Porch, Bethesda, close to the Sheepgate, with its five porches, the pavement named in Hebrew Gabbatha, Gethsemane, Golgotha, and Bethany. Passing thence through Samaria, he pauses to describe Jacob's Well, its situation at the opening of the lovely valley of Sichem, its depth; the piece of ground purchased by Jacob and given to Joseph, where the bones of the latter were deposited; the wide fields of corn waving in the breeze and whitening to the harvest; Gerizim, towering high above, and commanding a vast and varied prospect, with its temple built by Manasseh, the seat of Samaritan worship. Then entering Galilee he shows the same intimate acquaintance with its scenery, the grassy slopes east of the Lake of Gennesaret clad in spring verdure—"there was much grass in the place;" the sudden gusts that sweep down the mountain gorges and fall with such severity upon the lake, which is 600 or 700 feet lower than the bed of the Mediterranean; the size of the lake, as may be inferred by comparing Mark's statement that they were in mid-lake when the storm overtook them, with John's account that they had rowed twenty-five or thirty furlongs, exactly half across, the lake being some forty-five furlongs, or six miles at its broadest part; the elevation of Cana, the modern *Kana-el-jelil*, on the table-land, and the descent to Capernaum, *Tell Hum*, on the border of the lake, implied in the words: "as He was going down." His references to *persons* are equally noticeable. Besides the members of the apostolic circle, Andrew, Philip, Peter, and Nathanael, he names Nicodemus, Lazarus, Simon, Malchus, Pilate, Joseph of Arimathæa, the relationship of Annas and Caiaphas, the Greeks coming to Philip. He was equally at home in relation to *times*—that

is to say, not only the festal seasons of Passover, Tabernacles, Dedication, and the undefined feast in the beginning of the fifth chapter, whether Pentecost, Purim, or Trumpets, but even days of the week and hours of the day—namely, the tenth, the seventh, the sixth, also early morning, evening, night. Still more his perfect familiarity with Jewish *customs* and ceremonies, their marriage feasts, modes of purification, sites of sepulture, rock-hewn tombs, the Jews' method of embalming, so different from the Egyptian, the coinage of the country, the κερματιστής who changed large foreign money into the smaller half-shekels, and the κόλλυβος, the fee paid for such exchange, the outer court ἱερόν, and the sacred structure within ναός; again, the rigorous law of the Sabbath, the Rabbinical teaching, the Messianic hopes of Jew and Samaritan respectively, the worship of the latter; the difference of the features of the country north and south—the vineyards and sheepwalks of the south, with the corresponding parables of the Good Shepherd and true vine; the lakes and mountain scenery of the former, with the parables of the sower, birds, and fishing, adapted thereto. Nowhere is this more apparent than in the additional day and the two appendages introduced into the original festival of the feast of Tabernacles.

Those appendages consisted of drawing water out of the pool of Siloam and pouring it on the altar, and of lighting the lamps at night. As the feast itself commemorated the dwelling in tents in the wilderness, so the two appendages served as memorials of the two typical miracles—the water from the rock, and the pillar of fire by night during their wanderings. These and many such details are those of a man who lived and moved and had personal experience of all that he describes. No one but an eye-witness could by any possibility touch on so many topics with perfect ease and perfect exactness,—in other words, none but the veritable apostle whom Jesus loved.

(2) The writer's own testimony is in the same direction. He affirms that he was an eye-witness, and so had direct evidence of the facts he narrates. Thus (*a*) in John i. 14 he says: "We beheld His glory" (ἐθεασάμεθα), which denotes

careful inspection—gazing on, not mentally as θεωρεῖν, nor without attentive observation as ὁράω. When this is compared with 1 John i. 1–4, where ἐθεασάμεθα also occurs, and where thus the same verb and the same tense, denoting a historic past, are used, but where at the same time another verb and another tense are used (ἑωράκαμεν) to denote the abiding impression, there is found good and sufficient reason to understand it not of internal or spiritual vision, but of actual and literal eyesight. Again, (b) John xix. 35 is equally, if not more, explicit: "And he that saw it bare record, and his record is true: and he knoweth that he saith true, that ye might believe." The use of ἐκεῖνος, which generally refers to a third person or one remote, has been urged against identifying the eye-witness who beheld what is recorded, and the author who vouches for the truthfulness of that witness. But John's usage with respect to this pronoun completely sets aside this grammatical objection. That a speaker may apply this pronoun to himself is made abundantly evident by John ix. 37: "And Jesus said unto him, Thou hast both seen Him, and it is He that talketh with thee" (ἐκεῖνός ἐστι); while John i. 18: "The only-begotten Son, which is in the bosom of the Father, He" (ἐκεῖνος), and other passages, confirm a peculiar use of this pronoun to denote one eminently or exclusively possessed of a certain qualification for whatever business may be on hand. Besides, if the writer wished to distinguish himself from the witness in the case before us, he must needs make his meaning plain by saying, not *he knoweth*, but *I or we know*, that he saith true. Further, when it is said "his record is true," the word ἀληθινός, *genuine*, is employed; and when it is added, "he saith true," ἀληθής is the term; the difference is significant and important. The former assures us of the competency of the witness, and that the testimony proceeds from one who is properly qualified to act in that capacity; the second warrants his truthfulness in this particular case. Moreover, had the author referred to another's testimony and not to his own, he would most probably have used a historical tense; but his employment of the perfect (μεμαρτύρηκεν) evidences his abiding interest in it, or its continuance in his own self-consciousness.

(3) Certain objections, though in themselves deserving little attention and capable of easy refutation, may now be glanced at. The author of the fourth Gospel is charged with inaccuracy (*a*) in relation to "Bethany beyond Jordan," as if there were no such place, or only Bethany in the neighbourhood of Jerusalem. Yet (**a**) two places bearing the same name were no singular thing in Palestine. When, however, such occurred, the difference was specially marked by some adjunct or distinctive epithet, as in the case of Bethlehem Ephratah, which is thus distinguished from Bethlehem in the tribe of Zebulon; Cana of Galilee, from Cana of Cœlo-Syria; and Bethsaida of Galilee, west of the sea of Tiberias, from Bethsaida east of the lake in Gaulonitis. Just so Bethany is distinguished by the words "beyond Jordan," from Bethany on the eastern slope of Olivet. Indeed, the words "beyond Jordan" would be emptied of any proper significance if they did not indicate some such difference. It is also probable that the latter signifies *place of poverty* (Bethaniyyah), and the former *the place of the ferryboat* (Bethoniyyah). The name Bethany, though originally found in nearly all MSS., was changed to Bethabara of the received text by Origen, and this correction was adopted by Chrysostom and others. The place (*β*) might no doubt change its name, and all the more readily as both have like signification; for if Bethany, as just remarked, means *place of the ferryboat*, Bethabara signifies *place of the ferry*, both intimating the place of a ford for crossing the Jordan.

In *Tent Work in Palestine*, by Lieutenant Conder, there is an interesting note on this name. The following is an extract:—"'And the third day there was a marriage in Cana of Galilee' (John ii. 1). Here is the controlling passage. The hostile critics of the fourth Gospel have taken hold of it; they have supposed the traditional site" (*i.e.* the fords of Jericho) "to be undoubtedly the true one, and have thence argued the impossibility that in one day Christ could have travelled eighty miles to Cana. . . . We should therefore look naturally for Bethabara within a day's journey of Cana. The ford 'Abarah is about twenty-two miles in a line from Kefr Kenna, and no place can be found on Jordan much nearer or more easily accessible to the neighbourhood of Cana." He had stated previously that his attention was drawn to 'Abarah as the name of a ford; that on looking it out on the map he found it to be one of the main fords "just above the place where the Jalud river, flowing down the valley of Jezreel and by Beisan debouches into Jordan;" and further, that among the names of forty fords "no other is called 'Abarah."

But (*b*) the name Sychar is held to be a mistake for Sichem in chap. iv. 5. Now, (*a*) even in the LXX. version of the Old Testament the orthography of the name varies, being sometimes Συχέμ and sometimes Σίκιμος or Σίκιμα; this last, by a not unfrequent interchange of the liquids *m* and *r* becomes *Sikar*. Or (β) the change of name from Sichem to Sychar was meant to intimate some incident in connection with the place or its population—either the falsity of Samaritan worship, if the word came from שֶׁקֶר, or the intemperance of the people, if it be taken from שֵׁכָר, or Jacob's purchase of the parcel of ground hard by, if it be derived from סָכַר. Or (γ) what is still more probable, Sichem and Sychar were different places in the same locality, the latter being identical, at least in site, with the present poor village called *Askar*, according to Delitzsch and others, while Lightfoot ingeniously accounts for the troublesome initial *Ayin* by supposing the word a contraction for *Ayin-Sychar*, the "Well of Sychar."

Again, (*c*) the author of the fourth Gospel is credited with a jealous rivalry of Peter, and several most reckless inferences have been drawn therefrom. Among others is that of Baur, who sees in it an effort to exalt Paulinism in the person of John to the disparagement of Petrinism as represented by Peter. This is utterly baseless. The whole originates mainly in mistaking an incident which has a quite different bearing. Peter beckons John to ask Jesus the name of the traitor. The reason is obvious, and the result all the other way. On the couch Jesus was middlemost, the place of honour, reclining on Peter, who was at the head of the couch, and so in the second place of honour; John reclined on Jesus, and consequently was at the foot of the couch, and only third in place, but in a more favourable position for asking the question; and indeed this much is indicated by the expression ἀναπεσών ἐπί. At table John reclined on Jesus' bosom ἀνακείμενος ἐν τῷ κόλπῳ (*i.e.* the fold of the robe), as we learn from the 23d verse; but thus (οὕτως) situated, he changed his posture in order to put the question which Peter wished, having leant back towards the Saviour's breast, as we are taught by the words ἀναπεσὼν ἐπὶ στῆθος. But another phrase must here be taken into account. When John is called the disciple whom Jesus loved, the word ἠγάπα denotes moral preference, in Latin *diligebat;* but when Peter and John are together, John xx. 2, we find the word ἐφίλει (*amabat*), which, according to Trench, is at once more and less, signifying personal affection with which Jesus embraced them both alike and equally. When the fancied preference is a mistaken notion, what ground is left for unholy envy or unseemly rivalry? But we now hurry on to those matters in particular to which, as already intimated, exception has been taken.

1. Let us look at the *character of our Lord's discourses* as narrated in this Gospel. Comparing His teaching as set forth by the Synoptists and by John respectively, we find in the former short sententious sayings, proverbial expressions, and parables fully expanded; while the latter presents dialogues of some length, as with Nicodemus and the woman of Samaria, and discourses of considerable extent, but in a somewhat different vein and style. Even that longer discourse known as the Sermon on the Mount, recorded in full by Matthew and abbreviated by Luke, consists largely of a series of short pithy sayings, with sundry gnomic expressions; and at the conclusion in both is the parable of the wise and foolish builders as the application of the whole. In the synoptic Gospels we have the sententious saying or peculiarly weighty sentiment; in that of John we have the doctrinal statement; in the former we find the short simile or its expansion the parable, in the latter the simple metaphor, with occasionally its elaborated form the allegory, as in the case of the vine and its branches; in the former we have the παραβολή, in the latter the παροιμία; a comparison is no doubt implied in both, but in the one it is developed at full length, in the other condensed and concentrated. Not only so, the teaching of the Synoptists is eminently practical in its purpose, that of

John somewhat speculative in its caste; that of the former is plainly popular, that of the latter not a little philosophic in its character. Still more, the subjects most dwelt on by the Synoptists are the nature, extension, and consummation of the kingdom of heaven upon earth, with the character of all true members of that kingdom; while those in which John delights most are the unspeakable glory of that kingdom's head, even the Son of God, and His exalted dignity in closest relationship to the Father, together with the duties of true discipleship. The difference of style and subject we have thus presented as fully as is necessary for our purpose, and as faithfully as due regard to brevity permits.

Now the consideration of a somewhat parallel case, that has been often referred to and quoted, will, we think, serve best both to explain and illustrate this difference. We are all familiar, no doubt, with a comparison that is sometimes instituted between our blessed Saviour, the Son of God, and that greatest of Athenian sages Socrates, especially in relation to their moral teachings, life, and death. Some also have been pleased to institute a comparison between their respective biographers. The latter comparison is the parallel to which we would advert for a few moments. Xenophon and Plato have both left on record an account of the teaching and doctrines of their great master; but between the Memoirs of the former and the Dialogues of the latter there is the greatest possible difference of style; while Socrates himself, as seen in this picture and in that, appears quite a different person. There must be a background in the character and teaching of Socrates of which we can only catch an obscure glimpse, and that on rare occasions, in the account of Xenophon. In him who originated dialectics, the soul of all subsequent Greek philosophy, as also the subject that distinguished the earlier from the later method of inquiry, and who started the doctrine of those conceptions which Plato separated from the phenomenal world into independent existences or ideas, but which Aristotle replaced in the world of appearances as the very essences of things, both of them developing, each in his own way, the Socratic germ—in that philosopher who first treated morals scientifically, and who, besides giving such a mighty impulse to the perfect Socratics represented by Plato at the head of the Academics, and Aristotle at the head of the Peripatetics, was the founder of the three imperfect or one-sided Socratic schools, that is to say, the Megareans with their dialectics, the Cynics with their snarling and self-denial, and the Cyrenaics with their selfishness and self-indulgence, all of whom derived their system from some doctrine of this many-sided man,—in such a man there must have been more, much more, than appears from Xenophon. In that chatty old man who, according to the *Memorabilia*, tried to talk the people into good sense and right living, now entangling them inextricably in the well-woven web of his reasonings, again surprising them with the disagreeable discovery of their own ignorance, there must have been more of the speculative and philosophic element than is made apparent in Xenophon, and at the same time more of that practical business-like canvassing of the concerns of daily life than he is credited with by Plato. Few now-a-days find any difficulty in accounting for this diversity of delineation. There is a pretty general agreement at the present day that these two different representations are both truthful and both life-like—that instead of being discordant with, they are supplementary of each other. There was a manifoldness in Socrates, while Xenophon and Plato were the very intellectual antipodes of each other. Consequently each took up that aspect of his master that most coincided with his own cast of mind. Xenophon, the matter-of-fact military man and man of business, addresses himself at once in a style of crisp terseness to the practical side and everyday details of his master's teaching; Plato, combining the spirit of a poet with the subtilty of the philosopher, deals with the theoretical and discusses with exuberance of diction the principles of the Socratic philosophy. It is the same teacher withal, in different aspects of his deportment and doctrines, whom both represent. Moreover, different as these representations are, Socrates presented phases of doctrine and sides of character answering to both; while, now and again, even amid the bald dry details of Xenophon, passages crop up closely resembling, in their speculative turn and even more fluent style, the descriptions of Plato. Take, for example, *Mem.* i. 4. 8, where, speaking of the diffusion of intelligence through nature, he touches on the dialectic question about the correspondence between thought and being; iii. 10, where he seeks to lead artisans to correct conceptions of their several trades; and iv. 6. 1, where he aims at the formation of conceptions, not for the purpose of practical knowledge, but for the sake of knowledge itself, and tries to make men more skilled in dialectics (διαλεκτικω-τέρους). Again, in the account of the closing scene of the philosopher, the omissions of Xenophon are more than supplemented by Plato. Hence the opinion is fully justified, that Socrates and his teaching, though viewed from a different standpoint, are faithfully and truthfully exhibited by both.

If it be thus in the case of Socrates and his two friends, surely we may be prepared *a fortiori* to expect in relation to the Saviour and his biographers a like difference of style and manner of treatment, when they delineate the character and conversations of Him who was so truly many-sided, not only as the greatest of the sons of men but the incarnate Son of God. While the Synoptists are chiefly busied in relating the facts of the Redeemer's life, John discloses the inmost workings of His spirit and reveals to us the very heart of Jesus. The Synoptists sketch the outward events of His history; John the underlying thoughts that stirred the depths of the soul within; the former wrote for the Church in its infancy, the latter for the Church in its maturity. Besides, John writes subsequently, and so he may naturally enough be presumed to supplement the account of the Synoptists, supplying this and that omission, adding an incident here and a discourse there, in order to fill up and complete the outline.

Further, as has been already observed with regard to the Memoirs of Xenophon in relation to Plato, so in the Synoptists passages here and there occur in exact harmony with the Johannean style and spirit. Many passages in proof of this position might be cited, but our comparison must be limited to very few. In those few, however, to which we shall ask attention for a little, the correspondence is so marked and the resemblance so palpable, as to supersede the necessity of further references on that point. Turning to two passages in the Synoptists, one in Matthew and the other in Luke, we find exactly the same relation to the Father and the same reference to the Saviour's Sonship which so often meet us in the Gospel of John. The passage in Matthew reads thus:—"I thank thee, O Father, Lord of heaven and earth, because Thou hast hid these things from the wise and prudent, and hast revealed them unto babes. Even so, Father: for so it seemed good in Thy sight. All things are delivered unto me of my Father, and no man knoweth the Son but the Father; neither knoweth any man the Father save the Son, and he to whomsoever the Son will reveal Him." In a parallel passage of Luke the same sentiment is expressed in words all but identical. Now, any one at all familiar with the Gospel of John will have little difficulty in recalling to mind passage after passage of that Gospel, containing the self-same vein of thought and a closely similar manner of expression. In fact, the whole of our Lord's intercessory prayer, as recorded in the 17th chapter of John, is an expansion of such sentiments. How strikingly similar are the last verses: "Father, I will that they also, *whom Thou hast given me*, be with me where I am. O righteous Father, the world *hath not known* Thee: but *I have known Thee*, and these have known that Thou hast sent me. And I have *declared* unto them Thy name, and will declare it." Thus thoughts occurring in the Synoptists, not merely in germ, but in bloom and blossom, appear again in John as the fully-ripened fruit. Again, in John we catch occasional glimpses of that aphoristic teaching and of those short sententious or gnomic statements so common in the Synoptists. Take as examples the following:—"Verily, verily, I say unto you, Except a corn of wheat fall into the ground and die, it abideth alone: but if it die it bringeth forth much fruit;" also: "If any man serve me, let him follow me; and where I am, there shall also my servant be;" again: "Verily, verily, I say unto you, The servant is not greater than his lord; neither he that is sent greater than he that sent him;" and once more: "Verily, verily, I say unto you, He that receiveth whomsoever I send receiveth me; and he that receiveth me receiveth Him that sent me." In fact, numerous instances of coincidence in figure, in thought, and in expression might readily be pointed out. But of the many examples of this sort that might be adduced, and of the many arguments that might be urged on this head, even the one touched on will, we think, be sufficient to show how entirely arbitrary and flimsy the allegation is, which, from the difference of style and character of our Lord's discourses, as reported respectively by the Synoptists and by John, infers that the latter is post-apostolic, and therefore a forgery, and by consequence possessing no divine authority.

The other matter insisted on by those who affirm the post-apostolic origin, and consequently unhistorical character of the fourth Gospel, is the *difference in the course of events*. It is a well-known fact that the synoptic Gospels are mainly occupied with the Galilean ministry of the Saviour. From a superficial and less scrutinising reading of their narrative, the interval between His temptation and last passover at Jerusalem would appear to have been spent in Galilee. They do not expressly mention any visits to Jerusalem or ministry in that city or in its vicinity during that interval; whereas the Gospel of John deals chiefly with the Judean ministry, and records three visits of our Lord to Jerusalem, and a considerable stay there or in the neighbourhood during that time. Here then, say the opponents, is a divergence quite incompatible with the Johannean authorship and consequent historical credibility of this Gospel. But this conclusion is as baseless as it is hasty and rash. The whole probabilities of the case are against it. It were strange indeed that our Lord should stay all this time in Galilee, away from the capital—the seat and centre of Jewish life, the place of the religious solemnities and great festivals. It were stranger still that He whose "parents went to Jerusalem every year at the feast of passover," and who Himself, when twelve years old, went up with them "to Jerusalem after the custom of the feast," who was so scrupulous in fulfilling all the requirements of the law, and whose disciples after His ascension were so strictly observant of the obligation on all the males of the nation to appear three times a year before the Lord in Jerusalem, should turn His back on early training, national custom, and legal enactment, absenting Himself from Jerusalem time after time in the manner supposed. Had such been the case, and had our Lord confined His movements to the remote northern province, the strangest circumstance of all would be the conduct of the Pharisees in conceiving such deadly hatred against Him. It is commonly and constantly taken for granted that the synoptic Gospels are silent on the matter of these visits. The assumption is correct according to the Gospel narratives as contained in the received text; but there is one exception—a notable one—in the Gospel of Luke as read in some of the oldest and best manuscripts. Where it is written in the last verse of the fourth chapter of that Gospel that "He preached (more accurately, *was preaching*, that is, continued for some time to do so) in the synagogues of Galilee," six uncials, including such trustworthy authorities as the Sinaitic and Vatican, with some cursives and two versions of ancient date, read *Judea* instead of Galilee; thus: "He was preaching in the synagogues of Judea." The acceptance of this reading would of course be the short road towards removal of the supposed divergence; but as the weight of evidence has not been sufficient to gain it favour with the majority of critical editors, we do not insist on this disputed reading; nor is it indeed necessary to do so. For an attentive study of the contents of the synoptic Gospels leads to the inevitable conclusion that they presuppose on the part of the Saviour some such visits and certain periods of sojourn in or near the Holy City. Several circumstances recorded by each of the Synoptists cannot otherwise be accounted for, such as the discipleship of Joseph of Arimathea, who was a member of the great council of the nation, and had his residence at Jerusalem, which was also the place where he had provided the family sepulchre. Now, which is likelier, that Joseph travelled away to Galilee to attend our Lord's ministry there, or that he became a disciple of Jesus during the occasional visits of the latter to the capital? Another proof of the same sort, but somewhat stronger, at once presents itself in connection with that quiet peaceful village of Martha and Mary, on the eastern slope of Olivet, scarce two miles distant from Jerusalem, whither the wearied Saviour many a time, we doubt not, repaired for rest and retirement from the noisy bustle of the busy town, as well as from the malignant machinations of His enemies. The close and cordial relations of our Lord with the family of Bethany, the very cordiality of which unquestionably bespeaks an intimacy of some considerable standing, can only be satisfactorily explained on the same supposition. But what puts the matter beyond the shadow of a reasonable doubt is that most pathetic and impassioned utterance of our Lord which is reported by two of the Synoptists: "O Jerusalem, Jerusalem, which killest the prophets, and stonest them that are sent unto thee; *how often* (ποσάκις) would I have gathered thy children together, as a hen doth gather her brood under her wings, and ye would not." This apostrophe is utterly meaningless unless on the supposition of *repeated* previous efforts on the part of the Saviour, by teaching and preaching, in Jerusalem for the conversion of its perverse and doomed inhabitants. But it is painfully instructive to note the perverted criticism of Baur and Strauss, and their ridiculously absurd method of evasion. The former resorts to figure, and forces an interpretation; the latter in his last edition rejects all such subterfuges, saying: "Here all shifts are futile. . . . If these are really the words of Jesus, He must have laboured in Jerusalem oftener and longer than would appear from the synoptic reports." He then adopts a bolder course—scarcely attempting to loose the knot of his own making, he does not hesitate to cut it. After manipulating the parallel passages of Matthew and Luke, he pronounces the words in question a quotation from some lost book, and charges the evangelists with negligence or mismanagement in respect to the formula of citation; he decides that the one is mistaken in omitting it altogether, the other wrong in misplacing it; and finally, denies that our Lord ever used the words. Such is the reckless and irreverent way in which this sceptical critic quotes Scripture when it suits him, accuses it of mutilation or misplacement when it goes against him, throwing it overboard altogether when it becomes unmanageable; and all in support of a favourite but false hypothesis!

Several other considerations induce the belief of a somewhat lengthened ministry of our Lord in Judæa. There is the strongest likelihood leading, in fact shutting us up, to this conclusion. If we pass over the narrative of the Saviour's birth and boyhood, and fix attention on the commencement of His ministry, His labours in Galilee, and the closing scenes of that eventful life, we find that Luke, to a large extent, goes round the same circle of events with Matthew and Mark, and, like them, dwells chiefly on the Galilean ministry. But on approaching the end of the ninth chapter of his Gospel we are struck to find from that on to near the middle of the eighteenth a large section, comprising eight whole chapters, occupied with incidents and discourses of our Lord on His last journey to Jerusalem, not one of which is recorded by the two preceding evangelists. Does not this suggest a presumption, nay, does it not afford a strong probability, that other incidents and other discourses, left unrecorded by the three Synoptists, were taken up by John, and these in connection with the Judæan ministry? Recording only one discourse delivered by our Lord in Galilee, and only in four instances traversing the same ground, namely, in relation to the stilling of the storm, the feeding of the five thousand—that one common ground of all the Gospels, the anointing of the feet, and the circumstances of the passion, he omits the events fully recorded by the Synoptists; though with an occasional hint that those events were generally known, as, for example, the choice of the twelve apostles, and the difference between the place of the Saviour's birth and the place of His abode; or with a presupposition of the events detailed by the Synoptists, as of the miraculous conception, the sacraments, the ascension, the descent of the Spirit, and commission of the apostles. Contenting himself with indicating the spiritual import of the facts recorded by others, he confines his narrative to the journeys to the prescribed feasts and the work in Judæa; and all the more so as this fell in with his plan, not only to supply what was lacking in preceding accounts by a suitable supplement, but also to take advantage of that particular portion of our Lord's work as best adapted to counteract the leaven of gnostic speculation which was already beginning to insinuate itself to the detriment of the infant Church. This part of his plan was, doubtless, subordinate to his main design, which was twofold—historical, the subject being that Jesus is the Christ the Son of God; spiritual, the object being the life of believers in His name.

The probability just indicated becomes a certainty when, on turning to Acts, we read a statement made in a discourse of Peter, and recorded by Luke, that the gospel of Christ "was published throughout all Judæa, and began from Galilee, after the baptism which John preached;" while from the same inspired penman we learn that the apostles were to be "witnesses of all things which He (the Saviour) did, both in the land of the Jews (that is, Judæa) and in Jerusalem."

We omit those allusions to the multitudes following Him from Jerusalem and from Judæa (Matt. iv. 25), and to His departing from Galilee and coming into the coasts of Judæa beyond Jordan (Matt. xix. 1), and the legitimate inference of a period of ministry in those regions; also His withdrawing into Galilee (Matt. iv. 12), or coming into Galilee (Mark i. 4), clearly implying an earlier ministry elsewhere; but we may not overlook the necessary corollary that a change of locality implies a change of audience, and a change of audience a change in the mode of instruction. For place and people are correlatives, and method of teaching is a function that varies with respect to the latter. Hence it was that the parabolic method which our Lord employed so frequently in instructing the Galilean multitude, and which is so much dwelt on by the Synoptists, needed to be exchanged for a method better suited to Jewish rulers and the more cultured audiences of the metropolis. And of this abundant evidence is furnished in the Gospel according to John. Besides, on the other hand, there is plain proof in the somewhat fragmentary notices of John that he is well acquainted with our Lord's ministry in Galilee and Peræa as well as in Judæa; for example the following:—"After these things Jesus walked in Galilee" ($\pi\epsilon\rho\iota\epsilon\pi\acute{a}\tau\epsilon\iota$, imperfect denoting some duration); His going forth into Galilee, mentioned by John in his 1st chapter; his first miracle in Cana of Galilee, recorded in his 2d; his reception by the Galileans, recorded in his 4th chapter: "Then when He was come into Galilee, the Galileans received Him, having seen all the things that He did at Jerusalem at the feast." In this way what appeared a probability at the first blush of the matter becomes a certainty, and that certainty had its origin in a necessity—a necessity of adaptation to the persons addressed.

But a third objection to the genuineness of the fourth Gospel is derived from the *difference of style* between that Gospel and the Apocalypse usually attributed to John. We can only glance at this. There is undoubtedly a certain difference; in the former there is evidence of considerable Hellenic culture, in the latter a strong Hebraistic impress. It will be conceded that difference of subject demands difference of style; that the lapse of a decade or more of years, makes a change in the style of most writers; besides, the difference has been exaggerated. But apart from all this, when John wrote the Revelation, the rapid rush of oncoming events carried him away with it, while the visions with which he was privileged had much in common with those of the old Hebrew prophets; hence the less regular style and the Hebraistic impress may be sufficiently accounted for. Even of John's Gospel, one characteristic is a species of Hebrew parallelism. Church history informs us that the aged apostle spent the evening of his days in Ephesus; there, by a few years' residence in that centre of Greek colonial life, his facility in that language would greatly improve. There, too, amid tranquillity of outward circumstances and the calm serenity of advancing years, he had leisure to look back and contemplate those wonderful events through which he had passed in company with his Lord, and still listen to the echo of those equally wonderful utterances that had fallen from His lips. Not only so, away beyond the reach of Palestinian influences, and amid surroundings more conducive to breadth of thought, he could not fail to represent the Jews (οἱ Ἰουδαῖοι), who still continued Jews in all the narrowness of Judaism and rejection of the gospel, as enemies of the Saviour, former distinctions, as of Pharisees and Sadduccees, being now merged in one common apostasy; while his style could not choose but be affected by the expansive character of Hellenic speculation and philosophy.

But after making full allowance for difference of style between the fourth Gospel and the Apocalypse, there remain points of close resemblance both in sentiment and language. There are (*a*) the same designations of the Saviour in both; compare—

> (α) John i. 1: "In the beginning was the Word," ὁ λόγος.
> Rev. xix. 13: "And His name is called the Word of God," ὁ λόγος τοῦ Θεοῦ.
> (β) John iii. 29: "He that hath the bride is the bridegroom," τὴν νύμφην νυμφίος ἐστίν.
> Rev. xxi. 9: "I will show thee the bride, the Lamb's wife," τὴν νύμφην τοῦ Ἀρνίου.
> (γ) The name of "Lamb" itself, though it is ἀμνός in the Gospel and ἀρνίον in Revelation (the latter perhaps as a diminutive of endearment, or rather as antithetic in form to θηρίον).

There is (*b*) striking similarity of expression, thus:—

> (α) ὁ ἄρτος τῆς ζωῆς, the bread of life, John vi. 35.
> τὸ ξύλον τῆς ζωῆς, the tree of life, Rev. xxii. 14.
> τὸ μάννα ἔφαγον, did eat manna, John vi. 31.
> φαγεῖν ἀπὸ τοῦ μάννα, to eat of the manna, Rev. ii. 17.
> (β) τὸ ὕδωρ τὸ ζῶν, the living water, John iv. 11.
> τοῦ ὕδατος τῆς ζωῆς, of the water of life, Rev. xxi. 6.
> (γ) ἡ ἀνάστασις καὶ ἡ ζωή, the resurrection and the life, John xi. 25.
> ἡ ἀνάστασις ἡ πρώτη, the first resurrection (when the spirits rise and reign with Christ), Rev. xx. 5.
> (δ) Common use of σφραγίζω, σκηνόω, φῶς, περιπατεῖν μετά, τηρεῖν τὸν λόγον; also the frequent occurrence of μαρτυρία in both.

Many other (*c*) indications of oneness of authorship, of which these are only specimens, might be adduced. Minute though remarkable coincidences of sentiment point in the same direction, *e.g.* the change of person from the first to the third in the quotation from Zech. xii. 10; and the disciples' privilege of sharing their Master's glory; thus: (*a*) "They shall look upon *me* whom they have pierced," cited John

xix. 37: "They shall look on *Him* whom they pierced;" Rev. i. 7: "They also which pierced *Him*." Again, (β) John xvii. 22: "The glory which Thou gavest me I have given them;" Rev. iii. 21: "To him that overcometh will I grant to sit with me in my throne, even as I also overcame, and am set down with my Father in His throne." Even the evangelist's particularity in explaining matters connected with the customs and country of the Jews argues him a stranger, it has been alleged, whereas it can only be taken to imply that he had in view the instruction of strangers to Palestine, as the inhabitants of the district where he now lived and wrote undoubtedly were. The sneer at a Galilean fisherman being the author of such a Gospel as John's, and the slur cast on Peter and John as "unlearned and ignorant men," owe their origin—the former to a misapprehension, the latter to a misinterpretation. John's acquaintance with the high priest indicates the respectability of his social status, and such an amount of education as corresponded thereto; while the fact of our Lord's entrusting His mother to his care implies the possession of, at least, a competency; besides, the terms "unlearned and ignorant" simply signify the absence of learning in Rabbinical lore and of official position. Another most important element was the training received in the school of Christ. It must be further borne in mind that the chief charm of the Johannean Gospel is its narrative of our Lord's own words—a circumstance which, as much as anything else, perhaps differentiates its style from that of Revelation. If, again, the miracle of raising Lazarus occasion exception to be taken to this Gospel, we have in the Synoptists the raising of Jairus' daughter and of the widow's son of Nain, similar in kind, and differing only, if at all, in degree.

And this brings us back to the theory of Baur and his followers of the Tübingen school. That theory rests on two assumptions, both of which are entirely groundless. In addition to that of naturalism noticed at the beginning, is the fancied discord between the Petrine and Pauline theologies, or the Judaic and Gentile, that is Catholic, elements in Christianity; while he tries to make out that the tendency of John's Gospel is to harmonise these, and that it is a post-apostolic effort for that purpose, the ascription of the Gentile or Catholic element to Jesus in that Gospel being according to the same authority an anachronism. The *non-existence* of this discord is, however, fatal to his hypothesis; besides, in the Gospel of Matthew, to which he awards at once the priority and the pre-eminence, both elements are found. As examples of the Gentile or Catholic, may be mentioned the commendations of the centurion's faith; the taking of the kingdom from the Jews and giving it to another people; the injunction to preach the gospel to every creature; the prophecy that it should be preached to all nations; and the parables describing the universal spread of the gospel. Nay, in the teaching of our Lord Himself, as, for example, in His Sermon on the Mount and His parables, both co-exist. In like manner it might be shown that in the Epistles Baur rejects, using the same supposed difference between Paul and the older apostles as the test of date and authorship, as well as in the *four* he retains, the representation given of the Saviour is identical.

Strauss, it is true, gave the finishing blow to the naturalistic theory of Paulus; but his own mythical theory succumbed to the tendency theory of Baur, so that in the last edition of his *Leben Jesu* he resiles from many of his former views, being forced, though with undisguised reluctance, to adopt the conclusions of his superior in scholarship, and, while still clinging to the name, he has largely altered the nature of his system. Renan, again, notwithstanding all the errors of his legendary theory and his frequent vacillations, vigorously opposes the late date assigned to certain books of Scripture by Baur, and makes a very near approach in this respect to the orthodox view.

But when, we may ask in conclusion, will men bow in reverence before the word of God, or at least treat it with as much respect and fairness as an ordinary Classic? When, instead of theorising in favour of an adverse foregone conclusion, will they submit to the plain, honest teaching of the Scriptures? When, instead of reading a sense into Scripture that it cannot bear and was never designed to have, will they honestly endeavour to educe from Scripture that meaning it was meant to convey? When, above all, will men learn to despise those rotten rags of Rationalism, now cast aside, in great part, by the Germans themselves, and cease to import them for the purpose of rehabilitating some effete form of British infidelity? And when, too, shall the people of God give over their apprehensions about the cause of truth, as though the ark of God were in any real danger, or were ever likely to fall permanently into the hands of the Philistines of unbelief? Every now and again some new cry of alarm is raised—a pre-Adamite man has been discovered; but that pre-Adamite man, in the long run, turns out a myth or perhaps a salamander. Many a time have people fond of notoriety caused a stir and created a sensation, whether consciously or unconsciously; but ere long their vain trifling and unwisdom become transparent. Even in our short time we have seen many such bubbles burst.

CHAPTER IV.

RELATION OF THE LINES OF EVIDENCE.

BEFORE proceeding with our argument on the internal evidence, let us notice briefly the relation which the two lines of evidence, namely, the external and the internal, bear to each other.

It is somewhat curious that both Protestant and Catholic appeal to an objective standard; the latter deferring to the authority of the Church, the former to that of the Bible; while, on the other hand, the Rationalist and the Mystic agree in recognising a subjective standard alone, and only differ as to what that standard is; the former setting up subjective reason, and the latter subjective feeling, as the umpire. But while Protestant and Catholic both appeal to an objective standard, their mode of verifying Scripture is widely different. The method employed by the latter is mainly external, and resolves itself into the sole judgment of the Church deciding what Scripture is. To this extreme view of the Romanist there was an opposite reaction on the part of the Reformers, who confined themselves too exclusively perhaps to the internal evidence. So is it also with not a few at the present day; thus, for instance, the principal of a Scotch university, according to the report of a late address, asks: "Was that faith the deepest and truest which believed the Bible to be God's word because wonderful miracles had been wrought in support of it? No, it was not; but the true belief is that of self inner consciousness, under the influence of which a person could say that he knew and felt it to be the truth." Here, however, the middle course is the true, as it is the safe way. For, paying due attention to the external evidences, to which the Church may fairly be admitted as a *witness*, though

F

not as a *judge*, we willingly acknowledge that the Bible possesses a self-evidencing power, and is, as some of the Reformers termed it, αὐτόπιστος.

We must not, however, shut our eyes to the important fact, too often lost sight of, or put out of view, in this matter, that for a due estimate and right appreciation of either kind of evidence—external or internal, more particularly the latter—there must be a subjective *something*, not according to the sense of either Rationalist or Mystic, but in the sense of a spiritual discernment, or religiousness of disposition, or obedient temper, call it by any of these names you please. Our Lord Himself not obscurely hints at something of this sort when He says: "If any man will do His will, he shall know of the doctrine whether it be of God, or whether I speak of myself."

In order to illustrate the relation of the two kinds of evidence referred to, and the proper appreciative sense at the same time, let us suppose a case somewhat similar. A picture is found in some town or district of the Netherlands; it is affirmed that it was painted by one of the grand old masters of the Dutch or Flemish school; a picture, let us say, by Cuyp, or Vandevelde, or Wouvermans, or Ruysdael, or Teniers. In investigating the truth of the assertion two courses are open. There is the external evidence or history of the picture, embracing such inquiries as the place where it was found, the likelihood of a picture by such a painter being found in the locality, the circumstances under which the family or individual owner got it in possession, the veracity of the present possessor, and other similar matters of a historical or circumstantial kind. To conduct such an inquiry or to judge of the result, any man of good understanding and accustomed to weigh evidence would be competent. But that done, a second and more important, as well as more difficult task remains; and this is to be able to discern in the picture itself such indications as would serve to connect it with its author, in fact, to read the internal evidence furnished by the picture, and to be capable of specifying such peculiar points—such delicate touches or tints or outline; or such particular management of light and shade, as would give a certain clue to the discovery of the artist from whose hand the picture had proceeded. Now, who but one having taste for, or skill in, paintings—a real art critic or a true painter—could affirm that that atmosphere was just such as Cuyp used to make visible, and that landscape such as he lit up and set all aglow with the warm sunlight; or that those sandy beaches, shingly shores, breezy seas, and high-pooped ships, all so exquisitely finished and delicately exact, were precisely the sort that Vandevelde loved to paint; or that, in the wooded dell, and near the sutler's tent, that favourite white horse, so lifelike, so beautiful, and withal so spirited, is precisely such an one as figures so frequently in the paintings of Wouvermans; or that the sparkling transparency of that waterfall, or the gloom of that gathering storm, or those lofty and luxuriant trees in the outskirts of the forest, are the very features of a scene transferred to the canvas by Ruysdael; or that those jolly rustics, with broad and merry grin, are proof positive of the inimitable expression and touch of Teniers, or that that rare mixture of softness and sharpness was peculiar to the execution of his hand, or that that landscape is just such a veritable piece of Dutch land as Teniers was wont to produce? For all this the spirit of the genuine artist or skilled connoisseur, or painter with keen eye and appreciative soul, would be required. So the individual gifted with spiritual discernment, or endowed with a believing, obedient heart, has the truest, surest evidence that the truths of the Bible can only come from God; for those truths are spiritually discerned.

While the external evidence may probably be the best calculated to convince the gainsayer, the internal is that which ever makes the deepest impression on the mind of the honest inquirer; at the same time it is that which furnishes to the believer the strongest assurance of the foundation of his faith. With regard to external evidence, we prove that God has spoken in the Bible; in the case of internal evidence we take the fact for granted, and prove it from what is spoken; and doing so, we find ten thousand vouchers in the volume itself that it is nothing less than the truth of God. Still, while some may prefer one class of evidence as more calculated to arrest attention or produce faith, and some the other, these different sorts and sources of evidence must none of them be overlooked, because the effect of all combined is cumulative, and that in the highest degree. They are like so many different rays of light all converging in one focus; and we all know the powerful effect of such convergence.

CHAPTER V.

THE MORALITY OF THE BIBLE.

THE internal evidences of the Bible are concisely as well as correctly enumerated in a well-known formulary which reads thus:—"The heavenliness of the matter, the efficacy of the doctrine, the majesty of the style, the consent of all the parts, the scope of the whole (which is to give all glory to God), the full discovery it makes of the only way of man's salvation, the many other incomparable excellences, and the entire perfection thereof, are arguments whereby it doth abundantly evidence itself to be the word of God." Where excellences so abound, it rather weakens than strengthens the argument to detach one from the many; still, as the ancient moral systems were elaborated by master minds, and are in high repute still, it cannot be unsuitable to lay some of their salient points alongside the morality of the Bible.

We put aside the fact that the *subjective* side of morals, involving the question: Why is an action right, and why am I bound to do it? in other words, what constitutes duty? or "the relation of the individual will and consciousness—the moral subject to the good in life and action," was ignored by, or rather unknown to, the foremost of heathen moralists. For though Aristotle employs such words as δεῖ, ὡς δεῖ, δέον, the real conception of the "*ought*" formed no integral part of his system—it was, in fact, neither rightly understood nor clearly expressed. Even when he deals with the objective side, making virtue consist in *the mean between two extremes*, he only makes, as Kant has shown, a quantitative difference between virtue and vice, while he bases his Ethics on eudæmonism or utility. But Aristotle's mean is mainly for self-regulation, and irrespective of the relation between man and man; besides, he lays down no *standard* whereby to determine the mean itself; neither is he consistent in exhibiting the utilitarian principle; for, though it is assumed in the first and leading part of his Ethics, especially in Book VI., he notwithstanding makes acting according to right reason (κατὰ τὸν ὀρθὸν λόγον) the rule of practical life. At any rate, these two conflicting elements of his philosophy became the two antagonistic theories of the Epicureans and the Stoics; and thus the three great philosophies of antiquity, the Peripatetic, the Epicurean, and the Stoic, all owe much to Aristotle, bearing in a greater or less degree the impress of his mind; for while he was the direct founder of the first, he influenced to no inconsiderable extent the second and the third. Further, his proposed end of life, as already intimated, is happiness; but instead of identifying happiness with virtue, as Plato, he divides it between virtue and a complete life (βίος τέλειος). Thus the rule of life in relation to or in quest of happiness is unsettled; for while virtue points in one direction, the circumstances or requirements of a complete life may lead in another, and so the forces conflict or neutralise. His virtues have been characterised as a "mob," and, while this may seem severe, the list is undoubtedly arbitrary and unsystematic. While his division of virtues into ethical and intellectual is incorrect or meaningless, not only is his rule indistinct, confused, and uncertain, but his method is vague, indefinite, and unpractical; and yet his aim was to represent virtue as a practical habit of moderation, in opposition to Plato, who regarded it more as a species of science.

Plato again, the predecessor of Aristotle and the first great writer on ethical subjects, by making virtue a sort of harmony between the different parts of man's nature—the irascible, concupiscible, and rational, while each faculty kept strictly within the sphere of its own function, constructed a specious theory, but a mere theory and no more. His cardinal virtues were wisdom, courage, and temperance, with justice as the regulatrix, perfection, and uniting bond of them all. Their relation is the following:—right reason is wisdom, anger controlled by reason is courage, desire controlled by reason is temperance; and justice consists in each of the others keeping its own proper place, and while it assigns the primacy to reason, maintains the purity of the will, and keeps cupidity in subjection, it is thus itself the harmony and so the health of the soul. There is, however, another side to Plato's philosophy, and a side more purely Platonic. This stands in close connection with his idea of the *summum bonum* or supreme good, to which human action ought to tend and by which virtue is determined. The source and secret of virtue he accordingly places in love to the highest beauty which is goodness, and to the greatest goodness as existing in a pure but impalpable essence.

To give us a more vivid representation of his cardinal virtues, he illustrates his doctrine by the pleasing allegory of the chariot drawn by two steeds, the one wild and wayward, which is *appetite*, the other noble and generous, which is the *will*, while *reason* with skilful hand and steady rein acts the part of charioteer. These, no doubt, are the pretty fancies of a sublime dreamer, but just such fancies as come to us from dreamland.

We next turn to the Stoics, the followers of Zeno. In the development of their system there were three stages. There are the Stoics, as represented by Zeno, Chrysippus, and Cleanthes; then in the hands of Panætius and Posidonius it grew more practical, departing from the severe sternness of its early days, and became thoroughly eclectic; eventually, on the immense prevalence of Stoicism in Rome, the system was more than half unpaganized, as may be seen from its treatment by Seneca, Epictetus, and Marcus Aurelius. The Stoical theory made virtue to consist in *living according to nature;* but they distinguished between the *right*, or what was morally perfect, and the *suitable*, or what harmonised with the course of human life. Their perfect virtues they termed κατορθώματα or rectitudes, while their imperfect virtues were καθήκοντα, that is, proprieties or fitnesses. It was the doctrine of those imperfect but attainable virtues that constituted the sum of their practical morality. Coming to Cicero's work *De Officiis*, which is in great part borrowed from a similar work by the Stoic Panætius, entitled περὶ τῶν καθηκόντων, we have on the whole one of the best ethical treatises of which heathenism can boast. Cicero was, strictly speaking, an eclectic, now following the Academics, again inclining to the views of the Peripatetics, but chiefly, and especially in the department of morals, a Stoic. His Stoicism was thus of a modified but not inferior kind. In the treatise referred to he follows the usual quadruple division of the virtues into prudence, temperance, fortitude, and justice. This distinction is neither adequate nor distinct; parts overlap, benevolence is left out, while minute and unimportant details are dwelt on. Taking up the letters of Seneca, we see them darkened by the dread of death; their author too, instead of being humbled on detecting his failings, seems to pique himself on such detection; add to this that he speaks of suicide in terms of hearty approval. Now in Cicero and Seneca, especially the latter, we have the most favourable specimens of Stoicism; but whether the elevated morality of Epictetus be due to a higher source than paganism, admits at least a doubt. Whether the Epaphroditus, whose slave he had been, was that friend of whom Paul speaks or not, it is certain he was a courtier of Nero; and so his servant Epictetus may well have been one among those of Cæsar's household, who benefited by Christianity. Even the high moral tone of Seneca was attributed by the Fathers to his *Christianizing*. In forming an estimate of this or any other system, instead of depreciating, it is our duty willingly and even gratefully to accept whatever approves itself of real worth. Now the system of the Stoics is credited with grasping and, to a certain extent, developing the idea of independent morality, making duty paramount, and preferring the virtuous to the useful—the *honestum* to the *utile*. Its rejection of other ends of human aim and action, such as riches and honours, thus became a logical necessity; while its contempt of external things, especially in the wretched times of Roman tyranny, when all possessions were precarious and life itself so insecure, could not fail to be a powerful recommendation. It was, no doubt, a matter of much importance to draw men's minds from the external to the ideal, and so, in some sort, to raise them above the world. Its rule, too, of conformity to nature was at once simple and symmetric, provided that nature itself were incorrupt. But granting all this, still it must be acknowledged that at starting it struck too high a note, outstretching and overstraining the bounds of human nature, and so bordering on fanaticism. By and by the standard had to be lowered by compromises which were so many concessions to opponents. In the consequent modifications of their system the Stoics had to retract their dogma about the worthlessness of all external things, admitting that, though not morally good, some of them might deserve a preference, and be suitable objects of pursuit, and even helpful to a life in accordance with nature. Accordingly they were obliged to fall back on a sort of duplex morality, one species being attainable only by the ideal perfect man whose love of rectitude was supreme, the other accommodated to ordinary mortals whose motives were less pure and feelings more powerful. In itself, and at the first narrow and repulsive, Stoicism was doubtless improved, it may be at the sacrifice of consistency, by such modifications. On the whole, after a careful consideration of the doctrines professed by the leading philosophers of that sect, one cannot help feeling that there is an unreality about their theories, together with an exaggeration or even affectation in many of their sentiments; besides, their sanction to suicide is glaringly inconsistent with that constancy which they ranked so high. Their piety was little, if anything, more than a stubborn submission to the inevitable of fate; the tendency of their creed was to foster pride, and the spirit it breathed was not unfrequently that of self-complacency instead of self-denial. No doubt it did many a time crush down certain evil propensities of human nature, but it as often crushed out some of the best affections of the human heart. Thus it frequently happened that, instead of living according to nature, it was a living contrary to the true principles and real promptings of nature; instead of being a hearty, honest conformity to nature, it was often a haughty, high-minded contempt of nature. And what shall we say of its paradoxes? When it affirmed that all virtues and vices are equal, inasmuch as virtue is conformity to and vice deviation from nature, it exposed itself to the sneer of the satirist, and gave too much ground for the charge of absurdity. When it made a series of paradoxical affirmations about the wise man,—that he feels neither pleasure nor pain, is as free from faults as devoid of feeling, can neither deceive nor be deceived, is free in all places, rich in all conditions, and happy in all circumstances, that he is kingly, divine,—its warmest admirer cannot acquit the system of extravagance; and, what is worse, it cannot be denied that by such extravagant assertions it did much to encourage moral haughtiness and hypocrisy, and went far to produce artificial demeanour rather than excellence of character.

The rival system was that of Epicurus; he made virtue to consist in conduciveness to happiness. And, strange to say, Epicureanism, so congenial to the Greek, but so little adapted to the Roman who preferred energy to ease, and so inferior to Stoicism, became, from a concurrence of circumstances, the most permanent of all the ancient systems. It is not probable that this system, at least as it proceeded from its founder, was chargeable with the grossness of subsequent corruptions. He reclaimed against that misinterpretation of his doctrine that would place the chief good in the pleasures of sense. His idea of happiness was far different from the vulgar sentiment on the subject. With him it was more spiritual enjoyment than carnal pleasures,—a permanent tranquillity of soul, an inward satisfaction of spirit,—the absence of perturbation within, and, when properly attainable, the outward decencies and harmless enjoyments of life without. Men mar their own happiness by their keen demand for present pleasures, and the foolish dread of prospective evils according to the view of Epicurus. Hence he could consistently enough allege that virtue is inseparable from happiness, and happiness impossible without virtue,—that no one can live happily without living wisely, and no one can live wisely without living pleasantly. It will be acknowledged, we may presume, that Epicureanism cannot possibly be entitled to a more favourable representation than this. Even if in this way we shut out of view and take no account of the vicious excesses and sensual indulgences to which the system of Epicurus was supposed to lead, it is perfectly clear that he laid far too much stress on the *tendency* of virtue. Virtue promotes happiness; hence, and hence alone, virtue is to be practised. Such is a fair statement of their rule of action. According to this, the tendency to happiness was the measure of virtue, and rectitude did not exist apart from its results. That this system was most liable to abuse, and most likely to be abused, is obvious. With the present life as the whole extent of existence, and with present consequences as the only objects that offered themselves for consideration, and without any superior power to overrule the affairs of men, it was but natural that happiness should be identified with sensuality or confounded with animal pleasures, so that the motto of the system might be exactly expressed in the words: "Let us eat, drink, and be merry, for to-morrow we die."

Both these two great systems of ancient Ethics, Epicureanism and Stoicism, when contrasted, may be said, though in a somewhat limited sense, to have followed, the one the law of the members, the other the "law of the mind;" the one the feelings, the other the reason; the one the desires, the other the thoughts; the one acted on the principle that a thing is good because it is desirable, the other that a thing is desirable because it is good. Both took a partial view of the subject, looking at it only on one side; both erred by the extreme doctrines they broached, both being right, though not to the same extent, and both wrong, though not in the same way nor to the same degree. Singular enough it is that these two antagonistic systems have their representatives among moral philosophers till the present day, one section making utility and the other duty the standard. The theories of ancient times have been caught up and embodied in modern systems — that of Epicurus in those systems that make virtue consist in *prudence*, while those of Plato, Aristotle, and Zeno have been reproduced in those that place virtue in *propriety*. We do not quarrel with, however we may criticise, these theories; there is more or less of truth in them all, and they are all to be regarded as so many testimonies to the excellence of virtue; but who will deny their extreme vagueness? They are much too complicated, cumbrous, and unwieldy to be capable of easy application. Owing to this and other causes, they have been in a great measure inoperative and ineffective.

Now, over against all these theories of heathen Ethics that have passed one by one in review, stands out in grand and glorious contrast the moral system of the Bible. It goes deeper down than heathen morality; for, beginning with the beginning, it purifies the heart, which is the fountainhead; and then the streams, including the inward thoughts as well as the outward life, become pure. It is magnificent in its comprehensiveness; it is, in a sense, all-embracing, for it addresses itself to all the various principles and emotions on which other theories, as well of modern as of ancient times, are made to depend. More particularly, instead of the numerous and often frivolous as also wearisome details of heathen moralists, the Bible enunciates a few noble and never-to-be-forgotten principles of far-reaching tendency and most extensive applicability, such as that golden rule: "All things whatsoever ye would that men should do to you, do ye even so to them." Similar expressions, we are aware, have been quoted from Hebrew and heathen Ethics, but they fall short of completeness when brought into comparison with the gospel rule; they differ from it in character, because of the ground on which it is based, namely, likeness to God; and they lack altogether the accompanying power of performance. Another principle like to this, and closely allied, is that grandest, highest, holiest maxim of Christian benevolence: "Thou shalt love thy neighbour as thyself." But not only does it go down deeper and spread out farther—it ascends up higher, embracing man's relations to the Supreme Being, and adding the sanctions of a future life. Thus it has respect to God and immortality. Heathen Ethics, with some rare exceptions, are occupied, as might be expected, with man's relations as mainly, if not merely, mundane, with the relations of man to man, and leave out, for the most part, the relation of man to God, and seldom even hint the prospects of a future life. One of the most remarkable moral treatises transmitted from heathen antiquity—the *Memorabilia* or Memoirs of Xenophon —if we except some few instances of unquestionably false morality, states, with tolerable clearness and correctness, the relations of man to man. It recognises him as a being of this world, and gives him many prudent and judicious directions for his true honour and happiness in this world; but while it speaks of him as a moral and intellectual being, it ignores his immortality; and, with the exception of a few cold compliments to the goodness and wisdom of the gods, takes no further notice of those fabulous beings or of man's relation to them. How different the Bible! It unites morality and religion, binding them together by an indissoluble bond: "This is the love of God, that ($\~\iota\nu\alpha$ not the fact, but the aim or scope) we keep His commandments." It draws round him the threefold cord of duty to the Creator, his fellow-creature, and himself, when it urges him to live "soberly, righteously, and godly." And while virtue is to be practised for its own sake and in the right spirit, still it argues, we maintain, no base selfishness, but, on the contrary, true self-love, to be stimulated by the ennobling and elevating enforcement: "For great shall be thy reward in heaven." Such is the sanction. There is a simplicity in the Bible system of morals, and withal a grand sublimity—it is as sublime as it is simple; for its foundation is the immutable distinction between right and wrong. Its principle is love contemplating its two objects: "Thou shalt love the Lord thy God with all thy heart, soul, mind, and strength; and thy neighbour as thyself;" yet love affected by the remedial scheme, since God is the God of salvation, and in Christ reconciles the world unto Himself, not imputing unto men their trespasses. Its end is the divine glory, so that whether we eat, or drink, or whatever we do, we do all to the glory of God. Its motive is the goodness of God, including both the grace of His holiness and the holiness of His grace. Its standard is the divine will, for the thing that is well-pleasing to God is also right, while that will is partially made known to all by the light of nature, but fully revealed in the divine word and clearly manifested to the Christian. The mental faculty that judges authoritatively, and with accompanying feeling of approbation or disapprobation, is *conscience* discovering the law, so that those without the written law are a law unto themselves, ever proceeding on and pointing to the law, and yet needing itself to be quickened, enlightened, and elevated by the law. Such is the revealer of the law. Butler speaks of conscience as "a sentiment of the understanding, or a perception of the heart, or both," and yet there is no confusion of thought, nor is the language, though seemingly, really incongruous. He means that as an operation of the understanding it includes a sentiment or feeling, and as a feeling of the heart it involves a perception. Strictly speaking, conscience, we admit, is more limited in the sphere of its operation. Like consciousness, which is the knowledge of mental states, conscience is properly the knowledge of moral law. But its meaning is often extended. The prefix *con*, with, which is the first part of the compound, may mean knowledge of the law in conjunction with the lawgiver, or a joint knowledge of the law and of personal conduct, whether conformable or contrary thereto (συνείδησις), and so far it may be a witness-bearer testifying for or against. Now this knowledge prepares for coming to a decision, and so conscience acts the part of judge (ἐπίκρισις), accusing or excusing, acquitting or condemning. But the popular sense attached to the term goes even farther still, and in addition to moral judgments, comprehends those sentiments or feelings of approbation or disapprobation that are known to accompany such judgments. But, whether the language used be merely popular or strictly philosophic, the great fact remains, and that is, the supremacy of this power, which, like the eye of the soul, discerns the law of God and interprets its enactments.

The highest recommendation of Bible morality, perhaps, rests on the fact that it is so practicable and effective. What the ancient sage desiderated, we have here—an instructor sent from heaven with authority to reveal and enforce the duty of man. Human morality derived from the opinions and traditions of sages, and based on human observation and experience, however precarious by consequence it was in theory, failed most of all in practice. The morality of the Bible, being heaven-derived, is based on the authority of Almighty God; and, what crowns all, it is exemplified in the life and labour—the walk and work of His eternal Son. Hence the vast superiority of Bible morality is not only its unfaltering certainty and unfailing reality, but above all and beyond all, its bearing on practice. Some of the moral theories of those ancient heathens were, we cheerfully and readily own, ingenious and subtile; some of their maxims sublime; some of their dreamings splendid; but they were dreamings all the same. Scarcely practical in purpose, they made little way into the practical concerns of daily life. Knowledge and practice were as far apart as ever; or, like the curve and its asymptote, though continuing to approximate they fell short of coincidence. Even in the case of the philosophers, their systems were better than themselves; still more in the case of the multitude, between the theoretical and the practical a great gulf yawned, and there was no Curtius by leaping in to fill it up. In the life and death and resurrection of the Saviour that gulf was bridged across; a new impulse was given to humanity; God's laws were no longer engraven on tables of stone, the Spirit wrote them on warm human hearts. Life and light now came closer; knowledge and practice now joined hands; and though human practice, as human knowledge, is still but partial, the day will dawn and the time will assuredly come when, perfected in themselves, their union shall be universal as complete. May we not then with good reason conclude that the morality of the Bible gives evidence clear and conclusive that it is the word of God?

From this general view of ancient Ethics as contrasted with the principles of Bible morality, we may pass, for the purpose of further comparison, to some particulars of a still more *practical* kind. Without any attempt at a full enumeration of the practical defects of the ancient systems, a few examples of such in connection with the two most distinguished of those systems, and in comparison with certain precepts of Scripture, may be used as samples, and serve as an epitome of the whole. With regard to the system of Epicurus, the following particulars deserve to be noted :—

(1) Epicurus vacillates between polytheism and atheism. He speaks of the gods, but his gods are only ideal existences, or gods only in name. If they exist at all, they take nothing to do with human actions or terrestrial affairs. Having their supposed abode in cloudland, they live apart from earth and at ease; they are free from all care, and without concern of any kind. Accordingly, duty in the sense of piety towards

the gods had no place, and could have no place, in his system. (2) Downright selfishness was the mainspring of the Epicurean's system. At the best, his happiness was freedom from mental trouble and bodily pain, and his principle prudence. In practice, his rule of action was prudential avoidance of whatever would disturb his mind or pain his body. All self-denial, all self-sacrifice, all rendering of a service to friend or fellow-man, in case such sacrifice or service clashed with his personal pleasure or caused him pain, was out of the question. Epicurus himself, as we have seen, disavowed such an abuse of his maxim about pleasure as took it to mean gross sensual pleasure; on the contrary, Aristippus and the Cyrenaics did not mince matters, but casting aside all disguise, held bodily pleasure to be man's chief end and aim. (3) The ground on which Epicurus inculcated the avoidance of what was vicious or the observance of what was virtuous, was not the intrinsic evil of the former nor the meritoriousness of the latter; but because the present pleasures of a vicious course led to future and greater pains, while virtuous conduct conducted to pleasure or profit. Akin to this is his prohibition of crimes, not from any disinterested motive or generous principle, or because of the criminality itself, but for fear of detection and consequent punishment. As in other ancient philosophers, so in Epicurus there was a vanity of boasting combined with strange and glaring inconsistencies, as when he maintains that a wise man is happy though he should be suffering extreme pain; and this as though in forgetfulness of, or in direct opposition to, his own principle, that pain is the greatest or only evil, while pleasure is man's chief good.

(1) We turn again to the Stoics, who, it is admitted, did include in their creed piety to the gods; but in their case it was an acknowledgment not of one god, but of gods many. They were either polytheists or pantheists, and so their worship was either idolatry or a worship of nature. They worshipped they knew not what, and, if we judge from their diversities of mode, they worshipped they knew not how. Besides, their fear of the gods was a respectful reverence without any dread of their wrath against either ungodliness or unrighteousness.

(2) The Stoic philosophers spoke of benevolence as a duty; but with respect to the forgiveness of injuries, they were divided in their sentiments. Greeks were required to show this benevolence to Greeks because of kinship; but to barbarians, as all who did not speak Greek were called, hostility or hatred took the place of benevolence. Farther, in regard to forgiveness, some held that not to revenge an injury argued a defect of character; others, that it was a mark of indolence; others, again, that forgiveness might be extended once, but not a second time, to a person who repented of the injury inflicted, and in such a way or with the condition that others might be deterred from injuring; while a very few did hold the duty of forgiveness, and forbade retaliation in case of injuries. These sometimes urged the duty of forgiveness in forcible terms; but even when urging it, they not unfrequently placed the duty on a wrong basis, or enforced it by wrong motives. They pled for forgiveness on such grounds as these:—the persons who do the injury are to be forgiven, because they acted through error of judgment, and because that owing to such erroneous judgments they could not act otherwise. Thus it is unwillingly and ignorantly they did the wrong, and so they ought to be forgiven, since from their wrong notions they were under a necessity to act as they did. Thus conscience was stifled, and right and wrong confounded. Another argument employed by them in favour of forbearance and forgiveness is still more remarkable, and shows at once the extravagance and inconsistency of their system. It is, that their wise man or ideal good man is incapable either of doing or suffering injury; thus Seneca says: "Quod in sapientem non cadit injuria." But if no injury be sustained, there can surely be no room for the exercise of forgiveness, or at least no merit in such exercise. By a similar inconsistency, they held that a wise man was happy even under the evils of life, such as pain and poverty, distress and disaster, or rather, that these in reality were no evils at all; and yet, notwithstanding this, they recommended suicide as a remedy against, or relief from, such things, though, on their own showing, they could neither destroy nor even diminish a wise man's happiness. Moreover, when they placed a man's

happiness in his own hands, they were compelled, in order to keep up the semblance of consistency, to treat external things —advantages or disadvantages, over which a man can have no control, as indifferent—neither good nor evil, thus contradicting both reason and experience. (3) The greatest blot on their system was perhaps the looseness of their views with respect to purity and chastity. It is not strange, then, that impurity was so prevalent in the heathen world, when it was countenanced, to some extent at least, even by its most renowned philosophers. Another sad blemish was their laxity with regard to intemperance. Zeno was addicted to it, Cato practised it, Seneca commended it on particular occasions, and Chrysippus died of it. (4) Arrogancy of pride, self-sufficiency, and boastfulness of spirit were mixed up with their best performances. In their self-confidence they boasted that happiness as well as virtue was in their own power. They left no room for prayerfulness of spirit or humility of mind. As to the former, they recommended prayer for help in performance of duty; but why pray to the gods for what they possessed or had in their own power? And humility was out of the question in the case of those who claimed to be equals of, not inferiors to, the gods themselves. Seneca speaks of a consistent virtuous life in these words: "Hoc est summum bonum, quod si occupas, incipis deorum esse socius, non supplex."

In contrast with these, the Scriptures give us (1) the most exalted notions of the divine nature and character. They teach the unity of God; that He is a Spirit, self-existing and eternal, possessing every perfection, and with every high and holy attribute; that He is everywhere present, His power almighty, His wisdom infinite, His greatness unsearchable; that He is omniscient as well as omnipresent—all things being open and naked before His all-seeing eye; that He is our Creator and Preserver; that He guides all, governs all, and that His mercy is over all His works, while His goodness is unspeakable; that He is holy and just as well as good, righteous in all His ways and holy in all His works; that He is a God of unswerving truth and spotless purity; that, owing to His infinite goodness and our littleness and weakness, He is to be approached through the mediation of His Son, our Saviour, and that the riches of His grace have been manifested to man in the person and work of that Mediator; that He is to be worshipped in spirit and truth, with humble, penitent, and contrite hearts; that He is to be supplicated as the God that hears prayer; that He is to be praised for His wondrous works, for His mighty deeds, for the honour of His majesty and the glory of His grace; that He is to be loved with all our heart, soul, mind, and strength. (2) With respect to our fellow-creatures, the Scriptures forbid us to injure them by work or word or even thought; they require us to render good for evil; to do good to all men as far as we have opportunity; to help them in their struggles and sympathise with them in their sorrows; to forgive as we expect forgiveness; to render to all their due; to observe the duties that devolve upon us in our various stations and relations, as husbands and wives, parents and children, masters and servants, as rulers and ruled; in a word, to do justly, love mercy, and walk humbly with our God. (3) In reference to ourselves, they enjoin purity of heart, speech, and behaviour; they command temperance in all things; they forbid pride and high-mindedness; they condemn avarice and love of riches, teaching the rich not to trust in them, but to use them without abusing them—to regard themselves as stewards who must one day give account; they urge contentment with our lot and patience under the diverse ills that flesh is heir to, not, be it observed, apathy, as if we were persons devoid of feeling, nor as if such things were indifferent,—a course which is against, instead of according to, nature,—but with the impression that these ills are paternal chastisements, trials of faith and patience, and to be ultimately overruled for our highest good; they inculcate true courage, not needless exposure to danger, diligence in our calling yet heavenly-mindedness, self-denial but not asceticism, carefulness of health and life, as God's gifts to be used in His service and to His glory, and on no account to be neglected or recklessly cast aside; they enjoin freedom from all carking cares and harassing anxieties, casting our burden on the Lord, who careth for us. In a word, whatsoever things are true, and pure, and just, and lovely, and of good report, "if there be any virtue, and if there be any praise," we are to "think on these things."

Such are the precepts of the gospel; text after text of Scripture might be cited in proof of these and others similar. Our privileges as saints, as members of Christ, as children of God, and as heirs of heaven, require our obedience. The promise of divine aid is pledged for our help. The example of the Saviour is our pattern. The attempt in our own strength is like forcing water up a hill; but love makes labour light, nay, love all-constraining, and all-conquering love, makes the career of the Christian like the water-course downhill, now sweeping away the obstacles that impede, again forcing its way between narrowed banks, anon dashing over the rugged rocks, and pursuing its onward way in might and majesty to the main. The kaleidoscope consists of a few simple materials; these it presents under a variety of aspects, and with shapes and shades of surprising beauty; so in the kaleidoscope of Scripture, the different fundamental doctrines of morals are presented under a variety of beautiful shapes and forms, yet all united and harmoniously blended. One aspect is the eternal and unchanging rule of right and wrong, "Shall not the Judge of all the earth do right?" this is the objective side; another is the supremacy of conscience—God's monitor to and vicegerent in man, the inward faculty that makes man a law to himself, "Even of your own selves judge ye not that which is right?" this is the subjective side; a third is the consequences of conduct good or bad, "These things are good and profitable unto man;" this is the practical side. These three cardinal truths are the germs of the leading ethical systems, whether of ancient or modern times. Their separation is weakness, their combination is strength as well as beauty. In most human systems they are isolated from each other, in Scripture they are united; in heathen Ethics they are detached, in Scripture they are dovetailed together; they are easily distinguishable, but can never be dissociated; their separation is a disproportion, their close connection in Scripture makes a perfect whole of full and fair dimensions.

But the whole may be put into a few sentences. The morality of the Bible is all-embracing. It includes every creature and every case that can possibly emerge amid all the possibilities of moral conduct. It comprises everything that men commit or omit. It comprehends every thought, every word, and every work. It ranges all along the line of human conduct from one extremity to the other—from the roving fancy or evil imagination to the dreadful deed of blood. It is confined to no sphere, to no station, and to no sex. It makes its appeal to the conscience of young and old, of high and low, of rich and poor, of young man and maiden, of old men and children alike. There is no conceivable duty that it overlooks, and there is no duty that it misstates, or mutilates, or misplaces. Everything that man owes to himself, to his fellow, and to his Maker, is controlled by the same great rule of right and law of love. Again, it combines rectitude of conduct with correctness of motive. The thing must be right in itself, and the motive that prompts it must also be right. It welds together all the elements of right action. The particular line of conduct must approve itself as right to conscience; and conscience, in the popular sense, while interpreting the law, must be in agreement with the law, for there is weight in Whewell's paradox, that to act against conscience is always wrong, though to act according to one's conscience is not always right. But with an action accepted as right by an enlightened conscience, there must also be the right spirit. In other words, there is the right thing to do, and the right way including the right spirit, and the right motives to do it. Again, unlike the Epicurean system of old, or the Utilitarian in modern times, it sets before us an end and aim higher and holier than the love of pleasure, or of profit, or of power, or of worldly greatness, or earthly grandeur, or human glory of any kind, even the glory of God and the good of man. It is unlike Stoicism, with respect to the individual man as well as in relation to society; for while Stoicism refuses to acknowledge the ills of human life, Christianity seeks to relieve them; while Stoicism looks down with supercilious scorn upon the affections of humanity or tries to suppress them, the Christian system sanctifies them. Finally, its morality is unvarying as universal. Theories of virtue, framed even by those who have had the benefit of Bible teaching, vary according to the diverse opinions of the theorists themselves. With some it is founded in the nature of things, whether they place it in harmony with nature, as Cudworth, or in accordance with eternal fitnesses, as Clarke, or in conformity to both, as Wollaston; with others, in the nature of man, whether they represent it as benevolence with Shaftesbury or Hutcheson, or as that which excites moral sympathy with Smith, or as conduciveness to happiness, our own or others', with Paley and his school, or as living agreeably to nature under the supreme control of conscience with Butler. These, again, are separable into three classes according to their psychological method—some resolving the faculty that determines moral obligation into a sentiment or feeling, hence the Sentimental Theory; others making it partake of the nature of reason, hence the Rational Theory; and those also who maintain the supremacy of conscience. But the morality of the Bible is secure and unshaken, reposing on the very nature of God Himself; for while to us it is right because God wills it, God wills it because it is right, and His will is the manifestation of His nature. This relation has been beautifully represented by a mystic circle whose centre is goodness, whose area and radii are wisdom, and whose circumference is will—goodness directing the wisdom, and wisdom regulating the will. The moral system of Scripture is not a dogmatic creed, nor an ethical code, nor speculative conjectures about virtue; it is constant contact with the living God in the person of His Son and through the agency of the Spirit, and thus it resolves itself into the eternal rule of right and the ever living law of love.

And now we conclude this part of the subject, namely, the internal evidence, by an observation or two on what is called *experimental* evidence, consisting in the felt experience of the blessed influences and effects of the truths of Scripture on our hearts and lives. Leading us back to God, they prove themselves to have come from God. Divine in their influence, they are divine in their origin. In other words, the experimental evidence consists in a strict accordance between the statements of the Bible and the experience of the condition, wants, and, in the case of a true Christian, renewal of his own heart.

That poor invalid who had suffered so much and spent so much to no purpose, whom our Lord cured of her terrible malady of twelve years' standing, "felt in her body that she was healed;" and when our Lord challenged her touch amid the throng, and testified that "virtue had gone out of Him," her own happy experience coincided with and confirmed the statements, for, "knowing what was done in her," she came and fell down before Him, and told Him all the truth. So the sinner, who is conscious to himself of spiritual health and cure, has the witness in Himself that healing came by hearing, and hearing by the word of God, and that the word of salvation to his soul must be the truth of God.

The close correspondence between the Bible and man's heart, especially when that heart is renewed, is truly wonderful. The statements of the book and the pulsations of the heart are in unison. The hand that framed the one must have found its way among the cords and fibres of the other. The Bible so speaks to the understanding, to the conscience, to the affections, to all the emotions of his nature, and to all the circumstances of his life, that there must have been a previous and prearranged harmony. Take a similar case. A man has a well-executed portrait of himself on the wall of his chamber. The artist who executed the portrait puts into his hand a sheet of paper clean and white. Between the picture and the paper he sees no resemblance, nor is there; but, by the application of a chemical agent to the paper, lines and marks and features become gradually apparent, and by and by more clearly visible, until he sees on the paper an exact reflection of the picture on the wall, and both a correct representation of himself—the picture on the paper is a perfect counterpart of the portrait on the wall. He cannot help coming at once to the conclusion that they proceeded directly, or at least the one originally and the other by copying, but both in the one way or other, from the same hand; and that the hand of one who had known and observed and delineated him well. So, when any man becomes a new creature in Christ Jesus, and has his eyes enlightened by the Spirit, he sees in the Bible a portrait of his moral nature, while in his heart features come to light that had not appeared before, just like the picture on the paper. At all events, every lineament of his moral nature is portrayed in the Bible; to that portraiture is found a counterpart in every working of his heart. None but he who formed the one could have constructed the other. None but the self-same hand that touched that heart into life, could produce such an exact representation of its moral likeness. With reverence he acknowledges the hand of God in both.

PART II.

INSPIRATION.

CHAPTER VI.

NATURE AND PROOF OF PLENARY INSPIRATION.

WHILE no doctrine has suffered more severely at the hands of Rationalistic critics than the inspiration of the Scriptures, there is none, perhaps, more keenly sifted at the present time.

Inspiration presupposes revelation, and is preceded by it. In treating of inspiration, we must take for granted revelation. That God has revealed Himself to man must, we think, be manifest to any one who carefully and honestly puts together certain considerations and certain evidences within easy reach of every candid inquirer. Equally evident must it be that the Bible contains that revelation. It was attested by men who, under all the circumstances, could not possibly be deceived themselves, and who, if there be any truth in history, and any reliance to be placed on testimony, or any confidence reposed in honesty, could not deceive others. Without motive or reward, or any conceivable object, despite the loss of all that men hold dear,—in the face of bitter opposition, and bloody suffering, and painful tortures, and death itself in the most terrible form in which it can be inflicted, they persevered in their testimony to the supernatural revelation they had received from God and had been commissioned to record. Not to speak of the signs and wonders and mighty works, divers miracles, as well as prophesyings transmuted after the lapse of ages into the facts of history,—miracles not only of power but of knowledge,—there is the internal concurrent evidence of the record itself in its exact and entire adaptation to the intellectual, moral, and spiritual nature of man, in all his longings and aspirations, with all his wants, and woes, and weaknesses. But while fully persuaded that in the Bible we have a communication from God and a revelation of His will to man, we may further inquire what is the character of that communication. Is the record of the revelation, as well as the revelation itself, from God? or did God, after giving the communication, leave it to man to record as best he could? Whether is it a merely human or a divinely-inspired record? Or, admitting a divine inspiration, is that inspiration partial or plenary?

1. Here we begin the inquiry by a reference to the record itself; nor is there anything illogical or objectionable in such a mode of procedure. In the case of any honest history that has the ordinary claims on human belief, if we wish to know the method of the author or the nature of his composition, we consult the composition itself. Surely, then, it cannot be looked upon as an assumption of the conclusion, if we adopt the same plan with respect to the Scriptures. If this be conceded, as it must reasonably be, we shall not have to travel far for an explanation, clear and concise, sufficient and satisfactory, of the whole matter—of revelation and inspiration at the same time. In 1st Corinthians ii. the apostle declares, distinctly and decidedly, in reference to the revelation itself, that it is from God. He speaks of it as "the wisdom of God," and tells us that it consists of "the things of the Spirit." The doctrines he taught and the duties he enjoined were not derived from worldly wisdom, nor from human reason, nor from the workings of his own spiritual and intellectual nature, but from God. "God," he says, "has revealed them unto us by His Spirit." To God alone as its source it is thus traced. Then as to the record he is equally explicit, and even emphatic, for he adds, "Which things also we speak, not in the words that man's wisdom teacheth, but which the Holy Ghost speaketh, comparing (bringing together in order to compare, or explaining by comparison, συνκρίνοντες) spiritual things with spiritual," or, as Hodge explains the last-quoted

phrase, " clothing the truths of the Spirit in the words of the Spirit." But though the meaning which Hodge thus educes is true enough and suitable enough, still it is questionable whether it be strictly grammatical to supply, to two adjectives thus exhibited without their substantives, any substantive that is not of the most general kind. Not only should the substantive thus obviously suggest itself, but to both adjectives the same substantive would naturally be supplied. Luther supplies *Sachen* to the first, leaving the second indefinite, and translates : " Und richten geistliche Sachen geistlich."

It may not be out of place here to remark that the inspiration claimed is, of course, for the autographs of Scripture long since lost, and to which we find only a reference or two in the early Fathers, as when Tertullian speaks of the churches in which *ipsæ authenticæ literæ eorum* (apostolorum) are read ; while the efforts and appliances of Textual Criticism aim at bringing the apographs or copies into the closest possible approximation to those venerable documents, which had proceeded directly from the hands of the apostles themselves. Then and only then were they entirely free from all error, but no continued miraculous interposition was either promised or put forth to secure them against subsequent deterioration through transcription, lengthened transmission, and the accidents of time. True, the value set on them as the word of God, while it occasioned more frequent transcriptions, and so more numerous variations, did at the same time produce such carefulness in copying as to limit those various readings to the less important.

While fully convinced of the correctness of the view commonly known as *plenary* inspiration, we must guard against the so-called mechanical theory of inspiration, which would reduce men to mere machines, making them pens and not penmen. The dynamical theory, as it has been called, is much to be preferred, recognising, as it does, the human as well as the divine side of inspiration. An illustration will perhaps help to put the matter in a clear light. Every one acquainted with mathematical studies is aware that, while in algebra we have two kinds of quantities to deal with, the known and the unknown, in the higher calculus also we have two sorts of quantities to compare and calculate, namely, *constants and variables*. These have an interdependence and well-ascertained relation to each other; but the constants are uniform, never changing their value; whereas the variables, as the name imports, undergo frequent change, and so vary in amount. In like manner the Bible consists of two elements, the one a constant, the other a variable. The one element is divine, the other is human. The one creates unity in the whole, the other occasions variety in the different parts. Unity in variety is the law of nature, unity in variety is the law of Scripture, and in both it is the law of God. Hence, too, is the appropriateness of the expression, "which was spoken *by* God *through* the prophet;" the former ὑπό, the latter διά, equivalent to the *a quo* and *per quem* of the Latins, that is to say, the agent and the instrument.

The penmen of Scripture retain their peculiarities of thought and expression, their own intellectual characteristics, their own special idiosyncrasies; but one and the same inspiring Spirit, using them as His instruments, and using them according to their several gifts and endowments, moved them, and so made their words His own.

2. In the great commission given by our Lord after His resurrection, He appointed His apostles to be the *teachers* of all things whatsoever He commanded; while for their encouragement, He pledged His power and promised His presence. The precept is central between a promise preceding and a promise succeeding. "All power," He says, "is given unto me in heaven and in earth; therefore," He adds, "go forth and disciple the nations of the world . . . teaching them to observe all things whatsoever I have commanded you; and, lo, I am with you alway, even unto the end of the world." When one has danger to brave or duty to face, it is a mighty encouragement to have a strong arm to lean upon; but what is the strength that slumbers in the strongest human arm compared with that of an arm that reaches from heaven to earth and from earth to heaven, and that exercises the might of omnipotence in both? Encouraged by that command, leaning on that arm, strengthened by that power, the apostles went forth to Christianise the world. Nor did they need to fear that it would ever forsake

them. That powerful presence was to accompany them all days, even unto the end of the age. Again, immediately before His ascension, He further commissioned them to be *witnesses* unto Him, pointing out the path they were to pursue and the unlimited field they were to take possession of. From Jerusalem out into Judea, and on through Samaria, and then forward—ever forward, until ultimately the world's end should be reached. Once more, in view of this wide sphere of operation, with all the toils and trials the work would involve, He renews the encouragement, saying, "but ye shall receive power after that the Holy Ghost is come upon you." From these two general statements we naturally turn to inquire about the particulars comprehended under them, and for this purpose we fall back on previous intimations and previous instructions.

In that same Gospel in which the great commission occurs we read in chap. x. 18–20 : "And ye shall be brought before governors and kings for my sake, for a testimony *unto* them and the Gentiles. But when they deliver you up, take no anxious thought *how* or *what* ($\pi\hat{\omega}\varsigma$ $\mathring{\eta}$ $\tau\iota$) ye shall speak: for it shall be given you in that same hour what ye shall speak. For it is not ye that speak, but the Spirit of your Father which speaketh in you." The same sentiment, somewhat abridged, is found in Mark xiii. 11 : "But when they shall lead you, and deliver you up, take no anxious thought beforehand what ye shall speak, neither do ye premeditate: but whatsoever shall be given you in that hour, that speak ye: for it is not ye that speak, but the Holy Ghost." Another promise of like import occurs in Luke xxi. 14 : "Settle therefore in your hearts, not to meditate before what ye shall answer ($\mathring{a}\pi o\lambda o\gamma\eta\theta\hat{\eta}\nu a\iota$): for I will give you a *mouth* and *wisdom* ($\sigma\tau\acute{o}\mu a$ $\kappa a\grave{\iota}$ $\sigma o\phi\acute{\iota}a\nu$), which all your adversaries shall not be able to gainsay nor resist." So also in the same Gospel, Luke xii. 11 : "And when they bring you unto the synagogues, and unto magistrates and powers, take ye no anxious thought *how* or *what thing ye shall answer* ($\pi\hat{\omega}\varsigma$ $\mathring{\eta}$ $\tau\acute{\iota}$ $\mathring{a}\pi o\lambda o\gamma\acute{\eta}\sigma\eta\sigma\theta\epsilon$) or what ye shall say ($\mathring{\eta}$ $\tau\acute{\iota}$ $\epsilon\mathring{\iota}\pi\eta\tau\epsilon$): for the Holy Ghost shall teach you in the same hour what ye ought to say." Now these promises, —one in Matthew, one in Mark, and two in Luke,—at once suitable and comprehensive, have been misunderstood or misapplied in two ways. Some have restricted them too much, others have unduly extended them. The view of the latter, in regarding them as superseding ordinary pulpit preparation, does not deserve serious attention; but the former, referring them to those apologetic testimonies to which the apostles were frequently called, demands consideration. This view seems favoured by the words in Luke, especially ἀπολογήσησθε, and is no doubt true as far as it goes; while instances of the fulfilment of the promise in this sense are found in the appearances of John and Peter before the Sanhedrim, as recorded in the fourth chapter of Acts; of Stephen in the synagogue and before the Council, as narrated in the sixth chapter of the same book of Scripture; and in the case of Paul, when he says of himself, in 2 Tim. iv. 16: "At my first answer no man stood with me, but all men forsook me. Notwithstanding the Lord stood with me, and strengthened me; that by me the *preaching* might be fully known, and that all the Gentiles might hear." While, therefore, such special occasions are included in the promised help of the Holy Spirit, the last-mentioned example of fulfilment shows that it comprehended much more. In Paul's case there was not only strength graciously vouchsafed for the answer (ἀπολογία), but the proclamation (κήρυγμα) of the truth of the gospel was also contemplated, whilst the record of the promise in Matthew and Mark is freed from any limitation. It is there *speech* and *testimony* for which succour and support are promised.

The form of expression, if not borrowed from, has a close analogy with such passages of Old Testament Scripture as the following:—" Now therefore go, and I will be with thy mouth, and teach thee what thou shalt say," Ex. iv. 12; "Then the Lord put forth His hand and touched my mouth. And the Lord said unto me, Behold, I have put my words in thy mouth," Jer. i. 9; "Then flew one of the seraphim unto me, having a live coal in his hand, which he had taken with the tongs from off the altar: and he laid it upon my mouth. ... And he said, Go, and tell this people," Isa. vi. 6, in allusion to which Milton sings: "Sendeth forth His cherubim with the hallowed fire of His altar, to touch the lips of whom He will." If, then, we consider the passages of Old Testament Scripture to which the promise bears such striking resemblance, and to which it probably alludes, the absence of restriction in Matthew and Mark, the fact that it was for the general purpose of apostolic testimony this special aid is promised, and more particularly the broad commission in the background, we shall not hesitate to conclude that the promise has respect not only to such special and rarer occasions as those of the apostles' appearance before Gentile potentates and Jewish rulers, but to all those moments of supreme importance in their history when they (*i.e.* apostles) were required either by tongue or pen to testify or teach the truth of God. The oral teaching and the written record are, it must be observed, placed by the Apostle Paul on the same level, when, writing to the Thessalonians, he says: "Stand fast, and hold the traditions which ye have been taught, whether by word or our epistle." This is confirmed by the expression of the Apostle John to the effect: "These things are written, that ye might believe that Jesus is the Christ, the Son of God; and that believing ye might have life through His name."

3. But passing from the application of the promise to its actual import, we shall find that it contains most ample provision for all the varied exigencies of the case and requirements of the work. In the *how* and *what* ($\pi\hat{\omega}\varsigma$ $\mathring{\eta}$ $\tau\acute{\iota}$) are clearly included both the matter and the manner—the right material to be employed, and the proper mode of its exhibition; while under the *mouth* and *wisdom* ($\sigma\tau\acute{o}\mu\alpha$ $\kappa\alpha\grave{\iota}$ $\sigma o\phi\acute{\iota}\alpha\nu$) are as certainly comprehended the inward power of thought, and the outward power of expression. In both we have the underlying notions and their utterance—the internal thoughts and the external vehicle of speech—understanding and language whether oral or written—both ideas and words — in fact, the $\lambda\acute{o}\gamma o\varsigma$ $\mathring{\epsilon}\nu\delta\iota\acute{a}\theta\epsilon\tau o\varsigma$ and the $\lambda\acute{o}\gamma o\varsigma$ $\pi\rho o\phi o\rho\iota\kappa\acute{o}\varsigma$ of the Greeks, or the *ratio* and *oratio* of the Latins; that is to say, the mental conception with which the former is employed, and the verbal communication which embodies the latter.

4. On turning from the synoptic Gospels to the Gospel of John, we meet a similar, or even a still more explicit, assurance of complete divine guidance in the comprehension and

declaration of truth. In John xiv. 26: "The Comforter (or Advocate), which is the Holy Ghost, whom the Father will send in my name, He shall *teach you all things*, and *bring all things to your remembrance*, whatsoever I have said unto you;" then in chap. xv. 26: "The Comforter, even the Spirit of truth, which proceedeth from the Father, He shall *testify of me:* and *ye also shall bear witness*, because ye have been with me from the beginning;" and farther in the following chapter, viz. xvi. 13, it is written: "Howbeit when He, the Spirit of truth, is come, He will *guide you into all truth.*" The *first* of these Scriptures just cited contains two most valuable statements on the subject of inspiration—one with regard to future and full independent instruction, the other with respect to prevention of any possible lapse of memory. The "all things" ($\pi\acute{a}\nu\tau a$) must be taken in a limited sense because of its contrast with "These things ($\tau a\hat{v}\tau a$) have I spoken unto you, being yet present with you"—not all things absolutely, but all that was required to be added to the things which the Saviour had just taught. The time for instruction on the part of the Saviour was fast coming to an end; when it actually closed, whatever things or instructions remained unfinished, either from the apostles' inability to bear them just then, or from the need of application to their minds, all these the Holy Spirit would complete, not only making perfectly intelligible what had been left somewhat obscure, quickening their understanding, and directing attention to what had escaped their observation at the time; but concluding the lessons that needed still to be learnt, until the full measure should be attained. Nor would aught that had fallen from the Master's lips be lost, or allowed to slip from defect of memory or other cause; the Holy Spirit was to recall the Saviour's teaching, as well as supplement it, until the whole, in its entirety and just relative proportions, should take permanent possession of their mind and memory, and so remain at hand for transmission either orally or by written record. In the *second* passage cited from the Gospel of John, another point is prominently brought out. There is a two-fold testimony mentioned—the testimony of the apostles and the testimony of the Spirit. The testimony of the apostles had already commenced, and was to continue, for the verb is in the present tense, "and ye also bear witness ($μαρτυρεῖτε$);" the testimony of the Advocate proceeding from the Father ($παρά = from\ the\ side\ of$, signifies position, the reference being to His temporal mission, not to His eternal procession, in which latter case the preposition is $ἐκ = out\ of$, denoting source), and sent by the Son, would consummate this important testimony. Of many things the apostles were eye- or ear-witnesses, or both. The facts of His history, His life, His death, His resurrection, His ascension, His conversation while He went out and in with them, His discourses and His parables, were of the sort indicated. But there were other matters which, in the very nature of things, they themselves could not witness—things to which the Holy Spirit alone could bear testimony, such as the miraculous conception; and though, no doubt, the testimony of the Spirit was borne through human instruments, yet it was none the less distinct. The witness of the Spirit was thus at once concurrent and co-operative. This was the case with respect both to what the Spirit taught and to what He testified. This was certain to secure them against slips of memory. In this way the Spirit strengthened their memory, properly so called, in retaining, stimulated the suggestion that acts spontaneously under the laws of association, and helped their power of reminiscence. In retention and recollection alike His aid was needed, and the passages under consideration afford positive proof of that aid being vouchsafed, so that when, or if the lines became faded, they were freshened, colours dimmed were brightened, and characters effaced were retouched. Not only so; what was imperfectly understood at first, and so more likely to be forgotten, would, in accordance with the promise we are considering, be made clear to the apprehension, and so impressed on the memory. Still more, there were truths yet to be taught. And so the sphere of the Spirit's operation was widened by additional and independent teaching. As examples of this may be adduced the spiritual nature of Christ's kingdom, a truth which, notwithstanding all they had learnt from the Master Himself, they were ignorant of until they received the Spirit in Pentecostal power and plenty.

Some ten days before that marvellous event they still laboured under misapprehension in regard to the character of the Redeemer's kingdom, saying: "Lord, wilt Thou at this time restore again the kingdom to Israel?" They still clung, as is plain from this question, to the mistaken notion of a temporal kingdom. Another example of this independent and additional instruction, was the gift of tongues; this wonderful linguistic knowledge—this power of speech which opened the way to the hearts of so many strangers from many lands, was the bestowment of the Spirit, as we read: "They were all filled with the Holy Ghost, and began to speak with other tongues (probably each one speaking some new language, so that the strangers were addressed in their native tongue by one or other of the apostles), as the Spirit gave them utterance." In a manner somewhat analogous the Spirit instructed Philip, saying: "Go near and join thyself to this chariot;" and directed Peter: "while Peter thought on the vision, the Spirit said unto him, Behold, three men seek thee. Arise, therefore, and get thee down, and go with them, doubting nothing: for I have sent them." Whether, therefore, it was correction, or instruction, or direction that was needed, the Spirit's help met the exigency. So also in the matter of witnessing. He witnessed with and to the apostles; thus Peter says: "We are His witnesses of these things, and so is also the Holy Ghost;" somewhat similarly Paul says: "The Holy Ghost witnesseth (rather witnesseth *to me*, μοι, the reading of five uncials and many cursives, and approved by Lachmann and Tischendorf) in every city, saying that bonds and afflictions abide me." This was, in all probability, effected both by direct inward communication and such prediction as that of Agabus. This will account for the remarkable and otherwise almost inexplicable wording of the first synodical decree: "For it seemed good to the Holy Ghost and to us." There is joint operation in this decision, and joint authorship in its expression, whether it was that He directed it, and they drew it up, or that He sanctioned it, and they signed it, or, in the words of Hooker: "the Holy Ghost the author, themselves but only the utterers of that decree." It is not to be understood as meaning: "to us by the Holy

Ghost," with Grotius, who makes it a hendiadys; nor yet with Olshausen, as signifying: "to the Holy Ghost in us;" but rather, according to the remark of Calovius: "Conjungitur causa principalis et ministerialis decreti." At all events the two agencies are distinct yet consentaneous; their decisions, being thus come to under the guidance of the Spirit, carried with them infallible authority. Further, and *thirdly*, special consideration is due to that other promise of the Saviour: "I have yet many things to say unto you, but ye cannot bear them now. Howbeit when He, the Spirit of truth, is come, He will guide you into all truth." One great function of the Spirit is to deal with truth; it is with truth He takes to do. The expression Spirit of truth does not signify the same thing as truthful Spirit merely; it is more than a mere epithetic genitive, it is rather a genitive of the subject-matter of the Spirit's official work—that is, of the object on which, or the sphere in which, He operates. In that capacity He guided the inspired penmen into *the* truth, for so it literally is; the article restricts the meaning to that truth which, as divinely commissioned and divinely qualified instructors, the apostles were required to make known. It is neither intimated nor to be inferred that they were to be guided into all truth in general. With much truth, as lying in various departments of science, or belonging to different branches of philosophy, they might remain unacquainted; but into all the truth necessary for the particular object contemplated and the special end in view, into all the truth concerning Messiah's person and work, into all the truth about sin, and righteousness, and judgment,—in a word, into all the truth respecting the Saviour and salvation, they would be infallibly introduced. The Saviour is the way, the Spirit is the guide, while the fair domain into which they are conducted is the truth, and the truth in all its parts ($\tau\grave{\eta}\nu$ $\dot{\alpha}\lambda\acute{\eta}\theta\epsilon\iota\alpha\nu$ $\pi\hat{\alpha}\sigma\alpha\nu$, according to the right reading or true text).

But it may be proper now to notice in passing an objection against this view of the subject. A misapprehension here has caused confusion of thought and language about the nature of inspiration, as though inspiration was equivalent to or involved omniscience. But, in truth, it is neither omniscience in relation to all subjects generally, nor even omniscience with regard to the topics specially handled. The penmen of Scripture were not put in possession of all knowledge on all the various themes that occupy human thought, nor even in possession of all knowledge about those particular themes of which they treat. They were circumscribed in the communication of knowledge to themselves, and circumscribed also in their function of communicating that knowledge to others. On the other hand, all that they did communicate was absolutely true, all that they were commissioned to declare was thoroughly trustworthy. Whatever they vouched for, and to whatever extent they vouched for it, was to be received, as indeed it was, the truth of God, and to be unhesitatingly and confidently relied on. What they stated to be true was perfectly true, and as they stated it; what they declared to be fact was positively fact, and just as they declared it. It need not be thought strange, therefore, nor in any way incompatible with their high function, if they expressed at times uncertainty about some things, as when Paul says: "What I shall choose I wot not;" or unacquaintance with others, as in 1 Cor. i. 16, where he says: "And I baptized also the household of Stephanas: besides, I know not whether I baptized any other." Now, the promise of the Spirit's guidance embraced all necessary truth — all essential truth, as we have seen, both in the subject-matter and the manner of expressing it. Outside the sphere of the inspired penman lay many things about which he neither sought nor secured information; just as our Lord Himself said, in His reply to the apostles, immediately before ascending to His Father and their Father: "It is not for you to know the times or the seasons, which the Father has put in His own power." Again, of some particulars relating to matters within his sphere, as of the number of persons to whom he administered baptism, he admits, at least according to the common interpretation of the words, ignorance. This admission, even if it extend the length of uncertainty or ignorance according to the current exposition, is true, and truthfully recorded. Yet this statement, as generally understood, in which the apostle says: "Besides, I know not whether

I baptized any other," though sometimes urged against the doctrine of inspiration in general, is in no way either inconsistent or incompatible with that doctrine. Some baptized by him at Corinth might have removed elsewhere, or some baptized by him elsewhere might have removed thither, or some baptized by him might remain no longer in the land of the living, or some baptized by him might not now be remembered by him; and so he could not, from his own knowledge or recollection, or from information brought him by others, go beyond his present statement. Here we see the scrupulous exactness of the apostle, and his unswerving adherence to truth. In guarding himself from cavil, he admits the possibility of lapse of memory, or owns to uncertainty about the particulars, or even acknowledges ignorance of this one circumstance. But whether it was obliviousness, or uncertainty, or ignorance, it was in a mere matter of detail —a matter more secular than sacred—a matter, too, that no way concerned or touched the interests of religion; it was, in fact, a thing entirely unnecessary and unessential. Acquaintance with all matters of that sort would bespeak omniscience, which, as already seen, though an attribute of Deity, is no adjunct of inspiration; ignorance of such details as that referred to, only shows their insignificance; while his acknowledgment of the circumstance goes to prove the apostle's ingenuousness and candour. Of the main fact that he baptized few in Corinth, he is perfectly cognisant, and at the same time thankful that it had been thus ordered in Providence, so that the Corinthians could have no ground to suspect that he acted in the interests of sect or self. In inspiration, the individual's powers of mind were fully exercised, ordinary human means of information were duly taken advantage of, miraculous help was economised, but when really required, it was ungrudgingly granted; while in either case, and in every instance, the inspired writer was preserved from all error, so that his record was infallibly correct. Besides, silence about matters unimportant, or unessential, or without instruction to the Church, might as reasonably be pleaded, as ignorance or lapse of memory with regard to such matters, against the doctrine of inspiration. There is, however, another view that might be taken of the statement under consideration. The original words might possibly be understood as a mild and modified sort of affirmation, without any actual notion of uncertainty, to this effect: I am not aware of having baptized any other. So Wolf paraphrases them: "I am not conscious that I baptized any other." In like manner Semler understands them: *vix arbitror, dubito valde.* The translation by Conybeare and Howson, which is: "Besides these, I know not that I baptized any other," may be similarly understood. It is an acknowledged grammatical principle, that after verbs of feeling εἰ followed by the indicative is used, where ὅτι might be expected, inasmuch as the Greeks, even in matters of perfect certainty, preferred avoiding the tone of positiveness; for example, Demosthenes says of Meidias: οὐκ ᾐσχύνθη εἰ τοιοῦτο κακὸν ἐπάγει τῳ. He did not feel ashamed of bringing (lit. if or that he brings) such an evil upon a person. Besides, οὐκ οἶδ' εἰ is a sort of phrase implying either uncertainty or negation, as in the expression of the Medea: οὐκ οἶδ' ἂν (Porson: ἄρ', *al.* οὐκ οἶδα γ') εἰ πείσαιμι, I don't think I shall persuade him. In this last case the optative, not the indicative, follows the conditional particle, though this does not materially alter the meaning of the preceding clause.

5. The counterpart of the promises of Christ to His apostles is found in the claims which those inspired men themselves put forth, not directly or by way of display, but incidentally for the most part and unobtrusively; not formally, but in fact; not pretentiously, but nothing the less peremptorily. They stand in their Master's stead; they hold the place of His representatives; they act as His ambassadors; they speak in His name and on His behalf; they reveal the divine will, and record truth with infallibility; they plead His authority, they command, they decide, and their decisions are final; they demand obedience to their directions, and that obedience is unhesitatingly rendered; they excommunicate false teachers and stigmatise their doctrines; they instruct the Church in the name of Christ, by the authority of God, and under the inspiration of the Spirit. Passages of Scripture proving these allegations are too numerous to be cited in this

place, and too well known to need citation. Here and now we can only indicate a few such, some of them to be more fully considered afterwards. Besides Acts xv. 28, the following passages of the Pauline Epistles may be referred to in this connection: Rom. xiv. 14; 1 Cor. i. 10, ii. 16, v. 4, vii. 40, xii. 28, xiv. 37; 2 Cor. ii. 10, ii. 17, x. 7, 8; Gal. i. and iv. 14; Eph. iv. 17; 1 Thess. iv. 1, 2, 8; 2 Thess. iii. 6, 12, 14. This list might be easily supplemented by many other Scriptures from the Epistles of John and Peter; but such references will readily suggest themselves to any student of the divine word.

From a careful examination of Scripture according to any correct doctrine of inspiration, it will be seen that two phenomena must be taken into account. On the one hand, the inspired penmen wrote in the popular language of the place where, and of the period when they lived, while every one of them adhered to his own personal style. They employed the expressions common and current in human speech, each at the same time retaining unmistakably his individuality. On the other hand, they were under heavenly direction and divine guidance, so that they were led into all truth with respect to the subject of their communication, and controlled in the expression of it, so that they enjoyed exemption from all mistake. Thus their thoughts are truth, and their language, which is the embodiment of thought, is also and equally true. This doctrine is not hampered by that rigid theory which identifies inspiration with dictation, and which seeks its justification in the notion of God assuming the personality of the penmen, so as to reflect their style. On the other hand, it is not cumbered by those fluctuations of opinion about the nature of inspiration, varying as they do and rising through different gradations upward from the inspiration of human genius to mental elevation and spiritual insight, and from that again to the infallible declaration of religious truth, and from this infallible doctrinal teaching on to the unerring deliverance of such historical facts and events as are involved in religious doctrines, and from this to that other stage, where the whole record both of histories and doctrines are regarded as inspired, but in different degrees. The true doctrine of inspiration steers clear of such extremes as have been indicated on either side; and, what is more and better, it is founded on the promise of our Lord, established by the statements of His apostles, confirmed by the history of the Church, witnessed to by patristic writers of sub-apostolic and subsequent times, and embodied in the creeds and confessions of evangelical Christendom from the Reformation down to the present day.

6. We proceed to canvass more in detail the claim to authority set up by the sacred penmen themselves. Here there are three expressions that deserve a passing notice: they are γραφαὶ ἅγιαι, ἱερὰ γράμματα, and λογία Θεοῦ. The first of these, *Holy Scriptures*, traces the origin of Scripture to the agency of the Holy Spirit, and apprises us of its divine authorship; the second, though similarly translated in our Authorized Version, is somewhat different, and might perhaps be better rendered *Sacred Scriptures;* at all events, it implies the respect and veneration accorded to Scripture by men. If the one presents the God-ward aspect, the other exhibits the man-ward; both unite at the same time in attributing to Scripture a sacredness and a sanction which no other writings in the world possess. As to the third term, *Oracles of God*, it denotes the communications of God to man—those real responses called living oracles, because the same in potency now, and through all time, as when they first proceeded from the mouth of God,—oracles deriving their living essence and life-giving energy from the ever-living One Himself, and which His people shall not willingly let die. While generally expressed in the plural (Scriptures) in relation to their different parts, they are also spoken of in the singular (Scripture) to denote them as a well-known collective whole. And here we must have in recollection that the epithet conjoined with the expression γραφαί, or γράμματα, or λογία, whether that epithet be *holy*, or *hallowed*, or *divine*, or some other and still more explicit designation, applies not to ideas merely, but to the expression of those ideas—not to thoughts in the mind, but to thoughts embodied in language—not to what is mental only, but to what is manual at the same time—not to doctrines comprehended in the understanding of the penmen,

but committed to writing—not to the conceptions, but to the words in which these conceptions are couched. Now, it is affirmed that these "Scriptures must be fulfilled"—that they "cannot be broken"—that "one jot or one tittle (the smallest letter or projecting horn of a letter) shall in no wise pass from the law, till all be fulfilled"—that "holy men *of* God spake as they were moved by the Holy Ghost." Literally it is borne along, as a ship borne along before the breeze or wafted by the wind; while, instead of men of God spake, it may be men spake from God, that is, ἀπό the reading preferred by Tischendorf, the sense being that they spake, as authorised and instructed by God, what they had received from His lips or had seen in the light of His presence. It is further stated, that "if any man speak, it should be as the oracles of God;" not, be it observed, as the oracles of God speak, which is the explanation of some; nor yet let him speak, which is the current exposition, but, because of the participial construction of the preceding verse, if any man speak, *as one speaking the oracles of God*—not speaking them as though they were his own utterances or of human origin; nor adulterating them with the earthly, but handling them with that fidelity, solemnity, and reverence that of right pertain to the messages of God to man.

Again, we are taught that "all Scripture is given by inspiration of God," or, more literally, that *every Scripture is breathed or inbreathed by God*. In the passage just cited, exception cannot be fairly taken to the absence of the article from γραφή, nor is the force a whit weakened whether you take *given by inspiration* as a predicate or an epithet; for, with regard to the absence of the article, the word is used in its technical sense, and so partakes of the nature of a proper name, and, being thus sufficiently definite, can dispense with the article; but the absence of the article serves, in our opinion, another and important purpose—it *individualises*. The apostle had just spoken of the sacred Scriptures as a whole, and said that they are able to make wise unto salvation; here, in the verse next following, he takes them part by part, singly and severally, and affirms of each that every Scripture (the correct equivalent of πᾶσα γραφή) is inspired by God; or, as some prefer to construct it, being inspired by God is also useful. But we must reclaim against the restrictive sense attached to the phrase by some, who, besides taking it as an epithet, limit the sense : such limitation is erroneous, and introduces an idea which derives no countenance from the original. It does not mean that every Scripture *which* is inspired, or, *so far as* it is inspired, is useful for the purposes specified, as though there were some not inspired at all. This would foist an idea into the original, and force on it a modification never meant. The Vulgate, though rendering it as an epithet, gives no countenance to the wrong restriction indicated; it is, *Omnis Scriptura divinitus inspirata*, all Scripture, not which is, but being, or because it is, or as it is inspired. The Syriac, indeed, rather loosely renders by *davrucho ethkather*, which has been written by His Spirit, but not, as it appears to us, in any sense of limitation. This also must be attentively weighed, that all or every Scripture is inspired; not, you will observe, the meaning of every Scripture, nor the doctrines of every Scripture, nor the ideas of every Scripture, but the Scripture or writing itself, and that writing consists of words.

7. Another, and to our mind satisfactory, proof of verbal inspiration is involved in the fact that an argument is often made to hinge on a single term. Twice our Lord argues from the use of a particular word, as when, in reasoning with the Jews, He quotes from the Old Testament: "Is it not written in your law, I said ye are *Gods?*" Or when He poses them with the question: "How then doth David in spirit call Him *Lord*, saying, The Lord said unto my Lord?" Again, in the Epistle to the Hebrews, the reasoning in two instances proceeds on a special expression, or a single word, as where it is written: "And this expression, *yet once more*, signifieth the removing of those things that are shaken;" and also: "Thou hast put all things in subjection under His feet. For in that He put *all* in subjection under Him, He left nothing that is not put under Him." Nay more, our Lord bases the proof of such an important doctrine as the resurrection on the *tense* of a verb: "I am the God of Abram, and the God of Isaac, and the God of Jacob" (ἐγὼ εἰμι of the LXX. being equivalent to אנכי אלהי, that is, *I am*, not *was*). Further, a long chain of reasoning is linked by the Apostle Paul to the employment of the

singular number: "Now to Abraham and his *seed* were the promises made. He saith not, And to seeds, as of many; but as of one, And to thy seed, which is Christ." Now, we all know what becomes of an edifice when its foundation is weakened, or undermined, or in any way damaged. So with arguments based on the use of a particular expression, or on a single word, or a tense, or a number, if the sacred writer, who originally employed such expression, word, tense, or number, had only been guided in the *matter* merely, and not in the *manner* also; if he only possessed inspiration as to the ideas, but was left entirely to his own option in the choice of words to clothe them withal. In such a case he might have retained the sense and yet varied the expression, word, tense, or number at pleasure; and if he were at liberty to do so, or did so, or if the expression selected by him were not adequate or appropriate, or in any way not the best, no argument based on an expression, word, tense, or number thus left indifferent could possibly be conclusive. Unless the writer possessed verbal inspiration, no proof derived from his use of this or that particular form of expression could carry sufficient weight either to convince a gainsayer or confirm the faithful.

But admitting the application of all this to the Old Testament, how are we to prove its extension to the New? The words of the prophets of the Old Testament, and the commandments of the apostles of the New, are co-ordinated with respect to inspiration and authority, as when it is said (2 Pet. iii. 1): "That ye may be mindful of the words which were spoken before by the holy prophets, and of the commandments of us the apostles of the Lord and Saviour." Not to speak of those passages which thus put the apostles and evangelists on the same platform with the prophets of the Old Dispensation, we meet with such promises (some of which have been already cited) as: "It is not ye that speak, but the Holy Ghost;" "Whoso heareth you heareth me;" "The Holy Ghost, whom the Father will send in my name, He shall teach you all things, and bring all things to your remembrance whatsoever I have said unto you." To the fulfilment of this promise there is undoubtedly significant reference in the frequent "remembered" (ἐμνήσθησαν): "His disciples *remembered* that

He had said this unto them;" "Then *remembered* they that these things were written of Him." The Spirit was "to guide them into all truth," and to "show them things to come." The promises thus made by the Saviour were claimed by the apostles, and their claims were allowed, being ratified by signs following. But in addition to such assurances, we find Peter classing the Pauline Epistles with the Old Testament Scriptures, and assigning them just the same rank, when he says in reference to the former: "Which they that are unlearned and unstable wrest, as they do also the other Scriptures" (καὶ τὰς λοιπὰς γραφάς). Farther, Paul places side by side a citation from the Book of Deuteronomy in the Old Testament and a quotation from the Gospel of Luke in the New, assigning them co-ordinate rank and authority, and that in an Epistle to the very same person to whom he had asserted the inspiration and consequent practical excellence of all or every Scripture: "For the Scripture saith, Thou shalt not muzzle the ox that treadeth out the corn. And the labourer is worthy of his hire." Still more, in one of the four occurrences of the expression *Oracles of God*, the reference is to the New Testament, as the best commentators admit. Thus Webster (on Heb. v. 12) says: "*Oracles of God* may be applied to the Christian revelation, then in the course of oral disclosure. The apostle naturally, in writing to Hebrews, uses a word which puts it on a level with the earlier revelation." Similarly, Delitzsch (on the same passage) says: "Although, of course, it might be used to designate the Old Testament revelation (Acts vii. 38; Rom. iii. 2), yet here (Heb. v. 12), where Christians are addressed as such, it is the *revelation of the New Testament*, the whole word of God in relation to Jesus Christ, God's testimony to Him, and His own regarding Himself." The Oracles of God thus embrace the whole of His revealed will, whether in connection with the Old or New Covenant.

Not only is the Bible thus in its two great divisions of Old and New Testament the word of God, it is the word of God throughout. That some parts of it are inspired and others not; that some parts required a higher sort of inspiration; or that there are gradations in inspiration—that, admitting the inspiration of the whole, there are degrees, such as *Suggestion, Direction, Elevation,* and *Superintendence,* or name them as you please, are opinions which appear to us to be without warrant in the word of God. There is no such distinction made in Scripture itself between different kinds or different degrees of inspiration. There is no statement of Scripture leaving us to infer that, while the matter is inspired, the manner is left entirely to the writer's own discretion. The whole is a mere theory, and a theory, as we think, unsanctioned and unsustained by Scripture. Besides, what purpose can such a theory serve, except to unsettle people's minds in regard to what really originates with God and what only emanates from man; while it must needs detract materially from the respect and authority due to the word of God? The theory is cumbered with difficulties of a practical kind, and unworkable in detail; for where or how is the line of demarcation to be drawn between what is divine and what is human? Who is to discriminate? By what verifying faculty shall we be enabled to make the distinction? Surely, under such circumstances, the door is thrown open to our individual leanings, or prejudices, or even passions. In the end it comes to this, that by whim, or caprice, or preconceived opinion, or some other subjective standard, the word of God shall be tested, and, when so tried, accepted or rejected at pleasure. To such a fluctuating principle of inspiration, may we not, with the sense of a single term slightly modified, apply the question: "*An sua cuique deus fit dira cupido?*" A statement of Dr. Chalmers on this head deserves serious attention. "Strange," he says, "that with the inspiration of thoughts it should make pure ingress into the minds of the apostles; but, wanting the inspiration of words, should not make pure egress to that world in whose behalf alone, and for whose admonition alone, this great movement originated in heaven and terminated in earth. Strange, more especially strange, in the face of the declaration that not unto themselves but unto us they ministered these things; strange, nevertheless, that this revelation should come in purely to themselves, but to us should come forth impurely—with somewhat, it would appear, with somewhat the taint and the obscuration of human frailty attached to it."

Time would fail to enumerate all the proofs of verbal inspiration that meet us in Scripture, there is such a profusion of distinct and decided testimonies to this effect, while the general claim of inspiration made at the outset, or afterwards repeated, must be held to cover all the other recorded statements of prophet or apostle. We can only indicate a few of such testimonies, and these as characteristic of many more. Thus David says: "The Spirit of the Lord spake by me;" "The Holy Ghost spake by the mouth of David;" "Thou God, by the mouth of Thy servant David, hast said." Words spoken by the Psalmist are attributed to the Holy Ghost, as: "The Holy Ghost says, To-day, if ye will hear His voice." Words uttered by Moses, as we are informed in one passage, are identified with the commandments of God in another. A gracious promise recorded by Jeremiah is attributed to the Holy Ghost by the writer of the Epistle to the Hebrews, where he says: "The Holy Ghost also is a witness to us." Thus each of the three main divisions of Old Testament Scriptures—the law, the prophets, and the Psalms—is ascribed to the Spirit of inspiration. What Paul calls "my gospel" at one time, he designates "the gospel of God" at another. God identifies Himself with His word, so that what the Scriptures saith God saith. And in general it is said of God that He "spake by the mouth of His holy prophets, which have been since the world began." Going over the prophets individually, we would find such unmistakable statements as the following: "The word of the Lord came unto him;" "The Holy Ghost spake by Esaias;" "Behold, I have put my words into thy mouth;" "Write all the words I have spoken to thee in a book."

8. But it is urged by some that the sacred writers themselves do not claim inspiration for all the parts of Scripture they have written, and the words of the apostle in 1 Cor. vii. 6, 10, 12, 25 are appealed to in proof. The words are: "I speak this by permission, and not of commandment;" "I command, yet not I, but the Lord;" "But to the rest speak I, not the Lord;" "I have no commandment of the Lord, yet I give my judgment." From the last verse of the same chapter, viz., "And I think also that I have the Spirit of God," it is inferred that, even when the apostle does not disclaim inspi-

ration, he seems in doubt about its possession. Now, in regard to the objection drawn from the first-cited passage, it can only arise from a misunderstanding of that Scripture; for, when the apostle says: "I speak this by permission, not of commandment," he does not mean permission given to himself by God, but permission which he (the apostle) gives to the Corinthians; instead of binding them by a rigorous commandment, he permits them to use their own discretion in the matter referred to. It is an indulgence which he allows them, and not an injunction which he lays upon them; and so it is understood in the Vulgate: *Secundum indulgentiam*, by way of indulgence, as also in the Syriac, the exact rendering of which is: "But this I speak *as to the infirm*, not from commandment." Luther renders: "Aus Vergunst;" and Billroth pithily explains it: "Nicht als Befehl . . . sondern nach Vergunst, d. h. Ihr sollt daraus nicht sehen, was Ihr thun *sollt*, sondern was Ihr thun *dürft*." With regard to the second, it relates to an ordinance—that of marriage—revealed from the beginning, re-instituted by Christ, and recorded by the Evangelist Mark (x. 12); and the apostle plainly refers to that declaration, while in doing so he co-ordinates his subjective inspiration with the objective inspired record; and when he thus places the command he had received by direct revelation of the Spirit on a footing of equality with the command delivered by Christ Himself when on earth, he reduplicates the force of his instruction, as though he had said: "I command, yet not I (*only*), but the Lord." The next two passages, instead of presenting a contrast between the apostle and his Lord, or between the human and divine, or between Paul's own advice and an injunction of the Saviour, involves by implication inspired apostolic authority, in the *absence of any expressly recorded command*, such as existed in the preceding case. Here the circumstances were exceptional, the state of matters peculiar; for such no previous provision had been made, nor needed to be made, for the apostle himself was empowered to deal with such, and not only empowered, but enabled by that illumination of the Spirit, in virtue of which he says elsewhere in the same chapter: "So ordain I," and which he claims in the words (when rightly comprehended) of the last passage to which exception has been taken, namely,

"I think also that I have the Spirit of God." In one of the three cases considered there had been an explicit deliverance by our Lord Himself; this the apostle appeals to and enforces. In the other two there had been no such express decision, and so the apostle proceeds to deal with them on his own apostolic authority, and now he informs us of the source of the authority —it was the inspiration of the Spirit; and though he prefaces his assertion by "I think," it is only a modest statement of the claim in question,—it is an idiomatic expression,—here, as in other instances, not of doubt, but of courteous assertion— not of conjecture, but of conviction—not of uncertainty, but of assurance, as is quite capable of proof; for example, Eusebius in his Com. on the 118th Psalm says of God: δικαιότατος εἶναι δοκεῖ, implying no shadow of doubt. So also the word is used in the Greek Fathers as well as in the Greek Testament.

But another class of objections to verbal inspiration is founded on what are regarded as the *less important* or supposed *unimportant* statements of Scripture. To such it may be replied, that we are not always good judges of what is important or unimportant; not unfrequently great issues depend on seemingly trivial circumstances. If the film were removed from our mortal vision,—if some one did for us what the poet represents done for his hero,—

> "Omnem, quæ nunc obducta tuenti
> Mortales hebetat visus tibi, et humida circum
> Caligat, nubem eripiam,"—

if we could see things in the brightness of the upper sanctuary, or in the reflected light of eternity, how magnitudes would change proportions! How the little would be seen great, and the great become little! What an interspace would appear between the present with its phantoms and the future with its realities; for the things that are seen are temporal, but the things that are unseen are eternal! In this way we account for the fact that in the Bible things of great moment, according to our estimate, are briefly discussed or cursorily passed over, while things of less importance, as we think, bulk much larger. The structure of the world occupies a single chapter, that of the tabernacle extends over thirteen; and both with right good reason. The tabernacle typified the Church; the world was made for the Church. The world is but the temporary scaffolding, the Church is the completed and enduring edifice in all its grand magnificence. This we cannot understand till once we look at the material as subordinate to the spiritual, the temporal to the eternal; till once sitting loose to our present environments we become duly alive to the powers of the world to come, realising the worth of the soul, the value of salvation, and the paramount as well as permanent importance of spiritual and divine things.

But of the unimportant things charged against inspiration, are certain *directions* given to Timothy, and some *lists of names*. (1) But the directions to Timothy refer to matters connected with bodily health, and mental or moral culture. One is of the nature of a medical prescription to that young and faithful minister, whose energies had been overtaxed, and whose health had no doubt suffered in consequence. Another regarded an article of clothing necessary for a poor and aged man, the apostle himself, as a precaution against the inclemency of the approaching winter; while the books and parchments were for the intellectual improvement or spiritual edification of himself or others. Are these matters of small moment or trifling importance? Did the ancients set such store by the "*mens sana in corpore sano*," and most properly; and yet will a passing reference to the same, even in cases of emergency, by an apostle, be condemned as unworthy of his notice or too insignificant to employ his pen? Can it be deemed unworthy of that God, who condescends to feed the fowls of heaven, and clothe in loveliness the lily of the field, to stoop to directions about the supply of His servants' wants in matters and under circumstances where the consequences of neglect might be fatal?

But granting that all parts of the Bible are not equally important, that some are more vitally so than others, this concession cannot militate against the inspiration of the less important parts. The hairs on the head, and the nails on toes and fingers, are not so vitally important as the heart and head and lungs; but who will presume to pronounce them unnecessary in the physical economy, or derogatory to our Maker's handiwork? This world contains many wild and apparently worthless wastes, yet who will dare to affirm that their existence is a reflection on the Creator's skill?

Further, as to those names, or lists of names, that seem to some barren of instruction and better omitted, we would remark that names among the Hebrews were peculiarly significant, there is sometimes a whole history included in a name, not to speak of the important purposes served by the names occurring in genealogies; while such particularities as names, whether of places, or persons, or dates, are just the items that forgery eschews—such circumstantials are often the evidences as well as the tests of the true and real, in opposition to the fabulous and the false. One of the finest expositions we remember to have met with is occupied with two verses consisting mostly of names: no doubt the names are identified with geography and chronology, and so serve as the two eyes of the history. As a specimen of the identification of names with the truth of a narrative, we may be excused for quoting the exposition we have been referring to. It is from a lecture of Edward Irving (on Luke iii. 1, 2), and is as follows:—

"Instead of being slightly passed over as an uninteresting enumeration of names with which the mind refuses to be burdened, they should be used by the expounder of the record for that very purpose for which they were set down by the writer, as affording a clue by which to ascertain the veracity of the narrator, and the certainty of the things narrated. It is beyond a doubt that certainly within thirty years from the date of John's baptism this narrative was circulating on the spot where the very events narrated took place, and where the memory of events so singular must have been still fresh. Now do but conceive how strong a test this is to the truth of everything narrated. Suppose a similar case. Say that a book were published and circulated in London by a set of men as the foundation of their claims to belief; and that this their public document commenced by saying that, at the beginning of the century, in the 40th year of George III., when such a man was mayor of London, and such another high sheriff of the county, and such another lord bishop of the diocese. At that time, dated after the manner of the text, there came a man out of some neighbouring forest, say Epping Forest, to the banks of the Thames. That he was dressed in the most uncouth and savage attire, and fed on the roots of the earth, refusing all the comforts, and despising all the forms of civilised life. That he lifted up his voice day by day, sparing no rank nor description of men, and night by night retiring into the gloomy and savage wilderness, from whence he issued again only to take up his woful burden against the universal declension of the land; until the whole city was moved to its centre, and went forth with one consent to hear the savage and severe denouncer of their conditions. That, in our hearing, he pronounced our priests hypocrites, our rulers extortioners, our

I

soldiers spoilers, and all men gone astray and needing repentance; and having done his terrible office day by day, he returned night by night to the wilds of nature, and harboured with the savage tenants there. Let us be told, moreover, that the man was no raving fool, but of such terrible energy of eloquence that the common herd quailed before him, and every rank, stooping its particular pride, craved of him what he wished them to do—the priests, the governors, the soldiers; that the general inhabitants flocked to him, and rank after rank submitted to be schooled by him. Upon which he requires of every man the unseemly and inconvenient rule of allowing himself to be taken and by him baptized in the river, with certain solemn promises of repentance and reformation. Let us be told, moreover, that thirty years ago, while all this was going on, and multitudes were submitting soul and body to the terrible reformer, there came from the assembled thousands one youth, at the sight of whom the haughty preacher stood humbled and abashed; that the preacher refused to do the duty for him alone of all, declaring himself to need his ablution, and that he was not able to tie the latchet of his shoe. Let us be told, moreover, that in our sight and hearing the modest stranger declined the honour, and insisted upon submitting to the ritual; that upon his coming up out of the water, there descended, cleaving the clear blue heavens, a dove, which lighted and sat upon his head in the midst of the assembly, all forgetful of its timorous nature, whereupon the hollow vault was filled with a voice like the voice of thunder, and from the empyrean descended these solemn words: 'This is my beloved Son, in whom I am well pleased.'

"I say, let the followers of any religious sect that started into being thirty years ago—ay, I may say fifty years ago, or one hundred, or two hundred years ago—set forth such a story as this now related as the ground of their claim to divine origin, and insist thereon that we should break up our establishment of Church and State, and model ourselves upon their outlandish and novel doctrines. Would people, building upon so extraordinary a tale, so lately happened, so much in our power to remember, or so much in our fathers' power, or in our fathers' fathers'—would they obtain one single convert? The very publicity of the thing, the extraordinary nature of it, would at once expose its untruth, if so be it happened not. Any one who should set up his face for it would be hooted as an idiot, or silenced as a terrible liar. . . . But such was not the case with this narrative, though beginning with precisely such a tale; it was received and believed in, and made converts thousands in a day, who sacrificed all their wealth for it, and many of them their lives also. That, I say again, is to my mind the most indubitable proof that the whole affair actually happened as it is narrated; unless the people of Jerusalem were with one consent resolved to be duped, and for the sake of being duped, which men hate as they hate death, for this were resolved to sacrifice all possessions, life present, and hope of the life to come. Now all the weight of evidence rests mainly upon the narrative being dated "—

that is, upon the names, dry and barren as they are ofttimes considered.

But the quotations of the Old Testament in the New have been urged against plenary inspiration. Farrar, in an Excursus to his *Life of Christ*, borrows a numerically tabulated form of these quotations, with the express object, it would seem, of fortifying his readers, as well as himself, against plenary inspiration. This tabulated form, differing widely from other similar forms, we hold to be a gross exaggeration, erroneous in itself, and misleading in its tendency. A correcter statement of results would be this, namely, of formal and important quotations of the Old Testament in the New, two-thirds agree either exactly or virtually with the original Hebrew; of the remaining one-third, one-half — that is, a sixth — follows the Septuagint diverging from the Hebrew, while the other half, or remaining one-sixth, departs to some extent from both. In those instances (one-sixth of the whole) in which the Septuagint is followed in preference to the Hebrew, the Septuagint presents a version substantially correct, though somewhat paraphrastic, so as to involve an *explanation,* or is more distinctly expressive of a *particular aspect* of the truth indicated by the original. It is the same sense, but modified. The other sixth, deviating from the original as well as from the Septuagintal version, deviates for the very purpose of clearing up something *obscure* in the original, or of educing out of the fulness of Scripture some *latent* thought that otherwise might not have been readily apprehended, or of fitting it better for *applicability* to the conditions and state of things in gospel times. Thus the Old Testament passage and the New Testament quotation of it are one and the same function; but in the former case the function is implicit, and in the latter it is explicit. All the while, too, it is the same Spirit, who surely cannot be debarred from so modifying His own word as to make it more appropriate to the altered circumstances of the Church, or to the exigencies of the new dispensation.

Here let us, in connection with the subject of citation, hazard a statement that may seem paradoxical. There is an inaccuracy in one of the books of Scripture, which consists in a misquotation, or perhaps we should rather say an inaccurate quotation; and yet that quotation, faulty as it undoubtedly is, appears to our mind, and, we are persuaded, will approve itself to the reader's judgment also, one of the strongest possible proofs—incidental and undesigned, and therefore the more decisive—of the truth of the narrative, and the scrupulous veracity of the narrator. The passage we refer to is Acts viii. 32, and consists of a citation from the Old Testament; but then the citation is not from the original Hebrew, nor from a good translation of the Hebrew; on the contrary, it is from a translation which in this particular passage is both inexact and inaccurate, and yet this very inaccuracy is an indispensable element to the truthfulness of the entire passage. How so? you will naturally say. The Scripture quoted is from the 53d chapter of Isaiah. The eunuch was reading it when Philip joined himself to his chariot. That eunuch was an Ethiopian. Ethiopia bordered on Egypt. The capital of Egypt was Alexandria. Alexandria was the place where the Septuagint version was made. There is the strongest probability—a moral certainty, in fact—that the Bible of this Ethiopian eunuch was a copy of that Septuagint. And so, though the Septuagint rendering of the passage is inexact and inaccurate, still it was incumbent on the narrator, in relating the passage the eunuch was reading, to give it as it stood in the version which he used, however inexact and inaccurate that version of the passage might be. This the evangelist does, and in this are seen a punctilious exactness and an unswerving fidelity, that of themselves guarantee the thorough truthfulness of the man, and the perfect credibility of his narration.

But Scripture, it is alleged, contradicts science. To the theories of scientists it may run counter, but never to the facts of science. This charge lies equally or more against revelation than inspiration. Let us, for the present, just cast a passing glance at two or three of those common contradictions charged against the Bible, as specimens of the uncandid fragmentary mode of discrediting Scripture by urging a doubt here, a difficulty there — a cavil now, an objection again. (*a*) The geologist affirms the existence of our world during millions instead of thousands of years. Admitting the truth of his assertion, and supposing, what is certainly opposed to all analogies, that the formation of the earth at its origination proceeded according to the same laws of slow development that regulate its changes now after it has attained the maturity of its existence; but conceding all this, we find in the beginning of Genesis room, as far as the language of Scripture is concerned, for æons or milliards of years between the time when heaven and earth were created and the earth fitted up for the habitation of man, because the second verse of Genesis does not imply a period *contemporaneous* with the first, for in that case the verb would be omitted; neither does it imply a *close connection*, for that would be expressed by ותהי, the tense of connected narration, but, on the contrary, *sequence*, and so it is היתה, while in the intervening space myriads of years may intervene. Nor yet can the first verse be a mere heading; the copula and the prominence given to the repeated noun *earth* forbid that. Again, in the second verse it is stated that the earth had been or had become voidness and wasteness; but *synchronous* with the state of things so described, darkness was on the deep, and the Spirit was brooding on the waters. How long this lasted, or what changes were produced, God only knows. (*b*) It used to be proposed, as a sort of puzzle, how could there be light without the sun? Putting aside the production of light by electricity, galvanism, and combustion, the old *corpuscular* theory, which made light consist of luminous particles emitted by the sun, has, in the advance of science, given way to the *wave-theory*, which makes light consist of the undulations of a subtile fluid distinct from the sun. You will observe, it is not said that God *made* light or created light; it is stated God said, *let there be* light, possibly implying the previous existence of the material of light, but in a quiescent state,—the divine fiat calling it into action; while on the fourth day the sun was fitted up and prepared, not as the אור light, but the מאור, the *mem* generally signifying locality and sometimes instrumentality; and so henceforth the sun was made to produce the vibrations of that wondrous ether. The first act of the Creator, on the first day of creation, was to call into play those incomprehensible pulsations. And here, again, you will observe the appropriateness of this; for, according to modern physics, light force, with its accompaniments of heat and chemical action, is the basis of all physical energies, putting forth that strange actinic power that fosters plants and furnishes material for animal existence. (*c*) It is alleged that the earth's motion is negatived by the text: "The world is established, it cannot be moved." This quibble, though so often repeated, hardly deserves an answer. The word מוט there used is not the ordinary word for *motion* (which is נוע or נוף); it denotes *tottering, shaking, staggering,* and thus it is applied in Prov. x. 30 to the good man: "The righteous shall never be moved" (ימוט); and in 1 Chron. xvii. 19 to the people of Israel: "They shall dwell in their place, and be moved no more." In neither case is there a denial of motion—neither was to be a fixture immovably rooted in the soil or riveted to the earth. Accordingly, the same word applied to the earth means that it (the earth) shall never totter in its course, or be jostled out of its appointed orbital path. (*d*) Take one other example. In Genesis we read of grapes in Egypt, and a passage in Numbers implies that *vines* grew in Egypt; but Herodotus was quoted against the Bible, for he tells us that the Egyptians have no vines in their country. It was vain to quote, on the other side, Virgil's "*Sunt thasiæ vites, sunt et Marcotides albæ,*" or Horace's well-known "*Lymphatam Mareotico,*" signifying *Egyptian wine.* It is known now that the culture of vines was extensively carried on in Egypt, the most celebrated being those of Mareotis, Anthylla, Plinthine, Coptos, and the Alexandrian; while the "wine of the Northern country" is often (according to Rawlinson) mentioned in the lists of offerings in Egyptian tombs; "wines of various kinds were offered in the temples, and, being very generally placed by the altar in glass bottles of a particular shape, these came to represent in hieroglyphics what they contained, and to signify wine without the word itself." So, after all, the Bible was right and Herodotus wrong; or if his consistency must be preserved, he must be supposed to speak of the interior of the broad Delta, where the alluvial soil was not so suitable to the vine.

Inaccuracies sometimes appear on the surface; but usually they yield to a more painstaking investigation, or a correcter exegesis; sometimes, when thoroughly sifted and searched out, the seeming inaccuracy yields an indirect but most decisive testimony to the rigorous strictness of Biblical truth. There may be wrong theories in science and wrong interpretations of Scripture: rectify the one and amend the other; and you have harmony. An objection more against the exposition of Scripture than Scripture itself is, that a *double sense* is attributed to certain Scriptures, which generates a vague indefiniteness, contrary to the method adopted in the interpretation of an ordinary classic, and inconsistent with such a clear revelations as the Divine Being might reasonably be expected to give of His will. The very expression *double sense* is highly objectionable, as importing dubiety or ambiguity; but with a distinct and definite sense there may be a double application; or further, what is said of a type may be realised farther and more fully in the corresponding antitype. But look how the matter stands even in classic authors. Virgil, *e.g.*, in singing of the virtues and valour of his hero and his house, interweaves therewith allusions to the Roman emperor and the glories of the Julian line. There is certainly something of a double application, if not of a double sense, in the so-called and well-known *irony* of Sophocles. But to come nearer home, who does not know that Spenser, in his *Faery Queen*, while celebrating certain personified virtues, alludes in a manner unmistakable to certain distinguished personages, so that Sir Artigall at once represents *Justice* and *Lord Grey*; Duessa, *Falsehood* and the unfortunate *Queen of Scots*; the Red-Cross Knight, both *Holiness* and the *Church?* while Spenser's own letter to Raleigh clearly states the plan as follows: "In the *Faery Queen* I mean Glory in my general intention, but in my particular, I conceive the most excellent and glorious person of our Sovereign the Queen (Elizabeth), and her kingdom in Faery land. And yet in some places I do otherwise shadow her; for, considering she beareth two persons, the one of a most royal queen or empress, the other of a most virtuous and beautiful lady, this latter part in some places I do express in Belphœbe." Shall it be thought strange, then, that in the elevated language of prophets, a reference to present persons or scenes and circumstances should be coupled with a forecasting of their antitypical counterparts, especially of the great antitype in whom all the glory of their race and line at once culminated and centred? The deeper sense embodied by inspiration in the Old Testament is by inspiration evolved in the New.

God might have graven His word on stone, or inscribed it as the handwriting on the wall, or sent it by angelic messengers; but, speaking in the language of humanity, He addresses us in our own tongue and in accents familiar to us, the better to awaken our human sympathies and impress our hearts. There is thus the infallibility of God side by side with the individuality of man. Allied to the latter was that freedom which the sacred penman exercised in employing the usual materials of authorship, that is to say, what they had seen with their own eyes, or learnt by report, or heard from tradition, or known by earlier documents, to all which they were guided, and in recording all which they possessed immunity from error by virtue of inspiration. Again, when they incorporated the speeches, opinions, and sentiments of others, whether with approval or otherwise, the report of such, for which alone they were responsible, was in like manner infallibly correct. In every case the transcript was truth, without any alloy of misstatement. Also, they were free to view the same event under different aspects, and in different relations, and with consequent variety of description, while this very circumstantial diversity is a sure sign of substantial truth. Thus, as to the *hour* of the crucifixion, one evangelist uses the Roman method of reckoning time, and the others the Jewish; a comparison of the one with the other harmonises the report. Likewise, in regard to the *superscription* on the cross, the essential part of it, namely, "The King of the Jews," is the same in all the Gospels, and the record, as far as it goes, correct in each, though more complete in one by the addition of the name Jesus, which a Roman proud of the purity of his speech naturally omitted from the Latin title, and in another by mention of the place Nazareth; the prefatory words "this is" being omitted or inserted at pleasure. Or being trilingual, it is recorded as it occurred in the three languages by three of the evangelists, while Mark records the actual charge common to them all, viz. the assumption of royalty, as he says: ἡ ἐπιγραφὴ τῆς αἰτίας αὐτοῦ. Another explanation is the certainly ingenious one of Dr. Nicholson: "That Pilate wrote the rough draft, and that two or three men of different nationalities translated it freely."

Other matters of this sort are reserved for next chapter.

CHAPTER VII.

OBJECTIONS.

Sec. I.—*Supposed Contradictions.*

CERTAIN cavils arise from mistakes about supposed discrepancies among the inspired writings. The number of such has been gradually dwindling down and becoming small by degrees; and if we were in possession of all the facts and of all the circumstances of the few remaining cases, the last of those vanishing quantities would, there is little doubt, disappear entirely and for ever. But here we may premise, that in attempting to harmonise alleged discrepancies or to remove supposed contradictions, we must take into account two circumstances—(*a*) that our ignorance of all the data in each instance generally lies at the root of the difficulty, and tends to render a positive solution impracticable; and (*b*) that in consequence of a defect in this respect, that is to say, when the data are insufficient, there may be a variety of solutions, any one of which, in such a case, may be deemed satisfactory. To make our meaning clear, let us take the case of indeterminate equations in common Algebra. In such equations the data are deficient, inasmuch as the number of unknown quantities exceeds the number of independent equations. Consequently the number of solutions is indefinite or unlimited; the number, however, is diminished and confined within definite limits by certain restrictions, such as the rejection of all values not integral, or of negative values, or of numbers not square or cube, and so on. Still, after all deductions, a variety of solutions is possible; and any one of these solutions properly arrived at is accepted without hesitation. Just so with respect to the discrepancies referred to, the problem is often one that labours under deficiency of data, owing to which several solutions may be possible; any one of those solutions fairly made out meets the requirements of the case, and shows the feasibility of the attempted reconcilement.

I. The first class consists of antinomies which present themselves in Scripture, and which some mistake for real contradictions. They are, however, no contradictions at all, but rather contrasted or antithetical statements. This will appear to be so from a few familiar examples—some from the Old and others from the New Testament. In the proclamation of the divine name in the 34th chapter of Exodus, God is represented as " visiting the iniquity of the fathers upon the children, and upon the children's children, unto the third and to the fourth generation;" but in the 18th chapter of Ezekiel, at the 14th and 17th verses, we read : " Now, lo, if he beget a son, that seeth all his father's sins which he hath done, and considereth, and doeth not such like . . . . he shall not die for the iniquity of his father, he shall surely live." These two sentiments so apparently opposite are brought together in one passage of Scripture, namely, the 32d chapter of Jeremiah, at the 18th and 19th verses. " Thou recompensest the iniquity of the fathers into the bosom of their children after them," is the statement of the former verse, while that of the latter is to the effect that God " gives every one according to his ways, and according to the fruit of his doings." Both statements are perfectly true, and though sometimes urged as contradictory, do in no way contradict each other. The one respects our personal responsibility, the other results from our social unity. In accordance with the latter, the members of a community may have their condition injuriously affected by the conduct of their progenitors; the children of a criminal suffer disgrace and detriment from their father's crime; often, too, has the iniquity of vicious parents been visited on their unhappy offspring, whether that visitation come in the shape of disease, or debility, or dishonour, or degradation. The two statements, therefore, referring as they do, the one to social and temporal calamity, the other to personal and spiritual recompense, cannot contravene each other; like other similar statements of God's word, which, however apparently antagonistic, can never come into collision, because they traverse different and distinct planes. Similarly we read that God "ended His work, and rested on the seventh day from all His work which He had made." And again, in our Lord's answer to the Jews, He says: "My Father worketh hitherto, and I work." But here it is obvious that the contradiction is only apparent. The work which God completed was the work of creation; that which He continues to carry on belongs to the department of providence. In like manner God is represented as saying to the Israelites: "Let them make me a sanctuary that I may dwell among them;" on the other hand, we are informed that "the Most High dwelleth not in temples made with hands." Nor yet is there anything more than a mere seeming contradiction, for the one expression relates to His glory, the other to His grace; the one to His absolute dwelling-place in glory, the other to His gracious presence with His people on earth; the one declares His infinite majesty, the other expresses His ineffable condescension. So in Gal. vi., at the 2d verse, we read: "Bear ye one another's burthens" ($\beta\acute{a}\rho\eta$); while in the 5th verse it is affirmed that "every man shall bear his own burthen" ($\phi o\rho\tau\acute{\iota}o\nu$). Both are quite compatible, for the reference in the latter case is to individual responsibility, and in the former to social sympathy.

II. Another class comprises apparent discrepancies between the writers of the New Testament. There is need of being reminded that a discrepancy and a diversity are separated by a very wide interval indeed. The Augustinian axiom is as valuable as it is needful, and as needful now as ever, to the effect: "Locutiones variæ sed non contrariæ; diversæ sed non adversæ." Some of those so-called discrepancies that are still and most commonly insisted on, are readily set aside or adjusted. A few examples of such a kind as rule a number of similar cases may be adduced, and a few will be amply sufficient. (1) The healing of the blind man near Jericho is impugned on the ground of both number and locality. (*a*) Mark and Luke speak of one blind man, and Matthew of two. A case exactly similar in respect of number is that of the demoniacs of Gadara; Mark and Luke mention only one, Matthew two. Now a common maxim, with which Le Clerc is credited, disposes of both. It is: "Qui plura narrat pauciora complectitur; qui pauciora memorat plura non negat," which has been freely but correctly rendered: "The fuller account comprises the shorter, the shorter does not contradict the fuller." Ebrard is of opinion that two distinct cures were effected under similar circumstances—Luke narrating the one, Mark the other, and Matthew combining both. It is more likely the three records refer to one event. A very natural reason, then, for the mention of only one in each case by two evangelists, may be found in the peculiar circumstances or condition of the one mentioned, which may have made him better known or rendered him more prominent. This is hinted, not very obscurely, in Luke's words in reference to the demoniac: "There met Him out of the *city* a certain man," which seem to imply that he had once been a well-known citizen. Or perhaps the one mentioned in either case by Mark and Luke was the only survivor at the time. (*b*) Matthew and Mark represent the occurrence in the case of the blind man as taking place when Jesus was leaving Jericho, but Luke when He was entering that city. Now, (*a*) either the word ἐγγίζειν means, while Jesus was *still near* the city instead of *drawing near*, as in the following among other passages:—Deut. xxi. 2 (the LXX. version): "The city that is nearest to the slain man (ἐγγίζουσα)." (β) Or the one was cured by our Lord when entering, and the other when He was departing from the city. (γ) Or supposing our Lord to have stopped some days in Jericho, as seems implied in the words of Mark: "And they came to Jericho, and as He is going out," and making occasional excursions into the suburbs or surrounding district, on His return from one of these, as He approached the city, He performed the miracle. The cure was thus effected after He had gone out of or departed from the city, and yet as He drew nigh to it when coming back. (δ) Or the application was made by the blind man to our Lord as He entered the city, but it was not attended to, or rather the cure was deferred till He was leaving, by which time the second blind man had joined the first. (ε) There is another possibility or even probability in the case; for as Jericho consisted of an old town and a new, or had its villages, like the towns with their villages in Old Testament times, or contained extensive suburbs, all comprehended under the name Jericho, the miracle may have been performed while He departed from one part and was come nigh the other. (2) Another supposed discrepancy refers to the place where our Lord delivered His Sermon on the Mount, as it is commonly called. It was on the mount, according to Matthew; on the plain, or rather on a *level place* (ἐπὶ τόπου πεδινοῦ), according to the statement of Luke. This mountain, it is admitted, had two peaks, called Kurun Hattin or the Horns of Hattin at the present day; a level tableland, suitable for such a congregation as our Lord addressed, lies between. Thus it was both a mountain and a plain—a plain on a mountain, as indicated. The exact word for a plain, in the strict and ordinary sense, is different, being πεδίον or πεδινή; while ἐπί, with a local genitive instead of the dative, is thought by some to imply elevation. (3) A third instance is in connection with the healing of the centurion's servant. According to Matthew's narration of the cure, the centurion seems to come personally to the Saviour; but, according to Luke, he deputes the elders of the Jews for that purpose. This is an important case, as the principle of its solution rules several similar instances. Thus "Jesus," it is said, "made and baptized more disciples than John, though," it is added, "Jesus Himself baptized not, but His disciples;" John and James made a request to Jesus, but it was their mother who preferred it; Pilate scourged Jesus, but he must be understood to have done so by his officials. "Joseph laid the body of Jesus in his own new tomb, which he had hewn out in a rock," that is obviously, had got hewn out. Judas purchased a field with the reward of iniquity, that is, he caused or gave occasion to its purchase by the chief priests. The maxim that harmonises all such diversities of representation or seeming discrepancies, is the well-known one: "Quod facit per alterum, facit per se." This maxim holds good in law as well as in the common affairs of life, and is not called in question or objected to. Here we may introduce (4) the two seemingly conflicting statements about the death of Judas. In Matt. xxvii. 5, we are informed that, after he had thrown down in the temple the money he had got as the reward of treachery, he went away and hanged himself; but, according to the narrative of Luke in Acts i. 18, falling headlong, or on his face, "he burst asunder in the midst, and all his bowels gushed out." These two statements are neither inconsistent nor contradictory. Luke's account has the appearance of being rather abrupt, and supposes something to have preceded, but which has been passed over in the onward progress of narration. Matthew supplies the omitted and connecting link. There is no contradiction, for Luke does not deny that the traitor had hanged himself before falling to the ground, neither does Matthew contradict the sad sequel of his prostrate fall and frightful rupture. There is no inconsistency or incompatibility in the circumstances, for on the breaking of the branch, say, of a tree, to which the rope had been attached, or on the snapping of the rope itself by which he was suspended, the fearful fall would be the necessary result. And if, moreover, we conceive, as we may fairly do, the occurrence to have taken place on the verge of such precipices as overhang the valley of Hinnom, twenty, thirty, or forty feet in height, with or without a jagged rock projecting, the dreadful disembowelling would be no improbable consequence.

A parallel to the supposed discrepancy that has just been noticed is found in the Old Testament in relation to the death of Saul. Thus in 2 Sam. xxi. 12, it is stated that "the Philistines slew Saul in Gilboa;" in 1 Sam. xxxi.: "Therefore Saul took a sword, and fell upon it;" while in 2 Sam. i. 10, we are informed that an Amalekite despatched him: "So I (the Amalekite) stood upon him (Saul), and slew him, because I was sure he could not live after that he was fallen." Now, much as has been made out of this seeming discrepancy, there is only need of a careful examination of these passages and their context with ordinary fair dealing in order to effect a satisfactory reconcilement. The Philistine archers had shot at the unfortunate king and wounded him; sorely wounded in body, and smarting keenly in spirit under disaster and defeat, Saul longed for the end, and fell upon his sword; but in his nervous trepidation this self-inflicted wound did not prove fatal, at least not immediately; though he sought for death, he found it not. He may indeed have swooned from loss of blood or weakness, for the armour-bearer thought his master dead, when with less erring aim he slew himself. While lying on the ground, or partially and feebly raising himself by his spear, he sees the Amalekite, and eagerly solicits the finishing stroke at his hand. And so the life of the ill-fated monarch was brought to its sorrowful close by Philistine archer, by suicidal hand, and by Amalekite volunteer. Three acts ended the catastrophe, three agencies had their share in the work of destruction and death.

If any of these instances occurred in ordinary historic narrative, and proceeded from the hand of a secular writer, we would find no great difficulty in harmonising the seeming discrepancy, and could not refuse to credit the writer with honesty of purpose and acquaintance with the facts. Can less be conceded to an inspired writer?

(5) A more difficult example meets us in the narratives of Peter's denial of our Lord. Here both the *place* of that denial and the *persons* who provoked it are differently represented. But (*a*) in reference to the *place*, the first denial occurred by the fire in the high priest's hall (*i.e.* the αὐλή or quadrangular court under the open air); and the place of the third denial is not specified. At the second denial he went out, according to Mark, into the προαύλιον, and according to Matthew into the πυλῶνα, while according to John he stood and warmed himself. Now the fire, as we have seen, was in the αὐλή or open court; the passage from this αὐλή or open court out into the street was προαύλιον; the portal of this passage, or its entrance door, was πυλών, the same place more exactly defined. But though he had withdrawn a short way from the fire, he had not removed beyond the reach of its influence, nor ceased to share its warmth. (*b*) Again, as to the *persons*, the first question was put by a damsel who is described by John as the portress (ἡ παιδίσκη, ἡ θυρωρός). In the report of the *second* denial by Mark, Peter is noticed by the same damsel (ἡ παιδίσκη); but, what is often overlooked, she addresses her remark not to Peter himself, but to the bystanders—"them that stood by;" Matthew says, "another maid" (ἄλλη); Luke has "another man" (ἕτερος); while John uses the indefinite plural εἶπον, *they said.* This word gives us the clue to the whole proceed-

ing. The maid who this time accosted Peter *himself* was a different (ἄλλη) person from the portress; the portress (ἡ θυρωρός or ἡ παιδίσκη), on the other hand, addressed herself to the bystanders; they, it is probable, echoed her words; at all events, several (εἶπον, pl.) persons, male (ἕτερος) and female, now assailed him with their unwelcome interrogations. In reply to or repelling these various accusations, Peter repeats his denial, as is implied in the imperfect (ἠρνεῖτο = kept denying). Then at the *third* denial, still more of the bystanders, as may be inferred from the οἱ ἑστῶτες of Matthew and the similar οἱ παρεστῶτες of Mark, taxed Peter with being a disciple of Jesus; while another (ἄλλος τις of Luke) and still different individual acted, it would appear, as a sort of ringleader of the rest, drawing attention to the fact of his being a Galilean; while a kinsman of Malchus affirmed that he had seen him in the garden with Jesus. Thus the narrative in all its parts is thoroughly and truly consistent. Again, (c) in reference to the note of time, Matthew, Luke, and John represent Peter's denial as occurring before the crowing of the cock; but Mark is more specific, and says: " before the cock crows twice." As the first crowing of the cock near midnight is only or seldom heard except by few, we may safely say the second crowing before daybreak is that referred to by all the evangelists, though Mark is the only one who precisely intimates the fact.

(6) The time of the Last Supper has been questioned, and has given rise to much discussion. The synoptic Gospels place it on the evening of the Passover, that is, the 14th of Nisan; that of John seems to imply the night before, that is, the 13th of Nisan, as though our Lord and His disciples had anticipated the regular Passover, and partaken of a substitute the day before. The best and most satisfactory solution of this long and much mooted question is, we think, that of Robinson, who holds that the Lord's Supper was instituted at the legal time of the Passover, and interprets the seemingly contradictory passages of John in accordance with this view. These passages are John xiii. 1, xviii. 28, and xix. 14; and are harmonised with the Synoptists as follows:—(a) The " Passover" covers the whole *Paschal festival* or feast of unleavened bread, beginning with the Passover proper. (β) " To eat the Passover " is

equivalent to *keeping the Paschal festival*. And (γ) the "preparation of the Passover" is the ordinary *preparation for the Sabbath*, occurring in the Paschal week. This view, which has been largely adopted, removes all seeming discrepancy and difficulty.

III. Another class of difficulties consists of supposed or alleged discrepancies between the writers of sacred and those of secular history. One instance of this kind, though confessedly difficult, has been greatly exaggerated. In Luke ii. 2 it is written: "And this taxing was first made when Cyrenius was governor ($\dot{\eta}\gamma\epsilon\mu o\nu\epsilon\acute{u}o\nu\tau o\varsigma$) of Syria." Here it is alleged, on the authority of Josephus, that it was ten years after our Lord's birth when Cyrenius became governor of Syria. Several methods of solution have been suggested; but the most satisfactory is that which is furnished by the historical researches of Zumpt, who has proved the probability of Cyrenius having been *twice* governor of Syria. But a fuller discussion of this important subject will find an appropriate place in the following section, which treats of passages on which some new light has been thrown in recent times.

IV. A third class of discrepancies, supposed or alleged, is between the New Testament and the Old. The 7th chapter of Acts supplies the best examples of this sort—(1) The time of strangership and servitude of Abraham and his seed (that is, both in Canaan and Egypt, according to LXX., which adds $\kappa\alpha\grave{\iota}\ \acute{\epsilon}\nu\ \gamma\hat{\eta}\ X\alpha\nu\alpha\acute{\alpha}\nu$) is, according to Ex. xii. 40, four hundred and thirty years; according to Gen. xv. 13, four hundred years; and according to Acts vii. 6, four hundred years. The variation, which in reality is only apparent, may be easily harmonised as follows:—(α) The whole interval between Abraham's call or going down into Egypt and the exodus was 430 years; (β) From the birth or weaning of Isaac to the exodus the period was some 400 years; (γ) The verse of Acts should be read with a parenthesis, thus: "that his seed should sojourn in a strange land (and that they should bring them into bondage, and entreat them evil) four hundred years." Sometimes the round number and sometimes the exact number is quoted; while the whole reckoning stands thus:—

K

	YEARS.
From Abraham's arrival in Canaan to Isaac's birth, =	25
„ Isaac's birth till that of his twin sons, =	60
„ Jacob's birth till his going down into Egypt, =	130
	215
From Jacob's going down into Egypt till the death of Joseph, ... =	71
„ death of Joseph till birth of Moses, . =	64
„ birth of Moses till exodus, . . =	80
	430

(2) In Gen. xlvi. 27 it is written: "All the souls of the house of Jacob which came into Egypt were threescore and ten;" but in Acts vii. 14 we read: "Then sent Joseph, and called his father Jacob to him, and all his kindred, threescore and fifteen souls." (a) The number 70 consisted of the following:—Jacob's eleven sons and their descendants, with his daughter Dinah, amounting to 66; while Jacob himself, Joseph, and the latter's two sons make up the 70 of Genesis. (β) In Acts we have again the number 66, to the exclusion of Joseph and his two sons already in Egypt, and of Jacob, who is mentioned separately. To this number 66 must be added the 9 surviving wives of Jacob's sons (those of Judah and Simeon being already dead), and so we get the number 75.

(3) The difficulty that presents itself in Acts vii. 15, 16, though more formidable, is another of the same class, and will be considered at length in the following section.

SEC. II.—*New Light on Passages seemingly contradictory.*

It has been the fortune of our times to have light shed on sundry topics, both classical and Biblical, by modern research, by recent discoveries, by inscriptions, and otherwise. Much help has been obtained from such sources for interpreting, or illustrating, or in some way elucidating certain classical subjects, some of them difficult, others of them obscure, and all of them of more or less interest and importance. We might instance the true nature of the Agrarian laws among the Romans, the real object of Ostracism among the Greeks, and the right character of the Sophists, on all which and other subjects new important light has been shed. When we pass from the classical to the department of the Biblical the gain has been as great; for if not equal in quantity, it is superior in quality, because the gain in the former is confined to things temporal, the other is connected with things eternal. The respective results may be put in this way. Conceive a block of marble removed from its quarry, and roughly hewn into the resemblance of a man. Suppose beside it a well-formed marble statue—every feature finely chiselled, every limb exquisitely fashioned, every part polished, and the whole brought to the utmost excellence of form that the statuary's art is capable of. Then side by side with both place an actual human being—breathing, moving, and capable of all the functions and attributes of life. How striking is the difference between these three figures! Scarcely less is the difference between humanity,—first, in the savage state, rude, untutored, and barbarous; and secondly, humanity highly refined and polished by all the influences derivable from Roman civilisation and Grecian culture; and then, in contrast with both, humanity moulded by the plastic power of Christianity, animated by the lessons of that word which is spirit and life, and quickened into spiritual existence by the Spirit of the living God. Just in proportion to the superiority of the characters thus formed are the means of formation; and just in like ratio the records of classical antiquity, however humanising in their influences, are inferior to the records of that divine word by which men are born again into a new life, and begotten to a lively hope by the resurrection of Christ from the dead. Or view the matter in another light. Suppose a document came to us from abroad containing important and interesting information on various topics,—scientific, historical, political, or of any other kind,—we would naturally enough receive it gratefully and peruse it carefully; but suppose that document, over and above the information contained in it, made over to us an exceedingly valuable property or conveyed to us an unspeakably large legacy, with what surpassing joy and gratitude would we receive it, and with what unwearied and unwearying diligence would we read such a precious instrument! Every word would receive due attention, every expression would be weighed, every sentence pondered. The whole would be often in our hands, and always in our hearts. It is exactly so with Scripture truth; for, besides the information so exceedingly valuable, and nowhere else procurable, it apprises us of an inheritance incorruptible, undefiled, and that never fades away, which we are invited to make our own, and conveys to us a legacy which is no less than salvation—great, glorious, and everlasting. Once more, let us venture another comparison, and one taken from the field of history. The predecessors of Thucydides in that department occupied themselves mainly, as is well known, with the physical and sensible, describing, as they did, the geographical situation, physical aspect, natural products of the countries referred to, and the customs of their inhabitants, as also the military enterprises that had been undertaken by them or the hostile invasions made upon them, and ascribing the results to an arbitrary overruling power which controlled men's actions, together with an account of the works of art that met the eye or gratified the æsthetic sensibilities of the spectator. Thucydides departed from the beaten track thus trodden by previous historians; he struck out for himself a new method of narration; he confined himself chiefly to human actions as proceeding from the characters and situations of the actors, with the motives that dictated them and the influences exercised by them on mankind around. When he thus introduced a new feature, or rather employed an old feature in a novel way, interspersing his narratives with speeches, and that for the very purpose of assuming the character and placing himself in the position of the persons he described, and of thus exhibiting the springs of action that guided their course and shaped their conduct, and of allowing them an opportunity for the expression of their sentiments whether confirmatory or exculpatory of such conduct,—when he thus innovated in history, making provision for a true record of past events, and for the benefit of those who, from the aptness of human affairs to repeat themselves, might be similarly circumstanced in the future, he designated his work a κτῆμα ἐς ἀεί (a possession for ever). By this he meant not merely such a production as might be read on a single occasion for the gratification of an audience, but a possession which might be ever kept by them and ever ready at hand, and which might be conned over and over again for the guidance of the possessors; while the record of events was merely secondary to the practical end of training and directing, which was thus steadily kept in view. How much better entitled to the proud designation of a κτῆμα ἐς ἀεί, and how much more deserving of constant reference and frequent consultation are those holy Scriptures, which are able to make wise unto salvation, and which are profitable for doctrine, for correction, and for instruction in righteousness! Furthermore, if we hail the discovery of a new truth, or the formation of a correcter opinion, or the removal of a long-prevailing error, or the solution of some serious difficulty, or the rectification of a current mistake, or the unravelling of some mystery in an ancient classic, where only theoretic truth is in question, how much more gladly should we accept a similar benefit in relation to those truths that are imperishable in their nature and everlasting in their effects!

From these general remarks, which the nature of the case suggested, we proceed to the examination of some passages which, from supposed discrepancies or acknowledged difficulties, seem entitled to a more careful consideration, and on which, moreover, new light to some extent has been shed.

In Luke ii. 2, to which a passing reference was made in the preceding section, there occurs a brief chronological notice, which has sorely taxed the skill of interpreters and exercised their ingenuity. The difficulty of the passage arises from a supposed discrepancy between the date of Cyrenius' governorship of Syria as implied in the statement of Luke, and the date of the same event as ascertained from secular history, the latter date being some ten years later than the former. Now a discovery made by August W. Zumpt of Berlin, and recorded in his *Commentationes Epigraphicæ*, removes, we are persuaded, the whole difficulty and reconciles the seeming discrepancy. Before, however, applying to the elucidation of this passage the interesting fact happily discovered by Zumpt,—a fact which, as shall be seen, sets the subject in such clear light,—it may not be amiss just to glance at some of the theories formed by commentators and others in their attempts at interpreting the passage. The ordinary explanation makes πρώτη equivalent to προτέρα, the superlative identical with the comparative. But even in such parallels as πρῶτός μου and πρῶτον ὑμῶν, quoted in support of this, the superlative, while including, is still more extensive in meaning than, the comparative. Besides, the infinitive, rather than the participle, would in that case be the natural construction, though, it must be admitted, an instance of a similar use of the participle has been adduced from the LXX. Still this explanation must be regarded as unnatural, and an unfair treatment of the text; it looks so very like forcing a seemingly suitable sense upon it. A second method, adopted by Ebrard and others, is very ingenious. It consists in dropping the aspirate and reading αὐτή instead of αὕτη, so that the rendering would be: "the taxing itself took place for the first time when Cyrenius was governor of Syria." Thus the census ordered by Augustus was a preparatory step, the taxing (a meaning which the word ἀπογραφή also has) took place subsequently. This is admitted by one of the fiercest impugners of the evangelist's accuracy to be a solution of the difficulty; but curiously enough, he condemns it as an arbitrary alteration of the original, either in ignorance or forgetfulness of the fact that the earlier uncials as a rule have neither accents nor breathings of any kind. Middleton, again, taking πρώτη adverbially and in close connection with ἐγένετο, translates thus: "this census took effect for the first time under Cyrenius," and understands it to mean that the imperial decree for taking the census was carried out and completed by the actual levying of taxes under the rule of the Syrian governor; that the one was the means, the other the end; and that that end was only consummated when the ἀπογραφή became an ἀποτίμησις under Cyrenius. This, however, imparts to ἐγένετο a sort of pregnant sense, so as to imply that the ἀπογραφή or census not only took place, but became something else, issuing in an ἀποτίμησις or taxation, though that something else, instead of being explicitly mentioned, has to be imagined or supplied by a doubtful implication; while the distinction thus made between ἀπογραφή and ἀποτίμησις is questionable, both words being applicable to the census itself—the latter to the census in the city, the former to that in the provinces; while ἀπογραφή, as we have seen, has also the sense of taxing. A different way of evading the difficulty is resorted to by Wieseler. With codex B and Lachmann, he omits the article, and refers αὕτη to the decree of Augustus, accounting for its gender by attraction on the part of the predicate. The translation and sense would then be: "this (namely, the decree of Augustus) became a first census in Palestine when Cyrenius was governor;" that is, the census, though previously commenced and afterwards interrupted, was first completed then, and dated from the time of its completion. Not to speak of the awkward assumption involved in this construction, it is plainly too artificial, though a parallel for the change of gender in αὕτη may be found in several passages. Once more, Wordsworth gives two ways of rendering the expression under consideration; but he has himself misgivings about one of them, and acknowledges that it might appear to require a different order of the words. The other which he proposes has certainly the merit of no small degree of plausibility. It is as follows:—"This taxing or enrolment became (that is, began to be entitled) first when Cyrenius was governor of Syria." This rendering proceeds on the admission that there were two ἀπογραφαί or registrations—one in the time of Cyrenius, called by way of eminence "*the* registration," and an earlier one distinguished from it by the title of *the first registration*. Luke mentions both. In Acts he refers to "*the* registration," and here in the Gospel narrative he speaks of the earlier one, noticing the fact, as though parenthetically, that it had become necessary to distinguish this registration as *the first*, owing to the existence of that second one which took place under Cyrenius; and thus he directs to the first as that in which the registry of the Saviour's birth might be found. In opposition to all these, Ellicott insists that the plain grammatical sense of the words must be: "this taxing took place as a first one when Cyrenius was governor of Syria;" and with this rendering that by Winer nearly coincides: "this taxing took place as the first under the government of Cyrenius." This is obviously the plain, straightforward method of dealing with the passage, but then the difficulty already mentioned meets us at the outset, and must be grappled with. Here it is that the fact discovered by Zumpt and proved by him, as Merivale thinks, to a demonstration, enables us satisfactorily to clear up the discrepancy and honestly dispose of the difficulty. Zumpt, by a laborious and exhaustive process, discovers the successive governors of Syria from the days of Augustus till the time of Vespasian, that is, from 30 B.C. till more than 60 A.D., and puts it beyond a doubt that Cyrenius was twice governor of Syria—once at the time of Christ's birth, besides a second time some ten years afterwards. His governorship at the former period arose from the circumstance of his being at that time governor of Cilicia; and as Cilicia, after its separation from Cyprus, was annexed to Syria, so Cyrenius, being *de facto* governor of Cilicia, was *de jure* governor of Syria. Thus at the time of our Lord's birth Cyrenius held office in Cilicia, then become a province of Syria, and under the popular title of $\dot{\eta}\gamma\epsilon\mu\acute{\omega}\nu$ superintended the enrolment in question, while a few years later he obtained the actual governorship.

The mention of Cyprus calls up another circumstance, at once illustrative of our subject and elucidative of an expression of Scripture about which a doubt had been entertained. A certain title given to the governor of the island of Cyprus by the inspired historian of the Acts was called in question. It was supposed to be at variance with the title which that same governor bore in secular history; but the discovery of certain coins furnished, though not the first, yet powerfully confirmatory and conclusive evidence of the perfect propriety of the title. It is well known that the first Roman emperor, by a stroke of clever but cunning policy, contrived to retain in his own hand complete control over the military power of the empire, while he gratified the senate and people of Rome by the empty semblance of ancient liberties. Accordingly the provinces $\dot{\epsilon}\pi\alpha\rho\chi\acute{\iota}\alpha\iota$ were divided into senatorial and imperial. The power of appointing a governor to the former was vested in the senate, and to the latter in the emperor. The person appointed by the senate to a senatorial province received the title of *proconsul*, in Greek $\dot{a}\nu\theta\acute{\upsilon}\pi\alpha\tau\sigma\varsigma$. His district was supposed to be peaceful, his administration more of the character of civil rule, and, though he had the ensigns of power, was restricted in its nature and limited in duration, for his appointment lasted but a year. Achaia was a province of this sort, and hence we read that Gallio was its proconsul, or deputy according to our English version. So was Asia, of which the proconsuls or deputies are also mentioned. The governor of an imperial province, on the other hand, was called *proprator*, in Greek ἀντιστράτηγος. His province was less settled, requiring the presence of a strong military force to prevent internal revolt or external invasion. His command was that of a military chief, and his tenure of office depended on the emperor's pleasure. Syria was a province of this kind, and the technical name of its ruler was propraetor, unless when a more general term, such as ἡγεμών, applicable to any official command, was employed. A dependency or subordinate district of such a province was usually governed by a *procurator*, in Greek ἐπίτροπος, who attended to duties similar to those of *quaestor*, ταμίας, in the ordinary provinces. Judaea was a dependency of this sort in relation to Syria.

Now the correctness of the title ἀνθύπατος, deputy, applied to Sergius Paulus by the sacred historian in Acts xiii. 7, was questioned on the ground that Cyprus was an imperial province, and its ruler in consequence properly entitled a propraetor (ἀντιστράτηγος). But independently of the united testimony of Dio Cassius and Strabo, to the effect that a change had taken place, and that Cyprus, having been handed over by the emperor to the senate, had become a senatorial province and its ruler consequently a proconsul, a coin was found dating from the reign of the Emperor Claudius, with the image and superscription of Claudius Caesar on one side, while on the obverse are inscribed in uncials the words ἐπι κομινιου προκλου ἀνθυπατου, with κυπριων in the centre, meaning "in the time of Kominius Proclus, Proconsul of the Cyprians," while other coins—some in Greek, others in Latin, give the names of rulers that went before and that followed after Sergius Paulus, all bearing the title of proconsuls, ἀνθύπατοι. Thus, then, by the discovery of those coins and inscriptions, perplexed commentators were relieved from the difficulty they had felt, the doubt hanging over this expression of the divine word was dispelled, and the strict accuracy of the sacred historian triumphantly vindicated.

We may now appropriately address ourselves to that passage in Acts vii. 16, reserved from last section. It is confessedly one of the most difficult passages in the New Testament. The difficulty is twofold, respecting both the purchase itself and the place of burial. In both these there is a supposed discrepancy between the Old Testament and the New. The one difficulty consists in the circumstance that Abraham's burial ground was at Mamre, "the same is Hebron," not at Sychem; and the other in the fact that he purchased from Ephron the Hittite, not from the sons of Emmor (Hamor) the father of Sychem (Shechem); whereas (as if to complicate the matter still more) Jacob had purchased a parcel of ground near Shechem, of the children of Hamor, Shechem's father, but without any mention that it was for the purpose of a place of burial. (*a*) Some suppose that the two narratives have been confounded, and on this supposition various means of rectification have been resorted to. Some exclude the name Abraham altogether; but this wants MS. authority, and awkwardly introduces Jacob as the agent in the purchase. Some take Abraham as a sort of patronymic for Jacob, as though equivalent to ὁ τοῦ 'Αβραάμ; but this is quite unwarrantable. Some suppose an error to exist in the name, and that the error originated in the first letter *I* in *IAB*, the abbreviation for Jacob, being effaced, so that *AB* remaining was mistakenly written Abraham; this is simply conjecture. Other violent alterations of the text have been attempted, but with a like unsatisfactory result. (*b*) Scarcely more satisfactory is Fairbairn's attempt to remove the difficulty, by regarding the purchase by Abraham at Hebron and that by Jacob at Sychem (Shechem) as not distinguished, so that the purchase of Jacob is ascribed to Abraham who originated such a mode of procedure, but thrown together and treated as one—because one in the principle of faith in God, and one in its mode of manifestation by the purchase of a place of burial for their bodies, while as yet they had not a foot of ground in Canaan, and the promise of God was the only pledge of the inheritance. But to confound the agents because one motive actuated them, and to overlook the individuality of the acts because one principle pervaded them, is, to say the least of it, a very questionable principle of exegesis, and a rather curious method of making things plain, "nil agit exemplum quod litem lite resolvit." (c) Now, rejecting all these as undeserving of attention, there are two different translations of the verse, by either of which we sometime thought the difficulty could be removed. The reader will please turn up the passage in his Greek Testament. Now (a) one of these renderings takes the sentence as elliptical, and applies the scheme of καθ' ὅλον καὶ μέρος, while by the application of this well-known grammatical idiom the verses may be read thus: "So Jacob went down into Egypt, and died, he and our fathers, and were carried over into Sychem, and laid (*he*) in the sepulchre which Abraham bought for a sum of money (*they in that bought*) of the sons of Emmor the father of Sychem." There is thus an ellipsis of ἐν τῷ naturally suggested by these words in the preceding clause, and a common paraphrase of the preposition. This translation, if admitted, would agree with the tradition recorded by Jerome and Rashi, to the effect that, while Adam, Abraham, Jacob, and Isaac were buried in Hebron also called Kirjath-arba, or town of the four patriarchs, the other patriarchs were buried in Sychem. To this tradition we pay little attention, for the proposed solution is independent of it. The second (β) of the two translations proceeds on the principle of transposition, and runs thus: "And they (ver. 16) were carried over into Sychem, and laid *from among* the sons of Emmor, the father of Sychem, in the sepulchre that Abraham bought for a sum of money." This would accord with the tradition of Josephus, who says the other patriarchs as well as Jacob were buried in Hebron. This tradition may be right or may be wrong; with that we have nothing to do, further than to observe that both traditions represent Jacob as buried in Hebron, and both translations do the same. By either translation we gain a feasible solution of the discrepancy and consequent difficulty. (d) After all, we are disposed to think that the discovery of the true solution of the difficulty is that which has been hit on by Wordsworth, who dispenses with any change of rendering, and endorses the translation of the verse in our Authorised Version. He substitutes, however, *the son* instead of *the father* in supplying the ellipsis in the last clause, and restricts the subject of " were carried over " to " fathers " (not including Jacob) of the preceding verse, thus: " And they (*i.e. our fathers*) were carried over into Sychem, and laid in the sepulchre that Abraham bought for a sum of money of the sons of Emmor (*the son*) of Sychem." Thus both the difficulties, namely, that of the purchase and that of the place of burial, disappear. The substance of this solution is, that the purchase of Abraham, recorded in the verse we are considering, is not in any way to be confounded with that of Jacob subsequently in the same district; that it is, on the contrary, an altogether distinct and separate transaction; that, while there is no direct record of the transaction in the Old Testament, yet there are incidental circumstances which, if they do not suggest, seem at least to indicate or even postulate such a transaction. The following may be taken as intimations of this purchase, and consequent corroborations of this conjecture of Wordsworth:—(1) That spot near Sychem or Shechem, where God at the first appeared to Abraham in Canaan, and which was thence called Moreh or vision, and where Abraham erected his altar, must, there is every reason to believe, have been purchased by him, as he was not likely to trespass on others' ground or make free with strangers' property, nor was he wont to serve God with what cost him nothing. (2) In addition to or besides the land which Jacob acquired by purchase at Shechem, he held possession of a plot which he had taken out of the hand of the Amorite by his sword and by his bow. It is not surely an unreasonable supposition that that was the very plot or portion of territory which Abraham had purchased, but which the Amorites had usurped and taken forcible possession of, and from which Jacob by his valour expelled them, recovering it for and restoring it to his posterity. In this way the twelve patriarchs, including Joseph, were buried in Sychem, and their place of sepulture had been the original and veritable purchase of Abraham. (3) There is further evidence, Wordsworth thinks, for this being a distinct purchase from that of

Jacob, for the latter purchased from the sons of one Hamor the *father* of Sychem, while Abraham from the sons of Emmor, or Hamor, the *son* of Sychem, as τοῦ Συχέμ should naturally be rendered, while Hamor was the hereditary or general title of the prince of the place, like the Pharaohs of Egypt and the Cæsars of Rome. From the restriction of this Greek form of expression to *son* instead of *father* we must dissent, as the import of the idiom is much wider; this, however, does not affect materially the general solution, whether the vendor in the case was son or father of Sychem.

Sometimes a difficulty is eliminated, and an obscure passage elucidated, by a very simple process. For example, the reading of the Codex Sinaiticus, which omits the single word "therefore" from John vii. 22, rectifies the present awkwardness in the connection of the sentences, thus: "Jesus answered and said unto them, I have done one work and ye all marvel. Moses *therefore* gave unto you circumcision." Here the presence of *therefore* mars the sense, and its omission makes the meaning plain. This by the way.

We now direct attention to another passage of Scripture cumbered with serious antiquarian difficulties. Of course the usual amount of doubts have been expressed about it, and inaccuracy or ignorance has been charged upon the writer of it. It occurs in Heb. ix. 4, of which, with the preceding verse relating to the furniture of the sanctuary, it has been alleged with some reason: "maxima totius Epistolæ difficultas in verbis hisce consistit." The main difficulty is connected with the words: ἅγια ἁγίων χρυσοῦν ἔχουσα θυμιατήριον. In rendering the last of these words, translators fluctuate between *altar of incense* and *censer*. If the altar of incense be meant, how can the holy of holies be said to have it (ἔχουσα)? If, on the other hand, the censer be the object meant, how comes it that the altar of incense finds no place in the enumeration? Here we must premise that, whichever of the two objects be intended, it can scarcely be doubted that ἔχουσα must be distinguished from ἐν ᾗ of the second verse, by referring not so much to the contents as to the belongings of the holiest of all. At the same time, the arguments and authorities appear to us to preponderate in favour of the signification *censer* attached to θυμιατήριον in our Authorised Version. Besides the employment by the Septuagint of another expression for the *altar of incense*, namely, θυσιαστήριον or θυσιαστήριον θυμιάματος, and the absence of the article which accompanies it in nearly all the 250 places of its occurrence in that version, there is the stress laid by the Talmud on the employment of a golden censer on the day of atonement; to which may be added a very important point to which Alford gives due prominence, to wit, that the altar being only overlaid with gold, one would expect not χρυσοῦν, but κεκαλυμμένον χρυσίῳ πάντοθεν, as in the case of the ark.

But taking it for granted that it is the censer that is denoted, the question that then presents itself for solution is, How does it happen that an article of furniture so important as the altar of incense is in that case excluded from the sanctuary, while one of apparently less consequence is included? While we may not be able to assign the right reason, or perhaps any satisfactory reason for this exclusion, we are in a position to produce a parallel instance from a notable public monument, and so far forth to render the exclusion less improbable, if not altogether to confirm the likelihood of such exclusion. It is a remarkable circumstance that Josephus, when describing Pompey's entrance into the Jewish shrine and the objects he saw there, enumerates the table of shewbread, the candlestick, the censers, and much incense; yet, strange to say, in connection with these objects so likely to remind him of it, he makes no mention of the altar of incense. But a still more important fact, and one of great significance, as we think, in this instance, is the omission of this very same altar of incense from the triumphal arch of Titus in Rome. From that public monument light is thus shed on the passage we are considering. On that monumental record of the Roman general's conquest of and triumph over the holy city are still to be seen table and candlestick and censers, which he had carried away with him when he "made Salem's high towers his prey;" but no altar of incense is inscribed thereon—no such representation is there to be found.

There have not been wanting men possessed of such temerity

as to charge the inspired author of the Book of Hebrews with ignorance in the matter of the sanctuary furniture. And certainly if the articles in question were not fully known to him, or if their position were at all doubtful, it would be ignorance of a most astounding kind. No Jew, whether Palestinian or Alexandrine, whether native or foreign, could have been guilty of it. No Christian who pretended to any acquaintance with the divine word could have been unacquainted with these things, though we are free to admit that certain Fathers, misled probably by their own misreading of this very passage, have fallen into some strange mistakes on the subject. No one, surely, who was capable of writing such an Epistle, even if we leave inspiration entirely out of the question, could for one moment be imagined ignorant of such obvious facts; least of all a writer who evinces the most thorough knowledge of the old dispensation in all its institutions and in all its rites, even to the most minute details.

When will men, we may reasonably ask in concluding this chapter, forbear such precipitancy of opinion? When will men, when they meet with difficulties in the word of God, learn to suspend judgment until sufficient data are available for explaining or elucidating those difficulties, or, in the absence of such data, refrain from leaping to hasty conclusions when all the circumstances of the case are not before them? The divine word has passed through many a fiery ordeal, but it has usually come forth brighter and more beautiful than before. Many an attack has been made upon it, but, while such attacks have never resulted in permanently damaging the object of attack, they have not unfrequently brought discredit on him that made them. Many a shaft has been shot at it, but they have fallen harmless as the missile on the ancient shield—

"Telumque imbelle sine ictu
Conjecit ranco quod protinus ore repulsum
E summo clipei nequicquam umbone pependit."

Many a time the very assaults on truth have opened up the way for its admission to quarters that before had been fast closed as though hermetically sealed against it. Many a time those assaults have led to closer investigation and clearer views, so that, though the truth itself has never changed, erroneous interpretations of it long current and widely prevalent have been discovered and discarded. To the inspired word of God pertains in the truest sense that permanence which an ancient classic poet proudly claims for the inspirations of his own poetic genius, when he says, in an English version of his words :—

> "More durable than brass, the frame
> Which here I consecrate to fame!
> Higher than pyramids that rise,
> With royal pride to brave the skies ;
> Nor years, though numberless the train,
> Nor flight of seasons, wasting rain,
> Nor winds that loud in tempests break,
> Shall e'er its firm foundation shake."

CHAPTER VIII.

CONFIRMATIONS OF INSPIRED SCRIPTURE.

Sec. I.—*Direct Confirmations.*

BUT from the negative let us pass to the positive side, that is to say, from cavils about apparent but not real contradictions, to certain confirmations of inspired Scripture. Confirmations of the truth of Scripture present themselves in every department and on every side. They are far too numerous to be reckoned up in a brief space, or to be recorded within narrow limits. The most we can or need attempt is a selection of a few. In the undesigned coincidences traced out by Paley in his *Horæ Paulinæ* there is a multitude of such proofs; some of the subtlest, others of the most striking kind, while not a few address themselves to the commonest capacity, and lay no tax on the most ordinary memory. To two of this last sort, that is, to two of the plainest and most easily remembered, we turn for a little.

The Apostle Paul addresses letters to two churches. He writes to these two different churches on the same general subject, but in his treatment of that subject he assumes a quite different tone and spirit. That difference of style might have been necessitated had the subjects been quite distinct; but so far from that being the case, it is the great doctrine of justification by faith without the works of the law that is discussed in both Epistles. Now the difference in Paul's treatment of this same general question in the Epistle to the Romans and in that to the Galatians is remarkable. In writing to the Roman Christians he reasons out his subject by *argument*, in that to the Galatians he enforces it by *authority*. Let it be borne in mind that one of these churches, that of Galatia, he had himself founded, the other he had not as yet even visited. Who then will deny that the difference of tone corresponds most exactly and undesignedly to this difference of his relation to these two Christian communities respectively?

Another case of undesigned coincidence is so important and so impressive, that Lardner considers it a confirmation of the whole history of Paul's travels. The case in question consists in a geographical agreement between a passage in Romans and a statement in Acts. "So that from Jerusalem and round about unto ($καὶ\ κύκλῳ\ μέχρι$, literally, and round about as far as, or to the confines of) Illyricum, I have fully preached the gospel of Christ;" such is the passage in Romans. Jerusalem was the central point of departure, and the part of the circumference of his circuit that was nearest Rome was Illyricum. So far he had gone, but no farther on his way towards the Roman capital. Again in Acts there is no mention of Illyricum, but the following statement occurs in reference to the apostle's journey:—" He departed for to go into Macedonia, and when he had gone over those parts ($διελθὼν\ τὰ\ μέρη\ ἐκεῖνα$), and had given them much exhortation, he came into Greece." Though there is no mention here of Illyricum, yet his route through those parts of Macedonia must have brought him to the very boundary of that country, which adjoined Macedonia to the westward, on the way to Rome. There is likewise a coincidence in time as well as place. Paul had visited Macedonia previously; but that first visit being accurately traced in the history from Philippi to Amphipolis, Apollonia, Thessalonica, Berœa, Athens, Corinth, and thence back to Jerusalem, was confined to the eastern side of Macedonia, and away from Illyricum. But his second visit, which immediately precedes the writing of the Roman letter, was the time of his journey through Macedonia westward on to the confines of Illyricum.

In all authentic history we expect, of course, the narrative to be correct even in its details, but in Scripture the truthfulness of the records is vouched for by the most trustworthy and unintentional coincidences. Some instances of this kind may now be adduced from the Old Testament.

(1) A very interesting circumstance occurs in connection

with the means employed for the conveyance of the tabernacle and its utensils. Attention has been called to the circumstance by Graves and Patrick, while Blunt has noted it as an undesigned coincidence. The circumstance may be briefly stated thus. When the princes of Israel brought their offering of six oxen and twelve waggons, Moses, as is stated in the 7th chapter of Numbers, distributed these among the Levites for the service of the tabernacle. To the Kohathites he gave none, but the reason is expressly mentioned; it is "because the service belonging to them was that they should bear upon their shoulders." To the Gershonites he gave *two* waggons and *four* oxen, while to the Merarites he gave *four* waggons and *eight* oxen; and no reason is assigned or even hinted for this unequal distribution and seeming partiality to the one as compared with the other. Why is a double portion of both waggons and oxen assigned to the Merarites? Is the cause to be sought in the numerical superiority of the Merarites over the Gershonites? Though this ground of preference has not been hinted at by those who have called attention to the matter, still it existed, for from the 4th chapter of Numbers we learn that the number of the Merarites was 3200, while the Gershonites only amounted to 2630—a difference of 570. This difference, however, is altogether insufficient to account for the inequality of division referred to. The real reason, we believe, is that suggested by Graves, and which consists in the circumstance that the lighter furniture of the tabernacle—the curtains, the hangings, the cords, and linen material of the tabernacle were allotted to the Gershonites, but the heavier portion—the boards, bars, pillars, sockets, and pins were to be borne by the Merarites. Hence there was a necessity on their part for a supply of waggons and oxen so much larger. Yet there is no explicit mention of that necessity in the narrative. It is only by a careful comparison of portions considerably apart that the curious coincidence so unintentional and withal so confirmatory of the truth of the narrative comes to light.

(2) A curious case of a similar kind occurs in the desert wanderings. Two enumerations of the Israelites are recorded —one in the 1st chapter and the other in the 26th

chapter of Numbers. They were made, one, after leaving Egypt, in the wilderness of Sinai; the other, before entering Canaan, in the plains of Moab. In the interval of nearly forty years, most of the tribes had greatly increased, one, that of Manasseh, had almost doubled, and a few had diminished, but only very slightly. One tribe, however, had decreased considerably more than one-half, nearly two-thirds. From 59,300 it had dwindled down to 22,200. How or why was this? Did it constitute a less prolific portion of the Hebrew race? Had the mortality been greater than in the other tribes? What had raised the death-rate? What, in fact, had produced the anomalous diminution? No reason is assigned, no account is given; but here again a strange and striking coincidence is discoverable, not on the surface of the record, but by a painstaking and critical examination of the circumstances of the case. A great sin had been committed, a double sin had been indulged. Immediately before the second numeration of Israel the people had been guilty of idolatry with its frequent concomitant licentiousness. The swift vengeance of heaven had overtaken the guilty. Four and twenty thousand perished in the plague. On what portion of the people did the judgment fall heaviest? The natural answer would mark out for greatest vengeance the guiltiest part. Here then we gain a clue to the mystery. A prince and chief man of the Simeonites, Zimri, was struck dead in the very act of sin. Like prince, like people, no doubt, is applicable in this case. The evil example of the exalted in rank was too readily and too generally followed by the humble in station, and so the inference naturally follows that the Simeonites had suffered most because they had sinned most. Hence the sad diminution of their numerical strength. Corroborative of the same is an omission strange, yea passing strange, on the part of the leader and lawgiver of Israel. When he pronounced his parting blessings on the tribes he omitted one. When he blessed all the rest, he passed over that of Simeon. He had denounced vengeance against the Midianites, he could not commit the inconsistency of blessing their partners in crime. Not only so, in the allotments of the tribes the Simeonites were treated as an appendage to

Judah, and obtained the surplusage of their brethren's portion. How very solemnising! How very striking! How extraordinarily minute, and how wonderfully indicative of truth is such a coincidence!

(3) Every one is familiar with the events of Hezekiah's reign as recorded in 2 Kings xviii. and xix., and with the parallel account of the same transactions as contained in Isaiah xxxvi. and xxxvii. His kingdom was invaded by the mighty monarch of Assyria, most of the fenced cities of Judah had fallen, the holy city itself was about to be attacked, the Assyrian camp had already taken up its position near the capital, the Assyrian monarch himself still abode at Lachish to complete the siege. Meantime the most vigorous preparations for resistance had been made by Hezekiah. But all was to no purpose. The only means of safety was submission. An embassy was accordingly despatched with valuable presents, and in humble terms sued for peace, " That which thou puttest on me I shall bear." The large sum of 300 talents of silver and 30 talents of gold was imposed on the King of Judah. Now certain *bas-reliefs* exhumed from the palace of Koyunjik —on the site of ancient Nineveh, on the eastern bank of the Tigris opposite Mosul, and a palace, be it remembered, built by the Assyrian monarch Sennacherib himself—supply the Assyrian report of the same occurrences. The report contained in those excavated inscriptions is perfectly identical, in all the main facts, with the narrative of the Bible. The sovereigns are the same, the subjection to tribute the same, and the sum is similar in the two items of gold and silver, and exactly the same in the former. The version of the story from the Assyrian standpoint is more minute, giving, as might be expected, more prominence to such details as tend to exalt the might and majesty of the Assyrian conqueror and the prowess of his arms. Thus it gives the number of captured cities as forty-six, and the number of the captives as above two hundred thousand. The closeness with which the siege was pressed is graphically described in the terms: " Hezekiah himself I shut up in Jerusalem, his capital city, like a bird in a cage." After mentioning the fear of the power of his arms as falling on the King of Judah, the embassy of the chiefs and

elders sent from Jerusalem, and the amount of gold and silver which they brought, it adds, "and divers treasures, a rich and immense booty." The single discrepancy in the matter of the talents of silver, 300 according to the Bible, 800 according to the inscription, may probably be explained by a second demand on the part of Sennacherib, when Hezekiah, in his anxiety for the withdrawal of his enemy, "gave him," as we read in the Scripture account, "all the silver that was found in the house of the Lord, and in the treasures of the king's house." Besides all this, a sculpture represents Sennacherib seated on a gorgeous throne with captives crouching in an abject manner, in his presence, before the city of Lakis, understood by Layard and others to be Lachish, with the inscription: "Sennacherib the mighty king, the king of the country of Assyria, sitting on the throne of judgment before the city of Lachish. I give permission for its slaughter." Thus disinterred from beneath the mounds of the far distant Assyria, silent but sure witnesses have come forth to testify to the truth of God and to afford the most marvellous verification of Scripture, corroborating, as scarcely anything else could do, the accuracy of its statements and the perfect trustworthiness of its venerable and everlasting verities.

(4) Resembling the position of Nineveh on the Tigris was that of Babylon on the Euphrates, while they were the respective capitals of the two great early and Eastern empires. The fall of Babylon, the slaughter of its sovereign, and the transference of the kingdom into the hands of the Medo-Persians, are narrated with sublime brevity by the prophet, when he says: "In that night was Belshazzar the king of the Chaldeans slain. And Darius the Median took the kingdom." The night referred to was the last night of revelry in the royal palace of Babylon. No statement of Scripture has been more stoutly controverted than this. Infidelity supported by heathenism impugned the record with violence, one might almost add, with malignancy. The $\delta\grave{o}\varsigma$ $\pi o\hat{u}$ $\sigma\tau\hat{\omega}$ had been granted. A vantage ground was ready at hand for the enemies, on which they could plant their lever for the overthrow of the sacred record. Herodotus and Berosus had both come to their aid as timely and powerful auxiliaries. These

two historians agreed in giving an account of the matter altogether different from the Biblical. Here, then, the odds were against it. We sometimes try to reconcile Herodotus with himself; but who would think of reconciling him with Scripture, and all the more as Berosus confirmed his statement but contradicted that of Scripture? The knight-errants, whose dispute nearly came to blows about the metal of which a shield was made, those on one side asserting it was brass, those on the other that it was iron, and both turning out to be right with regard to the side directly opposite to them, might have suggested caution to the opponents of Scripture, but *they did not*. The King of Babylon is called Belshazzar in the Bible; but Berosus and Herodotus say it was Nabonidus. The Bible says he was in the city; but Berosus and Herodotus tell us he was in the country. The Bible gives a circumstantial account of how he was engaged that night in untimely riot with the grandees of his realm and the women of his harem; but Berosus and Herodotus state the cause of his absence from his capital to have been the collecting of an army in order to take the Medo-Persians in the rear, or compel them to raise the siege. The Bible represents the slaughter of the monarch as the closing scene of a dark picture; but Berosus and Herodotus, while admitting his capitulation, allow him to retire alive, and, if not with the honours of war, at least with a respectable provision. How then could two accounts so diametrically opposite and contradictory of each other in so many particulars both be true? How, especially, could we presume the Biblical account to be correct when such weighty authorities as Berosus and Herodotus were both opposed to it? And yet we might in our simplicity suppose that the Bible was entitled to be placed, by way of courtesy, at least on a par with profane history, and that, if no means of reconcilement had been found, it might have been allowed the benefit of the doubt; for, after all, Herodotus and Berosus are never reckoned, even by their most ardent admirers, to have been infallible. Still this would have been an amount of fair play which the Bible is not much accustomed to. Fortunately, however, for belief of the Bible and the credit of its narrative, two cylinders, two thousand years old and inscribed with contemporaneous history, were brought from Ur of the Chaldees. From those cylinders we learn that Nabonidus was the father and Belshazzar his son; that the father had taken the son to a partnership in the sovereignty; that they were joint-sharers in the government of the realm and in the kingly throne; that while one remained inside the city to defend it against the invaders that were beleaguering it without, the other was operating outside and facing the foe in the open field, in hope of gaining victory over the enemy, or of bringing relief to his friends. Thus the contradiction is converted into a confirmation, as singular as it is striking, of the inspired word of God.

(5) One other instance, where the removal of a difficulty has tended to the confirmation of the truth, may be added in this connection. After the great event of the exodus had taken place, and during those weary years of wandering in the wilderness, how was that great host of 600,000 men sustained? How were man and beast in the Hebrew camp supplied with food? This question has sometimes been put with puzzling effect. The difficulty it involves is to some extent modified, if not entirely removed, when, instead of forming our estimate from its present barrenness, we duly consider the capabilities of the desert in ancient times. Leaving out of the calculation the miraculous supply of manna regularly, and of quails occasionally vouchsafed, and setting aside the obvious circumstance of the Israelites spreading themselves far and near over the verdant wadies and fertile spots of the Sinaitic peninsula, where no doubt the pastoral portion of the people, turning to account whatever pasturage could be had, would employ themselves in their accustomed occupation, and where the agricultural would take advantage of every spot suitable for tillage,—setting all this aside, there are three considerations which, if we bear in mind, greatly reduce the difficulties of the case. (*a*) First, the deterioration of the country has been going on for ages. The trees, which once attracted the vapours floating up from the Indian Ocean on the south, have been mostly swept away by the torrents or the storms; while the acacias that still remain are rapidly disappearing to supply

the charcoal trade of the Bedawin. The result is a diminished rainfall, while the consequence of this again is the diminution or total destruction of the vegetation. And with the disappearance of vegetation the means of subsistence, of course, vanish. (*b*) Secondly, the remains of dwellings, churches, gardens, together with the names of places, of which nothing but the mere memory now remains, bespeak a population far exceeding not only the present number of inhabitants, but even any conception that might thence be formed in relation to their number in the past; while the powerful resistance which the Amalekites opposed to the march of the Israelites through the district, coupled with the fact that they were the first of the nations, must greatly enhance our estimate of the character and capabilities of the region, and correct our idea of its barrenness and desolation. (*c*) Thirdly, add to the present population of some 6000 the 5000 more that pass annually through the country on their pilgrimage to Mecca; but above all, take into account the effects of care and culture, as evidenced at the present day in two places, which Stanley has pointed out—one, the gardens at the Wells of Moses, under the superintendence of Europeans; the other, in the valleys of Jebel Musa, under the care of the monks of St. Catherine. These considerations duly weighed greatly diminish, if they do not cause to disappear altogether, any doubt or difficulty about the possibility of Israel's maintenance in the desert.

All this has been more than confirmed. In an instructive and interesting little book, entitled *Our Work in Palestine*, in the chapter about the Sinai Survey, we read the following:—
" Objections have been raised, based on the present barrenness of the peninsula, to the narrative of the Bible. They vanish before the results of the survey. The barrenness of the peninsula is due to neglect. In former times it was more richly wooded; the wadies were protected by walls stretching across, which served as dams to resist the force of the rushing waters; the mountains were terraced, and clothed with gardens and groves. This fertility lasted till modern times. The monks—there was formerly a large Christian community in the peninsula—carried on the old traditions of cultivation

(traditions, perhaps, as old as the Amalekites), and terraced, protected, and planted. Then came the bad times of Mohammedan rule, which let in the Bedawin to waste and destroy. Then the protecting walls across the wady were broken down; the green terraces along its sides were destroyed; the trees were cut down or carried away by the winter torrent."

Sec. II.—*Indirect Confirmations.*

In Scripture there is, or seems to be, a frequent anticipation of discoveries made in subsequent ages and centuries after the record. Reference has been already made to the undulating theory of light as having superseded the corpuscular, and the agreement in this respect between Biblical narrative and modern scientific research. In the present section we shall subjoin a few instances of a similar kind, regarding them as indirect confirmations of inspired truth.

(1) In a remarkable passage in the Book of Job there is a curious statement referring to two of the most important elements in nature, namely, the atmosphere that surrounds the entire globe, and the waters that occupy so much of its surface. In the 28th chapter and 25th verse of the book of Scripture referred to, we read: "To make the weight for the winds; and He weigheth the waters by measure." A slight modification of rendering will bring it into more exact agreement with the original, for תכן refers rather to adjustment or determination of relative proportions than to weight, while מִשְׁקָל in the preceding member of the sentence wants the article, and רוח is in the singular, so that a more accurate translation would be: "To make weight for the wind; and He hath adjusted or apportioned (*meted out* is the rendering of the Revised English Bible) the waters by measure." As רוח is both air and wind—wind being simply air in agitation, we have thus in a single verse the weight of the air and the measure of the waters reckoned by the writer among the arrangements of the Creator's skill and the evidences of His power. For many centuries after the statement of this text had been penned, certain facts of experience were expressed by the formula that "nature

abhors a vacuum." But this formula only darkened counsel by words without knowledge—it was itself at once a mystification and a mystery. It was only a convenient expression of ignorance. Nature's abhorrence of a vacuum remained to be accounted for—the cause was still for long unknown. At length Torricelli, early in the 17th century, found by experiment that nature's abhorrence of a vacuum was a variable quantity—differing for different fluids, and that in inverse proportion to their specific gravity. Here was the solution of the mystery, and Torricelli made the discovery that it was atmospheric pressure on the open surface of fluids that supported a column of water to the height of 32 feet and a column of mercury to the height of 30 inches. Hence, too, the fact became known that the air presses on every square inch with a weight equal to 15 pounds. Here, then, in a book so old as that of Job we have embodied in the words of a brief clause a scientific fact which was only discovered in the 17th century of our era, and a fact that has been utilised in a variety of ways. Whether Job himself understood the fact is not the question, for the prophets did not always comprehend the purport of the communications made to them, though they searched diligently to attain that knowledge. But be this as it may, the words of the Spirit contain a correct and accurate expression of the fact.

But wind being properly air in motion, its pressure is in proportion to that motion and in the direction thereof, so that when its velocity is ten miles an hour the pressure is $\frac{1}{2}$ lb. on the square foot; when 20 miles, equivalent to a good breeze, it is 2 lbs.; when 40 miles, or a gale, it is 8 lbs.; when 60 miles, or a storm, it is 18 lbs.; and when it reaches hurricane speed, from 80 up to 100 miles, its pressure rises in proportion from some 30 to 50 lbs. Further, not only are the weight of the air at rest and its pressure when in motion covered by this expression; but, variable as the wind is, that variation is regulated by law, and follows with more or less steadiness a certain order. The order of its variation was formulated by Lord Bacon thus:—

N : NE : E : SE : S : SW : W : NW : N ;

otherwise thus:—

S : SW : W : NW : N : NE : E : SE : S ;

while Dore in his *Law of the Rotation of the Winds* has ably elucidated the subject. Now, turning to Ecclesiastes i. 6, we read: "The wind goeth toward the south, and turneth about unto the north; it whirleth about continually, and the wind returneth again according to its circuits," or more exactly: "It goeth to the south, and turneth to the north; circling, circling, goes the wind, and the wind returneth again on its circuits." The passage of the wind from north to south, and from south back to north, not directly and immediately, but for the most part circling through the intermediate stages, could not be more briefly, and at the same time beautifully, expressed in this 19th century by the most skilful student of the laws of atmospheric change. But if there is this constancy in the changeful—this fixity in the fickle—this regularity in the fluctuations of the wayward wind of temperate climes, still more is this the case toward the region of the tropics. The statement that the wind returns again on its circuits has, we think, a special appropriateness in relation to the perennial trade-winds of the tropics, tracing and retracing their north-east circuit in the northern hemisphere and their south-east circuit in the southern; to the periodicity of the monsoons or season-winds, moving for the winter half-year from the north-eastward and south-eastward, north and south of the equator respectively, but reversing their course during the summer months; as also to the diurnal alternation of the sea-breezes and the land-breezes, the former in the morning, the latter in the evening.

But while the air has weight, the waters have been regulated by measure. It seems, on the first blush of the thing, somewhat singular that so much of the earth's surface is covered with water, the approximate proportion being three to one. Still more, the distribution is equally surprising. There is much less water in the northern hemisphere than in the southern, much less also in the eastern than in the western. The land in the northern hemisphere is two-fifths of the whole, but in the southern it is only one-eighth. Thus the land greatly preponderates in the north-eastern, and the water in the south-western region of the globe. The greater part of the land, moreover, is situated in the north temperate zone, while the greater part of the sea is in the torrid. These curious arrangements are not the result of chance. Under the influence of the sun's heat a portion of the waters of ocean is carried up by evaporation into the atmosphere. The clouds have been compared to aqueducts for conveying these waters at seasonable times and in suitable measure to the different regions of the globe. Descending in rain and dew, they refresh tree and herb and flower, they fertilise the face of the earth, they minister to man and beast, they supply the freshet of the mountain, the springs that run among the hills, and the rivers that roll onward in magnificence to the ocean, carrying blessings with them as they go. Without this great cistern earth would be a desert, and the land a dry and parched wilderness, without grass for the cattle or herb for the service of man; vegetable and animal life would languish or become extinct. We don't speak of its beneficial effects in preventing the stagnation of noxious vapours, or the facility it affords for communication between different and distant lands. We confine our remarks to its refreshing effects by means of evaporation, and its equalising influence in the matter of temperature. It has been asserted as the result of experiments, that the proportion of water to land on the surface of the globe, large as it may appear, is just the quantity which scientific measurement proves to be requisite for all the purposes of evaporation, and for all the exigencies of the various tribes that compose the vegetable and animal kingdom. The Almighty has meted out the waters with skilful as well as beneficent hand, and in due measure. But the same careful adjustment of the waters is indispensable for maintaining the proper equilibrium between the temperature of our planet and the structure, modes of life, and other conditions of the organic existences that tenant it. It has been made manifest that a considerable diminution of the waters of the ocean, or a different distribution of those waters, would injuriously disturb that equilibrium. If the mass of waters were greatly diminished or greatly increased, or if they were distributed much otherwise than now—if, in a word, the measure were materially changed, or the present proportion much modified, or the present arrangement greatly altered, such alteration would produce a most detrimental effect on the temperature. Nay, it is more than possible, it is highly probable that it would prove destructive to the very existence of the plants and animals that at present exist upon our globe. So true it is, that the Creator has settled the waters of that great sea by measure, allotting land and water not only their proper place but right dimensions.

(2) We advance now to the position of the earth, or its suspension in space. Another extraordinary statement of Scripture defines that position. It is found in Job xxvi. 7, and reads in our Authorised Version as follows: "He stretcheth out the north over the empty place, and hangeth the earth upon nothing." This rendering may be somewhat improved by a close adherence to the original. More literally it reads: "He stretcheth out the north *upon emptiness* (תֹהוּ = voidness); He hangeth the earth upon nothing." There is surely, it must be acknowledged, a most striking concord between this affirmation of the divine word and the correct account of matters as disclosed to us by modern physical astronomy. Without assuming that Job was acquainted with the sphericity of the earth, or the nice balancing of those forces, centrifugal and centripetal, that keep it in its orbit, or that law of attraction in particular that binds it to the central sun, we cannot help feeling that the words in question accord better with the Copernican than with the Ptolemaic system that had prevailed for fourteen hundred years. The transference of the centre of motion from the earth to the sun by Copernicus was a new departure in astronomy. From that time forward astronomical science advanced with firm step. Kepler's three laws—(1) that the *radius vector* or line from a planet to the sun describes equal areas in equal times; (2) that the orbits of the planets are ellipses with the sun in one of the foci; and (3) that the squares of the periodic times are proportionate to the cubes of the distances—were three mighty and magnificent strides. But the principle that bound these laws together, and from which they flowed as consequences, remained to be found out. The crowning discovery was reserved for the genius of Newton. The great law of universal attraction or of gravitation, acting in all directions in direct proportion to the quantity of matter

and in reverse proportion to the square of the distance, was made known. And so the secret of the earth's position was revealed. It now became clear how it was suspended in empty space without support—how it was poised in vacant air, with no foundation underlaid or underlying it—how, as Milton has said, " Earth, self-balanced, from her centre hung " —how, in words more sublime and more precise than those of the poet, God " hangeth the earth upon nothing ;" and that by virtue of those wonderful impulses which His almighty hand impressed on it at the first. With the velocity of projection that would speed it onward into space, He combined the force of attraction, so that in an elliptical path it circles round the sun. Whether known or unknown to Job, there lies imbedded in his words an anticipation of the great Newtonian discovery, or rather of the result of the law that philosopher discovered, by which the earth though unsupported still keeps its place, and though suspended upon emptiness holds on its way.

(3) We pass, however, from earth, prepared and preserved for the abode of man, to man its great inhabitant. In Deuteronomy xxxii. 24 we read מְזֵי רָעָב. The first of these words Gesenius compares with מצה, and renders " sucking ;" while Fürst prefers connecting it with מסס, and translates " melting or wasting." Our Authorised Version has " burnt with hunger," and is supported by two of the most distinguished Hebrew expositors,—one of them, Ibn Ezra, explaining it by שׂרוּף, *burnt*,—and by many of the ancient Christian expositors. It can claim, besides, other support than that of such authorities however eminent. Being an ἅπαξ λεγ., and occurring nowhere else, we cannot have recourse for help to a precisely parallel passage in Hebrew ; but in the Chaldee of Daniel, אֵזֵא, a word radically the same, is found in the signification of *hot*, applied to a furnace ; and a similar effect is ascribed to famine in Lamentations v. 10 : " Our skin was black like an oven (*i.e.* blackened by the fire) because of the terrible famine." If, then, the common and current translation be accepted, the words express the curious physiological fact first expounded clearly by Liebig, who says that " in the animal body the food is the fuel ; with a proper supply of oxygen we obtain the heat given out during its oxidation or combustion ;" and again,

referring to death by starvation, he says, "The flame is extinguished, because the oil is consumed; and it is the oxygen of the air which has consumed it." He is at pains to explain how the oxygen combining with food fuel produces a process of combustion; but when food fails, the proper fuel is wanting, and then "the substance of the organs themselves, the fat of the body, the substance of the muscles, the nerves and the brain, are unavoidably consumed," and by combustion. Thus persons dying by famine are literally "burnt with hunger."

In the last chapter of the Book of Ecclesiastes we read: "Or the pitcher be broken at the fountain, or the wheel broken at the cistern." The whole passage is a most impressive one. The young are urged to a remembrance of their Creator and consecration to His service in youth, before the decrepitude and discomforts of age succeed to youthful vigour and enjoyment, and before dissolution comes to close the scene. A lively representation is given of the stages of decay, as also of death itself. The whole consists of striking allegorical expressions, and as such these expressions have been differently expounded. Yet they are so plain and clear that no soberminded interpreter needs mistake their meaning. And, indeed, there has been a pretty general agreement among expositors in relation to their meaning. The expression just quoted, in regard to its single particulars, is as difficult as any that occurs in the passage, though its import on the whole is unmistakable. Some understand it to refer to the heart and lungs and their reciprocal action; and, speaking generally, this is a tolerable exposition of the meaning. It is adopted by some eminent commentators. Still it is scarcely precise enough. A fountain and a cistern are a good deal similar in use. The fountain sends out its life-giving fluid, and the cistern parts with its contents when requisite. The pitcher and the wheel are the appropriate means by which fountain and cistern are respectively discharged. The fountain and the cistern may not improperly be referred to the cavities of the heart; but we would venture to reverse the usual order of their application. Thus the fountain would correspond to the left cavity, consisting of auricle and ventricle, whence the purified blood proceeds; while the pitcher is the great artery called the aorta, which with its branches conveys away the blood from the heart through the entire system. The cistern would then be the right cavity, consisting also of auricle and ventricle, while the wheel is venæ-cavæ, bringing back the impure blood to the heart, and especially the pulmonary artery, which forces the blood that has now circulated through the entire body forward into the lungs for the purpose of being purified. Wunderbar, as well as many others, takes it for granted that the author of the book understood the nervous system and the circulation of the blood; but Oetinger, as quoted by Delitzsch, expresses himself more guardedly. He says: "As far as concerns my opinion, I dare not affirm that Solomon had a knowledge *systematis nervolymphatici*, as also *circuli sanguinis*, such as learned physicians now possess; yet I believe that the Holy Spirit spake thus through Solomon, that what in subsequent times was discovered as to these matters might be found under these words." True it is that Delitzsch in citing this judgment of Oetinger expresses his dissent from it, denying that the figure of death in the passage is an anticipation of modern discoveries, adding, however, that "it is as true to fact as it is poetically beautiful." It is surely a most surprising fact that a book so old as any part of the Old Testament should harmonise, for this is the lowest ground that can be taken, so exactly and minutely with, even if it does not anticipate, a discovery which was made known to the world only at the close of the first quarter of the 17th century, when William Harvey published his celebrated treatise, entitled *Exercitatio Anatomica de Motu Cordis et Sanguinis*.

(4) Nearly allied to the circulation of the blood is its *vitality*. A truth as old as the days of Moses, and enunciated by him in a statement as concise as it is comprehensive and correct, namely, "The life of the flesh is in the blood," was proved demonstratively by the experiments of John Hunter, also in the beginning of the 17th century. Its capability of resisting heat and cold, as only living agents can do; its power of uniting living parts; mortification and death from cutting an artery, and other similar facts, abundantly evidence the truth of its asserted vitality.

(5) The book of Scripture called Acts presents all the appearance of actual history, even to a superficial reader; but the close examination of a single chapter cannot fail to convert that appearance into an acknowledged reality. Let any one peruse with a moderate amount of thoughtfulness the 27th chapter of that book, and especially let him read it in the light of those illustrations which may be found in *The Voyage and Shipwreck of St. Paul*, by J. Smith, Esq. of Jordanhill, and there can be little doubt of his concurrence in the opinion just expressed. It is not to be wondered at that since the publication of Mr. Smith's interesting volume, nearly all commentators have largely availed themselves of its most instructive details as explaining the chapter referred to. The internal proof furnished by this chapter, when elucidated in the manner indicated, is of the most astonishing kind. That it was written by an eye-witness—one who had been a partner in the voyage, and passed through all its perils, and had been present in the final wreck—is all but demonstrated. Now the author who narrates with such unerring fidelity one most important scene, and a scene the most difficult to be described of all in a truly eventful history, surely gives a guarantee for his veracity in the remainder. But the historian of these events, which took place in A.D. 58, refers to a previous history written by him, how much earlier in point of time we do not know, but, it may be fairly inferred, equally entitled to credit. That history was the Gospel according to Luke; and if Matthew's preceded, as there is good reason to believe, the latter must carry us back to a date considerably earlier than a quarter of a century from the death of Christ.

In this chapter we find so many incidents of the most thrilling and interesting kind, that one regrets being obliged by want of space to pass over so many particulars. We can only, however, note, and that briefly, a few of the most striking points.

(*a*) The first thing that impresses itself on one is the frequent and precise use of nautical terms met with in this chapter. There are no less than ten such expressions descriptive of the ship's movements as related to the rate of speed, or distance from the land, or direction of the wind.

For example, there is πλέω, to sail, and ἀποπλέω, to sail away; ἀνάγομαι, to launch, get under way, or set sail, with its opposite κατάγομαι, to come to land; again, they ran to the leeward of Clauda, ὑποδραμόντες; they sailed to the leeward of Cyprus and Crete, ὑπεπλεύσαμεν; they sailed the whole length of the sea along the coast of Cilicia and Pamphylia, διεπλεύσαμεν; they proceeded slowly, βραδυπλοοῦντες; they coasted along with difficulty, παραλεγόμενοι; also αἴρω, to weigh anchor, if τὰς ἀγκύρας be the ellipsis, or set sail, if the supplement be τὰ ἱστία.

(b) The course of the ship was devious, being determined by the direction of the wind. First, they had a speedy and successful run from Cæsarea to Sidon (now Saida); then they steered northward, keeping Cyprus on the left, though the direct line would have been westward, or, at least, to the north-west; but this was prevented by the wind blowing from that quarter, as is usual to the present day during the summer etesiæ; after that, they did proceed westward, taking advantage of the local land breeze and usual westerly current, to Myra, where they changed ship and worked to windward as far as Cnidus. Thence they ran south to the leeward of Crete, as far as its easternmost extremity Salmone. From that point they coasted along the south of the island westward, though with difficulty, by help of a weather shore and western current as before. In the account of all this, Luke's knowledge of his subject is so perfect, and his language is so extremely accurate and precise, that the reckoning has been wrought, the course of the vessel tested and traced, and the voyage itself reconstructed as clearly and correctly as if the whole had been laid down in the log-reckoning of a modern ship.

(c) Luke's account is in strictest correspondence with all that is known of the structure of ships and method of seamanship, whether in foul or fair weather, in ancient times. When the typhoon, or levanter, as it would now be called, came down upon them, after taking the boat on board, they frapped the ship, passing undergirders or large ropes several times round the hull. Next, they lowered the gear or heavy yard with sail attached, and in this plight they were borne along or drifted at the mercy of winds and waves. But the storm still increasing, they proceeded to lighten by throwing overboard such things as could be most easily dispensed with; then with their own hands they cast out the furniture or moveables of the ship. The same graphic and exact style continues to be employed in the subsequent part of the narrative. When the seamen suspected that land was approaching ($\pi\rho o\sigma\acute{a}\gamma\epsilon\iota\nu$ αὐτοῖς χώραν = land nearing them, "the graphic language of seamen, to whom the ship is the principal object"), they cast out four anchors from the stern. Eventually they were obliged to complete the process of lightening by throwing the cargo itself into the sea, and prepared to run the ship aground, cutting away the anchors, loosing the rudder bands, and hoisting the foresail.

(*d*) A comparison of the narrative with the localities where the events referred to occurred, and the identification of the various places named, show still further and more fully that the historian was personally engaged in the events, and that the correctness of his language is thus a transcript of his actual and accurate observation of each occurrence, and of the spot where it took place. The Adramyttian ship was no doubt homeward bound, that is, to Adramyttium, a seaport of Mysia on the eastern shore of the Ægean opposite Lesbos, while the Alexandrian ship was bound directly for Italy. But why is the Alexandrine ship found at Myra, due north from Alexandria, instead of standing right across the Mediterranean and pursuing her voyage westward? Apart from a probable occasion to touch there for commercial purposes, the same westerly winds that forced the Adramyttian to steer east of Cyprus drove the Alexandrine ship to Myra, which, as Smith has shown, was the mode of navigating those seas at that season under similar circumstances. This ship was a merchantman, for its lading is mentioned in the 10th verse; the character of the cargo, which we only learn incidentally in the 38th verse to have been wheat, and the season of shipment, were in exact correspondence with all we know about the trading in those days between the granary of the East and the great metropolis of the West. The

Fair Havens have been identified with two roadsteads of Calolimounias or Limenes Kali, a name of the same import, on the south coast of Crete, a few miles east of Cape Matala, while two hours eastward from Fair Havens the ruins of Lasea, a city mentioned by no ancient geographer and long unknown, were discovered in 1856 in a remarkable manner and beyond any possibility of doubt. Port Phœnice is identified with Lutro, and by a coincidence of equal importance it is ascertained from an inscription that Alexandrine ships did anchor there, while the shipmaster's name in the same inscription is $κυβερνήτης$, and that of the ship's sign is $παρασήμω$. Further, Clauda is the modern Gozzo.

(c) The Maltese tradition about St. Paul's Bay in Malta being the actual scene of the shipwreck, has been verified. But several singular circumstances deserve to be noted here. (a) By certain strictly mathematical calculations of Mr. Smith, in which, after the most thorough investigation, he assumes as the elements of his calculation the size of the ship evidently one of large dimensions, the force of the gale to be moderate, and the probable rate of drift of such a ship, hove to in such a gale and working against a north-east wind, to be about 36 miles in 24 hours, it is computed that a ship starting in the evening from Clauda, under the conditions specified, would drift over some 476 miles, and would thus be within less than 3 miles of Koura point, at the entrance of St. Paul's Bay in Malta, by midnight on the 14th. But ($β$) not only is there this very remarkable agreement between the distance drifted and the time so spent, but the direction of the ship's drift in order to escape the Syrtis corresponds in similar exactness with the bearing of St. Paul's Bay from Clauda. This also was subjected to strict mathematical reckoning, in which the mean direction of the wind as deduced from the narrative, the angle of the ship's head with the wind, and the leeway supplied the data; while the result was the singularly curious correspondence just stated. Further, ($γ$) another fact of no less significance as well as singular coincidence is connected with the soundings and nature of the soil where anchor was cast. At the first sounding they found the depth of the water was 20 fathoms; and after advancing a short distance, it was 15 fathoms. The self-same soundings may be taken at the present day by a ship approaching Malta in the same direction. Not only so, the anchorage retains to the present time the same striking peculiarity that allowed four anchors to be cast successfully under such disadvantageous circumstances. The ground is of such peculiar tenacity, that as long as the cables hold, there is no danger of the anchors starting.

From such coincidences, of which only specimens have been adduced, the circumstantiality and vivid character of the whole narrative, the appropriateness of the descriptions, the expressiveness of the words employed, the use of nautical terms at once clear and correct, the accuracy with which the course of the voyage is traced, and the direction of the winds indicated, the hints in reference to the structure of the ship, the intimations of the method of seamanship, the accurate geographical notices, the distances navigated, the times consumed, all the numerous incidents even to the geological character of the sea-bottom,—from all these, expressed with such precision of language and rigid adherence to admitted facts, we infer with certainty that the narrator was not only well acquainted with the sea, but must have been present as an eye-witness and actual observer of all that he has so faithfully recorded.

No one who studies this one chapter of the one book, and takes pains to acquaint himself with the points noticed and many others that might be added, viewing them in the light of modern geographical research and of improved acquaintance with ancient navigation and practical seamanship in the Levant, can possibly deny that a firm basis is furnished by this chapter for an argument of great weight and much importance in favour of the authenticity, genuineness, and credibility of the whole Book of Acts, and by consequence of the Gospel by the same author. Not only are the facts narrated shown to be real, but the account of them is by one contemporaneous with the events, and who, moreover, observed them with his own eyes, and actually took part in the transactions. Nor is this all; they are described not by a landsman, who would be inadequate to the task, nor yet by a seaman, who would be likely to discuss not only *what* was done, but to dwell on *how* or *why* it was done; while the present narrative, most accurate and graphic though unprofessional, of what was done, is such as could only proceed from a real eye-witness and direct as well as correct observation of the whole.

CHAPTER IX.

THE SOLOMONIC AUTHORSHIP OF ECCLESIASTES.

A REMARKABLE feature of the books of Scripture is the unity of the whole, notwithstanding the variety of the parts. These books, sixty-six in number, have been written by different persons, following different pursuits, in different places, at different periods, and under different conditions and circumstances, and on topics not a little diverse; and yet one purpose pervades them all. Among the penmen of Scripture we find the greatest difference of natural gifts, of degrees of culture, and of social position. Some were plain men, with little or no learning except what they were taught of God; again, we have Moses trained in all the learning of the Egyptians, and Paul brought up at the feet of Gamaliel, and Luke educated and practising as a physician; some are of royal rank, as David and Solomon; some of courtly dignity, as Isaiah and Daniel; and some of priestly descent, as Jeremiah, Ezekiel, and Ezra; others were taken from lower walks in life, like Amos from tending the herd, or Matthew from the seat of custom, or Peter and John from the boat of the fisherman. Equally various are the species of composition. There is history comprising three-fifths of the whole; there is poetry — lyric, elegiac, didactic, and even dramatic in a restricted sense; there are epistles to Churches and Church members; while more than a millennium and a half separated the first penman of revelation from the last. The topics treated are almost countless, comprehending God's dealings with man, and man's doings in relation to himself, his fellow-man, and his Father in heaven. And notwithstanding all this variety of persons and pursuits, there is perfect unity of purpose. The whole is but the history of redemption in its two great parts—the salvation of man and the service of God. To this one great purpose everything else is subordinated. When fresh revelations of that plan of mercy are vouchsafed the record expands, if they are withheld it contracts. Thus, in the initial stage the record of 2000 years, that is, from Adam to Abraham, is contained in a few chapters; while 200 years, that is, from the death of Jacob to the exodus, are compressed into three chapters. Again, the deliverance from Egypt, the settlement in Canaan, the commencement of the line of inspired prophets with Samuel, the establishment of the kingdom of David, the overthrow of idolatry by Elijah, were each a new departure; and, as a consequence, the record becomes fuller and the details more copious. Three books cover the post-exilian period, and without any miracle save God's miraculously providential preservation of His people in time of greatest peril. Then comes an interruption of some four centuries, for the stars must disappear before the rising sun, after which interval the record recommences with the life and labours, the doing and the dying, the resurrection and ascension of our Lord; continues with the progressive history of the rapidly-growing Church; and passes on to Paul's proclamation of the gospel in the capital of the world, and thus in parting leaves us a hint of its great purpose for obedience to the faith among all nations, and a pledge that all flesh shall see the salvation of God. One gracious purpose thus unites all the books and all the penmen of Scripture, bringing them into contact, however far apart in space or time, and binding them together like pearls united by the cord on which they are strung. Like the river that, rising in the lofty Andes, pursues its course across an entire continent, now passing through mountain gorges deep and beautiful, again receiving its tributary streams,—one on this side, others on that side,—then winding through primeval forests, anon spreading out like a sea in the plains, and never stops till it reaches the Atlantic 4000 miles from its source; so the stream of the divine purpose flows on through history, and prophecy, and poetry, and psalmody, sometimes narrower, sometimes wider. This unity amid elements so numerous, and conditions so distinct, and persons so diverse, bespeaks one moulding, modifying, plastic hand, or rather, to sum it up in a word, one inspiring mind. Among the writers themselves concert is out of the question, and from the nature of the case clearly impossible. Yet they imply each other, and quote each other,—for example, the Gospels are quoted more than fifty times in the Epistles,—and allude to each other in instances more numerous than is generally supposed; while the threads of their narrations are so interwoven that no human hand can disentangle them. Neither do cases of disputed authorship militate against this. They only enhance the marvel and increase our wonder as they contribute to this astonishing unity—a unity which of itself bears testimony to the divinity of its origin.

Among those books of Old Testament scripture that have been subjected to the most scathing criticism of modern times is the Book of Ecclesiastes, so much so, that the position assigned it by certain critics is incompatible, as it appears to us, with its inspiration. That it might be a production later in its origin than the time of Solomon, or that it might proceed from other authorship, without its claim to inspiration being necessarily discredited or disproved, is quite conceivable. But that a late production should be palmed off on the Church or the world as Solomon's, or that such a production should be made to enhance its value by the credit of his name, might be the disingenuous attempt of a literary pretender or low personator, but could not possibly, we think, consist with the character of an inspired penman. Here, then, we find ourselves at issue with some of the advanced critics of the present day. The writer of an article in a recent number of the *Encyclopædia Britannica* speaks contemptuously of the very idea of adhering to the old belief in Ecclesiastes being the production of Solomon, and regards the attempt to prove the non-Solomonic authorship of the book in the same light with adducing facts to prove that the earth does not stand still. After affirming that such is the current of opinion "on the Continent, where Biblical criticism has been cultivated to the highest degree, and where Old Testament exegesis has become an exact science," he proceeds to say: "In England, however, some scholars of acknowledged repute still adhere to the Solomonic authorship. Their principal argument is, the unanimous voice of tradition declares it to be so. We at once concede the fact. The Jewish synagogue undoubtedly believed that Solomon wrote Canticles when young, Proverbs when in middle life, and Ecclesiastes in old age, and the Christian Church has simply espoused the Jewish tradition."

In this state of matters, let us examine the subject carefully yet concisely. The *name* of this book in the original furnishes one ground of objection. That name is קֹהֶלֶת, a noun of the feminine gender, and a word variously interpreted. Some understand it (*a*) in the sense of συναθροιστής, a *collector*, that is to say, a collector of truths from an induction of facts furnished by a long experience, or a collector of proverbs, παροιμιαστής, as Symmachus renders it, or even a compiler of the sayings and opinions of others. To this view both linguistic usage and the character of the book are decidedly opposed, for the meaning of the root-word is not at all to gather things inanimate together, but to call living persons to a meeting-place; while the book is not a series of isolated maxims strung together, but has a well defined plan, and presents a full development of most important thoughts in a style partly rhetorical and partly dialectical. Others take the name to mean (β) an *assembly*, but this is entirely incompatible with the very first sentence of the book, namely: "The words of קֹהֶלֶת the son of David, king in Jerusalem," and with a similar statement at the 12th verse: "I קֹהֶלֶת was king over Israel in Jerusalem." Considerably different is (γ) Ewald's view, that the word, which is a participle in the feminine, agrees with חָכְמָה, wisdom, understood, with the signification of *preaching wisdom*, and as a sort of symbolic proper name. This, no doubt, is ingenious as an effort to account for the feminine gender of the word, and to reconcile at the same time its general construction with a verb in the masculine; but it has the same difficulties to encounter as the preceding. The common and long-current explanation of this word (δ) by ἐκκλησιαστής, a preacher, not in the technical sense, but one who speaks in a public assembly, is at once well supported, and possesses the advantage of entire suitability. This opinion has the support of the LXX., of Jerome, who translates it *concionator*, and of most respectable Jewish authorities; also of Gesenius, Knobel, and others among modern scholars. The root קָהַל,

connected with קוֹל, the voice, and cognate with the Greek καλέω, and even the English *call*, implies this sense; while the feminine, as (*a*) an abstract name of office, is used with the meaning of the concrete, in other words, for the person invested with or exercising that office. Two other words have often been quoted, and most properly quoted, as similarly employed, namely, סֹפֶרֶת, Sophereth, that is, scribe, Ezra ii. 55 and Neh. vii. 57; also פֹּכֶרֶת, Pochereth, that is, snarer, Ezra ii. 57 and Neh. vii. 59, while both are used as proper names. Hence, too, it comes to pass that this grammatically feminine word is by a common *constructio ad sensum* construed in every instance except Ecclesiastes vii. 27 with a masculine verb. But (*b*) to this explanation of the feminine it is objected that those feminine forms that are used to denote office are abstract nouns, whereas this feminine is an active participle. The analogy of the Arabic feminine, which is sometimes used collectively to designate the properties of a class, is considered to furnish a sense more grammatically correct. Still the meaning will be the same, or rather stronger, viz. one who unites in himself all the properties of a preacher.

1. But the advocates of personated authorship urge in favour of their theory particular statements, and the style of language, as also the general subject of the book. The first (*a*) of these statements is that which speaks of a king in Jerusalem, and seems to intimate a long succession of kings from ancient days. "Above all (lit. every one, כֹּל) that were in Jerusalem before me" occurs with only a trifling variation both in chaps. i. and ii. Now it is argued that as his own father and immediate predecessor had established the seat of government and royal residence in Jerusalem, the expression quoted seems to clash with this, and leads one to conclude a long line of royal ancestors. But (1) it must be observed that "all" is quite indefinite, it is not said all *kings*, it is more likely that the word refers to *men* than to kings; (2) it is acknowledged that Jerusalem had been an ancient royal city from the time of Abraham and earlier, for "Melchizedek king of Salem," that is, Jerusalem, met him and blessed him as he returned victorious after the defeat of the allied kings; (3) an expression closely resembling the one before us, both in form

and purport, occurs in reference to Solomon in 1 Chron. xxix. 25: "And the Lord magnified Solomon exceedingly in the sight of all Israel, and bestowed upon him such royal majesty as had not been on any king before him in Israel." The statement is thus immensely enhanced. With advantages greater, experience wider, an induction more extensive, and wisdom higher than any person or any king that had been in Jerusalem, whether in patriarchal and primitive or more recent times, Solomon had conducted his investigations and come to a conclusion that did not satisfy—had made trials that resulted in failure. The next (*b*) statement found fault with is that in which Solomon speaks of "the oppressions that are done under the sun," the power of the oppressor, and the tears of the oppressed; and again, of "the oppression of the poor, and violent perverting of judgment and justice in a province," in chaps. iv. and v. It is contended that such a state of violence, oppression, miscarriage of justice, and provincial misrule, with the consequent sufferings and miseries, are inconceivable under the wise sway of such a sovereign as Solomon, and at a period of such unprecedented and unparalleled prosperity. To this it may be replied—(*a*) that it is abundantly obvious that Solomon does not confine his remarks to the condition of matters and the state of things that prevailed through his own dominions, wide as they were, and many as its judicatories were. He takes a much wider sweep and a far more extensive survey, for does he not himself inform us that in his most comprehensive outlook he contemplates the oppressions that are done *under the sun*, from the rising of the sun to where he has his fall, whether in the far east or distant west, whether in those remote lands visited triennially by his fleet, or in those neighbouring kingdoms to the north and to the south that were ruled over by allied sovereigns? But (β) even within the limits of his own extensive empire, notwithstanding all the wisdom of his rule and all the equity of his laws, was the executive equal to the legislative power of the state? was the administration of the laws always equal to their excellence? were all the deputies, lieutenants, or other subordinate functionaries so free from blame, so inaccessible to bribes, so uncorrupt and upright as to procure for themselves the approbation of the sovereign, and promote the wellbeing of his subjects? I trow not. If, as the proverb has it, a mishap may occur in the best ordered families, much more is this the case in well-regulated but extensive kingdoms. Solomon, moreover, must be regarded as speaking of evils that are liable to exist, with more or less abatement, at all times and in all lands; not only so, exceptional cases did doubtlessly occur in a kingdom so extended and with so many agencies necessarily employed in its administration, especially in those ancient times and in those Eastern lands.

But a third (c) objection is stated to be Solomon's advice to resist tyrannical oppression, not in the capacity of individuals, but by taking advantage of a time of general revolt. The beginning of chap. viii. is specified as inculcating this doctrine. On examining the passage, however, we shall find that no such unkingly advice is tendered. The 9th verse furnishes the clue to those that precede, and shows that the reference is to despotic oppression: "There is a time when a man rules over a man to his hurt." But instead of counselling the suitability of a time of general rebellion for confederate, not individual resistance, the passage imports the very opposite. It inculcates dutiful allegiance on the part of the subject to his sovereign: "Keep the king's commandment, and that because of the oath of God," the submission of subjects to their sovereign is thus stated as a religious duty; the oath of God, that is, the oath of obedience, is that compact between king and people which includes virtually, though not nominally, all the subjects of a kingdom. The 3d verse warns against the perilous thoughtlessness of revolutionary measures: "Join not in an evil matter; for he (the king) executeth all that he desires." The 5th verse enforces what goes before by the consideration that a wise man, instead of being hurried into acts of disloyalty and rebellion, even under despotic oppression, will bide God's time, for He will at length bring it to an end, and God's judgment, for He will punish it. The 6th verse implies that the wickedness of the oppressor is no safeguard; once the cup of his iniquity overflows, divine vengeance swift, always sure, and sometimes sudden, overtakes the oppressor. Thus the passage inculcates prudent and dutiful conduct, even towards a tyrannical monarch, moderation and wise submission even in a time of misrule, leaving the whole matter in God's hand with the conviction and consolation that in due time God Himself will interpose to right the wronged and wreak vengeance on the oppressor.

A fourth (*d*) objection is found in the description given of an intemperate pleasure-seeking and spendthrift king, and the misery thus brought upon a country. This objection is founded on the close of chap. x.: " Woe to thee, O land, when thy king is a child, and thy princes eat in the morning!" the opposite state of things forms a happy contrast, " when the king is the son of nobles, and thy princes eat in due season, for strength, and not for drunkenness. By much slothfulness the building decayeth; and through idleness of the hands the house (*i.e.* the kingdom or state) droppeth through."—Again: " Money answereth all things." With respect to these statements and the objection founded on them, it is clear (*a*) that the severity of this description falls more heavily on the princes than on the king himself; (β) that the language is specially appropriate as coming from a royal teacher, proper for warning kings and princes against courses at once riotous and ruinous, and perhaps prophetic of dark days to come; at all events, had his son and successor wisely laid the warning to heart, it might have saved him from mismanagement and mistake, as well as much misery consequent thereon. But (γ) granting that Solomon, when reviewing the past, reflects upon himself, what of that? Is it not so with all that truly repent, and is it not in the character of a penitent he comes before us in this book? Is not such language in perfect accord with the state of feeling when persons sorrow after a godly sort; " what carefulness it wrought in you," says an apostle, " yea, what indignation—yea, what revenge!" If we compare the language of another royal penitent, we find him reflecting on himself with much greater severity, while his self-upbraidings are greatly more aggravated: " I acknowledge," he says, " my transgressions: and my sin is ever before me. Against Thee, Thee only, have I sinned, and done this evil in Thy sight."

But to these objections, trifling and frivolous as some will be disposed to consider them, an undue importance has been attached by others; the molehill has been made a mountain. As there is a religiousness that strains out a gnat while it swallows a camel,—that tithes mint and rue and anise, but neglects the weightier matters of the law; so there is a criticism which, overlooking the broad comprehensive features of the Bible, deals in infinitesimals—a hair-splitting, fault-finding, carping sort of criticism, ever raising objections to or finding fault with traditional beliefs. There is again a manly, honest, upright criticism, that seeks to go deeper and ever deeper down into the rich unfathomable mine of gospel truth, and ever and again brings from thence nugget after nugget of the precious metal. This is calculated to accomplish, as it has already accomplished, much good. Far be it from us to speak disparagingly of straightforward reverent criticism, or to depreciate its results, even when constrained to differ from them. But there is a self-styled "higher criticism" of a pretentious kind, which has been called, and unfortunately in some cases too well merits to be called, the "lower scepticism." Its aim is rather to find flaws in than fetch truth out of the divine word.

2. Let us now compare some events of Solomon's life and reign, as recorded in the historical books, with statements in Ecclesiastes, and see how closely they correspond; while this correspondence cannot fail to confirm the currently received authorship of the book in question.

1. 1 KINGS iii. 12.
"Lo, I have given thee a wise and an understanding heart; so that there was none like thee before thee, neither after thee shall any arise like unto thee."

2. 1 KINGS vii. 1, 2, 8.
"So was he seven years in building it (*i.e.* the house of the Lord)."
"But Solomon was building his own house thirteen years, and he finished all his house. He built also the house of the forest of Lebanon. . . . Solomon made also an house for Pharaoh's daughter."

1. ECCLES. i. 16.—*His wisdom.*
"Lo, I am come to great estate, and have gotten more wisdom than all they (literally, every one) that have been before me in Jerusalem: yea, my heart had great experience of wisdom and knowledge."

2. ECCLES. ii. 4.— *The houses he built.*
"I builded me houses."

3. 1 Kings ix. 15.

"For to build the house of the Lord, and his own house, and Millo, and the wall of Jerusalem, and Hazor, and Megiddo, and Gezer.

"And Solomon built Gezer, and Beth-horon the nether. And Baalath, and Tadmor in the wilderness, in the land. And all the cities of store that Solomon had, and cities for his chariots, and cities for his horsemen."

3. Eccles. ii. 4.—*His great works.*
"I made me great works."

4. 1 Kings x. 14, 15, 22.

"Now the weight of gold that came to Solomon in one year was six hundred threescore and six talents of gold. Beside that he had of the merchantmen, and of the traffic of the spice merchants, and of all the kings of Arabia, and of the governors of the country. Once in three years came the navy of Tarshish, bringing gold, and silver, ivory, and apes, and peacocks."

4. Eccles. ii. 8.—*His gold, silver, and treasures.*
"I gathered me also silver and gold, and the peculiar treasure of kings and of the provinces."

5. 1 Kings viii. 46.
"For there is no man that sinneth not."

5. Eccles. vii. 20.—*Universality of sin.*
"For there is not a just man upon earth, that doeth good, and sinneth not."

6. 1 Kings iv. 32, 33.
"And he spake three thousand proverbs. . . . And he spake of trees, from the cedar tree that is in Lebanon even unto the hyssop that springeth out of the wall: he spake also of beasts, and of fowl, and of creeping things, and of fishes. And there came of all people to hear the wisdom of Solomon."

6. Eccles. xii. 9.—*His knowledge.*
"And moreover, because the preacher was wise, he still taught the people knowledge; yea, he gave good heed, and sought out, and set in order many proverbs."

7. 1 Kings xi. 3.
"And he had seven hundred wives, princesses, and three hundred concubines: and his wives turned away his heart."

7. Eccles. vii. 26, 28.
"I find more bitter than death the woman, whose heart is snares and nets, and her hands as bands: whoso pleaseth God shall escape from her; but the sinner shall be taken by her.

"One man among a thousand have I found; but a woman among all those have I not found."

8. 1 KINGS xii. 13, 14.

"And the king (Rehoboam, son of Solomon) answered the people roughly, and forsook the old men's counsel that they gave him. And spake to them after the counsel of the young men."

9. 1 KINGS viii. 57, 58.

"The Lord our God be with us. . . . That He may incline our hearts unto Him, to walk in all His ways, and to keep His commandments, and His statutes, and His judgments."

8. ECCLES. ii. 18, 19.—*Presentiment of his son's folly.*

"Because I should leave unto the man that shall be after me. And who knoweth whether he shall be a wise man or a fool? yet shall he have rule over all my labour wherein I have laboured, and wherein I have showed myself wise under the sun."

9. ECCLES. xii. 13.

"Let us hear the conclusion of the whole matter: Fear God, and keep His commandments: for this is the whole duty of man."

3. The great stumbling-block, however, is the style of the language—its impurity consisting in Chaldaisms and later Hebraisms. This class of objections has been greatly magnified. Exaggerations, like an immense heap of overlying rubbish, had to be cleared away. This part of the work was fully and faithfully accomplished by Herzfeld, upwards of forty years ago. Since then the Græcisms and Rabbinisms, once supposed to exist in it, have been surrendered, and even the later Hebraisms have been searched and sifted. The result is, that the residue of corrupt forms and expressions is made up of little more than a dozen later Hebraisms, and of less than a dozen Chaldaisms or East Aramaisms.

When we turn attention to the style, we find (*a*) the following Aramaic words:—בְּטֵל, *to cease* or *stand still*, a common Semitic word occurring in Syriac, Arabic, and other dialects, as well as in Chaldee; זְמַן, *time*, which is also found in the cognate dialects, as well as in Esther and Nehemiah; it corresponds to the Greek καιρός, and means a *seasonable* or *fitting time*, and could not be properly replaced by מוֹעֵד, as Gesenius believes, for the latter word is an *appointed time*; פִּתְגָם, *sentence* or *decree*, frequent in Syriac, and found in Daniel and Ezra; גּוּמָּץ, *a ditch*, also found in Syriac. So also the particle כְּבָר, *formerly, already*, occurs in Syriac. Then (*b*) we have, of words supposed to indicate modern Hebrew, אִי, *woe, alas*, instead of the older אוֹי, a word of onomapoetic formation, connected with אָנָה, *to cry out*, and lying at the root of a bird, אַיָּה, of peculiar note, probably doleful, mentioned more than once in the Pentateuch. The word would thus appear to be rather ancient than modern. אִלּוּ, *if*, is generally regarded as compounded from אִם, *if*, a condition usually affirmative, and לוּ (= לֹא, comp. Ezek. iii. 6), a negative condition; but more correctly, perhaps, considered by some an uncompounded conjunction which should omit the Daghesh, and take Seghol under Aleph in its punctation, and would answer to אֲרוּ of the Chaldee and Syriac. It occurs in Esther vii. 4. But whether compound or simple, it can scarcely be adduced as a modern Hebrew word. Another particle admittedly compound, בְּכֵן, *in such a manner*, then *so*, found also in Esther, though of rare occurrence, is no proof whatever of a modern formation, but its formation proceeds on the old lines of לָכֵן, עַל־כֵּן, and אַחֲרֵי־כֵן. Its unfrequent occurrence has been accounted for from the circumstance that it expresses a notion not often needed in the simple style of Hebrew composition, being equivalent to the *quæ cum ita sint*, it being so, of the Romans. מַדָּע, found in Chronicles and Daniel, commonly taken in the sense of γνῶσις, *knowledge*, or rather *inner consciousness*, is more correctly rendered by the LXX. συνείδησις, *conscience*. It thus differs from the more common word דַּעַת, in being the place of knowledge (the heemantic Mem usually indicating locality) rather than the knowledge itself. יוֹתֵר, *more*, is an old word, and really a participial adjective denoting that which remains, *the rest*, and occurs in this sense in 1 Sam. xv. 15; it is only its employment as an adverb of comparison, instead of the ordinary syntactical arrangement, that is urged as a mark of modern Hebrew; but it may be satisfactorily shown to be more significant and emphatic than the common comparison made by מִן. It denotes something *over and above*. The word מְדִינָה, *a city, province*, or more literally, a place of jurisdiction, occurs in several books of the Old Testament, even in 1 Kings xx., and is just such a word as we might expect in the writings of a king, whose rule extended over so many cities and provinces, in which numerous circuits and courts of jurisdiction naturally and necessarily found place. Again, (c) there are many words with terminations in וֹן, ־ִין, and וּת which have been pointed to as evidences of late date. Thus we meet with יִתְרוֹן, *profit*; רַעְיוֹן, *vexation, desire,* or *endeavour*; חֶשְׁבּוֹן, *account, reason* (of things); כִּשְׁרוֹן, *prosperity,* with which may be compared כֹּשָׁרָה in Ps. lxviii. 7; שִׁלְטוֹן, *rule*; עִנְיָן, *object, occupation, business, travail*; סִכְלוּת, *folly*; שַׁחֲרוּת, *youth*; שִׁפְלוּת, *idleness.* Though a few more words are added by Pusey, and a considerable list of additional words and forms is supplied by Delitzsch as pointing to a recent period of the language, yet those here enumerated are chiefly the ones to which exception is taken. (*d*) Other peculiarities are the frequent use of the participle, the rare use of Vav consecutive, the interchange of *Lamed-Aleph* with the forms of the Lamed-He verb, the frequent employment of the personal pronoun with the verb, as אָמַרְתִּי אֲנִי.

In view of these peculiarities of words and expressions which characterise this book, how, we naturally ask, can it be shown that these peculiar characteristics, relied on by many in proof of a late date, are notwithstanding perfectly consistent with its Solomonic authorship? The answer to so wide a question must necessarily comprise several particulars. The following considerations will at least indicate the line of reply:—

(1) The numerous abstract forms in וֹ, ־ִי, and וּת are only evidences that the author adapts his style to his subject, and proofs of that correspondence that should ever exist between thought and language. To treat philosophical subjects connected with the great problems of life and death, duty and human destiny, without such abstract forms of speech would amount to a manifest incongruity, if not an absolute impossibility. Besides, many of those abstracts are the natural offshoots of good old Hebrew roots. (2) The use of the pronoun with the verb, which occurs some eleven times, will clearly appear, on a careful examination of such occurrences, no mere pleonasm or proof of modern composition, but the result of a definite purpose, which was to emphasise as personal an experience so varied and so extensive as that of the royal author is acknowledged to have been. Besides, this emphatic use of the pronoun is not confined to this book; it occurs in Hosea viii. 13, xii. 11, and in Ps. xxxix. 11 and lxxxii. 6, the only difference being one of position, as the

pronoun in these instances goes before the verb. (3) That the imperfect with Vav consecutive to continue a historical narrative is infrequent in Ecclesiastes,—occurring only three times,—while the perfect with simple Vav copulative is proportionately frequent, we admit; but the cause of this is, we hold, not the lateness, but the peculiarity, of the composition. Regular sequence in the historical record of past events is required; but when one recalls his own past experience, or rehearses the communings with his own spirit, the case is quite different, just as the strictly historical differs from the ethically didactic or devotional. This circumstance of difference accounts for the usage referred to. (4) After making all reasonable deductions from the number of Aramaisms and Hebrew peculiarities with which this book has been represented as abounding, there is undoubtedly an Aramaic colouring discoverable throughout it. While some have recklessly multiplied peculiarities of this kind, others have quite needlessly laboured to minimise them. The truth lies between the two extremes; and its explanation is found not in lowering the date of the composition, but in looking at the districts it was designed to influence, and the probable design of the writer. In the reign of Solomon the kingdom was widened away beyond its former limits, while it was especially in an eastward direction that this enlargement took place, embracing the Aramaic-speaking peoples onward to the Euphrates. Without taking any account of the freer and more frequent intercourse which this extension of territory would necessitate between the sovran and his subjects through ambassadors and governors, and without trying to estimate the influence which his many wives may have exercised on the original purity of his Hebrew speech, we may not overlook nor understate the inducement which Solomon would have to adopt a form of speech which would be best understood by and most acceptable to his subjects. The Aramaic colouring would bring him into closest contact with the peoples of that wide region which owned his sway to the east. By such an accommodation and approximation to their dialect, he would occupy a vantage ground in securing their attention to the great subjects, ethical and religious, discussed in this book. He would thus place himself in full accord with their sympathies, enlist their affections, and make his most effective appeals to both head and heart. The Book of Ecclesiastes would thus be a great missionary manifesto to the heathen inhabitants of those lands. Amid all the perplexities that embarrass human life, and all the dissatisfaction attendant on human pursuits, it would acquaint them with the living God as the true source and centre of all real happiness. It is no small confirmation of this view that God is not presented under the designation of Jehovah, the name by which He was known in His covenant relation to Israel, but as *Elohim*, the God of all the nations and peoples that call upon His name. Not only so, in that portion of 1st Kings that treats of Solomon and his reign, curiously enough numerous Aramaic forms mingle and interchange with the purer Hebrew. Farther, the subject of the highest good, which receives so much attention in this book of Scripture, was so familiar to the chosen people, and so fully and frequently set before them, as to preclude the necessity of its special treatment as far as they were concerned. Not so with those who dwelt in other lands, where the cry went up from yearning hearts and numerous tongues: "O who will show us any good?" According to this apprehension of the matter, Solomon would be acting in the spirit and aiming at the great object of Israel's mission, so little understood and so often forgotten, a mission at once conservative and cosmopolitan—conservative of the worship of the true God, cosmopolitan with blessings to all mankind. The work of the royal preacher and the word of the royal psalmist would thus be in beautiful harmony with each other, and find fit expression in the utterances of the 67th Psalm, saying: "Let the people praise Thee, O Lord, let all the people praise Thee,"—all Israel, though like the sands of the sea or the stars of heaven for multitude; but the aspiration does not stop there, it stretches far beyond Israel: "O let the nations be glad, and sing for joy." A case analogous to the linguistic peculiarities sought to be explained was the deterioration of the language of Greece from Attic to Hellenic, consequent on and occasioned by the extension of the kingdom of Macedon, when the different tribes and nationalities subject to the sceptre of Alexander contributed more or less of individual dialectic peculiarities to the speech of Greece—no longer Attic in its purity, but common in its compass.

The plain statements of the book cannot be quibbled away nor lightly set aside. They are: "The words of the preacher, the son of David, king in Jerusalem;" and again: "I, the preacher, have been (and *am* הָיִיתִי) king over Israel in Jerusalem." It has been objected that, if Solomon were the author of the book and still continued to reign, the pronoun and noun אֲנִי מֶלֶךְ = *I am king*, would be used; that the preterite הָיִיתִי denotes: *I was once king, but am so no longer*. On the contrary, the preterite connects the past and present, and expresses the required idea, namely, that he was king when he acquired his varied experiences, and that he is king still while recording them. Moses, speaking of his sojourn in Midian, says: I have been הָיִיתִי a stranger in a strange land, and he continued so at the time he spoke (Ex. ii. 22). However far deception may be from a writer's design, it is difficult for ordinary people to distinguish from fraud that mode of composition known to the higher criticism as personated authorship. Neither is the voice of tradition, Hebrew and Christian, to be silenced or disregarded in deference to mere subjective theories. The late dates assigned by the destructive critics, so very many and so very diverse, some three centuries apart from each other, show how little reliance can be placed on any of them, while their advocates thus confute each other. Where at those late dates were those numerous literary productions, those "many books," to be found? The Solomonic era was surely a more likely period for such. How, besides assuming those late dates to be correct, can we account for the entire absence of that Oriental theosophy or Alexandrian Greek philosophy, so apparent in the books of the Apocrypha? The plan of the book has been misunderstood. It sets the fear of God before our eyes as the object never to be lost sight of, and leads us up from the unsatisfying vanities of the world to delight in God as the highest happiness and greatest good. It rebukes avarice, ambition, pleasure-seeking, murmuring, and bootless speculating; at the same time it inculcates a temperate enjoyment of the good gifts of God, and vindicates the ways of God to man, replying to the sceptical objections of the time; and all by an appeal to an unusually large experience. After each new experience, at the close of each of the four divisions, comes the sad and solemn summing up—vanity of vanities. It is midway between Job and Proverbs. It resembles Job in dealing with the perplexities of mortal life, and the doubts about human destiny. Job dwells in those perplexities and mysteries of providence that present themselves in connection with the sufferings of the righteous; Koheleth pictures the failures that men encounter in the pursuit of happiness; the former takes to do with the sufferer, the latter with the pleasure-seeker. But then comes the difference; Job is poetry, but Ecclesiastes is only rhythmic prose. Again, it resembles Proverbs in those sayings and maxims which embody the wisdom of experience, urging prudence and the present discharge of the duties of practical life, and refers the full solution of all human difficulties and divine dealings to the present rule of the righteous Creator, and the future allotments of the just Judge. Not till then shall the crooked be made straight, and disorders of time for ever done away. Here again is a difference. Proverbs is also poetry, and is more lively and cheerful in its caste. The motto of Koheleth may be written in the words: present duty, true wisdom, earthly vanities, and the fear of God. At all events these subjects are treated pointedly, practically, and profitably, in this most instructive and interesting book of sacred Scripture. If space allowed, we might materially strengthen our position by instituting a comparison between portions of Ecclesiastes, especially of the 7th, 8th, 9th, and 10th chapters, and passages of Proverbs; and likewise by comparing Ecclesiastes with Canticles, as also with the record of Solomon's eventful reign in Kings and Chronicles. The singular resemblance of sentiments in Ecclesiastes on the one hand, and in Proverbs or Canticles on the other, bespeaks a common paternity.

If the authorship of Ecclesiastes were a mere literary question, we would doubtless be prompted by the love of truth to seek and search it out. But what makes us yet more earnest in our endeavour to vindicate the traditional belief of its Solomonic origin, is the feeling that it touches somewhat closely, as we conceive, the doctrine of inspired truth. Though learned and excellent men may take the opposite view, and yet hold fast by inspiration, still we are persuaded that that view tends to lower the standard, or at least to lessen our attachment to it.

In closing this part of our subject, a few practical remarks cannot be out of place. What enhances the value of inspired truth is the practical consideration that it is the means which God employs to sanctify and save. It is our privilege, as it is our duty, to hail the light of truth whencesoever it may come. We hail accordingly every additional ray from whatever quarter it proceeds, or on whatever object it may fall. There is truth in science, for science properly so called is the exposition of nature, and nature itself is an effect whose cause is God. There is truth in art, for it turns to account the facts of science, and employs the laws of nature for the benefit of man. There is truth in astronomy, calculating, as it does, the dimensions, distances, periodic times, and other circumstances of the planets, or tracing the fair-haired comet in its erratic tour throughout the remote invisible space. There is truth in the facts of geology, though not always in the hypotheses of geologists, diving down into the bowels of the earth, examining its strata and their formation, with the fossils and other remains therein imbedded. There is truth in the events of history, for what is history but philosophy teaching by example? There is truth in physiology, showing the structure of plants and animals, and the high position of man, so fearfully and wonderfully made, in the scale of being. There is truth in chemistry, with its wonderful combinations and curious analyses. There is truth in ethics, sounding the depths of human consciousness, dealing with the human conscience, and expounding the duties of man. But while elevating all, and to some extent ramifying through all, yet high above all, is the truth of God —the truth as it is in Jesus, and which sanctifies and saves the soul. Hence the petition in the great intercessory prayer: "Sanctify them through Thy truth; Thy word is truth."

The Christian's life may be fitly compared to a voyage. This world is the troubled sea, heaven is the port in prospect, the truth of God is the Christian mariner's means of safety. It serves the double purpose of compass to show the direction, and of chart to save from the shoals and rocks and dangers of the deep. The importance of its function will clearly appear if for a little you view with the mind's eye the voyage. As a picture of that voyage, you may contemplate the mighty vessel ribbed with mountain oak, plated with metal, and rigged with care, then launched from the stocks, and sent forth to plough the main. From the time it leaves its home in the mountain, or its station in the harbour, it traverses the wide waste of waters. Many are the dangers it encounters, and many the difficulties it meets. Sometimes its track is circuitous, frequently it is chequered—there are the sunshine and the calm, often days of gloom and nights of darkness. The winds of winter buffet it, the wild waves roll round it and dash over it. It mounts up to the heaven, it goes down again to the depths. It reels to and fro, and staggers like a drunken man. By and by the tempest becomes a calm, and the waves are still, the perils of the voyage are past, and the gallant ship, having weathered every storm, speeds her homeward way, laden with a rich and precious cargo. Yonder you see her skim the wave like a true ocean bird, with full sail and flaunting flag. Onward she comes, with sunshine above and smooth sea below, while amid cheers from the crew on deck and the crowd on shore, she enters the port gloriously and triumphantly. That is just a figure of the Christian guided by this truth of God through all the vicissitudes of his perilous voyage, till he reaches at last the "fair havens" above, when an abundant entrance, through faith in that Saviour whom this word reveals, and by the grace of that Spirit by whom it was inspired, is ministered to him into the kingdom of Christ and of God. So may reader and writer at last be brought into the desired haven!

PART III.

THE CANON.

CHAPTER X.

WHAT DETERMINES CANONICITY.

OUR next investigation has respect to the canon of Scripture. If God has been pleased to reveal His will to men, and if that revelation has been committed to writing under the inspiration of His Spirit for the benefit of His people all down the ages, it cannot but be a matter of great importance to ascertain the exact limits of the record containing that will. We are thus led to inquire, What are the books in which the divine will is recorded, and which God has been pleased to give by inspiration? By what process of proof do we discover them? And on what evidence do we accept them?

It is a matter of some moment at the outset to seek a correct definition of the term *canon*, as wrong definitions have led to low and unworthy notions about the nature of the entire subject. The canon is not a list of books read in the Christian assemblies, as Semler and others would have it, for this leaves out the main element, that of inspiration, from which the canon derives its true value. Neither is it merely a catalogue of sacred books, for this also lowers the idea and deprives it of much of its worth. The canon, as properly understood, is *the rule of faith and morals divinely recorded in Scripture.* The Scriptures are a standard of supreme authority. They are authoritative because they are infallible, and they are infallible because they are divinely inspired.

As to the word canon, its origin and meanings have been

carefully traced. The word is immediately derived from the Greek κάνη, which is the representative of the Hebrew קָנֶה. Like other Semitic words denoting Asiatic products and articles of traffic, it made its way through Phœnician commerce into Greece along with the object denoted by it. That object was a reed or cane. Thus derived, canon denotes something straight; something to keep straight; then something as the test of straightness, like a rule; also passively, something ruled or measured off. But from material measurement the word was transferred *figuratively* to things mental and moral; while, from this signification of a rule or standard applicable alike to matter or to mind, to things civil or sacred, it came by a natural association of ideas, in virtue of which the mind forms a connection between the rule itself and what contains it, to denote that book or collection of writings in which the rule or standard is found; in other words, the Scriptures, as containing the authoritative rule of faith and practice. Its application to the Scriptures is by way of eminence, as implying such a standard of doctrine and duty as we are morally bound to conform to. Those who assign a *passive* signification to the word understand by it the Scriptures themselves measured and defined, as consisting of certain books which have been ratified and received by the decision of the Church. Even in its later ecclesiastical usage, as applied by the Fathers during and after the fourth century to a catalogue or list, it does not seem to have been employed synonymously with κατάλογος to denote a mere list, but in a higher sense and with reference to an ulterior purpose—that is, as a standard whereby to settle the character of different books, or determine the question of canonical authority. Owing to the labour expended on it, the carefulness with which it was framed, and the scrupulous inquiry into the character of the books admitted into it, it was clearly distinguished from a mere κατάλογος, being elevated to an authoritative position, or allowed the place of umpire in deciding the pretensions of other compositions. It is acknowledged that, though the word occurs twice at least in the New Testament, it is not applied by the New Testament writers, nor by the early Christian Fathers, to the Scriptures as a volume. That application was first made by

Amphilochius, after an enumeration of the books of Scripture. The same application is found in Athanasius. But though the word canon itself was thus late in its application to the sacred Scriptures, several of its derivatives, such as *canonical, canonise*, had been employed in this way by Origen, or even earlier. Still it was not till early in the fourth century that this usage of them became common and current.

More important for us than the derivation or application of the name, is the nature of the thing which that name denotes. We do not mean to enter on a history of the formation of the canon, as that history is closely interwoven with the history of the early Church. The one was the complement of the other, the doctrines of the canon first had their living embodiment in the members of the Church; but before the first founders of the early Church passed away, a written permanent record of the doctrines taught with their lips and illustrated in their lives became at once a necessity and a natural outgrowth. We mean to confine attention to the authority of the canonical books, and the evidence by which that authority is supported.

It may be proper for us here to glance at some of the principal theories of canonicity. The question is often asked, What constitutes canonicity? Without a formal definition of canonicity, it may be sufficient for our purpose to say that we understand by it the right of a book to take rank among and form part of that collection of writings which contain a revelation of the divine will. Accordingly we associate with a canonical book the idea of sacredness of character, and consequent authoritativeness in all matters of doctrine and duty. It is another and a distinct question how we are to ascertain the canonicity of a document, or what is the standard of appeal in such a case, or the test to be applied. But, though a separate consideration, it touches the former inquiry at several points, the one in fact frequently involving or at least overlapping the other. To both questions the same or a similar answer is occasionally, and rightly too, returned.

Here, however, there is considerable variety and no little diversity. To the question, What constitutes canonicity, or what determines it, and how are we to make sure of it? the reply of some is *ecclesiastical authority*. This is the teaching of the Latin Church on this important subject. It is for the Church to say what writing is canonical and what not, and to bestow or withhold its sanction accordingly. The pronouncement of the Church decided the case. The Anglican Church in its 6th Article decides the matter thus: "In the name of the Holy Scriptures we do understand those canonical books of the Old and New Testaments of whose authority was *never any doubt* in the Church." The Reformers, loath to accept anything at the hands of a Church against the doctrines of which they protested, and setting canonical Scripture above the Church, looked within for the settlement of the matter, and rested satisfied with the *witness of the Spirit*. This was their test. Convinced on the one hand of the self-evidencing power of Holy Scripture, and assured on the other of the inward testimony which the Spirit of God bears to the word of God, they required no other or higher standard, and sought no further proof. A subjective standard of this sort necessarily varied. Thus Luther founded the proof of canonicity on testimony to *the doctrine of Christ*, and rashly rejected an Epistle where he failed to see that doctrine stand out with such clearness and distinctness as satisfied him. The *contents* of Scripture again have been appealed to in proof of canonicity; some fixing on the peerless purity of Scripture ethics, others on the adaptation of Scripture to our spiritual needs, as Coleridge, when he speaks of Scripture "finding us," by which he meant its wonderful suitability to the varied cravings and necessities of our nature. Again, *apostolic authorship* has been set up as the standard. This no doubt is coming nearer to the true state of the case. Cunningham, in the recently published volume of lectures, resolves canonicity into apostolic authorship. Lardner long ago had done the same, but with a certain reservation or restriction. He confined that authorship to what was *doctrinal* or *preceptive*. In this way he sought to evade the exception that might be taken to the alleged non-apostolic authorship of two of the Gospels. But while he steered clear of a supposed difficulty on one side, he involved himself in defect on the other.

Without urging the particular objections that lie against

each of these, it must be obvious that they all labour under one common defect, and that is onesidedness. It may be readily conceded at the same time that there is an element of truth in every one of them, but then it is only a part of the truth. It is truth drawn from a different aspect of the subject, and expressed according to a particular standpoint. Like a figure of several sides which are all differently coloured; those that look only at one side, while the rest are concealed or out of view, may maintain that the colour of the object is blue; those that look on a different side under similar circumstances may affirm that it is green; others in like manner may assert it to be red. Each is right as far as he sees, and each wrong. It is only on examining all the sides that truth is eventually reached. So to some extent with the conflicting theories of canonicity. The sanction of Church authority neither constitutes nor confers canonicity, any more than the signpost creates the city to which it points the way; nor has a section of the Church, and that a section by many deemed degenerate, any right to arrogate to itself such authority; and yet the authorisation of the primitive Catholic Church has a most important bearing on the subject. It is not the inward witness of the Spirit that constitutes canonical proof, though such evidence we hold to be of prime importance. It is not the contents, pure as they are, and needful as they are, and suitable as they are, and unspeakably blessed as they are, that meet all the exigencies of the case, though they undoubtedly go far in the way of proof. The undoubted or never doubted recognition even by the ancient Church only goes a certain length, for a few portions, which men hesitated to accept for a time, were subsequently and in due course received and acknowledged. Though apostolic authorship comes, perhaps, nearest of all to a satisfactory solution of the problem, yet without modification it cannot be proved fully adequate. We are of opinion that by substituting *inspired authorship* for apostolic authorship, we come fully up to the mark we aim at. This inspired authorship meets all the requirements of the case, and is the main constituent in canonicity. But how is this inspired authorship to be ascertained? How can it be proved? What are its criteria? There is a threefold testimony available for the purpose—there are three that bear record in this business. The testimony of the Church from earliest times and in all its sections to the acceptance of the books and acknowledgment of their authority; the testimony of the Spirit, not only to the individual consciousness, but in the whole body of believers—the voice of God by His Spirit in the Church universal; and the testimony directly to apostolic authorship, or indirectly to apostolic sanction and suggestion, or other source of divine instruction; while the character of the contents necessarily come in also for a share in this department of evidence.

After this general view of the theories of canonicity we may now consider some of them a little more in detail. We have seen that some rest the authority of Scripture entirely on the decision of the Church; others plead the external evidence afforded by the concurrent testimony of the Jewish and Christian Church with regard to the Old Testament, and of the latter in relation to the New; while others again profess themselves satisfied by the internal evidence derivable from the surpassing excellence of the books themselves. But the first of these views involves the surrender of the right of private judgment, as also the vicious circle of the logician, which goes to establish the Church by the canon and then the canon by the Church. The second is inadequate, though the testimony of such early and respectable witnesses to matters of fact is most valuable. The third theory is incomplete, and requires a historical basis. If, however, we combine the second and the third, we are more likely to reach a satisfactory result. That result depends partly on historical research, and partly on moral reasoning. The former enables us to ascertain what books were admitted by the Jews into the Old Testament canon, and what books were received by Christians into that of the New. This is purely a matter of history. But we may not stop here, we must further inquire, Were the Jews and Christians respectively justified in their choice, and had they sufficient grounds to go upon? And in connection with this part of the subject such questions as the following seek and need solution:—Did the writers of the books, received and regarded as sacred, assume on their own behalf and assert for themselves the possession of divine instruction and guidance in the composition of those books? Did they afford to others such tokens of divine help as under the circumstances were possible, and such as to their contemporaries were satisfactory? Were they regarded by those with whom they came into contact, and who from proximity in time and place had the best means of judging, as writing by divine warrant and under divine direction? Was there a general concurrence in this verdict by the great body of believers? And has there been an unanimous or all but unanimous acquiescence in the same, on the part of the various Churches of Christendom, from the period immediately adjoining the close of the canon all along the centuries till the present time? These are questions ascertainable by historical research, and, as far as ascertainable, capable, we are convinced, of an affirmative answer.

Then follows the internal evidence touching on the contents of the books, their perfect consistency in themselves, their complete correspondence with the language, customs, and other conditions of the time in which they appeared, their entire agreement with what is universally known of God's works and ways in creation and providence, their unspeakable moral grandeur and transcendent excellence. Are these and their other characteristics such as bespeak them to be divinely inspired? For on the ground of such inspiration they were allowed a place in the canon at first, and their position there guarantees to after-times the fact of that inspiration.

The subjects of genuineness and authenticity, which fall under the head of canonical authority, are after all secondary to that of inspiration. They can only be referred to here in general terms. Such investigations in regard to particular books have been usually relegated to the department called "Introduction," and have been, on the whole, disposed of by reasonably candid and honest critics in a manner confirmatory of the conclusions generally held by the Church universal. Neither space nor time at present permits us to investigate the genuineness of the books of Scripture individually. Such investigations may be found in several excellent works of the kind just referred to, in which an attempt is made, and made in almost every instance successfully, to ascertain that the sacred books were written severally by the author whose name they bear, or, in case of an unnamed author, that they were written at the time, in the place, and under the circumstances which they indicate, and that they are thus free from spuriousness. Their authenticity at the same time is abundantly established, so that their contents are shown to be a narrative of facts as opposed to what is false or fictitious. To some particular points of internal evidence of genuineness we shall have occasion afterwards to refer; while regarding the external, every one acquainted with the matter will agree with us when we affirm, that there is ten times stronger and more satisfactory evidence for the genuineness and substantial integrity of the books of Scripture than for the histories of Tacitus and Thucydides, of Livy and Xenophon, about which no scholar ever entertains a doubt. If, beginning with the present generation or present century, we trace the writings of the New Testament, for example, backwards and upwards along the stream of time to the very source, we shall find them accredited by each foregoing generation and by the men of each preceding century till we reach the days of primitive Christianity itself, when we find them universally believed by the early Christians to be the works of their eight reputed authors, and quoted as such by the earliest Christian writers, the contemporaries and successors of the primitive penmen. Add to this the testimony of neutrals, apostates, heretics, foes as well as friends of Christianity. What more conclusive proof of authorship can reasonable criticism demand, or the archives of human literature produce, than this combined and concurrent testimony to the genuineness of the sacred Scriptures?

If after such evidence of authorship we turn attention to proofs of integrity, we find abundant means of authentication. If we were to institute a comparison between the secular classics and Scripture, we should find a vast preponderance of evidence on the side of the latter, and that arising from a combination of distinct particulars. Among these may be reckoned the unusually large number of manuscript copies; for, while in the case of an ordinary classic twenty manuscripts are above the average number, and five are deemed amply sufficient, and even one, as of the Roman history of Paterculus, is relied on; of the New Testament alone we have nearly sixteen hundred; some of these contain large portions of it, and twenty-seven contain the whole. Their great antiquity is another important element; for, while the dates of most manuscripts of the classics range between the 10th and 15th century, and not more than half a dozen rise above the 6th, we have at least two New Testament manuscripts dating from the 4th century, probably from an early part of it; two with several large fragments from the 5th; seven at least from the 6th, and so on in increasing numbers down the succeeding centuries. But without dwelling on the particulars enumerated, we need only mention, in addition to those already specified, the early and wide diffusion of copies of the Scripture, the high estimate formed of them, and consequent care in guarding them as well as pains taken in copying them, the numerous early versions, quotations, and references, the wide dispersion and jealous divisions of the custodians of the books of Scripture, together with the mighty influence exerted and the wonderful effects produced by these books. No more cogent argument for the antiquity, genuineness, and integrity of Scripture can be urged than that which is furnished by the ancient versions still extant; so much so, that it has been asserted by a very high authority, that "when accordant translations of the same writings, in several unconnected languages, and in languages which have long ceased to be vernacular, are in existence, every other kind of evidence may be regarded as superfluous." But with this proof of genuineness coexists a testimony to their credibility. It has been laid down as almost axiomatic in matters of this sort, that the genuineness of the writings proves the truth of the narrative. "No such suppositions," says Taylor, referring to supposed instances of falsehood being believed, "meet the case of various public transactions, taking place through some length of time, and in different localities, and which were witnessed by persons of all classes, interests, and dispositions, and which were uncontradicted by any parties at the time, and which were particularly recorded, and incidentally alluded to, by several writers whose works were widely circulated—generally accepted and unanswered, in the age when thousands of persons were competent to judge of their truth." On the disbeliever in such narratives rests the *onus* of accounting for the writings, if the events narrated never occurred. But reverting to the subjects of genuineness and authenticity, no one can pretend to gainsay the fact that they have been established on a hundredfold more solid historical basis than any of those literary productions of classical antiquity which nobody ever thinks of calling in question.

CHAPTER XI.

THE NEW TESTAMENT CANON.

Sec. I.—*Formation of the Canon.*

WE are now prepared to examine more minutely the subject of the *New Testament* canon. Though Luke in the beginning of the Acts makes mention of his former treatise, which was his Gospel, yet the first reference to any collected portion of the canon occurs in the 3d chapter of the Second Epistle of Peter. In that passage he refers to a collection of the Epistles of Paul, either in whole or in part, placing them on the same platform with Old Testament Scripture. The character of the reference clearly indicates that the collection in question was known and acknowledged in the Churches then planted, and accepted as Scripture among the Christians who constituted the membership of those Churches; for Peter in that Epistle addresses not one individual believer, or one single community of believers, but all the believers in all the Christian communities then in existence, as far, at least, as the circulation of the letter might extend. This is plain from the 1st verse of that Epistle: "Simon Peter, a servant and an apostle of Jesus Christ, to them that have obtained like precious faith with us." It has also been inferred from the supplementary character of the fourth Gospel, that John must have been acquainted with the other three Gospels, and in all probability had them before him in a collected form when he wrote. His acquaintance with them scarcely admits a doubt; but whether they circulated as separate treatises, or were brought together for more convenient perusal and comparison, can only be a mere matter of conjecture. Equally or rather more uncertain is the tradition which attributes to John the collecting and sanctioning of the books to be admitted into, and so the closing of, the New Testament canon. This tradition, however, seems to have no other foundation than John's survival of his brethren in the apostleship, together with the circumstance that his Gospel concludes the histories of the Saviour's life on earth, and his Revelation completes the history of the Church on to the consummation of all things. Perhaps, too, the solemn prohibition at the close against adding to or taking from the words written, and the things recorded in that book, by an extension of its application to the whole of Scripture, may have had something to do with that tradition. But be this as it may, the settlement of the canon cannot be regarded as the result of direct determination by apostolic authority. Still less can we ascribe it to the decision of an ecclesiastical council; for, before any such council had pronounced on the subject, the canon had been fully completed and finally closed. The work of a council went no farther than to record what had been already done, thus giving its sanction to and setting its imprimatur on the result. Neither need we resort to the supposition of an immediate miraculous interposition in the case; for, according to that law of parsimony, which uses the fewest and simplest means to reach a given end, God never employs the supernatural when natural means are sufficient for the accomplishment of His purpose. At the same time, that the ordinary means and agencies employed to effect the work were under divine direction and special divine superintendence, no Christian will be disposed either to doubt or to deny. Not only would God's care for His own word, the importance He attaches to it, and the high and holy interests which He makes that word subserve, warrant such a presupposition, but the circumstances of the case abundantly confirm it; for otherwise it were difficult to account for such remarkable oneness of purpose which, as we have already seen, prevails amid such variety of subject and style,—such completeness of result amid compositions so diversified and independent,—such wonderful condensation in a case where, if all the things done and all the words spoken had been written, it would be no very extravagant hyperbole to say that the " world itself could not contain the books that should be written,"—such marvellous productions emanating from men, most of whom, from rank, habit, and occupation, were unacquainted with and naturally averse to literary labours, all combined into one harmonious whole.

But while, no doubt, under divine guidance, the formation of the New Testament canon was natural and gradual; yet as in worldly matters demand and supply are mutually regulative, so here the books that eventually composed the canon were issued to meet the rising requirements of the time or urgent necessities of the Church—in every case to supply existing wants. From the time of the Pentecostal effusion of the Holy Spirit, ten days after our Lord's ascension, the apostles, rendering a ready obedience to their Master's commission to disciple all nations, and having received the necessary power from on high, entered at once on their career of vigorous and continuous evangelisation, preaching and teaching orally the gospel of the kingdom. The consequence was that disciples multiplied daily, Christian associations were formed, neighbouring districts and even distant lands were visited, while everywhere at home and abroad the preached word had free course and was glorified. Then and not till then were proper persons prepared to take charge of written records of Christianity. It was only when societies of faithful men had been called into existence or had continued to exist for some time, that safe and suitable depositories of the forthcoming documents of the new faith were provided. Then, too, and not till then, did such documents become a necessity. As long as the apostles engaged in the ceaseless activities of their ministry and the constant itinerancies of their mission, the words of the Lord proceeded fresh and glowing from the living preachers' lips, and there was little occasion and less leisure for written compositions. But when an apostle was about to remove permanently to another and distant sphere of labour, it was natural as well as necessary that he should leave behind a permanent record of his oral teaching. It was thus that Matthew, after having proclaimed the gospel to the Jews in Palestine, and before setting out for other lands, committed to writing the Gospel which bears his name for the benefit of his countrymen. Also an apostle, in anticipation of his decease, and before quitting the earthly scene of his labours, would make suitable provision for the permanent instruction and edification of believers. This is exactly the course pursued by the Apostle Peter, who, speaking of the present, and indicating his arrangement for the future, says: " Yea, I think it meet, as long as I am in this tabernacle, to stir you up, by putting you in remembrance; knowing that shortly I must put off this my tabernacle, even as our Lord Jesus Christ hath showed me. Moreover, I will endeavour that ye may be able after my decease to have these things always in remembrance." Again, when circumstances of a peculiar nature or emergencies of one kind or other arose in connection with the Churches already formed, apostolic interference was required. Thus Paul refers to the report that had reached him about the state of matters and the spirit of party in the Church of Corinth: " It hath been declared unto me of you, my brethren, by them which are of the house of Chloe, that there are contentions among you;" and subsequently states the object of his letter: " I write not these things to shame you, but as my beloved sons I warn you." To another Church he says: " To write the same things to you, to me indeed is not grievous, but for you it is safe." Even a single individual convert enlists his sympathies and employs his pen, when he writes on his behalf to Philemon, to whom he says: " Having confidence in thy obedience, I wrote unto thee, knowing that thou wilt also do more than I say." By and by, too, the complete organisation of Churches some time formed claimed more attention, and hence came the pastoral Epistles. In some such way as this the twenty-seven books composing the New Testament canon originated, issuing necessarily yet naturally, spontaneously yet providentially, from the hands of some eight apostolic men, or, if not all apostolic, at least all inspired men.

SEC. II.—*Claim to Divine Direction or Inspiration.*

Now, having seen that what the apostles wrote was the natural sequel to what they spoke, and sprang out of special circumstances, it remains for us to consider the importance which of necessity attaches to apostolic authorship. The fact of a book having been written by an apostle, or having received his sanction, is of itself sufficient to stamp it with divine authority. Let it once be proved that an apostle wrote the book with his own hand or by an amanuensis, or sanctioned it when written by another, and it follows that the book is an unerring record. The reason of this is obvious, for the apostles of our Lord were His accredited witnesses, and their testimony He identifies with His own; for hath He not said: " He that heareth you heareth me"? But while to some this mode of treating the canon may seem the most satisfactory, as undoubtedly it is the simplest, still others may prefer a wider induction and a fuller analysis. Meantime we may notice, in order to obviate, an objection that may fairly enough be made against the apostolic origin of all the books in the canon of New Testament Scripture, namely, that though there is a general agreement that six of the eight penmen were apostles, it is readily acknowledged that the remaining two, that is to say, Luke and Mark, were not. There is, however, a perfect consensus of ancient authorities for the opinion that Luke committed to writing the gospel which Paul preached, just as Mark wrote down that proclaimed by Peter. In evidence of the former statement, Irenæus, Origen, Tertullian, Eusebius, Jerome, and others may be quoted; while most of the same authorities may be cited in proof of the latter.

The connection between Paul and Luke was exceedingly close and cordial. From the Acts, of which Luke is acknowledged the penman, we learn their constant companionship. Luke accompanied him in his first voyage to Macedonia, as is reasonably inferred from the employment of the first personal pronoun, for example, " Loosing from Troas *we* came with a straight course to Samothracia," and so on to Neapolis, and thence to Philippi. A short interval of separation is intimated by Luke narrating the apostle's further journeying in the third person, saying: " When *they* had passed through Amphipolis." Ere long, however, Paul is in Greece the second time, and Luke is with him, for he resumes the use of the first person:

"These going before tarried for *us* at Troas; and *we* sailed away from Philippi." Paul, on the other hand, associates Luke with himself in salutations to the Church of the Colossians, thus: "Luke the beloved physician and Demas greet you;" and in the salutations to Philemon, where he calls him "Lucas, my fellow-labourer;" while towards the close of the apostle's career, in his second letter to Timothy, he mentions him as his sole companion: "Only Luke is with me." A strangely curious and interesting circumstance arising out of this close companionship, and singularly confirming it, is the remarkable manner in which Paul and Luke act and react on each other with respect to modes of thought and expression. That the apostle influenced the style of the evangelist is pretty well known, but it is seldom suspected that the converse is equally true. In illustration of the former circumstance we may refer to *similarity of phrase* in their respective accounts of the Lord's Supper; in the maxim recorded by both to the effect that "the labourer is worthy of his reward;" in the expression, "whatsoever is set before you eat," occurring in Paul's letter to the Corinthians, as compared with "eat such things as are set before you" in the 10th chapter of Luke; also to the use by both Paul and Luke, and by them alone, of *certain words*, or words in a certain sense, as κατηχέω, to instruct orally; πληροφορεῖσθαι, to be fully believed; and παρακολουθέω, to understand perfectly. Hence it would seem that there is some ground for the opinion of Origen, that the Gospel of Luke is cited and approved by Paul, and that it is to Luke's Gospel Paul refers when he says in two different places, "according to my Gospel," and speaks in another Epistle of "the afflictions of the gospel." Now let us see how the matter stands on the other side, and how Luke influences the language of the apostle. Luke, as a physician, is accurate in the diagnosis and technical description of disease,—for example, to persons whom the other evangelists speak of as *whole* or strong, Luke applies the term *healthful;* where they speak of the case of a particular *leper*, he says *full of leprosy*, showing his correctness in characterising disease; when they simply mention a case of *fever*, he terms it a *great fever*, showing his superior acquaintance with that class of illness. Many more instances of a similar kind might be adduced. Frequent intercourse and close contact with the special culture of the beloved physician exercised a very sensible and clearly perceptible influence on the apostle's modes of expression, as may be seen from the few striking examples that follow :—When Paul refers to *sound* doctrine, he terms it *healthy* ($ὑγιανούσῃ$); *doting* about questions is *diseased* about questions; a *seared* conscience is literally a conscience *cauterised*; persons *puffed up* are really persons seized with the delirium of typhus fever ($τυφωθείς$); the spread of error is that of *cancer*. These are only samples of many such.

Let us, however, examine briefly the evangelist's own account of his Gospel history. In the reasonable and scriptural theory of inspiration here advocated, the inspired writer must be conceived at liberty to use at his discretion such materials as suit his purpose, and on which he can lay his hand, being guided in the selection and guarded from error all the while. In accordance with this principle we might construct a theory from the style and contents of Luke's Gospel, about the materials of which the evangelist availed himself. Theorising in this way, we might arrive at a plausible and even somewhat seemingly probable conclusion about the factors employed. The genealogy of the 3d chapter bespeaks a Judean element. The deep Aramaic colouring, clearly perceptible through the light Greek shading, in the style of the first two chapters, implies a purely Hebrew source—a document, say, in the family of Mary or Joseph. In the long middle section, extending from near the end of the 8th to the 15th verse of the 18th chapter, a Judeo-Christian element prevails. In the account of the institution of the Supper the origin is unmistakably Pauline. In the history of the Passion, again, the style being freer from Hebrew and more purely Greek, seems to have a basis in oral narratives or antecedent Greek accounts. Even on such a supposition the evangelist would make those materials subservient to his purpose, selecting and arranging, correcting and completing, or moulding and modifying. In a word, as a great historian avails himself of all sources of information open to him, and makes all available materials his own, the sacred historian employs in a similar manner all trustworthy means and sources of knowledge; the difference consisting in the fact, a very significant one, no doubt, that the secular historian has to depend on his own instincts and genius, while the sacred historian acts under the unerring guidance of the Holy Spirit. These and kindred theories about the genetic origin of the Gospels, and their relation to each other, however plausible such theories may appear, can only be regarded as mere theories and no more. They must not be allowed to assume or usurp the place of well-ascertained facts. At the same time, we have some reliable information with respect to Luke's *method*, which deserves our most careful attention; that information is furnished by the evangelist himself. We are consequently at liberty to canvass and scrutinise to the utmost the information thus afforded without being chargeable with seeking to be wise above what is written. The information which Luke is pleased to give us is, in regard to the materials somewhat meagre, with respect to his method quite full, while in relation to the result it is most satisfactory. With respect to his *materials* or sources of information, it would appear to resolve itself into apostolic tradition (παράδοσις), by which is meant the oral testimony of the apostles, or the instruction imparted by the apostles to the infant Church, called in Acts ii. 42 the διδαχὴ τῶν ἀποστόλων.

The preface to Luke's Gospel, similar but superior to that of Herodotus or Thucydides, here claims our attention. It is at once modest, simple, and concise, commencing in the following familiar words:—Since (ἐπεί), as is well known (δή), and as might be expected from the nature of the case (περ), many have taken in hand to set in order a narrative of the events fully accomplished or surely believed among us. This undertaking is rather commended than condemned by the evangelist; nor does the Word ἐπεχείρησαν of itself contain a reflection, as some have thought, on the writers. This is made clear (*a*) by their narratives being in conformity with (καθώς) the tradition of apostolic men, that is, of those who had been eye-witnesses from the beginning, and had become, probably after the Pentecostal effusion of the Spirit, ministers, not of the eternal Word, nor yet of the thing related, according to the mistaken views of some interpreters, but of the word in its ordinary sense; as well as (β) by the fact that the evangelist places himself to a certain extent in the same rank when he says, it seemed good to me also (κἀμοί) to compose a history. Still, though he does not censure their well-meaning efforts, or even insinuate their absolute incompetency, yet he certainly implies the inadequacy of their narratives. Otherwise why should he increase by one the number of the πολλοί so engaged? Not only so, he clearly claims, and has a perfect right to claim, superiority over them, and that on several grounds. And here he gives us considerable insight into his *method*. He not only possessed the apostolic tradition and the documents of those predecessors, though whether he used the latter, or how, or to what extent, we are not informed; but he had traced the stream of the history to its source (ἄνωθεν). Besides, he had made himself acquainted with all (πᾶσιν) the circumstances. In doing so he did not content himself with the acquisition of such information as was needful for his work; the use of the dative παρηκολουθηκότι instead of the accusative is thought to imply that he had so assimilated that information as to make it part of his mental constitution, "a quality inherent in his person." Further, he had used all diligence to attain exactness and precision (ἀκριβῶς) with regard to the facts of his history; nor are we at liberty to imagine that his inspiration superseded, or was ever intended to supersede, the vigorous exercise of his mental faculties, and the careful investigation of all accessible means of correct information. Still more, after all these pains, and this patient, persevering industry, he finds himself in a position to give a correct consecutive account (καθεξῆς = in order), whether this is to be understood of a systematic classification or of strict chronological order. And now we come to the grand *result* which was to crown the whole, and which, notwithstanding all his efforts, could not have been attained without the teaching of God's Spirit. For though he does not specifically mention or make any parade of the superior aid and agency at work, he makes no secret of the effect produced—an effect corresponding with the end in view, namely, ἀσφάλειαν, unfailing certainty or unerring correctness—in other words, infallibility. The immediate purpose was the attainment on the part of Theophilus of full knowledge (ἐπιγνῶς) of the perfect reliability of the oral instruction he had previously received, and the more remote consequence was of course the *infallibility* of the record.

If, then, we accept the tradition already referred to of Irenæus, Jerome, and others, that what Paul calls " my Gospel " in Rom. ii. 16 and xvi. 25, as also in 2 Tim. ii. 8, was that written by Luke, it consequently follows that it was written with the apostle's sanction, if not suggestion and supervision; and further, if the supposition of Origen, Jerome, Chrysostom, and many others, that Luke is referred to in 2 Cor. viii. 18, 19 as " the brother whose praise is in the Gospel in all the Churches," be admitted, then the expression just cited is a sort of distinctive appellation marking him out almost as distinctly as a proper name; and while the reference may be to his written Gospel, as Chrysostom maintains, saying διὰ τὴν ἱστορίαν ἥνπερ ἔγραψε, he is thus singled out not merely as an oral teacher, for there were many such, but as one otherwise as well as pre-eminently distinguished. The generality and grace of the gospel as preached by Paul would thus be shown by Luke to have been proclaimed by our Lord Himself even from the beginning, and so the Gospel of Luke, affording support to the Pauline doctrine, might most appropriately be styled Paul's Gospel. Such a Gospel, moreover, would serve to " introduce," as a modern commentator expresses it, " beneath the vast ecclesiastical edifice raised by Paul, the only foundation which could in the end prevent it from falling." Though this statement appears somewhat strong and even bold, it may, with certain modification, be regarded as founded in fact.

Again, Mark's intimacy with Peter appears to have begun in the house of Mark's mother, in Jerusalem; for after Peter's release from prison it was to her house, as his home, that he repaired. His conversion was due to the instrumentality of Peter, who speaks of him with such tenderness when he says, " And so doth Marcus, my son." On Paul's first missionary tour Mark discharged the duties of attendant or minister, making the necessary arrangements for the various stages of the journey, and the supply of their bodily necessities. When, afterwards, Silas took his post, as it would seem, with Paul, Mark attached himself in the same capacity to Peter. To both apostles in turn he had been what Paul says of him, "profitable for ministering" (εὔχρηστος εἰς διακονίαν).

The patristic testimonies to the connection of Mark with Peter, and the relation of Mark's Gospel to Peter's teaching, come down to us from the very border-land of apostolic times. We may only select a few as follows:—*Irenæus* (latter half of 2d century) says: "Mark, the disciple and interpreter (ὁ μαθητὴς καὶ ἑρμηνευτής) of Peter, even he delivered to us in writing the things that were preached by Peter." The testimony of *Clemens Alexandrinus* to the same effect is twice quoted by Eusebius in the second and also in the sixth book of his history. In the former passage he says: "With various entreaties they solicited Mark, who was Peter's attendant, and whose Gospel we have, that he would leave them in writing a record of the teaching they had received by word of mouth.... The apostle having ascertained what was done by revelation of the Spirit, was delighted with the zealous ardour of these men, and authorised the history to be read in the Churches." *Origen* says: "Mark composed it (the second Gospel) under the guidance of Peter (ὡς Πέτρος ὑφηγήσατο αὐτῷ), who, therefore, in his catholic Epistle, acknowledged the evangelist as his son, saying ... and Marcus, my son." *Tertullian* (beginning of 3d century) says: "It (the Gospel published by Mark) may be ascribed to Peter, whose interpreter (cujus interpres) Mark was." *Eusebius* himself (end of 3d century), in his *Demonstratio Evangelica*, says: "It had all along been currently reported that Mark, who had become his (Peter's) familiar acquaintance and attendant, made memoirs (ἀπομνημονεῦσαι) of his discourses concerning the doings of Jesus." Similarly Epiphanius. *Jerome* (end of 4th century) says: "Mark, disciple and interpreter of Peter, wrote a brief Gospel at the request of the brethren in Rome, in accordance with what he had heard related by Peter. This Gospel, when read over to Peter, was approved of and published by his authority to be read by the Churches" (probavit et ecclesiis legendum sua auctoritate edidit). From the external testimonies of the Fathers we turn to the internal evidence of the Gospel itself.

As between Paul and Luke, so between Peter and Mark there is a resemblance of style, but the resemblance here is of a more minute and subtile kind. Two instances of this kind must suffice. One is the circumstance that the word "interpretation," which is used once by Peter and nowhere else, has its verbal representative in Mark, where it is rendered "expounded" ($\dot{\epsilon}\pi\dot{\epsilon}\lambda\upsilon\epsilon$), and only in one other passage in all the New Testament. The other is the omission of the word "law" ($\nu\acute{o}\mu o\varsigma$) by both Peter and Mark—a word elsewhere of such frequent occurrence in Scripture. Besides coincidences of style, other accompanying circumstances point in the same direction. The extreme picturesqueness of the style of this Gospel, and the numerous graphic touches with the exceptional minuteness of detail and vividness of delineation, such as the *hired servants*, the *pillow in the hinder part of the ship*, the *green grass in the desert place*, the *sitting in ranks and companies by hundreds and by fifties*, the *exceeding white as snow, so that no fuller on earth could whiten them*, the *young man running and kneeling*, the *certain young man with the linen cloth round his naked body*, the embrace of the little children whom *He took up in His arms;* the looks of our Lord, the very expressions of His countenance, and the identical Aramaic words He uttered, as when He said to the little damsel, *Talitha cumi*, or to the deaf mute, *Ephphatha*—all these and more bespeak unmistakably an eye- and ear-witness, and leave the strongest possible impression that such graphic touches must have proceeded in the first instance from one who had seen and heard, and had been personally present through the whole. Akin to this, and alike leading to the same conclusion, is the unsparing exhibition of Peter's failings, as the repeated denial of his Master so circumstantially related, and the frequent omission of the more favourable incidents of his history, as the blessing pronounced on him and the promise of the keys of the kingdom; while the word *immediately* or *straightway* ($\epsilon\dot{\upsilon}\theta\acute{\epsilon}\omega\varsigma$), occurring upwards of forty times in the Gospel of Mark, is certainly very peculiar. A word so often written must have been often spoken; nor can it be regarded as a straining of matters to connect it with the activity of service and promptness of ministry on the part of one who had been a minister or attendant on two apostles. It is a very noteworthy circumstance that Peter's confession forms in part the commencement of Mark's Gospel. That confession, recorded in Matt. xvi. 16, is: "Thou art the *Christ, the Son of the living God*," while the Gospel of Mark commences with the words: "The beginning of the Gospel of Jesus *Christ, the Son of God*." This correspondence, slight as it may seem, is nevertheless very suggestive and strongly corroborative of the relation in which, as is generally understood, the evangelist and the apostle stood to each other. Very observable, too, is the small point of minute detail in the notice of Peter's joint occupancy of the same house with his brother Andrew, mentioned only by Mark, who, instead of calling it Peter's house as Matthew does, or Simon's house as Luke does, speaks more exactly of it as the house of Simon and Andrew. Still more remarkable is the circumstance of Peter being singled out and specified separately from the other disciples in the message of mercy: "Go your way, tell His disciples and Peter." Redundant as it appears, it serves to reassure the disciple, who had denied his Master, of that Master's unchanging love and full forgiveness. How touching this record of the evangelist, and how true to life, when we regard it as repeated from Peter's own lips! Especially so, when we reflect that the dark shadow of that foul denial and fearful fall never departed, as it seems, from the apostle's mind and memory, for the darkest deed that he could picture to himself or point out to others was such denial: "Ye denied the Holy One and the Just;" "Ye denied Him in the presence of Pilate," Acts iii. 13, 14 (Peter's speech); while the brightest blessing he could conceive was to be kept from such a fall: "If ye do these things, ye shall never fall," 2 Peter i. 10; "Beware lest ye also fall from your own stedfastness," 2 Peter iii. 17. Put all these circumstances together, the undesigned and quite remarkable coincidences between Luke and Paul on the one hand, and the several peculiar circumstances connecting Mark and Peter on the other, and you will have no difficulty in appreciating the unanimous testimony of antiquity, that though neither Luke nor Mark was an apostle, yet both wrote under the guidance, and the latter probably under the dictation, of apostolic men.

Thus all the books of the New Testament, with certain apparent exceptions afterwards to be noticed, are ascribed to apostolic authorship, or what amounts pretty much to the same thing, to apostolic sanction, as in the case of Mark and Luke, though Luke's own statement of the result ($ἀσφάλειαν$) attained by him, as we have seen, falls nothing short of his claiming independently for his writings inspired authorship. We are now in a position to answer one of our questions at the outset, with respect to the divine assistance and instruction which the authors of the sacred books assumed or asserted for their composition. The very fact of apostolic authorship carries with it the full persuasion of divine help, and so of divine authority, for an apostle—one who had seen the Lord, and one who could work miracles, and one whose testimony the Saviour ranked on a par with His own—must have been divinely qualified as well as divinely commissioned for the undertaking. But we are not left to inference in the matter. The penmen of the New Testament state plainly and positively the ground on which they rest their claim to divine direction. Of these statements a few will serve as a specimen, and set the subject in a clear light. Thus Paul says: "I have received of the Lord that which also I delivered unto you;" Peter says: "We have not followed cunningly devised fables, when we made known unto you the power and coming of our Lord Jesus Christ, but were eye-witnesses of His majesty;" John says: "That which was from the beginning, which we have heard, which we have seen with our eyes, which we have looked upon, and our hands have handled, of the Word of Life—this, then, is the message which we have heard of Him, and declare unto you, that God is light."

Sec. III.—*Evidence of Divine Help.*

The next question that requires to be answered respects the tokens or evidence of this divine help by which they were enabled to convince others. There were miraculous operations not standing out separate and detached, but intertwined with the very framework of the Christian system. The miracles which they witnessed in conjunction with many others, and the miracles which they wrought in presence of numbers, were the most palpable tokens both of their mission and their message. The contemporaries of our Lord and His apostles were in the habit of asking: "What sign showest thou?" The Jews looked for a sign, and nothing less was likely to satisfy them. This was the case all along from Old Testament times; thus, the woman whose son Elijah restored to life said to Elijah: "Now by this (*i.e.* miracle) I know that thou art a man of God, and that the word of the Lord in thy mouth is truth." In relation to the Master we are informed that, in the hearing of Jews and Jerusalemites, as well as of the eleven apostolic brethren, Peter affirmed, not only without any risk of contradiction, but with the entire acquiescence of the multitude, that signs of the most convincing kind had been shown them. Hear his bold appeal: "Ye men of Israel, hear these words; Jesus of Nazareth, a man approved of God among you by miracles, and wonders, and signs, which God did by Him in the midst of you, as ye yourselves also know." But the same seal which God by His own hand set to the teaching of the Master was graciously granted to His apostles; for, in close connection with that most beautiful picture which represents the primitive Church "continuing stedfastly in the apostles' doctrine and fellowship, and in breaking of bread, and in prayers," we are informed that "fear came upon every soul; and many wonders and signs were done by the apostles." Immediately after, Peter, in company with John, heals a man lame from birth, and "all the people saw him walking and praising God." Rulers, and elders, and scribes, with the high priest at their head and his kinsmen, in fact the great council of the nation, held a conference, and confessed not only the reality, but the magnitude of the miracle, saying: "What shall we do to these men? for that indeed a notable miracle hath been done by them is manifest to all them that dwell in Jerusalem; and we cannot deny it." Again we read that "by the hands of the apostles were many signs and wonders wrought among the people." Paul cures a cripple at Lystra, and brings to life a certain young man named Eutychus at Troas. Thus, as the apostles went forth proclaiming the gospel of salvation, the Holy Ghost accompanied them with signs following, than which nothing could be more satisfactory as evidence of divine help. The power of their Lord was delegated to His apostles. The divine aid that prospered their oral teaching would be appealed to as proof of similar help in what they wrote. It would serve as the seal on the outside of the letter, but the contents within, from the heavenliness of their matter, would correspond to this sign-manual of heaven's King.

Sec. IV.—*Authentication and Dissemination of the Inspired Writings.*

But there was still something more and further to be attended to. It was not enough to assume to themselves and give assurance to others of divine guidance in their writings; the penmen of the New Covenant were careful, in the prosecution and for the prosperity of their work, duly to *authenticate* their writings, and diligently to further their circulation for the instruction and edification of individuals as well as of Churches. We find the clue to this in a notification at the close of the first Pauline Epistle. At the conclusion of that first letter to the Thessalonians he adds: "The salutation of Paul with mine own hand, which is the token in every letter: so I write." This was the signature which was to render spurious imitations impossible. Similarly in the last chapter of Galatians we read: "Ye see in what large characters I have written with my own hand." Again, in the end of First Corinthians we have: "The salutation of me Paul with mine own hand." Whether a letter was written by the apostle himself or an amanuensis, the signature, sometimes the salutation, was by his own hand; thus again in the last verse of Colossians we have the statement: "The salutation by the hand of me Paul." Nor was this all; in those early times, so long before printing was invented or the power of the press known, it was necessary to adopt suitable means for the publication of the apostolic writings. When a communication from an apostle was sent to an individual, it was of course a sacred deposit; but it was not to be secreted or selfishly hoarded, it was to be imparted to others. When a letter reached a Church, it was received, as we have good reason to believe, with supreme respect and superlative attachment; and consequently it was preserved inviolate and inviolable. Yet here also the same course was to be pursued. Churches were to exchange such communications, and reciprocate each other's attentions in this matter. Thus they mutually helped each other's faith and diffused its records. The document, whether Epistle or Gospel, when received by one Church, was copied and sent to a neighbouring community of Christians; by them it was forwarded to a society more remote—this Church sending it to that Church, and that Church to another Church, and that other Church to the Church beyond it again, till the sacred document or a carefully taken copy of it had gone the round of Christendom and arrived at the farthest off society of the faithful. This is no fancy, it is founded in fact, as we know that the Church at Colosse and that at Laodicea were to exchange with each other in this manner, for it is enjoined as follows: "And when this Epistle is read among you, cause that it be read also in the Church of the Laodiceans; and that ye likewise read the Epistle from Laodicea." Otherwise a circular letter was written, and copies sent to different Churches; thus the Epistle to the Ephesians may have been originally a circular letter of this kind to the Asiatic Churches. Paul sent copies of it by Tychicus to the several Churches of the district, and eventually it got its name from the metropolis of proconsular Asia. On this wise the records of the faith passed from hand to hand and from Church to Church. The autographs were kept with greatest vigilance, but copies were, no doubt, sought for with avidity, as no Church would knowingly or willingly fail to possess itself of such; and no Church would be so unfaithful to its trust and to an apostle's expressed requirement as to neglect to send such. Documents so venerable and precious, with the truths of which men's best interests for time and eternity were bound up, were thus not merely as a matter of course, but as a matter of imperative duty, circulated with greatest diligence. Not only so; as they multiplied, they were collected together as a thing of course, they were classified as a matter of convenience, and so we find a very early reference to the two chief portions of the canon as "Gospel and Apostolicon," which, though a collection mutilated by the heretic Marcion for the purpose of his heresy, testifies to fuller and earlier collections of the New Testament writings. But if, as we are sure, these documents were diligently circulated, they were treasured in the various Churches with peculiar and uncommon care. Of this there is abundant evidence in Tertullian, when he refers to the several Churches then in existence as witnesses to as well as guardians of the autographs of the New Testament Scriptures. For, making all due allowance for the rhetorical style of that Father, we are sure there must be a solid substratum of underlying facts in his challenge to certain of his contemporaries when he says: "Run through the apostolical Churches, in which the chairs of the apostles still occupy their places, in which their own autograph letters are read aloud, resounding the voice and representing the face of each one. Achaia is very near to you, you have Corinth. If you are not far from Macedonia, you have Philippi; you have Thessalonica. If you can steer your course into Asia, you have Ephesus. But if you border on Italy, you have Rome." Thus the different portions of the canon grew, were disseminated, distributed into the corresponding classes, and compacted into a complete whole, so that by the time the last surviving apostle had passed away from earth, or shortly afterwards, the books of the New Testament emanating, as we have endeavoured to show, from men divinely instructed, authenticated by the writers themselves, gladly accepted by thankful communities, rapidly and extensively circulated among the Christian societies, carefully collected from every available quarter, and properly classified, noiselessly and gradually found their way into and formed our canon. And all this took place in a way at once perfectly natural and necessary, in full accord with the individual Christian consciousness and the spiritual instincts of the whole Christian Church. And who can shut his eyes to the divine supervision in all this? Surely the same Providence that guides the sparrow in its descent to the ground, and numbers the hairs of our head, and counts His people's tears, putting them into His bottle and writing them in His book, is not less careful of the lessons of that truth that saves, and of that good news which is the gospel of the glory of the blessed God.

And here there are two allegations that require to be met and set aside. On the one hand, it is alleged by the Romanist that the Church was before the canon, in other words, that it is more ancient than Scripture, and that the authority of the latter is consequently derived from and dependent on the former; on the other hand, the Rationalist seeks to show the late formation of the canon, and so to throw doubt upon the inspiration of its contents. To the first allegation we reply that it is based on a false assumption, and that assumption arises from confounding the *spoken* word and the *written* word of God. The Church itself is based on the word of God, for it is "built on the foundation of apostles and prophets, Jesus Christ Himself being the chief corner-stone;" the inspired teachers that preceded, and the inspired teachers that succeeded the Saviour, laid the foundation of the Church by their teachings; the great central truth taught by both was the truth as it is in Jesus. The Church is the custodian of the truth, the pillar and ground of it, or the pillar and pedestal of it. Like a monumental pillar, it makes it prominent and visible, directing attention to it; like a pedestal, it upholds and supports it. Chrysostom inverts the text just alluded to, reading its meaning thus: "The truth is the pillar and ground of the Church." This is perfectly correct in relation to truth by itself and in the abstract; but it is inapplicable to the truth in its reception by man and acknowledgment in the world. The Church's foundation is the truth, but the Church's function is the propagation and diffusion of the truth; its commission in part being to defend and maintain the truth of God in opposition to all error and every heresy. For this very purpose the word of truth needed to be written in order that it might not only be preserved, but kept pure and entire. Thus truth spoken is more ancient than the Church, but truth written is less so. This distinction is well explained by Wordsworth.

As soon as written the word was to be read, not only by private persons, but in the public assemblies of the faithful. The apostle in two passages, namely, Colossians iv. 16 and 1 Thessalonians v. 27, enjoins this public reading of the written word in the Christian congregation. One part, and a principal part of divine service, consisted in this public reading of Scripture; and as the Law and Prophets had been read in the synagogue, so the Gospels and Epistles took their place, or rather took place alongside with them in the worship of the early Christian societies. And now it needs to be carefully observed that this reading of the New Testament writings was a public sanction to the divine origin of those writings, and a public authorisation of their inspired contents. By this very fact of their being read publicly, and solemnly enjoined by apostolic command to be read, in the public worship of God, these writings were virtually canonised. In that very Epistle which contains an injunction for this public reading of Scripture, we are informed of the character of the sanction thus given, and of the consequent reception suited to these writings. "When," says Paul to the Thessalonians, 1 Thess. ii. 13, " ye received the word of God which ye heard of us, ye received it not as the word of men, but as it is in truth, the word of God." Again, in 2 Thess. iii. 14, the same apostle claims implicit obedience, saying: "If any man obey not our word by this Epistle, note that man, and have no company with him, that he may be ashamed." Accordingly the word, when written and thus read in the public religious assemblies, was thereby publicly declared to be the truth of God. The veneration with which it was regarded tended at once to its wide circulation, and to its being kept inviolate, so that nothing was added to it and nothing taken from it, and no tampering with it in any way allowed or even possible; or if anything of the kind was attempted, as by the heretic Marcion, it was sure to end in signal failure, and to expose the person who made the attempt to the severest reprobation and rebuke. But it has been asked, Why are there so few *direct* quotations of Scripture in the apostolic Fathers? The answer is not far to seek; for, while it must be admitted that their quotations of and allusions to Scripture are very numerous, any want of directness, where that occurs, is probably owing to the two following circumstances :—first, the Apostolic Fathers took for granted their readers' familiarity with the New Testament writings, and did not feel under any necessity to name the individual writer ; and secondly, most if not all of them having enjoyed the oral teaching of the apostles, and retaining, as is natural, a more lively impression of what they had learned from the living voice than of the written record, allowed the personality of the writers to fall into the background. This, however, only serves to enhance their testimony, because it is thus twofold, where direct, to the authorship, and where indirect, to the substance of New Testament Scripture.

With respect to the rationalistic theory about the lateness of the period at which the canon was formed, the Councils of Laodicea and Carthage have been appealed to as though they had for the first time formed the canon. In this way their work is entirely misunderstood or strangely misinterpreted. The work of those councils was in no sense formative, it was simply and solely declarative. The formation of the canon had taken place long before, and had taken place in the manner indicated. Written by the apostles of our Lord, or by their intimate associates, and with their sanction and supervision, they were received as inspired by those to whom they were sent. The accompanying injunction for the public reading of them in divine worship, introduced and recommended them to the Christian assemblies. The reading of them in those assemblies under such circumstances procured them at once a place in the canon, for they were thus accepted, and rightly accepted as divine, while this very acceptance secured their inviolability and exempted them from wilful corruption, at least to any considerable extent. When, therefore, synods or councils in the course of time took the matter up, they did not attempt to authorise, nor could they mean to do so, the canonicity of this or that other book ; they only affirmed their belief, or bore witness with regard to the canonicity of those books ; or rather repeated the affirmation of earlier synods or councils on the subject. They did no more than state or rather re-state the Church's sentiment in reference to it. Theirs was no creative act or formative process ; it was only a reiteration of opinion that had prevailed from the beginning—an endorsement of what the Church had done soon as the written record of its faith and charter of its privileges had been put into its hand. By Church in this connection we must of course understand the Church Catholic; not any single branch of that Church by itself, such as the Eastern or Western, the Roman or Reformed, the Anglican or Gallican; but the Church universal, and that, as already intimated, of primitive and apostolic times.

We must now refer in passing to a few apparently exceptional cases, that is to say, certain books that were slower in finding acceptance and gaining admission into that recognised collection. Those books referred to were for a time *antilegomena* or disputed. Though they were accepted from the first as canonical by the Churches to which they were addressed, it cannot be counted strange that they were some time in reaching, and thus somewhat slower in attaining authority with Churches far remote. An event which occurs in Ireland is reported and accepted as a fact in England before it has time to reach Australia; but by and by, when the report has made its way to that distant land, it gains credence there also. So with the few controverted books, it was only a matter of time as affected by distance, perhaps also by a season of persecution interrupting the free intercourse of Christian Churches and the public reading of circular letters addressed to them, and in two instances by a certain indefiniteness of address, which retarded their full, final, and universal recognition. Accordingly the Epistle of James and the Epistle to the Hebrews were recognised from the first by the Churches to which they were specially addressed; for the former having been written in Palestine, and addressed to the Jews under the name of the twelve tribes, and the latter being intended for Hebrew converts, were both received at once by the Eastern or Syrian Church. It is not at all strange, however, that some time necessarily elapsed before their recognition by the Church of the West, while the concealment of the author's name in the case of Hebrews contributed to the same result. Again, the Apocalypse was received and acknowledged from the earliest time in the scene of John's labours in Asia Minor.

Then with respect to Jude and Second Peter, the indefiniteness of address—in the former of the writer, and in the latter of the persons addressed—retarded and restricted their spread. But notwithstanding the delay thus in part at least accounted for, we have only to combine the earliest canon of the East and the earliest canon of the West, and with one exception they mutually supplement each other. For while the Latin canon omits James and Hebrews, the Eastern has them; and while in the Eastern Jude and Revelation (the latter not from lack of external evidence, but, as we shall see, because of its contents) are wanting, the Latin contains them. The exceptional case of Second Peter, omitted in both, is covered by probable allusions in two of the Apostolic Fathers, an adaptation of a passage of the epistle by Theophilus, a reference to another passage by Hippolytus, quotations from it in Rufinus' Latin translation of Origen, and a distinct recognition though somewhat later by Firmilian of Cappadocia, the very region into which the Epistle had been first sent, to which may be added the most striking verbal coincidences (to be noticed hereafter) between Second Peter and First Peter, between Second Peter and the speeches of Peter as recorded in Acts, and the adoption by Jude of some of the very words of the Epistle in question.

SEC. V.—*A more detailed Account of certain Books of the New Testament Canon.*

Papias, Bishop of Hierapolis in Phrygia, gives us the earliest account of the Gospels. He flourished at the beginning of the 2d century. He was a contemporary and companion of Polycarp and others who had known the apostles. He was not only a friend of Polycarp, but a personal disciple of John, according to Irenæus, who speaks of him as "a hearer of John and a companion of Polycarp" ('Ιωάννου μὲν ἀκουστής, Πολυκάρπου δὲ ἑταῖρος γεγονώς). But whether it was John the apostle or John the presbyter, has been questioned; some holding, with Eusebius, who grounds his opinion on the preface of Papias, that it was the latter; others understanding Irenæus, who had other and better means of information on such a point than Eusebius, to refer to John the apostle. At all events, Papias professes to derive his information from two sources, namely, the elders and their immediate disciples, and so from Aristion and John the presbyter—personal disciples of Christ; probably too from John the apostle; possibly also from Andrew and Philip, who had withdrawn into the same district; but more especially from the followers and friends of these primitive disciples. The sources of Papias' information are detailed by him in the preface to his work in five books. In that preface as preserved by Eusebius, Papias says: "I will not be loath also to arrange for you along with the interpretations whatever I learnt correctly, and remembered correctly in time past from the elders, guaranteeing truth about them." This statement includes, of course, the oral information he received from the elders. Farther on he refers to the information he derived not directly from the elders themselves, but mediately from their followers, saying: "But if anywhere there came one who had followed the elders, I would inquire about their discourses—what was said by Andrew, or by Peter, or by Philip, or by Thomas or James, or by John or Matthew, or any other of the Lord's disciples, and what Aristion and the elder John, the disciples of the Lord, say."

The title of the work of Papias here referred to is, *Exposition of Oracles concerning the Lord* (λογίων κυριακῶν ἐξήγησις), that is to say, oracles not spoken *by*, as κυρίου might mean, but *of* the Lord. This title has been twisted and tortured in order, as it would seem, to make it mean that the object of Papias was to give a narrative of our Lord's discourses from current oral traditions, in other words, to write a gospel himself. But this perverted interpretation of Papias' meaning has been once and again refuted and proved utterly untenable for the following among other reasons:—(1) the word ἐξήγησις signifies naturally and commonly *explanation*, not *narration*, which is properly διήγησις; while the expression ταῖς ἑρμηνείαις in the preface fixes the meaning of this word in the title; (2) the material on which his exposition is exercised consists of the λόγια, presumably the evangelical narratives of Matthew and Mark, to which he afterwards refers; (3) the oral traditions, which he introduces along with his interpretations, were for the purpose of illustration; while (4) when he speaks in the preface, already mentioned, of getting less benefit from the written books than from the living and abiding voice, he refers not assuredly to books containing the Gospel narrative, but to interpretations like his own, or rather to misinterpretations of a gnostic or otherwise erroneous tendency.

Renan's admission, both with regard to the weight that attaches to the testimony of Papias, and with respect to the Gospels themselves, may here be referred to as deserving attention. After identifying Luke, the companion of Paul, as the writer both of the Gospel that bears his name and of the Acts, and after inferring the date of the third Gospel, from the 21st chapter, as following immediately after the destruction of Jerusalem, he proceeds to say: "But if the Gospel of Luke be dated, those of Matthew and Mark are dated also; for it is certain that the third Gospel is posterior to the first two.... We have besides in this respect an important testimony dating from the first half of the 2d century." In his 13th edition he writes: "from the middle of the 2d century." "It comes," he goes on to say, "from Papias, Bishop of Hierapolis, a grave personage, and laden with traditions, who all his life was careful to collect what could be known of the person of Jesus. After declaring that in such a matter he gives the preference to oral tradition over books, Papias mentions two writings on the acts and words of Christ: 1st, a writing by Mark, the interpreter of the Apostle Peter, short and incomplete, not laid out in chronological order, comprising things said and things done ($\lambda\epsilon\chi\theta\acute{\epsilon}\nu\tau\alpha$ $\mathring{\eta}$ $\pi\rho\alpha\chi\theta\acute{\epsilon}\nu\tau\alpha$), composed from the recollections and information of the Apostle Peter; 2d, a collection of sayings or oracles ($\lambda\acute{o}\gamma\iota\alpha$) written in Hebrew by Matthew, which each translated as he could. It is certain that these two descriptions correspond well with the general physiognomy of the two books now called 'Gospel according to Matthew,' 'Gospel according to Mark;' the first characterised by its long speeches, the second specially anecdotic, much more exact than the first in small matters, concise even to aridity, poor in speeches, indifferently composed.... In other terms, the system of the life of Jesus in the Synoptics rests on two original documents: 1st, the words of Jesus collected by the Apostle Matthew; 2d, the collection of anecdotes and personal particulars which Mark wrote according to Peter's recollections. It may be said that we still have these two documents . . . in the first two Gospels." Further, Renan expresses his doubt about the Johannean authorship of the fourth Gospel somewhat flippantly as follows:—" Pour moi, je n'ose être assuré que le quatrième Évangile ait été écrit tout entier de la plume d'un ancien pêcheur Galiléan;" he then goes on to say: "But that upon the whole this Gospel proceeded, towards the end of the first century, from the great school of Asia Minor, which attached itself to John; that it presents us with a version of the Master's life, worthy to be taken into high consideration and often to be preferred—this is what has been demonstrated, both by external testimonies and by the examination of the document itself, after a manner that leaves nothing to be desired." This admission of Renan about the fourth Gospel, defective though it is, displeased the negative critics; in consequence of which he re-examines the whole subject at considerable length and with critical minuteness in an Appendix to the 13th edition of his *Vie de Jésus;* but the conclusion he comes to, instead of diverging farther from, approaches more closely to the traditional belief on the subject. "We have three Epistles," such is the summing up at the close of the Appendix referred to, "which also bear the name of John. If there is anything probable in critical results, it is that the first of these Epistles is from the same pen as that which wrote the fourth Gospel. The author of this Epistle, like the author of the Gospel, represents himself as an eye-witness (1 John i. and iv. 14) of the evangelical history. At the first view of the subject, the most natural hypothesis seems to be that all these Scriptures are truly the work of John, the son of Zebedee. For me, I see only one issue. It is to hold that the fourth Gospel is certainly in a sense 'according to John,' though not written by John himself. Did notes or dictations left by the apostle serve as the basis of the text we have in our hands?"

In this extract from Renan we have his individual criticism on the Gospels, together with his comment on the testimony of

Papias. With respect to the common ground thus covered by both, a few remarks are needed to correct the misinterpretation of the former, and bring out clearly the meaning of the latter. (1) By the λόγια ascribed by Papias to Matthew, Renan with other critics of like tendencies understands only the discourses or a collection of our Lord's sayings by Matthew. This view Renan explains more fully in the following words: "The original λόγια (speeches, sayings, oracles) of Matthew are without doubt represented by the discourses of Jesus, which fill a considerable part of the first Gospel. Indeed, those discourses, when detached from the rest, form a pretty complete whole." This is an undue restriction of the meaning of λόγια. In this way λόγια, oracles, is identified with λόγοι, sayings; whereas it has been proved demonstratively from the usage of λόγια in the New Testament, in the Apostolic Fathers, in subsequent patristic writings, in Papias himself, that this word comprehends doings as well as sayings, and is, in fact, synonymous with Scriptures, embracing facts as well as sayings, incidents as well as discourses. It thus applies not to a detached collection of sayings or discourses, but to the whole Gospel narrative. At the same time, it is specially appropriate to that Gospel which contains such a full record of our Lord's discourses. The exhaustive discussion of this term by Lightfoot has cut the ground completely from under the feet of those who deny the application of λόγια to a gospel at all, or at least to the Gospel of Matthew as we now have it, and who limit its meaning to certain discourses or sayings of the Saviour. But (2) another objection has been founded on the statement of Papias, that "each translated them (*i.e.* the λόγια) as he was able." From this it is argued that there could be no authentic or generally recognised Greek version of the Hebrew original of which Papias speaks. But this again is a perversion, for his expression refers to a previous period of time, and by implication to a state of things that existed no longer. Had the necessity continued till his own day, he could not have used a past tense, but must have employed the present. He would have said, "each translates them as best he can;" but instead of this he speaks of a past and no longer existing necessity, when he says: "each translated them as he was able." We are not much concerned about Papias' view of the relation of the Greek Gospel to the Hebrew original; whether he regarded the Greek as a duplicate of the Hebrew and proceeding from the same pen, or the former as a reproduction of the latter, it would seem certain that he regarded it as a genuine reflection and stamped with apostolic authority.

The testimony of Papias to Mark's Gospel has been impugned from the same quarter, but on different ground. Papias intimates a want of completeness and an absence of continuous chronological order. Both are satisfactorily accounted for by Papias himself, from the fact that Peter adapted his preaching at once to his audience and to the occasion, and by consequence without any intention of unbroken continuity or strict chronological order, while the evangelist in his reminiscences of the apostle's preaching adopts the same method. Such at least is obviously the purport of Papias. Keeping these hints in view, we shall not likely misread the testimony of Papias or misinterpret its meaning. That testimony is as follows:—(1) In reference to Matthew he says: "Matthew compiled the oracles (συνεγράψατο τὰ λόγια) in Hebrew; but each one interpreted them as he was able." (2) Of Mark he writes: "And the elder (John) used to say this also; Mark, having become the interpreter of Peter, wrote down accurately everything he remembered (or everything he, *i.e.* Peter, mentioned)," as it may with equal propriety be rendered: "though he did not record in order what was either said or done by Christ. For he neither heard the Lord nor did he follow Him, but subsequently, as I said, (attended) Peter, who adapted his instruction to the requirements (of his hearers); but not with the design of making a connected narrative of the Lord's discourses (or oracles). So then Mark made no mistake as he thus wrote down some particulars as he remembered them (or as he, *i.e.* Peter, mentioned them); for he took good care of one thing, not to omit anything of what he had heard, or to make any false statement in his record." This testimony of Papias is confirmed, as we have seen in the case of Mark, by succeeding Fathers of the Church from Irenæus downwards;

and in the case of Matthew they give similarly confirmatory testimony. Thus Irenæus says: "Matthew put forth his written Gospel among the Hebrews in their own dialect." In like manner, Origen, Eusebius, and Jerome testify to the authorship of Matthew's Gospel. But suppose the writer's name were wanting in the case of either Gospel, and that the "according to Matthew" and "according to Mark" did not exist in our oldest MSS. or in the earliest references, would the omission mar the credibility or militate against the authority of a narrative which the primitive Church had accepted as the product of inspiration, and which the Church circulated as such, and upon which, in the exercise of that correct and clear-sighted discrimination seen in other similar instances, it thus set its seal? The absence or omission of the writer's name would rather indicate a public, authentic, and authoritative document so well and widely known that no name was needed for authentication, any more than the creeds of the Church—for example, the Nicene Creed, or Augsburg Confession, or similar formulas—need to have the names of their framers attached. Again it is denied, and denied without evidence, and so without reason, that the Gospels referred to by Papias are coextensive with the Gospels of Matthew and Mark as we have them. We are not bound to prove a negative, nor to do more than contradict a baseless assertion. It is only necessary in the case of Matthew to have in recollection that the term λόγια, as we have seen, is not restricted to the discourses of our Lord to the exclusion of the record of works done, miracles wrought, or other incidents; but, on the contrary, covers the whole ground. With regard to both Gospels, if considerable additions, or interpolations, or other changes had been made, how comes it to pass that we find no notice of such alterations, and no mention of them in any quarter? Why is Irenæus, who was taught by one friend of Papias, and who traces most of his traditions to other companions and countrymen of the same person, ignorant of or silent on the subject? Why does he even include in Mark's Gospel the few last verses (from the 9th to the 20th), which certain critics both in ancient and modern times impugn? Mark's Gospel, as we have it with its fancied uncritical ending and all, was just that Gospel as Irenæus was acquainted with it. Why, it may be further asked, does Clement of Alexandria and Tertullian of Africa observe the same reticence about any change, if indeed they had heard anything of it, or known anything about it? Or how could they have been ignorant of a shorter text, if such had in reality existed, or of the MSS. that contained it? Even later on, some hint of it might be supposed to have reached down to the days of Eusebius.

Coming now to the Gospel of John, we have already seen Renan's admissions in reference to its early date, that is, the end of the 1st century, and the preference he accords to that Gospel, as well as the high probability he assigns to the critical conclusion which makes the Gospel of John and the First Epistle of John proceed from the same pen. With the second point, as being a matter of taste, we take little to do; but the first and third statements are of moment, as bearing on the antiquity and credibility of this fourth Gospel. Papias, we are told by Eusebius, " has employed testimonies from the First Epistle of John, and likewise from that of Peter." Now Papias' knowledge of the Epistle of John implies his acquaintance with the Gospel by John; for not only, according to the admission of Renan and others, were both by the same writer, but we have evidence of a close organic connection between them. Whether the Epistle held the place of preface or postscript, it makes little difference as far as our present inquiry is concerned. The latter relationship has many plausible reasons in its favour, and seems most in harmony with the circumstances of the case. We may here notice the exceedingly ingenious and very probable conjecture of Lightfoot, that the sudden transitions to the second person were occasioned by and give evidence of this Gospel being addressed to a circle of hearers consisting of the older members of the Church, and some of them, like Aristion and John the presbyter, personal disciples of Christ, and eye-witnesses of the leading events of His life. To these the apostle is supposed to appeal for confirmation of his narrative, saying: " These things are written that *ye* might believe," and " He that saw it hath borne record ... that *ye* might believe;" while the last chapter and last verse but one contains their confirmatory response: "This is the disciple which testifieth of these things, and wrote these things: and *we know* that his testimony is true." Then comes the Epistle as the application, doctrinal and devotional, of the Gospel history, while to the close of the Gospel the commencement of the Epistle is linked on by the plural number in which John includes the elders, as vouchers for the authenticity and genuineness of the narrative, saying: "That which was from the beginning, which we have heard, which we have seen with our eyes, which we beheld and our hands handled, of the word of life . . . that which we have seen and heard declare we unto you."

Papias' acquaintance with the fourth Gospel has also been with much plausibility inferred from the somewhat singular arrangement of the names in the section of Papias already quoted from Eusebius, namely: "What was said by Andrew, or by Peter, or by Philip, or by Thomas or James, or by John or Matthew." This order has all appearance of being suggested by the position respectively held by them in the fourth Gospel. Of the first four, Peter alone occupies a position of prominence in the other Gospels; Andrew remains in obscurity; while Philip and Thomas have their names only mentioned in the number of the apostles. In the Gospel of John, on the contrary, they hold a much more distinguished place, and hence the order of Papias; while in the same arrangement John and Matthew are bracketed, as it were, together, on the ground of being evangelists and having each written a gospel. Otherwise we cannot help thinking that the order would have been different. The natural order would certainly have been that of precedence, viz. Peter first, James the Lord's brother second, and John third, Matthew fourth; while Andrew, Philip, and Thomas would have ranged themselves in a lower list. There is now little doubt that Irenæus is alluding to the exegetical work of Papias, when he records the interpretation by the elders of certain words of our Lord in the Gospel of John as follows: "As the elders *say*" (the present tense here employed is held to refer, according to Irenæus' usage, to a written document), "then also shall they which have been deemed worthy of the abode in heaven go thither, while others shall enjoy the delight of paradise, and others again shall possess the brightness of the city . . . that therefore our Lord has said: 'In my Father's abode are many mansions' . . . the presbyters, the disciples of the apostles, say that this is the arrangement and disposal of them that are saved." Further, if, as is generally believed, and as we have seen there is good reason to believe, there exists such a close connection between the First Epistle of John and the fourth Gospel, the quotation of the 4th chapter and 3d verse of the former by Polycarp, when he says: "For whosoever confesses not that Jesus Christ is come in the flesh is Antichrist," implies that Father's acquaintance with the latter. These and other considerations, which need not be dwelt on, all combine to confirm the antiquity of the fourth Gospel, fixing its date subsequent indeed to the other Gospels, but somewhere about the close of the 1st century. This, as has been said, is the conclusion as to date which Renan came to, though less scholarly and less candid critics would fain plead for a later period, and that in opposition to all the probabilities of the case. Can it be that the wish here, as elsewhere, is father to the thought, and that the attempt to lower the antiquity of the writing proceeds from the desire of lessening its credibility?

Proceeding now to the portions of New Testament Scripture, which we have not yet particularly treated of in relation to canonicity, we find that of the Epistles—some addressed to certain Churches in particular, some to the Church at large or Christian community in general, and others to private or individual Christians, as the pastoral to Timothy and Titus, and a special Epistle to Philemon—thirteen by Paul have been acknowledged by the various sections of the Christian Church from their very first appearance, being found in the Peshito Syriac of the Eastern, and enumerated in the Muratorian canon of the Western Church; while the Church Fathers of the East and West appealed to them with like unanimity. Even Marcion the heretic, notorious for mutilating Scripture to make it square with his peculiar dogmas, included ten of them in his *Apostolicon*. More singular still, the Tübingen critics, famous or rather infamous for tomahawking the word of God, admit the authorship of four of them, namely, Romans, Galatians, and First and Second Corinthians. The First Epistle of Peter and the First Epistle of John may be regarded as unchallenged. It remains to make a few remarks on Hebrews, Second Peter, James, and Jude, in their relation to the canon, in addition to our previous brief reference to them.

The authorship of the Epistle to the Hebrews has been a vexed question, and one of considerable difficulty; some maintaining its Pauline authorship, and others denying it, so that in a certain sense it may be said, *sub judice lis est.* Still the arguments in favour of the Pauline authorship, we are persuaded, predominate. (1) Of external authorities in favour of this view may be adduced (*a*) the Alexandrine Fathers, Pantænus, Clemens Alexandrinus, and Origen, the most learned and critical of them all, who says: "It is not without reason that the ancients have handed it down as Paul's;" with almost the whole of the Greek Fathers; and (*b*) many of the most eminent of the Latin, as Jerome and Augustine; also (*c*) the Eastern Churches generally. Eusebius, one of the most eminent men belonging to those Churches, and certainly the most painstaking in critically investigating the subject of the canon of Scripture, quotes the Epistle to the Hebrews as the work of Paul; for, in book ii. chap. 17, speaking of certain sacred writings, he says: "Such as are contained in the Epistle to the Hebrews, and many others of St. Paul's Epistles;" again, in book iii. 3 he informs us: "The Epistles of Paul are fourteen, all well known and beyond doubt;" also in his *Commentary on the Psalms* he quotes it frequently, ascribing its authorship to Paul; (*d*) The Syrian Church also accepted it as Pauline, and had it in their ancient version of the Peshito; while their leading theologians, Jacob of Nisibis, Ephraem the Syrian, and Ebedjesu, acknowledge and quote it as Paul's; while (*e*) in the most ancient MSS., namely, א A B and C, it is placed among the Pauline Epistles after Second Thessalonians, and before the Pastoral Epistles. It was the Latin Church, admittedly inferior in learning and critical ability to the Alexandrian, which in its two sections, Roman and North African, entertained doubts on the question from the middle of the 2d till some time in the 4th century. At a later period the Churches of the West concurred with the decision of the Greek and Eastern Churches; and what is of still more importance, there is reason to believe that at an earlier time the Western Church had accepted this Epistle as Pauline, at all events as canonical. We may feel our way here by the help of certain tolerably reliable indications. In doing so we find that Clement of Rome, though his citations are mainly from the Old Testament, quotes on several occasions expressions found in the Epistle to the Hebrews, such as: "Let us be followers of those also who went about in goatskins and sheepskins," compared with Heb. xi. 37; "For nothing is impossible with God, but to lie," compared with Heb. vi. 18; "Who being the brightness of His glory, is by so much greater than the angels, as He hath by inheritance obtained a more excellent name than they," compared with Heb. i. 2, 3; "*For so it is written,* who maketh His angels spirits, and His ministers a flame of fire," compared with Heb. i. 7; "The *Scripture* also bearing witness 'that He shall quickly come and shall not tarry,'" compared with Heb. x. 37, and several others. These references show not only an intimate acquaintance with this Epistle on the part of Clement, but a proper appreciation of its contents. They prove, moreover, the high antiquity of this Epistle, as Eusebius says: "He" (that is, Clement) "shows most clearly that the work" (viz. Hebrews) "was not of a recent date." The last two quotations are prefaced with words which imply an appeal to inspired Scripture, namely, *it is written* ($\gamma\acute{\epsilon}\gamma\rho\alpha\pi\tau\alpha\iota$), and *the Scripture* ($\tau\hat{\eta}\varsigma$ $\gamma\rho\alpha\phi\hat{\eta}\varsigma$). Further, when we take into consideration the position of Clement in relation to Paul as his friend and fellow-labourer (Phil. iv. 3), and the generally acknowledged fact that early ecclesiastical writers of the Western Church seldom or ever quoted non-apostolic writings, we are convinced that there is much to countenance the inference that Paul was the apostle whose Epistle Clement was so familiar with, and which he quoted with such comparative frequency. The same acquaintance with, and appreciation of, the Epistle to the Hebrews may be fairly assumed of the intelligent members of the Roman Church over which Clement presided. But days of persecution came, and some fell away from the faith; the

Church was divided in reference to the treatment of the lapsed; the major part took the most favourable view of such weakness, and felt disposed to restore them in the spirit of meekness; but Montanists, and subsequently Novatians, determinedly opposed such restoration. In their fanaticism and violence they were glad to make their appeal to Heb. vi. 4-6, and urge the impossibility of renewing again to repentance those that fell away. Thus Theodoret, commenting on this passage of the Epistle, says: ταῦτα οἱ Ναυάτου κατὰ τῆς ἀληθείας ὁπλίζουσι τὰ ῥητά, that is, the Novatians employ these words as an objection against the truth. Unfortunately, imperfect views, as it would seem, of this mooted passage betrayed their opponents into the error of sacrificing Scripture when it seemed to jar with their sentiments or to support the heretics. We can understand how in this way the Epistle to the Hebrews fell for a time into disrepute, so that both its genuineness and canonicity were questioned. Wetstein, and after him Hug, held that opposition to the error of the Montanists and Novatians occasioned the denial of the Pauline authorship and consequent authority of this Epistle by the Latins. The proof text of the heretics against the readmission of the lapsed into the Church was differently treated by the Greeks and Latins. Hug regards their conduct in this respect as characteristic, and contrasts them in the following terms: "The conduct of the two Churches with regard to one and the same subject was very different. The Greeks endeavoured to evade the argument by their mode of interpretation, while the Latins rejected the Epistle entirely." The opponents of the Pauline origin of the Epistle, it is true, seek to overturn this position by denying that there is anything analogous to this rejection of a book of Scripture on dogmatic grounds, in forgetfulness, it would appear, of Luther's treatment of the Epistle of James for dogmatic reasons. But time brings its revenges; and eventually, after a considerable interval of doubt, the Western Church conceded the just title of this Epistle to a place in the canon, and concurred with the Eastern and Greek Church, that all along held by the truth on this important subject. The change was brought about by the increased ecclesiastical intercourse between East and West, by Ambrose's acquaintance with and respect for the writings of Origen, but especially through the biblical research and critical knowledge of Jerome, and the great influence of Augustine.

(2) The impugners of the Pauline authorship of this Epistle depend chiefly on its alleged difference of style from the other confessedly Pauline Epistles, and on certain peculiar characteristics of this Epistle, notably on the statement in Heb. ii. 3 : "Which at the first began to be spoken by the Lord, and was confirmed unto us by them that heard Him." This, it is urged, must imply that the writer received the gospel message at second hand from the personal hearers of the Saviour, and consequently that some other than Paul was the writer. But this objection is not so very formidable, for the apostle may be regarded here as identifying himself with those whom he addressed, as elsewhere he identifies himself with sinners, "of whom," he says, "I am chief." This is all the more feasible, as he says "confirmed," not proclaimed, or preached, or announced. Confirmation seems to imply previous reception, and that in whatever way. Paul, it is true, was not a personal hearer of our Lord in the same sense that the other apostles had been; he received the gospel by special revelation. But it is further objected that the style of this Epistle differs considerably from that of the other Pauline Epistles. So indeed it does, but the style does not differ more than the subject itself does, nor more than that subject requires. In all his other Epistles he addresses converted Gentiles mainly, in this he addresses converted Jews only. On the one hand, the converted Jews of Palestine were subjected to severe persecution by their fellow-countrymen; on the other hand, there was the gorgeous ritual of Judaism, after which, no doubt, there was a hankering on the part of some, just as on the part of their forefathers newly emancipated from Egypt there had been a longing for the leeks and onions of the land they had left. From one or other, or both causes, there was danger of a relapse into Judaism. The great purpose of the Epistle is to prevent that relapse. In order the better to effect his object he contrasts the Jews' religion with Christianity, and shows that the latter has nothing to lose by such comparison. Splendid as the Jewish service undoubtedly was, that splendour

was external, while Christian worship had all the elements of intrinsic value. The one was gilding, the other gold. The gilding may be very bright, and very beautiful, and very suitable in its place; but gold, though dimmer and darker, has the sterling worth. The one dispensation was ordained by angels in the hand of a mediator, but the author of the new dispensation is Christ, superior to angels, because nearer to the Father; superior to Moses, for He is a son, not a servant. The old dispensation had the ministrations of the Aaronic priesthood, but the Christian High Priest is more sympathetic and more potent—the former presented the blood of bulls and goats, the latter pleads His own blood. The old covenant wanted perfection, the new makes perfect as pertaining to the conscience. It is thus apologetic for the gospel by one intimately acquainted with Judaism. A Hebrew of the Hebrews, and a Pharisee of the strictest sect, was, humanly speaking, just the man to develop and defend the gospel from the Jewish standpoint. It was a theme worthy of an apostle, and one that gave full scope to the eloquence of one who of orators was chief. Paul's apostolic authority was not called in question, but the authority of the other apostles, by whom the Hebrew Christians had been instructed, is properly pleaded.

But (3) while the style is suited to the subject, and consequently somewhat singular, we must not overlook the similarities. There are (1) close similarities in words, constructions, and expressions, as follows:—

(a) We have similarity in words, e.g. νεκρόω, ἀπόλαυσις, ἀφιλάργυρος, ἀνυπότακτος, ἐνεργής, ἐφάπαξ, and many others which occur in the Epistle to the Hebrews as well as in the Epistles of Paul, but nowhere else in the New Testament. (b) There is similarity of construction, for example, (a) a neuter adjective for a noun of quality is common to Hebrews, as τὸ ἀμετάθετον, vi. 7, with Paul's Epistles—a peculiarity, by the way, often met with in Thucydides; (β) Another Pauline peculiarity of grammar found in Hebrews is that construction of a passive verb by which the remote object, instead of being in the dative, becomes the subject, as ὁ λαὸς . . . νενομοθέτητο, vii. 11; so πεπίστευμαι τὸ εὐαγγέλιον, Gal. ii. 7. (c) There is a striking similarity in *agonistic* expressions, viz. (a) afflictions are called a *fight*, x. 32, so in Phil. i. 30 and Col. ii. 1; (β) the Christian life is a *race*, xii. 1, so in 1 Cor. ix. 24 and Phil. iii. 12–14. (d) We find also a similarity in general expressions, thus (a) subjection to bondage, ii. 15, so Gal. v. 1 ; (β) the Jewish ritual a service, ix. 1, 6, so Rom. ix. 4 ; (γ) good conscience, xiii. 18, so Acts xxiii. 1 in Paul's address; and again in his address in Acts xxiv. 16 and 2 Cor. ii. 12 ; (δ) bonds and imprisonment, xiii. 3, 23 and x. 33, so Eph. iii. 1.

(2) Certain peculiarities of style common to Paul's writings occur in Hebrews—(a) a frequent paronomasia or play upon words of like sound, as μετέσχηκε . . . προσέσχηκε; (β) going off at a word, as Paley terms it; (γ) repetition of some favourite word; (δ) citations from the Old Testament connected by καὶ πάλιν, and again, i. 5 and ii. 12, so Rom. xv. 9–12.

(3) The personal notices in the 13th chapter of themselves go far towards proving the Pauline authorship of the Epistle. We have (a) intimation of a present, or at least recent imprisonment, with the confident expectation of being soon restored to his friends (ἀποκατασταθῶ) ; (β) he promises those to whom he wrote that "our brother Timothy," now *released*, as some understand it, or *sent away* (probably on a mission to Philippi), as others explain it (ἀπολελυμένον), will visit them, xiii. 23, with which we must compare Phil. ii. 19 : " But I trust in the Lord Jesus to send Timotheus shortly unto you" (the Philippians); (γ) a personal visit (ὄψομαι) of the apostle in company with his friend is also promised them, xiii. 23, and 19 according to the meaning some attach to the verb in the second clause of this verse ; (δ) believers in Italy (οἱ ἀπὸ τῆς Ἰταλίας) send their salutations. These direct personal allusions must have been well understood by the early Church that got this Epistle in charge, or else they are unaccountable. We naturally prefer the former alternative, and are persuaded that it proceeded from an author so well known as to render the mention of his name unnecessary ; and as the Epistle comes with the authority and breathes the spirit of an apostle, there can be little doubt that the apostle, known to have been a prisoner in Rome—known as a personal friend of Timothy—known as having purposed and

promised to send Timothy to Philippi to know their state and make known his own, and on his return to proceed in company with him elsewhere—is none other than the Apostle Paul himself. There was much in the circumstances of the times to make this opinion probable. If we assume, as we may, that the Hebrews addressed were the believing Jews or Jewish Christians of Palestine; and if we conclude, as we have reason to do, that it was a period of persecution,—this promised visit of the apostle to encourage them and this present letter to establish them fit in admirably with the course of events. We have several indications in chaps. viii., ix., and xiii. that the temple and its service, and consequently the Holy City, were still in existence, and yet alongside of these there are intimations in chaps. vi., viii., x., and xii. of the approaching doom. Combined with such notes of time, the exhortation to remember their own rulers who had spoken to them the word of God, and to imitate their faith, "reviewing as spectators the end of their course" (τὴν ἔκβασιν τῆς ἀναστροφῆς), identifies the recent persecution of the Palestinian Church with that by Ananus the high priest about A.D. 62, when James the Just and other leaders of the Church were put to death at Jerusalem. Still exposed to persecution and in danger of apostasy, they stood sorely in need of such an exhibition of Christ and of the Christian system, and of such exhortations to stedfast perseverance as the Epistle contains.

(4) There is still more convincing similarity in such doctrinal statements as the following :—

(*a*) God is the chief end of all creatures, "for whom are all things and by whom are all things," Heb. ii. 10, compared with Rom. xi. 36 and 1 Cor. viii. 6. (*b*) Christ is the image (εἰκών) or visible manifestation of Deity, i. 1–3, compared with 2 Cor. iv. 4 and Col. i. 15. (*c*) His humiliation for the sake of man, and consequent exaltation, ii. 8, 9, compared with Phil. ii. 8, 9. (*d*) His death, sacrificial and typified by the Jewish sacrifices, vii. 27, compared with 1 Cor. v. 7 and Rom. iii. 25. (*e*) He died once for all to put away sin by the sacrifice of Himself, and to secure the spiritual and everlasting life of all who trust in Him, ix. 26, 28, compared with Rom. vi. 8–10. (*f*) He through death destroyed the power of death, ii. 14, compared with 2 Tim. i. 10 and 1 Cor. xv. 54–57. (*g*) He lives to intercede, vii. 25, compared with Rom. viii. 34. (*h*) His session and sovereignty at the right hand of God till all enemies are subdued, x. 12, 13, compared with 1 Cor. xv. 25. (*i*) His reappearance to judge the world, and save those that look for and love His appearing, ix. 27, 28, compared with 2 Tim. iv. 1, 8. (*j*) The Pauline triad of faith, hope, and love, vi. 10, 11, and x. 22–24, compared with 1 Cor. xiii. 13. Also, (*k*) without particular references, the following doctrines will be found in Hebrews in common with the Pauline Epistles :—(α) The headship of Christ compared with the same doctrine in Ephesians and Colossians; (β) The righteousness which is by faith, x. 38 and xi. 7, compared with Romans and Galatians *passim*; (γ) Gradations in Christian life and character from babes needing milk to those of matured experience requiring strong meat; (δ) Freedom of access to the Father secured to us by Christ; (ε) Certain doctrinal expressions peculiar to Paul occur in this Epistle, such as mediatorship and the word *mediator* itself, $\mu\epsilon\sigma\acute{\iota}\tau\eta\varsigma$; the designation of God as the *God of peace*, while His word is the *sword of the Spirit*.

These are a few, and only a few, of the arguments that may be adduced in favour of the Pauline authorship of Hebrews. To enter into a full discussion of the subject, and examine with minuteness the reasons that induce us to adhere to the belief which the great body of the Christian Church held of its Pauline origin, as also the objections urged against it, would far exceed the compass and scope of our work. It would, in fact, require for itself a separate treatise. There is, however, one objection much insisted on which we may glance at. It is the absence of a superscription which had its share in causing doubt about the authorship. This omission has had various reasons assigned for it. Pantænus, in his attempt to explain it, alleged that as Paul's business was not to preach the gospel among the Jews, he in consequence suppressed his name. Clement of Alexandria, with greater probability, affirmed that in order to disarm Jewish prejudice he withheld his name from the beginning of his letter. Hug, with more clear-sightedness, accounted for the omission on the ground that this Epistle so called is more of the nature of a treatise than of a letter, and that therefore the usual introductory salutation at the beginning would be quite out of place. A still more satisfactory reason, as we think, is that the omission of the superscription was designed to indicate that the Epistle was for the use of Jewish Christians everywhere as well as in Palestine and its capital.

Hug, one of the ablest and most distinguished critics of the Fatherland, after a thorough investigation of the subject, came unhesitatingly to the conviction of its Pauline origin. His own words at the conclusion of his examination are the following:—" Wie mehr ich mit den Schriften des Apostels bekannt werde, desto mehr bin ich versucht, den Brief an die Hebräer für sein Meisterstück zu halten. Er trägt das Siegel der Vollendung, wie die an die Thessaloniker den Anfang seiner schriftstellerischen Laufbahn Vezeichnen."

We must now consider carefully, yet cursorily, the canonicity of Second Peter. With regard to Hebrews, in dealing with the question of authorship, we have seen, we think, sufficient reason to justify us in ascribing it to Paul; but even if the proof were insufficient to establish its Pauline origin, still we have had abundant evidence of its inspired authorship, and consequently of its canonicity. Even the testimony of Clemens Romanus should satisfy on that head. The case is different with Second Peter; its canonicity is involved in, and inseparable from its authorship, because the writer styles himself "Simon Peter, a servant and an apostle of Jesus Christ." As the external evidence against the canonical authority of this Epistle is purely negative, that is to say, there is no proof alleged against it, but simply a lack of conclusive proof for it, we shall only add to our previous statement on this head the weighty words of Tregelles : " Internally it claims to be written by Peter, and this claim is confirmed by the Christians of that very region in whose custody it ought to have been found." With regard to the internal evidence of authorship previously referred to, we are warranted in placing much reliance on the following circumstances :—

(1) Verbal coincidences between First Peter and Second Peter.

(2) Verbal coincidences between Second Peter and the

speeches of the Apostle Peter as recorded in the Acts, and which are more numerous in Second Peter than in First Peter.

(3) Certain words that have a special significance in connection with that apostle's experience.

(4) Testimony derivable from the Epistle of Jude.

It appears best to quote the passages in full, but in doing so we must consequently confine ourselves to a few. Thus under (1) we have the following:—

(a) 1 Pet. i. 19, ἀμώμου καὶ ἀσπίλου,=2 Pet. iii. 14, ἄσπιλοι καὶ ἀμώμητοι, without blemish and without spot, without spot, and blameless.

1 Pet. iii. 1, 5, ἰδίοις, their own;=2 Pet. ii. 16 and iii. 17, ἰδίας ... ἰδίου, your own, your own.

1 Pet. ii. 12 and iii. 2, ἐποπτεύειν,=2 Pet. i. 16, ἐπόπται, eye-witnesses. behold,

1 Pet. iv. 3, πεπορευμένους ἐν ἐπι-=2 Pet. ii. 10, ἐν ἐπιθυμίᾳ πορευομένους, that θυμίαις, walk in, walk in the lust.

=2 Pet. iii. 3, κατὰ ... ἐπιθυμίας πορευόμενοι, walking after lusts.

1 Pet. i. 15, 17, 18, ii. 12, iii. 1, 2, 16, ἀναστροφῇ, conversation, ἀναστράφητε, pass, =2 Pet. ii. 7, 18, iii. 11, ἀναστροφή, conversation. ἀναστριφομένους, who live.

1 Pet. i. 7, 19, τίμιος, precious, =2 Pet. i. 1, ἰσότιμον, like precious.
1 Pet. iv. 11, χορηγεῖ, supplieth, =2 Pet. i. 5, ἐπιχορηγήσατε, add.
1 Pet. iv. 3, ἀσελγείαις, lascivious,=2 Pet. ii. 18, ἀσελγείαις, wantonness.

(β) We have some words common to both Epistles, but occurring nowhere else in the New Testament; thus—

1 Pet. iii. 21, ἀπόθεσις, putting away, =2 Pet. i. 14, ἀπόθεσις, putting off.
1 Pet. ii. 9, ἀρετάς, praises or virtues, =2 Pet. i. 3, ἀρετή, virtue.

This latter word, though it occurs once besides, viz. in Phil. iv. 8, is nowhere else applied to God, except in the passages of Peter just cited.

Of (2) the following instances sufficiently illustrate the principle:—

2 Pet. i. 1, λαχοῦσι, obtained, =Acts i. 17 (Peter's speech), ἔλαχε, obtained.
2 Pet. i. 3, 6, 7, εὐσέβειαν, godliness, =Acts iii. 12 (Peter's speech), εὐσεβίᾳ, holiness.
2 Pet. ii. 8, ἀνόμοις ἔργοις, unlawful=Acts ii. 23 (Peter's speech), διὰ χειρῶν deeds, ἀνόμων, by the hands of the wicked.

2 Pet. ii. 1, ἀρνούμενοι, denying (the =Acts iii. 13 (Peter's speech), ἠρνήσασθε, Lord), ye denied.
2 Pet. ii. 13, ἐν ἡμέρᾳ, in the day-time, =Acts iii. 5 (Peter's speech), third hour of the ἡμέρας.
2 Pet. iii. 10, ἡμέρα Κυρίου, day of the =Acts ii. 20 (Peter's speech), ἡμέραν Κυρίου, Lord, day of the Lord.

In regard to (3) we have two curious coincidences with that most remarkable occurrence in the life of Peter—his presence at the transfiguration. Words he spoke on that occasion, as recorded by the evangelist, and words which occur in that chapter of Second Peter, and in the very context where reference is made to that same transfiguration scene, carry with them to any candid mind an unquestionable evidence of Petrine authorship; thus—

2 Pet. i. 13, { σκηνώματι, } tabernacle, =Evangelists (Peter's words), σκηνὰς
14, { σκηνώματός, } τρεῖς, three tabernacles.
2 Pet. i. 15, ἔξοδον, my decease, =Luke (transfiguration), ἔξοδον, his decease.

With respect to (4) no fewer than (a) eleven passages in the short Epistle of Jude refer to or rest on similar statements in Second Peter. The (β) priority of Second Peter to Jude, though denied by some, seems determined by the 17th and 18th verses of Jude, where we read: "Remember ye the words which were spoken before of the apostles of our Lord Jesus Christ; how that they told you there should be *mockers in the last time, who should walk after their own ungodly lusts.*" The corresponding statement is in 2 Pet. iii. 3 : "There shall come *in the last days scoffers, walking after their own lusts.*" Peter's statement usually is shorter, that of Jude longer; the earlier statement being the germ is shorter, the later statement being the development is longer; the original, like a text, is condensed; the subsequent, like paraphrase or comment, is more expanded.

In addition to the foregoing, we might enumerate certain miscellaneous correspondences between Second and First Peter, such as (a) a grammatical peculiarity found in some passages of both, and consisting in the omission of the article; (b) a historical reference to the flood and the destruction brought on the old world, with the exception of the eight souls saved, occurs in both; (c) similar doctrinal statements; for example, (*a*) the inspiration of the Scriptures; (β) regeneration by means of the divine word urged as a motive for abstention from worldly lusts; (γ) the judgment that will eventually overtake the disobedient and deceivers; (δ) calling and election; (ε) brotherly love (φιλαδελφία); (η) the Saviour's purchase of His people; (θ) the same salutation, consisting in the multiplication of grace and peace, in both.

Two main objections against the Petrine authorship are based on two passages in the 3d chapter. The first of these is found in the 2d verse of that chapter, and is as follows:— "That ye may be mindful of the words which were spoken before by the holy prophets, and of the commandment of us, the apostles of the Lord and Saviour." The objectors translate it "of our apostles of the Lord and Saviour," so that the writer, according to this rendering, shuts himself out of the company of the apostles. But the true reading of the text, according to the best MSS. and best critical editors, is ὑμῶν, so that the right rendering is, "of your apostles of the Lord and Saviour," or, as Alford more fully translates it, "of the commandment of the Lord and Saviour given by your apostles." In this way the writer does not separate himself from the apostles, but specifies them as a class, and speaks of himself as one, and only one, of that class. But the second passage to which exception is taken is in the 15th and 16th verses of the same chapter, and reads thus: "Even as our beloved brother Paul also . . . hath written unto you. As also in all his Epistles, speaking in them of these things . . . which they . . . wrest, as they do also the other Scriptures" (γραφάς). Now it is alleged that such a collection of the Pauline Epistles, in other words, that such a settlement of the New Testament canon as this implies, was subsequent to the apostolic age, and also that the term γραφή was not applied to the New Testament canon so early. The one allegation is a misconception, the other a mistake. Peter may have read all the Epistles of Paul that had been written up till that time; he may have read the extant Epistles separately as they appeared, or even in some collected form. This passage has a most important bearing on the subject of the canon generally, as well as on the authorship of the portion of the canon under consideration.

The term γραφαί was reserved as a distinctive title of the sacred Scriptures, and restricted to them, so that in some fifty places where it occurs it is applied only to the sacred writings of the Old or New Testament. Whether, therefore, the expression "other Scriptures" refers to the Old Testament, or to the first three Gospels, Acts, and earlier Epistles of the New Testament, in either case the application of this term proves that the Epistles of Paul then extant, or other New Testament writings as far as they then extended, were recognised by the Church as sacred—inspired, and so canonical. We do not deem it necessary to dwell on the differences of style and statement between Second Peter and First Peter, which have been urged against the genuineness of the former. The following judicious remark of Alford in reference to the mention of the coming of our Lord in both Epistles, appears to us a sufficient reply: "Now, would it not have been more just," he says, "in this case to say that the circumstances and persons in view cannot be the same, rather than that the writers (*i.e.* of Second and First Peter) cannot?" This observation of the Dean may be extended to the whole. The difference of occasion on which the apostle wrote, and the difference of object in view, do, we are convinced, satisfactorily account for the differences in question.

With respect to Second John and Third John, the former contains only thirteen verses, of which eight are found substantially in First John; while the remainder, as also Third John, bear, as far as it is ascertainable from such brief fragments, the impress of the Apostle John's style and spirit.

Having compared the style of Revelation with the Gospel of John, we shall only add here that the earliest Church tradition decidedly favoured the canonicity of this book of Scripture, and that it was subjective considerations which occasioned any delay in its reception by the Church, or doubts causing that delay. Those doubts originated in opposition to millenarianism and the somewhat obscure symbolism of the book.

In reference to James and Jude, we have only space to notice the objection which appears to be the strongest, and which is urged on the ground that in both cases the word "apostle" is not employed to designate the author.

In the one case it is "James, a servant of God and of the

Lord Jesus Christ," and in the other, " Jude, the servant of Jesus Christ and brother of James;" and in both instances the apostolic title is omitted. To deny the apostolic authority of either Epistle from this omission is not a whit more reasonable than for a student of Virgil, the Roman poet, to deny the existence of the largest lake in Italy, at least in Virgil's day, or to assert Virgil's ignorance of it, from that passage of the 2nd Georgic, as poetic as patriotic, in which he celebrates the praises of Italy, but in which, strangely enough, he makes honourable mention of Larius, the modern *Lago di Como*, and of Benacus, now *Lago di Garda*, but passes over in silence the largest lake of all, namely, Verbanus, the modern *Lago Maggiore*, saying:

" Anne lacus tantos ? te Lari maxime, teque,
 Fluctibus et fremitu adsurgens Benace marino ?"

Commentators, like certain critics, much exercised by the poet's omission, have tried their hand to make him say what he did not mean, or to supply what in their wisdom they regard as an unaccountable oversight, by detaching the adjective *maxime* from Lari, and by making it do independent duty as a poetic epithet taking the place of a substantive, that is to say, " O greatest," in other words, " O Verbanus," or according to the present name, " O Maggiore." Thus Fabricius and others have corrected the poet's geography, or fancied ignorance of the geography of his native land. There is just about as much taste in such corrections as truth in the conclusions frequently drawn from such omissions as the one we are considering.

SEC. VI.—*The Inspiration of New Testament Penmen acknowledged by their Contemporaries.*

The next topic is to answer the question, whether the penmen of the New Testament were regarded as writing under divine direction and guidance by their *contemporaries and immediate successors*, and whether such conclusion has been acquiesced in by the great body of believers in subsequent times ? Beginning with sub-apostolic writers, we cannot fail to perceive the superior rank conceded by them to the writers of the New Testament, and this superiority is more of kind than of degree; while writers in the next centuries, in increasing numbers, unfalteringly affirm the same. Clement (A.D. 96) is honourably mentioned by Paul in the last chapter of his Epistle to the Philippians as a fellow-labourer, and one whose name is in the book of life. In his first letter to the Corinthians, Clement places himself on the same level with those to whom he wrote, but points them to the apostle as away above him at a far higher elevation. He says: "These things, beloved, we write unto you, not only to admonish you of your duty, but to remind ourselves" (chap. vii.); but when he refers to the apostle, his tone and style are quite different. He says: "Take in your hands the Epistle of the blessed Paul the apostle. What did he first write to you in the beginning of the Gospel? In very truth he wrote you by the Spirit (πνευματικῶς, *divinitus inspiratus, Vet. Int.*, by the inspiration of the Spirit) concerning himself and Cephas and Apollos, because even then you had fallen into parties and factions" (chap. xlvii.). Again, he writes: "The apostles have preached to us from our Lord Jesus Christ, Jesus Christ from God. Christ therefore was sent by God, and the apostles by Christ. Thus both were orderly sent according to the will of God. For having received their commandment, and being thoroughly assured by the resurrection of our Lord Jesus Christ and convinced by the word of God, with the fulness of the Holy Spirit they went forth proclaiming that the kingdom of God was at hand" (chap. xlii.). In addition to the citations from the Old Testament, Clement has upwards of forty references or allusions to the New Testament Scripture, though he only quotes by name First Corinthians. He shows acquaintance with statements in the three synoptic Gospels, Acts, Romans, Corinthians, Hebrews, to which, according to some, may be added Galatians, Ephesians, Philippians, Colossians, First Thessalonians, Timothy, Titus, James, and First and Second Peter.

Barnabas has been regarded by some as a companion of the Apostle Paul. In his Epistle (A.D. 70–120) he addresses those to whom he wrote as follows:—"Not as a teacher invested with authority, but as one of yourselves, I shall lay before you a few things that your joy may abound;" and again: "Let us give heed, lest perchance we be found as it is written, 'Many are called, but few chosen.'" Here we must not overlook the significancy of the formula (*sicut scriptum est* = ὡς γέγραπται) by which Barnabas introduces this quotation from the Gospel of Matthew; nor the fact that the Greek text of cod. ℵ corresponds to and confirms the Latin version in which this formula is found. It is most important, and must be admitted as evidence, that he attributed to that Gospel the character of Holy Scripture. This is freely acknowledged by Hilgenfeld. Here too, let it be observed, is the first recognition of the canonical authority of a book of the New Testament. Besides two direct quotations, the applications of or allusions to New Testament texts amount to some twenty.

Polycarp, the personal friend and disciple of John, as also an early martyr and faithful servant of Christ, draws the line of distinction clear and broad between the inspired apostles and men like himself. He makes frank confession to this effect: "These things, brethren," he says (A.D. 116) to the Philippians, "I write unto you concerning righteousness; not that I take anything on myself, but because you yourselves before invited me to do so. For neither can I nor any other such as I am come up to the wisdom of the blessed and renowned Paul" (chap. iii.). And this he says by way of apology for writing to a Church that had been privileged with the instruction of the apostle. Not only so, he expresses profound respect for the Scriptures, and takes it for granted that the same sentiment will be readily responded to by those to whom he wrote. Thus he says: "I trust that ye are well exercised in the Holy Scriptures, as in these Scriptures it is said: 'Be ye angry and sin not.' 'Let not the sun go down upon your wrath'" (chap. xii.). And elsewhere he speaks of the "oracles of the Lord." Here is a most important testimony, on the part of a companion of the apostles, to the high estimate, as well as the existence of the major portion of the Holy Scriptures even at that early day. Nor is this all. In the one letter which he writes to the Philippians, and which is the only extant work of this holy man that we possess, he quotes from most of the books of the New Testament—

from the Gospels and Acts, from ten of the Pauline Epistles, probably also from Colossians and Hebrews, from the First Epistle of Peter, and the First Epistle of John. In his one short Epistle he refers directly or indirectly between thirty and forty times to New Testament passages, thus furnishing a testimony as unanswerable as it is undesigned to books comprised in the canon of the New Testament.

In like manner Ignatius, bishop and martyr, who lived forty years after the ascension, and who had conversed with the apostles, and who was rather disposed to magnify than disparage his office, places himself in an altogether different and lower category than that of the apostles, confessing his inferiority to this effect: "Not as Peter and Paul do I command you," he writes (about A.D. 115) to the Romans; "they were apostles, I am a condemned man." He also speaks of the Gospel and Apostles, which were the two divisions of New Testament Scripture from the earliest times. He thus implies a collection of the Gospels and Epistles, or of the New Testament in general. "Fleeing," he says to the Philadelphians, "to the gospel as the flesh of Jesus, and to the apostles as the presbytery of the Church." He puts in a plea for Old Testament Scripture at the same time, saying: "Let us also love the prophets, forasmuch as they also have preached in reference to the gospel, and hoped in Christ and expected Him. In whom also believing, they were saved." Thus in his turn Ignatius gave evidence to the writings of the canon. Even in the three short Syriac epistles he refers to two of the Gospels, the Acts, and five Pauline Epistles; in the shorter Greek epistles, seven in number, he refers or alludes plainly to the Gospels by Matthew, Luke, and John, Acts, eleven Epistles of Paul, Hebrews, First Peter, First and Third John.

Another similar and nearly contemporaneous testimony may be adduced from the Epistle to Diognetus, if the date now generally assigned to it be admitted. Some of its references are as beautiful as they are plain and distinct. But what invests these references with additional interest is the fact that the author of the Epistle places the writings of the New Testament and those of the Old on exactly the same platform. "The fear of the law is sung, and the grace of the prophets is known; and the faith of the gospel is established, and the tradition of the apostles is kept, and the grace of the Church rejoiceth exceedingly." That by the Law and the Prophets is meant the Old, and by the Gospel and the Apostles is meant the New Testament, is abundantly evident, while their equality in the estimation of the writer of the letter is sufficiently obvious, and needs no comment.

But a more remarkable document, known as the "Testaments of the Twelve Patriarchs," claims attention here. It is true that the date is variously fixed. Still the limits within which it must lie are not so very widely apart. That it was written after the destruction of Jerusalem in A.D. 70 is clear, and that it was written before the troublous times preceding the insurrection of Barkokab may reasonably be conceded. Thus it falls somewhere within the last decade of the 1st and the first two decades of the 2d century, in other words, between 90–120 A.D.

Its doctrinal facts are those of the New Testament, its ethical teaching is an echo of the Epistle of James, and its prophetic portion a reflection of the Apocalypse; while its language throughout is that of the New Testament writers. Thus, for example, fifty-one rare words peculiar to Paul, of which thirty-nine occur in no other writer of that age, are found in the "Testaments." From a most painstaking collation, by Sinker and others, of the whole with the New Testament, the conclusion that must be come to from he identity of facts, of doctrines, of words, of phrases, of general diction, is that the mind of the author must have been deeply imbued with the spirit of the New Testament, and that he must have been thoroughly conversant with almost all the books of the New Testament. There is, moreover, an important statement in the form of prophecy, like the rest of the book, concerning Paul, as follows:—"He shall be in the congregations of the Gentiles, and among their rulers, as a strain of music in the mouth of all. And in *the Holy Books* he shall be inscribed, both his work and word (καὶ ἐν βίβλοις ἁγίαις ἔσται ἀναγραφόμενος, καὶ τὸ ἔργον καὶ ὁ λόγος αὐτοῦ); and he shall be the chosen of God for ever." If, then, this conclusion be admitted, and it can scarcely be denied by any one who has given due attention to the subject, it follows that the canonical books of the New Testament were in existence about the commencement of the 2d century, and quite as much valued and in equally high repute then as now.

But before quitting the subject of the Apostolic Fathers, with their references and allusions to the various writings included in our canon of New Testament Scripture, a few general observations naturally suggest themselves :—

1. The books of Scripture were not only unique in their own character, they were peculiar in the power which they exercised over the people of sub-apostolic times. The Apostolic Fathers and others in those days not only bowed to them with reverence, quoting them with unqualified approval, and acknowledging their vast superiority to their own; they deferred to their authority as supreme. They not only expressed to a wonderful extent their thoughts in the words of Scripture as affording a perfect vehicle of speech, they appealed to their sanction as possessing exceptional value. And once that sanction was secured, they felt satisfied that it settled any matter that might be at issue, and that the controversy was at an end. It was, in fact, a decision from which, in their opinion, there lay no appeal. It is undeniable, therefore, that the productions of the inspired penmen of the New Testament, from their first appearance, were not in roll with ordinary writings. In order, however, duly to appreciate the whole of this statement, we must examine with some attention the exceedingly numerous citations of the New Testament by the writers of sub-apostolic times, as collected by Lardner or Kirchofer.

2. From their singularity these writings could not fail to impress themselves on all into whose hands they came. From their substance, as making known to sinners the way of safety, all who felt their sin and sought a Saviour could not but feel the deepest interest in them, as well as profound veneration for them. From their similarity they could not long remain separate; for, uncommon as they were among all the writings that immediately went before or followed after, they are united by a common bond of fact and doctrine, of principle and precept, of duty and devotion. If like loves like, if the adage—*pares cum paribus facillime congregantur*, apply to writings as

to men, if likeness be a principle that makes human productions as well as human persons gravitate towards each other, then these writings, in the hands of appreciative readers, could not in the very nature of the case continue unconnected or apart from each other for any considerable length of time.

3. The Old Testament was usually named from its constituent parts, especially from its two leading portions, "The Law and the Prophets;" so in several of the above references to the New Testament we find that its two principal divisions were called in like manner "The Gospel and the Apostles;" so they stand in Ignatius, so in the Testaments of the Twelve Patriarchs, so in the Epistle to Diognetus, and so likewise they were subsequently named by Clemens Alexandrinus, as also by Tertullian, Marcion, and others, for the custom of so designating the New Testament continued for long in the Church. But while this appellation bespeaks a collection of the New Testament—in fact, implies a canon—there is still further confirmation of this in the rank assigned them. They are set side by side with the prophets of the Old Testament; they are not only placed on a par with them as entitled to equal respect and rank, they are pronounced like them to be βίβλοι ἁγίαι—part and parcel of the same. Now such terms were used by the Jews and early Christians not as a mere figure of speech; they stood for a fact, and a fact full of significance in connection with this subject.

4. We might appeal in corroboration to the *Exposition of the Lord's Oracles* (κυριακῶν λογιῶν ἐξήγησις), by Papias, or the twenty-four books of *Exegetical Commentary* (ἐξηγητικά) on them by Basilides,—all within the first quarter of the 2d century, or very nearly so.

Passing from the Apostolic Fathers or the personal disciples of the apostles, we come to the Apologists for Christianity. Justin, in his first Apology to Antoninus Pius in the year 140, describing the mode of Sabbath worship in the Christian assemblies, includes in it, as a usage not recent but already long established, the reading of the books of Scripture. "The Memoirs of the Apostles or the writings of the prophets are read as long as the time permits." This public reading of portions of the New Testament along with those of the Old in their solemn Sabbath services, proves that they held equal rank and dignity as inspired and canonical Scripture. He had previously said: "The apostles, in the Memoirs made by them, which are called Gospels, have handed down that Jesus thus enjoined on them." This fixes sufficiently to any unbiassed mind what he meant by Memoirs. And here it deserves attention that in another passage he specifies particularly that the writers of these Memoirs or Gospels were not only apostles but their followers, when he writes: "In the Memoirs, which I say were composed by the apostles and those who followed them," and then quotes a passage from Luke, the follower of an apostle. Besides, it is worthy of remark that the word παρακολουθησάντων used by Justin in this connection is an echo of Luke's παρηκολουθηκότι. Similarly he elsewhere refers to the Memoirs of Peter for a fact found only in the Gospel of Mark. And thus, though he does not assign to all the Gospels exclusively apostolic authorship, he attributes to all of them apostolic authority; while his acquaintance with and employment of the principal remaining books of the New Testament—Acts, Romans, Galatians, Ephesians, Philippians, Colossians, Second Thessalonians, Hebrews, Second Peter, and Revelation (the only book he expressly quotes, ascribing it to John)—can be gathered with certainty from his writings.

But as the 2nd century advances, we come to the Controversialists against heresies within the Church. At the head of these stands Irenæus. Here it may be observed in passing, that the three most distinguished Fathers of the second century were Irenæus, Tertullian, and Clement of Alexandria. They may be fairly taken as representing the teaching and tradition of their respective Churches, so that in their writings we have a reflection of the doctrines current in the Churches of Gaul, North Africa, and Alexandria. But before examining the evidence furnished by Irenæus, it may not be out of place to advert to the canon of Marcion, and to the Muratorian. The first canon was that of Marcion the heretic, who flourished about A.D. 130; but this was a mutilated canon, consisting of the Gospel and Apostolicon, the former being an adaptation of Luke, and the latter embracing ten of Paul's

Epistles. His object was to eliminate from Christianity every Jewish element. Consequently he rejected the Old Testament and any such portions of the New as contained the obnoxious element, or referred to the incarnation and sufferings of the Saviour. That a larger canon had been previously in existence of which his was a mutilation, and that in his selection of canonical books he was guided, not by historic evidence, but purely dogmatic considerations, can scarcely be questioned. Nor does it follow from his denying the authority of any book that he doubted its authenticity. More interest attaches to the canon of Muratori. The MS. of this fragment being found by Muratori in a church of Milan goes by his name. It is a rude and literal Latin translation of a Greek original. Its author was contemporary with Pius, bishop of Rome, about the middle of the 2nd century, as we learn from the author's own words in excluding the Shepherd of Hermas from canonical authority because written "very recently, in our own times by Hermas, while his brother Pius was bishop of the see of Rome." It is the first public testimony of the Church to the contents of Holy Scripture, and contains all the books of our present canon, with a few exceptions, thus proving a general, or rather an all but unanimous, agreement about those contents even at so early a period—certainly not later than A.D. 160–170. The excepted omissions, consisting of James, Hebrews, and Peter, may possibly be accounted for by chasms, or the mutilated state of the text which was copied in the 8th century from a MS. of high antiquity already mentioned.

Let us now revert to Irenæus, the pupil of Polycarp, who himself had been the disciple of John. He was thus connected by a single link to apostolic men and apostolic times; but this single link embraced two individuals whose lives were contemporaneous throughout or nearly so. Not only by his preceptor Polycarp in Asia Minor, but also by his predecessor Pothinus in Lyons, who lived till the advanced age of ninety, was Irenæus united by a single link to apostolic days. He bore to Rome the report of the martyrdoms at Lyons and Vienne in the persecution by Marcus Aurelius; he helped also to moderate the violence of Victor, bishop of Rome, on the Easter controversy; he publicly opposed Valentinus the

Gnostic; he remonstrated with Florinus, a former fellow-disciple, who had fallen into the heresy of making God the author of evil; he controverted the doctrine of Montanus, who had fancied himself the Paraclete; he was the uncompromising antagonist of all errorists, and his great work, still extant in five books, is a refutation of heresies, according to its Latin title, *Adversus Hæreses*. But while his important mission to Rome was an interesting episode in his active life, we must keep in mind other equally important facts of his eventful career. Though the date of his birth is uncertain, it is supposed to have taken place about A.D. 120. At all events, he flourished in the second half of the second century. Bred and born in Asia Minor and trained by Polycarp, he engaged in a mission to Gaul, where he eventually became bishop of Lyons, A.D. 177, and continued in that position during the last quarter of the second century. Before utilising these facts of his history in their important bearing, as we shall see, on the subject of canonical Scripture, we shall find this perhaps the most convenient place to notice the close connection that links together the testimony of Irenæus and that of Polycarp; and all the more as a very special importance attaches to the relation which they bear to each other. These two outstanding Churchmen are a positive and personal disproof of that discontinuity between the close of the 1st and the close of the 2nd century, which the Tübingen theory of the late origin of the books of the canon would necessarily involve. This alleged lateness would imply a most unaccountable break in the progress of the Christian Church and in the formation of the Christian canon. But this whole period is bridged across by the lives of these two men, and the existence of the inspired books of the New Testament near the beginning of that period is proved beyond all possibility of reasonable doubt by their writings. Polycarp suffered martyrdom, as is now generally admitted since the new light cast on the chronology of this period by Waddington's scrutiny of the Fasti of the Asiatic provinces, in A.D. 155 or 156; he served Christ, according to his own statement, eighty-six years; his birth dates consequently from at least A.D. 70, the year of the destruction of Jerusalem. Thus the time available for his intercourse with the Apostle John was considerable, as Polycarp must have been bordering on thirty years of age at the death of John towards the end of the century (98 A.D. or thereabouts). Thus, too, it is safely conjectured that any time during the decade and a half of years closing the first half of the 2nd century Irenæus may have been a disciple of Polycarp. What is perhaps still more important, Polycarp, brought up under the influences of the Apostle John on the one hand, and yet on the other quoting so frequently and making such honourable mention of the Apostle Paul, scatters to the winds as the merest figment the antagonism supposed by the Tübingen school to have existed between those two apostles.

We are now prepared to estimate aright the position of Irenæus, and duly to appreciate his opportunities of intimate acquaintance with the books of Scripture. And here, with respect to his special advantages in this regard, three things must be noted: (1) His testimony is not that of a solitary witness, it is rather that of the representative of the sentiments of three Churches—the Church of his early days in Asia Minor, the Church in Rome where as a deputy he sojourned, and the Church of his closing years in Gaul. (2) His many encounters with heretics, and the fact of his taking an active and leading part in all the polemics of that stirring time, necessitated on his part more than usual familiarity with those Scriptures which, as we know from his writings as well as from other sources, formed the standard to which the orthodox and heretical alike appealed. In his capacity of controversialist, as we have seen, he confronted Montanism, Gnosticism, Monarchism in one of its phases, besides mediating in the Paschal controversy. These various theological conflicts undoubtedly required a knowledge at once minute and extensive of the sacred writings; and that he possessed this exceptional knowledge, no one conversant with his great work on heresies will for a moment question or deny. (3) But the peculiarity of his work, relating as it did to matters of doctrine in dispute among Christians, and needing for their determination a decided reference to those Scriptures that were acknowledged by all Christians in common, required a more direct and distinct recognition of canonical Scripture than any previous patristic writer. The writings of the Fathers that preceded Irenæus were of such a nature—being epistolary, or devotional, or historical, or apologetic—that only incidental notices or allusions or indirect references could be expected in them. How then does the matter stand with this distinguished man who represented the opinions or beliefs of several Churches, enjoyed so many and great advantages and such special opportunities, and whose work imposed on him the necessity of a close acquaintance with and constant reference to the Christian oracles? The answer is plain and positive. This able controversialist and eminent Christian co-ordinates the Old and New Testaments as oracles of God; he puts them on the same platform; he quotes them with the same reverence; he treats them in every way with the same respect. He represents the Valentinians fetching arguments "not only from the evangelic and apostolic writings (*i.e.* the New Testament), but from the law and the prophets" (*i.e.* the Old Testament). Speaking of the Gospel, he says: " Which Gospel they preached, and afterwards by the will of God committed to writing (per Dei voluntatem in Scripturis nobis tradiderunt), that it might be for time to come the foundation and pillar of our faith." Again, he tells us that " after our Lord rose from the dead, and they (the apostles) were endued from above with the power of the Holy Ghost coming down upon them (induti sunt supervenientis Spiritus Sancti virtutem ex alto), they received a perfect knowledge (perfectam agnitionem) of all things." He also informs us of their " having all of them, and every one alike, the gospel of God." He concludes in the following words: " He who does not assent to them, despiseth indeed those who knew the mind of the Lord; but he despiseth also Christ Himself the Lord, and he despiseth likewise the Father, and is self-condemned, resisting and opposing his own salvation." Further, he calls the Scriptures " the oracles of God " ($\tau\grave{a}$ $\lambda\acute{o}\gamma\iota a$ $\tau o\hat{v}$ $\Theta\epsilon o\hat{v}$); he terms them divine Scriptures: " It is read in the divine Scriptures," and " Scriptures of the Lord." Such is the way in which Irenæus treats the Scriptures of the New Testament; while at the same time he gives the names of the different writers, and assumes a certain knowledge of their writings among the Churches of Christ from the beginning, as also a ready recognition of them by all to whom he then wrote. The books of the New Testament of which Irenæus expresses this high estimate, and from which he quotes times almost without number, are the following:—the four Gospels, the Acts, twelve of Paul's Epistles, Revelation, which he ascribes to the Apostle John; and of the catholic Epistles, First Peter and First and Second John. The brevity of Third John and Philemon may account for their absence from the list. References there are to most, if not all, of the remaining books of the canon, but so obscure as to leave the matter somewhat doubtful, or, at all events, to make such references of little value. Thus, though nowhere professing to give a list of the books of Scripture, he has quoted from nearly all the books of the New Testament. He not only affirms their divine origin as Scriptures of the Lord and oracles of God, asserting their inspiration and authority as dictated by the Word of God and His Spirit, but attaches to them a paramount and permanent value as "the rule of truth" and supreme standard of appeal. The teaching of Polycarp on these subjects remained specially fresh and vivid in his memory. His affectionate reminiscences of his friend and father in the gospel are very touching; and as some of them have a direct and important bearing on the subject before us, we need no apology for citing two extracts containing such reminiscences. The first occurs near the commencement of his *Adversus Hæreses*, book iii. 3, and in an elegant translation of the passage reads as follows:—" And so it was with Polycarp also, who not only was taught by apostles, and lived in familiar intercourse with many that had seen Christ, but also received his appointment in Asia from apostles, as bishop in the Church of Smyrna, whom we too have seen in our youth, for he survived long, and departed this life at a very great age, by a glorious and most notable martyrdom, having ever taught these very things which he had learnt from the apostles, which the Church hands down, and which alone are true. To these testimony is borne by all the Churches in Asia, and by the successors of Polycarp up to the present time.... He also, when on a visit to Rome in the days of

Anicetus, converted many to the Church of God from following ... heretics, by preaching that he had received from the apostles this doctrine, and this only, which was handed down by the Church as the truth." The second passage is in the faithful remonstrance which he addressed to his former friend and comrade Florinus, and is preserved by Eusebius in his *H. E.* v. 20 : " These doctrines, Florinus," he there writes, " to say the least, are not of sound understanding ; these doctrines are not in harmony with the Church, but calculated to involve those adopting them in the greatest impiety ; these doctrines even heretics outside the Church have never ventured to broach ; these doctrines the presbyters before us, who also were immediate disciples of the apostles, never handed down to thee. For I saw thee when I was yet a boy, in Lower Asia with Polycarp, while thou wast moving in great splendour at court, and endeavouring to stand well with him. I distinctly remember the incidents of those times better than events of more recent occurrence. For the studies of youth, growing with the growth of the soul, become identified with it, so that I can describe the very place where the blessed Polycarp used to sit and speak, and also his outgoings and incomings, his manner of life, his personal appearance, the discourses he addressed to the people, and how he described his intercourse with John, and with the rest who had seen the Lord, and how he related their words. And whatsoever things he had heard from them about the Lord, and about His miracles, and about His doctrines, Polycarp, as having received them from eye-witnesses of the word of life (or life of the word), recounted all in full accordance with the Scriptures (πάντα σύμφωνα ταῖς γραφαῖς). To these discourses I used to listen at the time with attention by the mercy of God which was bestowed upon me, noting them down, not on paper, but in my heart; and these things, by the grace of God, I am always in the habit of recalling faithfully to mind.'

Proceeding from the controversialists against heresies to the Alexandrine school of philosophic theology, we meet Clement of Alexandria less than twenty years later than Irenæus. He succeeded Pantænus as head of the Catechetical school in that city towards the end of the 2nd century, and was linked through him to the apostolic age. Of his three chief works still extant—his *Exhortation to the Greeks*, which is apologetic; his *Tutor*, which is ethical, and in three books; and his *Stromata*, Patchwork or Miscellanies, which is dogmatic and in eight books; the last, as might be expected, abounds most in citations of Scripture. His statements show the high esteem in which he held the writings of the New Testament, and the profound reverence with which he regarded them; thus he says in reference to the Gospels: "For proof of this, I need not use many words, but only to allege the evangelic voice of the Lord;" "the Lord will confirm this by what He says in the Gospel." In referring to the Pauline and other Epistles, he speaks on this wise: "The Holy Spirit in the apostle says (τὸ ἐν τῷ ἀποστόλῳ ἅγιον πνεῦμα λέγει);" "Excellently well the divine (θεῖος) apostle directs us to put on Christ." Speaking of the Scriptures of the New Testament in general, he calls them "the holy books," "divine Scriptures," "divinely inspired Scriptures (κατὰ τὰς θεοπνεύστας γραφάς)." He, too, puts the "Scriptures of the Lord," that is, the New Testament Scriptures, on the same footing with the law and the prophets, or books of the Old Testament. "Both the law and the gospel," he says, "are the energy of one Lord, who is the power and wisdom of God." He speaks of all the Scriptures—the law, the prophets, and the blessed gospel, as "ratified by almighty power." He acknowledges that his writings are only "the shadow and outline of what he had heard from men who preserved the true tradition of the blessed doctrine directly from Peter and James, from John and Paul, the holy apostles, from father to son, even to our time." From these samples we can judge of the estimation in which he held the canonical Scriptures; while by his quotations he manifests acquaintance with all the books of the New Testament except three, viz. James, Second Peter, and Third John. Here, however, it is again necessary to be reminded that, as his quotations are incidental, and as he does not undertake to give a special catalogue of the sacred books, his silence, so far from proving the absence of those books from the canon, does not even show with certainty his want of acquaintance with them.

Origen was by twenty years the junior of Clement; he was linked by him through Pantænus with the apostolic age. His was the greatest name in all the Eastern Church; he was the most illustrious of teachers, the most indefatigable of writers, the ablest scholar of his time, and the first biblical critic. Born some dozen years before the end of the 2nd, he flourished during the first half of the 3rd century. His writings embrace criticism, exegesis, and practical exhortation. Besides his great critical work, the Hexapla or first Polyglott Bible, are his exegetical works, consisting of *Commentaries* on whole books of Scripture, of which a great many survive only in Latin translations by Rufinus or Jerome; *Homilies*, preserved also in translations; while his Scholia or short notes on difficult passages have all been lost. Of apologetics is his *Contra Celsum* or *Answer to Celsus* the Epicurean, in eight books; and of dogmatic writings is his *Principiis* (περὶ ἀρχῶν), or work on the First Principles of the Christian Faith, in four books, of which the fourth treats of the divine origin of the Holy Scriptures and the right method of studying them. His practical works comprise a treatise *On Prayer*, and an *Exhortation to Martyrdom*. There is also the work called *Philocalia*, or extracts from his writings by Gregory Nazianzen and Basil the Great. The judgment of such a man in relation to the Scriptures must be regarded as specially valuable. Besides, his quotations are so numerous, that though many of his works have perished in the lapse of time, and some of those that have survived are defective, yet in those still extant in Greek his citations of Scripture amount, as has been calculated, to two-thirds of the whole New Testament. Nor is it unworthy of remark in passing, that with him originated the name of New Testament or covenant (ἡ καινὴ διαθήκη). When he speaks of the Apostolic Fathers, he treats their writings with respect, but marks strongly his sense of their inferiority to the books of the canon; when he refers to apocryphal books, he pronounces decidedly on their rejection; and when he enumerates the canonical books, his canon is nearly that of Clement. The substance of his teaching on the subject has been thus summed up by Westcott: " He was acquainted with all the books which are received at present, and received as apostolic those which were recognised by Clement of Alexandria. The others he used, but with a certain reserve and hesitation arising from a want of information as to their history, rather than from any positive ground of suspicion." The books of the New Testament which he thus received as apostolic and acknowledged in the highest sense, are the following:—the four Gospels and Acts, thirteen Epistles of Paul, First Peter, First John, and the Apocalypse; with respect to the remaining books, he quotes them, but admits that they were not so universally acknowledged as those enumerated, and so leaves every one to exercise his own discretion on the subject, and to be persuaded in his own mind. His opinion of the inspiration and divine authority of the books thus included in the canon, he expresses in the strongest and most unqualified manner. "The sacred books," he says, "are not writings of men, but have been written and delivered to us from the inspiration of the Holy Spirit, by the will of the Father of all, through Jesus Christ." Again he says: "The true food of the rational nature is the word of God." And further he adds: "Let us come daily to the wells of the Scriptures, the waters of the Holy Spirit, and there draw and carry thence a full vessel. The greatest torment of demons is to see men reading the word of God, and labouring to understand the divine law."

Though we have placed Origen next to Clement of Alexandria because of the connection of both with the school of Alexandria, yet chronologically Tertullian preceded Origen by a quarter of a century. He represents the practical North African school. His numerous writings fall into four classes—(1) Apologetic, the chief of which is his *Apologeticus*, the best of its kind and the first plea for toleration; (2) Polemical, levelled against the Gnostic heresies, particularly those of Marcion and Valentinian, and his tract against all heretics, entitled *De Præscriptione Hæreticorum*, or a demurrer against the right of heretics to be heard; (3) Practical, on a variety of subjects—idolatry, and theatrical entertainments; an address to martyrs; on prayer, penance, and patience; (4) besides his Montanistic tracts. Of this remarkable man it has been said: "He has left writings which will charm as long as the Latin tongue is read, and a name which will live while courage is a Christian virtue." His quotations of Scripture are very frequent, so much so that Lardner affirms that in this one author there are more numerous and more extended quotations of the small volume of the New Testament than there are of all the works of Cicero in writers of all characters for several ages. He calls the Scriptures of the Old and New Testament a "divine instrument." He attributes the writings of the apostles to the inspiration of the Holy Spirit; thus, "the Spirit of the Lord (Spiritus Domini per apostolum) has declared by the apostle that covetousness is the root of all evil;" "the apostle recommends charity with all the force of the Holy Spirit" (totis viribus Sancti Spiritus); "we come together to recollect the divine Scriptures (literarum divinarum): we nourish our faith, improve our hope, confirm our trust, by the sacred words" (sanctis vocibus). His statements are very full and very explicit. "In the first place," he says, "we lay this down for a certain truth, that the evangelic Scriptures have for their authors the apostles, to whom the work of publishing the gospel was committed by the Lord Himself, and also apostolic men. And if also it have for authors apostolical men, it has not them alone, but with the apostles and after the apostles" (non tamen solos sed cum apostolis, et post apostolos). "Among the apostles, John and Matthew teach us the faith; among apostolical men, Luke and Mark refresh it, going upon the same principles as concerning one God, the Creator, and His Christ born of a virgin, the accomplishment of the law and the prophets." Again he says: "If it be certain that that is most true which is most ancient, that most ancient which is from the beginning, that from the beginning which is from the apostles; it will in like manner be assuredly certain that that has been delivered by the apostles which has been preserved inviolate (sacrosanctum) in the Churches of the apostles. Let us then see what milk the Corinthians received from Paul, to what rule the Galatians were reduced, what the Philippians read, what the Thessalonians, the Ephesians, and also the Romans recite, who are near to us; with whom both Peter and Paul left the gospel sealed with their blood. We have also Churches which are the disciples of John, for though Marcion rejects his revelation, the succession of bishops traced up to the beginning will show it to have John for its author. We know also the original of other Churches (that is, that they are apostolical). I say, then, that with them, but not with them only, that are apostolical, but with all who have fellowship with them in the same faith, is that Gospel of Luke received which we so zealously maintain. . . . The same authority of the apostolical Churches will support the other Gospels which we have from them, and according to them (that is, according to their copies), I mean John's and Matthew's, although that likewise which Mark published may be said to be Peter's, whose interpreter Mark was, for Luke's digest also is often ascribed to Paul." "These," he goes on to say, " are the summary arguments which we employ when we discuss the Gospels with heretics, maintaining both the order of time, which excludes the later works of forgers, and the authority of Churches, which upholds the tradition of the apostles; because truth necessarily precedes forgery, and proceeds from those to whom it has been delivered." In another place he says: " The first point to be determined is, which of the two (*i.e.* heretics and the apostolic Churches) is in possession of the genuine Scriptures, and of their true interpretation. How then is this point to be determined? By inquiring what doctrines are held, and what Scriptures received, by the apostolic Churches; for in them is preserved the truth as it was originally communicated by Christ to the apostles, and by the apostles, either orally or by letter, to the Churches which they founded; so that whatever doctrines and Scriptures are so held and received, must be deemed orthodox and genuine." Further, Tertullian clearly distinguishes between spiritual illumination which, though it discover no new truth, yet leads to the right discernment of truth already revealed, and which is therefore an essential element in sanctification and common to all true believers, and that special influence of the Holy Spirit which was peculiar to the prophets of the Old and the apostles or writers of the New Testament Scripture, and endued them with power for the high function of being accredited witnesses for Christ and teachers of the truth. Thus he says: " Even all believers, it is true, have the Holy Spirit; but all believers are not apostles" (spiritum quidem dei etiam fideles habent, sed non omnes fideles apostoli). Then soon afterwards he explains the difference, by stating how the apostles in a sense peculiar to themselves have the Holy Spirit in works of prophecy, power of miracles, and gifts of tongues, not partially as other Christians. His words are: "Proprie enim apostoli spiritum sanctum habent in operibus propheticæ et efficacia virtutum, documentisque linguarum, non ex parte, quod cæteri."

Here then is a consensus, not only in the expression of opinion concerning the divine succour and sanction enjoyed by the penmen of New Testament Scripture, but also an equally remarkable and equally satisfactory consensus in regard to the books of which the canon is composed. And a circumstance that makes this consensus the more valuable is, that it embodies the almost unanimous sentiments of all the different sections of the primitive Church. Asia, Africa, and Europe are all represented; the Churches of the East and of the West and of the South harmonise in their adherence to the extent as well as to the divine authority of the canon. While Irenæus represents the sentiment on this subject of the Churches of Asia Minor, and even, as we have seen, of Gaul and Rome; the Peshito Syriac, that venerable version made soon after the death of John, and wanting only Jude, Second Peter, Second and Third John, may be regarded as giving silent testimony to that of the more distant East. Clement Alexandrinus and Origen vouch for Egypt and its capital Alexandria, that centre of literary and ecclesiastical life. Tertullian, again, not only speaks in the name of the Churches in Africa along the southern shores of the Mediterranean, but joins his voice with the old Latin which, formed about the middle of the 2nd century, omits only Hebrews, James, and Second Peter, in support of the canon of the West. All these, and more which we may not stop to specify, unite from distant lands and in different languages, in wondrous harmony; and with one loud and long acclaim, accord to the books of the New Covenant a pre-eminence distinct and decided over all the works, however excellent, of any even the highest merely human authorship.

An observation may here be made with respect to the difference between the canonical books of the New Testament and the writings of the Apostolic Fathers which immediately succeeded them. Between the compositions of these two periods, viz. the apostolic and the sub-apostolic—between the apostles themselves and the apostolic men who were their intimate friends and immediate followers, there is a most surprising disparity. Though the two periods touch, and the persons who wrote, and spoke, and taught in them respectively came into closest contact, yet the difference between their productions is rather one of kind than of degree, it is a contrast rather than a comparison. Nor is the difference in form more than in essence; it extends equally to matter and manner—to substance and style alike. Between the writings of the apostles themselves, as we have them in the canon, and the writings of their disciples and direct successors, there is, as it were, a great gulf fixed. Nor is there any explanation of this feasible or even possible, except the recognition of the existence of inspiration in the one case and its absence in the other. In the one case the finger of God, if we may so speak, touched the pen of the writer, in the other case no such favour was vouchsafed. The statements of Daille in this regard are as appropriate as they are apparently paradoxical when he says: "God has allowed a fosse to be drawn by human weakness around the sacred canon to protect it from all invasion."

As the darkest hour of the night is that which immediately precedes the dawn, so, before Christianity was exalted to the throne of the Cæsars and became the religion of the empire, the tenth and most terrible storm of persecution swept over the Church in the reign and by the edict of Diocletian. One ugly feature of this persecution was, in addition to the demolition of the Churches, the destruction of the copies of the sacred Scriptures. In this last respect it was peculiar, and stood alone among the persecutions of the Christians under the heathen Roman emperors, and was only paralleled by that of Antiochus Epiphanes against the Jews. One chief object of attack in both was the sacred writings—those of the Old Testament by the latter, those of the New Testament by the former. Some weak Christians surrendered the sacred volume and were branded as *traitors* (traditores); others substituted heretical, or apocryphal, or otherwise useless books, and thus sought to escape. But while persecution raged without, perils rose within. The Donatist schism originated in a demand for more rigorous treatment of the lapsed. But here, as elsewhere, God brings good out of evil. The line between canonical—a word now come into common and more frequent use—and uncanonical books, though long ago drawn, became in consequence harder, faster, and more firmly established; while the testimony of Augustine assures us that Catholic and Donatist did reverence to the same canonical Scriptures. "And what," he asks, "are these but the Scriptures of the law and the prophets? To which are added the Gospels, the apostolic Epistles, the Acts of the Apostles, and the Apocalypse of John."

If space allowed, many more authorities to the same purpose might be quoted, such as Dionysius of Corinth (A.D. 170), who speaks of the "Scriptures of the Lord," or "Dominical Scriptures." The Epistle of the Churches of Vienne and Lyons, which has been called "the finest thing of the kind in all antiquity," without express citation, alludes plainly to the Acts, Romans, Corinthians, Ephesians, Philippians, First Timothy, First Peter, First John, Revelation, the Gospel of Luke, and that of John. In this last reference, namely, to John xvi. 2, occur the words: "Then was fulfilled that which was spoken by the Lord," from which we learn the estimate of Scripture, as divinely inspired, by those Churches. We omit also the references of Hippolytus, whose *Philosophumena*, or treatise "against all heresies" (the complete work or nearly so), discovered at Mount Athos 1842, and published at Oxford in 1851, "affords," according to Schaff, "valuable testimony to the genuineness of the Gospel of John," both from Hippolytus' own words and from his quotations of Basilides (A.D. 125), who had been a later contemporary of the apostle; while the writings of this same author (Hippolytus), besides containing citations from all the acknowledged books of Scripture except Philemon and First John, have, according to Tregelles, two references to Hebrews and one to Second Peter.

Believing that a due consideration of the testimonies already referred to will serve sufficiently the purpose for which they have been adduced, we proceed to an examination of the Old Testament canon.

CHAPTER XII.

THE OLD TESTAMENT CANON.

IT now remains for us to carry our reasoning up from the New Testament to the Old. Having ascertained the divine authority of the New, we now collect with care the testimony borne by the writers of the New Testament to the Hebrew Scriptures of the Old. Having first proved the moral and intellectual worth of the New Testament writers as witnesses, we now employ their evidence in relation to the Old Testament. This narrows the field of discussion, for having once fully satisfied ourselves about the character and competency of the penmen of the New Testament, we are in a proper position to take advantage of their statements with regard to the sacred character and binding nature of that collection of books composing the Old Testament Scriptures.

SEC. I.—*Fact of Recognition of the Old Testament in the New.*

Every reader of the New Testament must be aware of the fact that the references to the Old Testament contained therein are both numerous and various. This is a fact that lies on the very surface of New Testament Scripture, and a fact so patent that it cannot fail to be observed by the most cursory reader. It behoves us, however, to attend to the nature and extent of such recognition. In examining the nature of the recognition in question, the *manner* of New Testament quotation deserves a passing notice. While these quotations are very many, in the mode of quotation there is considerable diversity.

(1) *Manner of New Testament Quotation.*

Sometimes the reference is to a (*a*) *single book* of Scripture, whether mentioned by name or not, from which one or more passages may be cited. Thus the evangelist refers (*a*) *by name* to the book of the prophet Esaias, saying: "For this is he that was spoken of by the prophet Esaias, saying, The voice of one crying in the wilderness." Again, (β) *without adding the name*, he quotes the prophecy of Micah in regard to the birthplace of Messiah, thus: "And they said to him, In Bethlehem of Judæa: for thus it is written by the prophet." In this way many books of Old Testament Scripture are quoted and recognised individually. A second and more comprehensive mode of appealing to the Old Testament is (*b*) by that *threefold division* of those Scriptures with which every reader of Scripture is familiar. Thus in the well-known passage of the Gospel according to Luke, xxiv. 44, which is the *locus classicus*, we read: "All things must be fulfilled which are written in the Law of Moses, and the Prophets, and the Psalms, concerning me." Occasionally, for the sake of brevity and facility of quotation, by synecdoche, a common figure which puts a part for the whole, (*c*) some *one* of these three prominent divisions is put for the whole. In this way sometimes the whole Old Testament Scriptures are designated (*a*) the *Law*. Thus in John x. 34 it is written: "Jesus answered them, Is it not written in your law, I said ye are gods?" when the reference is to the 6th verse of the 82d Psalm. So also we speak of the Law and the Gospel, meaning by the former the Old Testament, and by the latter the New. The second leading division gives its name in like manner to the entire collection of the books of the Old Testament, as in Acts xxvi. 27, where Paul in his earnest appeal addresses his royal auditor: "King Agrippa, believest thou (β) the *prophets?* I know that thou believest." A third mode of reference, and one at the same time more general in its nature than either of the former two, is that by which the whole of the Old Testament is summed up and included under the expressive designation of (γ) the *Scriptures* (αἱ γραφαί). Now this, which is the most general name of all, corresponds, it will be at once perceived, to the third component part of the triple division already referred to, for כְּתוּבִים, that is, γραφαί or Scriptures, the terms being equivalent, was the proper designation of that third part. Instead of *Kethuvim*, however, the word Φαλμοί, or Psalms, was substituted, because the Psalms formed the first and most prominent portion of that division, and that on the well-known principle of *A potiori nomen fit*. The references of this class are so numerous that any one may at once recall some of them to mind. A striking and instructive example occurs Rom. xv. 4: "For whatsoever was written aforetime was written for our learning, that we, through patience and comfort of the *Scriptures*, might have hope." Again, we occasionally meet with a title given to the Old Testament, not from one part of the threefold division nor from the three portions all together, but from (*d*) *two of them combined*, as in the expression: "The Law and the Prophets," or "Moses and the Prophets."

(2) *Conclusions, from the manner of Quotation, in regard to the fact of Recognition.*

What, then, are the conclusions that may be legitimately drawn from the manner of citation adopted by the writers of the New Testament with respect to their recognition of the books that compose the Old Testament Scriptures? From the repeated citations of the Old Testament under the various designations which have been noticed — the Law, and the Prophets, and the Psalms; the Law; the Prophets; the Scriptures, frequently Scripture in the singular; the Law and the Prophets, or Moses and the Prophets — we cannot but conclude that the references are of such a nature as clearly to take for granted and plainly to imply a *well-known and publicly acknowledged body* of Hebrew writings. In one of the passages already cited, namely, Luke xxiv. 44, we read: "These are the words which I spake unto you while I was yet with you, that all things must be fulfilled which were written in the Law of Moses, and in the Prophets, and in the Psalms, concerning me;" while after this threefold division, there follows, in the verse immediately succeeding, a term at once explanatory and confirmatory, for in the 45th verse it is added: "Then opened He their understanding, that they might understand the Scriptures." This scarcely needs comment.

It seems clear as noonday that the expressions referring to the Old Testament in the 44th and 45th verses respectively are equivalent; they cover the same ground, they designate the same area. In the one case that area is partitioned into three compartments, in the other those three compartments are taken as a whole. There can be no reasonable doubt that "the Scriptures," which are mentioned in the 45th verse, comprehend and are identical with "the Law of Moses, and the Prophets, and the Psalms," spoken of in the 44th verse. It is manifest, then, that the writings of the Old Testament had thus a distinctive appellation—an appellation, moreover, well and publicly known. Were it otherwise, our Lord's words already quoted must have been palpably, and, we may even add, culpably unintelligible. If the triple designation of "Law, and Prophets, and Psalms" on the one hand, and the single equivalent term "Scriptures" on the other, did not denote a well-ascertained and definite collection of writings, the Saviour's words must have sounded mysteriously in the ears of His disciples, and must have lacked altogether the usual plainness and simplicity of speech which He was wont to employ; while the disciples must have been bewildered by the strange nomenclature, and must have failed to comprehend the language of the great Teacher. We maintain the very contrary. Common sense, reason, the very nature of language, all ally themselves on our side in asserting the contrary. Our Lord's words must have had due significance pointing to an assemblage of writings well known, consisting of a number of books strictly defined, and restricted to a certain set of compositions of which the words in question would at once remind every Jew to whom they were addressed. It is just as if we referred to the Odes, and Satires, and Epistles, and in the next sentence spoke of the writings of Horace; or if, in like manner, we should refer to the Bucolics, and Georgics, and Æneid, and in the next breath mention the works of Virgil; where is the classical scholar that would not in either case immediately and fully understand the reference? Where is the scholar that would not have a clear and correct notion of the compositions thus referred to, either in their threefold division or as a collected whole? Whether, therefore, our Lord appealed to the Old Testament under the triple designation of "Law, and Prophets, and Psalms," or by the one general name of "the Scriptures," every Jew that listened to His words must necessarily, and in the very nature of things, have understood without any effort the Saviour's reference as made to a collection of writings as distinct and definite as any fixed quantity employed by the mathematician. Not only so, every one of his auditors would comprehend clearly and with certainty the individual books included in and united together in that collection.

We have unmistakable *evidence* of this. In Matt. xxii. 29 our Lord charged the Sadducees with shameful and guilty ignorance of the Scriptures, saying: "Ye do err, not knowing the Scriptures nor the power of God;" while again, in John v. 39, He commanded the multitudes attending the Jewish festival to "search the Scriptures," adding, "for in them ye think ye have eternal life, and they are they that testify of me." Now, if the Scriptures were not a well-defined and generally known collection of writings, would it not be passing strange that none of his auditors questioned his statement or sought an explanation? His opponents, it must be owned, were forward enough to put captious questions for sinister purposes —witness the twofold question of the deputation from the Sanhedrin about the nature and source of His authority; the ensnaring political question of the Pharisees and Herodians about the tribute-money; the insidious doctrinal question of the Sadducees about the resurrection; the speculative question of the scribe about the greatest commandment; the treacherous question of discipline about the woman taken in adultery. Even His disciples were ready enough to ask an explanation, in case their Master gave utterance to any saying which seemed to them dark or difficult. But neither friend nor foe solicits an explanation or requests a definition of the term "Scripture." Why, it may be asked, was this? Why, simply and clearly because no one failed to comprehend it, no one misunderstood it—it was universally intelligible. So also it is in the Acts of the Apostles; so, too, in the apostolic Epistles. The inspired writers of those books, when using the word Scriptures, did not think it necessary to specify the application of the word, and those addressed did not need to make any inquiry on that head. Why was this so? For the plain reason that the term αἱ γραφαί was universally intelligible as denoting a body of writings so well understood, so publicly known, and so universally recognised, as to be beyond the reach of question or cavil. Still more, those very sects that hated the Saviour, and hated one another, never once ventured to make it an object of doubt, or of difficulty, or of ensnaring interrogatory. Another circumstance of utmost importance in connection with this fact of the recognition of the Old Testament Scriptures is that, when our Lord taxes the Jews with ignorance, or unbelief, or disobedience, He never for a moment thinks of upbraiding them with unfaithfulness in their trust as guardians of the Scriptures, or with interpolating them, or with mutilating them, or with corrupting them, or with tampering with them in any way whatever. He evidently assumes that they had been preserved pure and entire, and that they remained up till that time wholly uncorrupt.

SEC. II.—*The Character of the Recognition in question.*

We proceed to inquire in the next place in what terms the New Testament writers refer to Old Testament Scripture. What is the character of their references? What is the nature of their appeals? There can be no hesitation and no uncertainty about the answer that must be returned to these questions. The terms in which they refer to the Old Testament are manifestly of such a kind as to mark unmistakably the peculiarly high estimation in which they held them, and the singularly exalted character in which they recognised them. They regarded them as sacred, they looked upon them as of divine authority, and quoted them as the supreme standard of appeal. By them doctrine is proved, by them duty is enforced, by them virtue is stimulated, by them piety is commended, by them every question whether of faith or morals is determined. In all matters of religion the Scriptures of the Old Testament are referred to as an umpire from which there lies no appeal. In all cases, and on all occasions, they are expressly cited as, or tacitly conceded to be, the highest authority. Our Lord Himself commends these writings to the careful perusal of the multitudes in the familiar words already quoted, when He enjoins them to "search the Scriptures." He states expressly in John x. 35, that "the Scripture cannot be broken." He assures us that He came "not to destroy the Law and the Prophets, but to fulfil." He refers to several of the books of Scripture, sometimes to the whole volume, as the word of God. He quotes the Law, the Prophets, and the Psalms, or Hagiographa, as all and equally of divine authority. Our blessed Lord Himself thus sets His imprimatur upon them, stamping them with a sacred character. So with the apostles, they quote the volume of Old Testament Scripture, and, with a full recognition of all the writings contained therein, sanction in the fullest manner their divine authority. While in their writings, whether Gospels or Epistles, they ascribe the ancient economy to Moses, forasmuch as he was so prominently connected with its announcement and administration, they trace it at the same time to higher authority, assuming and asserting the divinity of its origin by designating it the law of the Lord. In like manner, with respect to the prophetic portion, it is affirmed: "For the prophecy came not in old time by the will of man: but holy men of God spake as they were moved by the Holy Ghost." With this decided utterance of Peter that notable statement of Paul already referred to in another connection is perfectly in accord, when he declares that "all Scripture is given by inspiration of God." But it were tedious, and at the same time superfluous, to enumerate all the testimonies of like kind to the sacredness and divine character with which the writers of the New Testament invest the writings of the Old.

SEC. III.—*The Means and Method of Identification.*

It now only remains for us to determine the books of which the canon of the Old Testament consisted. What were its component parts? That that canon, whatever its constituent elements were, is acknowledged by our Lord and His apostles, and that it is affirmed by them to be divine in its origin, sacred in its character, and binding in its authority, has been already sufficiently proved. All then in reality that is further needed to complete our argument for the canon of Old Testament Scripture, is to show that the canon, thus sanctioned, contained the same books and no others that are now included in the Old Testament Scriptures. Can we produce documentary evidence coeval with the apostle to prove that the term "Scripture" (γραφή), as understood by us, is of the same compass and extent, having the same comprehension, and embracing the same identical books, which Paul included in that term? Certain sacred books of the Hebrews are evidently referred to in the expression "all Scripture;" and, since all Scripture, or more accurately *every* portion of the writings so signalised, is declared to be inspired by God, the question of the canonical authority of the books comprehended under that term is settled by inspiration itself, that is to say, by the apostle writing under the inspiration of the Holy Spirit. This helps to narrow the subject, and the duty that now devolves on us is the work of identification. The New Testament recognises all the books of the Old Testament canon collectively, and a great number of them individually; and the problem we have to solve is to prove that the Scriptures of the Old Testament, as they have been handed down to us, and as we at present possess them, contain exactly the same books that were contained in those Scriptures which our Lord and His apostles quoted, and which they honoured with the designations already examined. Are we in a position to do this? Have we documentary evidence contemporaneous with the apostles, and coming down to us from their times, which will enable us to ascertain the books included in the Old Testament canon, as quoted by the penmen of the New, and so to identify those books with the Old Testament canon, as we at present have it? We can, we think, answer such questions with a decided affirmative.

Happily we are able to produce for this purpose a witness

whose evidence is unexceptionable and precisely suited to the case, we mean Josephus, who was born in the thirty-seventh year of our era, and whose testimony is enhanced by a variety of circumstances. Among these may be reckoned not only his general trustworthiness as a historian, but also certain special qualifications. He was a Jewish priest intimately acquainted with the history, religion, and literature of his nation, as also with the views and feelings of his countrymen. The treatise, in which his evidence on the point is found, having been written near the close of a career eminently distinguished by learned labours and literary research, contains the results of his most matured investigations and reflections. Besides, in the instance referred to, he does not speak in his own individual name, nor in order to express his own individual opinions, but in the name and on behalf as in defence of his countrymen. This plainly appears from his employment of such phrases as ἡμεῖς, παρ' ἡμῖν, πᾶσι 'Ιουδαίοις, so that he is giving expression not to his own private or peculiar views, but to the long established and generally accepted opinions of his nation. The statement referred to has been often quoted, and is generally known, but none the less does it need to be repeated here and now. It occurs in his treatise against Apion the Alexandrian grammarian, and in a defence of the Jewish people, their religion, sacred books, and especially the historical faithfulness of those books. It is as follows:—" Forasmuch as not every one that pleased was permitted to write, and as our writings contain no contradictions, the prophets only, being taught by divine inspiration, have narrated the earliest and most ancient events, and have recorded with fidelity the history of their own times. With us there are not myriads of books inharmonious and conflicting, but two-and-twenty books only, containing the records of the whole time, and rightly believed to be divine. Of these, five are those of Moses, which comprise as well the matters of law as the account of the generations of man, to the time of his death. This period is little short of 3000 years. But from the death of Moses to the reign of Artaxerxes the king of Persia after Xerxes, the prophets after Moses wrote what was done in their times, in thirteen books. The four remaining books contain hymns to God, and suggestions to men as to their lives. From Artaxerxes down to our own times events have been recorded, but they have not been accounted worthy of the same credit as those before them, because the exact succession of prophets existed no longer. And it is evident, indeed, how we stand affected to our own writings. For, so long a period having now elapsed, no one has dared either to add to or to take away from them, or to change anything; it being a thing implanted in all the Jews from their first birth, that they should account them as oracles of God, and abide by them, and, if there were need, gladly die for them." Such is the statement of Josephus—a statement which is valuable in various ways; it helps to determine the time when the canon was closed, and assigns a sufficient reason for its close; but for the work of identification in particular it is most serviceable. True, it does not give us a catalogue of all the books of the canon, it only counts them; neither does it give the names of all the books in each of the three divisions, it only numbers them. There is besides a difficulty—a difficulty which at first sight appears formidable, and yet more apparent than real. It consists in the fact that, while we reckon thirty-nine books as making up the canon of the Old Testament, Josephus in his enumeration makes them consist of only twenty-two. This seeming discrepancy admits a simple and satisfactory solution. It will be borne in mind that among the ancients, both Jew and Gentile, a sort of *memoria technica* prevailed. They were fond of mnemonic words and mnemonic numbers. The letters of the alphabet were very suitable for this purpose. Accordingly, the two great heroic poems of Greece—the *Iliad* and *Odyssey*—are divided into books on this principle. The letters of the Greek alphabet are twenty-four in number. Each of those poems is divided into twenty-four portions or books, while each book has a letter of the alphabet as a mark of numeration. In like manner, the 119th Psalm is divided into twenty-two pieces. The letters of the Hebrew alphabet are twenty-two, and each portion of that Psalm is marked by one of these letters. On precisely the same principle, the enumeration of the books in the Old Testament canon, as given by Josephus, proceeded. Neither is there anything far-fetched or unnatural in the combinations that are made of those books, in order that the number of the whole may exactly amount to twenty-two. On the contrary, a common-sense principle underlies such combinations, for they are formed on the principle of natural and mutual connection. The following tabular view will make the correspondence between the present enumeration and that of Josephus manifest:—

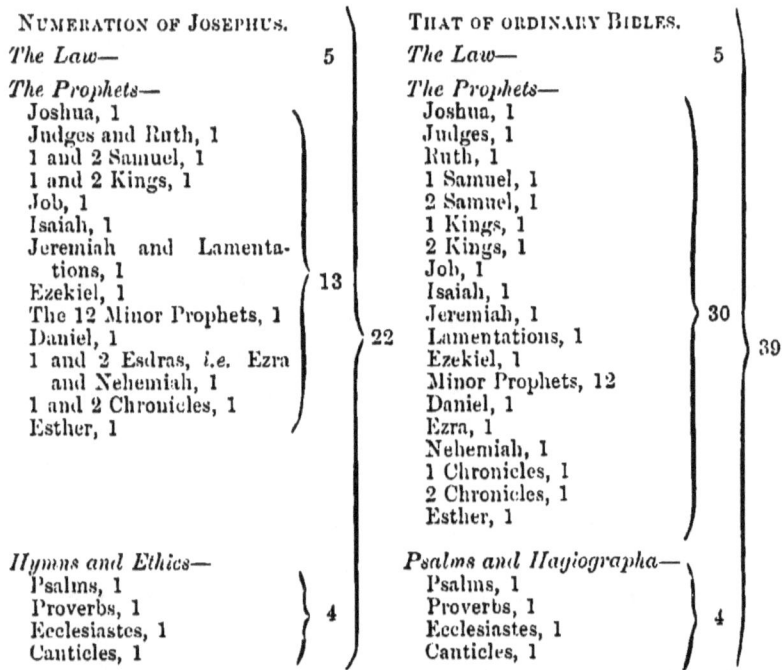

Numeration of Josephus.		That of ordinary Bibles.	
The Law—	5	The Law—	5
The Prophets—		The Prophets—	
Joshua, 1		Joshua, 1	
Judges and Ruth, 1		Judges, 1	
1 and 2 Samuel, 1		Ruth, 1	
1 and 2 Kings, 1		1 Samuel, 1	
Job, 1		2 Samuel, 1	
Isaiah, 1		1 Kings, 1	
Jeremiah and Lamentations, 1	13	2 Kings, 1	
Ezekiel, 1		Job, 1	
The 12 Minor Prophets, 1		Isaiah, 1	30
Daniel, 1		Jeremiah, 1	
1 and 2 Esdras, i.e. Ezra and Nehemiah, 1		Lamentations, 1	
1 and 2 Chronicles, 1		Ezekiel, 1	
Esther, 1		Minor Prophets, 12	
		Daniel, 1	
		Ezra, 1	
		Nehemiah, 1	
		1 Chronicles, 1	
		2 Chronicles, 1	
		Esther, 1	
Hymns and Ethics—		Psalms and Hagiographa—	
Psalms, 1		Psalms, 1	
Proverbs, 1	4	Proverbs, 1	4
Ecclesiastes, 1		Ecclesiastes, 1	
Canticles, 1		Canticles, 1	

Totals: 22 and 39.

Now, what attaches great and grave importance to this enumeration of Josephus, and the identification which it so materially helps, is the circumstance already intimated, that he is not writing in the interests of a sect, nor is he giving us the expression of his own private opinion, but rather the embodiment of the public faith of his nation. But in addition to Josephus' own express and explicit declaration regarding the canon, we find in his casual quotations every book of Scripture referred to except four. The four exceptional cases are Proverbs, Ecclesiastes, Canticles, and Job;

while the case of the former three is covered by the circumstance that from the eighth book of his *Antiquities*, where he refers to Solomon as an author, it may, with strong probability, be inferred that he regarded him as their author; and that of Job is accounted for by the fact that the events recorded in that book have no point of contact with the histories of Josephus.

If necessary, it might easily be proved that in the interval between the close of the canon and the time of Josephus *no change* in the books thereof had taken place. We might adduce several authorities to this effect. The same threefold classification that is found in the New Testament and in Josephus, occurs in the preface to the translation of Ecclesiasticus out of Hebrew into Greek by Sirachides. The lowest date assigned for the translation of Sirachides is 130 B.C., and consequently that of the original by his grandfather must have been at least forty years earlier, say about 170 B.C. Three times in the prologue of this work is this very threefold division of the canonical books referred to; thus, he says: "Whereas many and great things have been delivered to us by the Law and the Prophets, and the rest that followed their steps;" that is, the other books that followed in the same spirit. Again, he refers to "the reading of the Law and the Prophets, and the other books of our fathers." And a third time he speaks of "the Law and the Prophets, and the remainder of the books." In this way Sirachides, when referring to the divine authority of the Old Testament Scriptures, makes express mention of that self-same threefold division of them which existed in the days of our Lord and in the time of Josephus. Here it is indisputable that by τῶν ἄλλων, twice repeated, and by τὰ λοιπά a third class of sacred writings is designated—a class occupying the same common platform with the Law and the Prophets, though not yet bearing a technical name. The miscellaneous nature of those writings would perhaps make difficult, and so delay, the designating of them by one appropriate general name. An instance somewhat analogous is noticed by Thucydides in reference to Homer's mention of the Greeks, at the time of the Trojan war, by their tribal designations of Argives,

Achæans, Dorians, Ionians, and Danaoi, for want of one national, all-embracing common name. It is obvious, at the same time, that the designation of *the others* or *the rest* would have been utterly unintelligible to his readers unless in the supposition of a distinct, well known, and clearly defined class of writings. Here, too, must be observed the definite terms in which Sirachides mentions these books comprised in the third division. They are not others that follow, but " the others;" not other books of our fathers, but " the other books ;" " the rest of the books." A similar reference occurs in Philo, who flourished 40 B.C., for in describing the practices of the Essenes, he refers to " the laws, and oracles predicted by the prophets, and hymns and other writings by which knowledge and piety are increased and perfected." It must also be kept in mind that the Septuagint version, made before the middle of the 3rd century B.C., though it errs by excess, as we shall see, yet contains all the books of the canon of Josephus. But a sure guarantee for the unchanged condition of the canon before the time of Josephus was the jealous rivalry of the two opposing sects of Judaism, namely, the Pharisees and Sadducees, who were the ritualists and rationalists, or rather, the traditionists and Scripturists of that day, for the opinion about the Sadducees only holding by the Pentateuch has been exploded for many reasons that cannot be specified here. Further, if the watchfulness of these conflicting sects was a voucher for the unchanged condition of the canon up till the time of Josephus, a similar vigilance of the two contending parties, that is to say, Jews and Christians, is a warrant for the absence of change or of any tampering with the books or text of the canon since the days of Josephus.

The first authority in confirmation of the view just referred to is that of the old Syriac, dating from early in the 2nd century. There is good reason to believe that the books of this version coincided exactly with those that constituted the Hebrew canon. This might naturally be expected, for, translated directly from the Hebrew Scriptures, it adhered strictly to the books contained therein. Immediately connected with the Hebrew original, it comprised all the canonical books of the Old Testament, but no more and no less. This was the state of matters at the first, and even down till the time of Ephraem the Syrian, A.D. 370, as is certain from the fact that his commentaries embrace all the canonical books and no others. This is further evidenced by the quotations of Ebedjesu, while the same conclusion is confirmed by the postscripts to certain MSS. published by Pococke.

Scarce a century had elapsed from the time of Josephus till that of Melito, bishop of Sardis. This eminent man was born, there is reason to believe, near the beginning of the second century, not long after the death of the Apostle John, and so was a contemporary for many years of Polycarp and Papias. He flourished A.D. 150-170, when we find virtually the same enumeration of the sacred books by the Christian bishop as that made previously by the Jewish priest and historian Josephus. A special importance attaches to the testimony of Melito. His position, his intelligence, his spirit of inquiry, and critical taste, all combine to increase its value. He had journeyed from his residence in Sardis to Palestine for the express purpose of ascertaining with cautious discrimination and utmost accuracy (ἀκρίβειαν) the number, names, order, and other circumstances connected with the books of Old Testament Scripture. The result of his researches and inquiries is contained in a letter to his brother Onesimus, who was like-minded with himself, and animated with the same earnest inquiring spirit in relation to the records of salvation. In that letter, which is still preserved in the fourth book of the Church History of Eusebius, Melito gives a list of the books of the Old Testament. In the list handed down from this trustworthy and accurate witness—the first Christian writer who has been at the pains to give us such a list, we have proof positive of the sameness of the Old Testament canon from the first. Two things, however, are noteworthy in this catalogue. Melito after the Proverbs of Solomon (Σολομῶνος παροιμίαι) has the words ἡ καὶ σοφία, by which some have understood the apocryphal book called "Wisdom;" but this is obviously erroneous, for the ἡ is not the article, which would be out of place, but the relative, the meaning of the whole being, *The Proverbs of Solomon, which is also called*

Wisdom. The other matter for remark is, that under the general title *Esdras,* Melito comprehended Ezra, Nehemiah, and Esther.

Passing over several respectable vouchers for the same canon, we arrive at the age of Jerome, at once the best Hebraist and the most learned as well as critical of all the Fathers. This distinguished scholar distributes the canonical books into the three familiar classes of Law, Prophets, and Hagiographa, making the whole number of books comprised under these divisions to correspond with the number of the letters that make up the Hebrew alphabet, that is, twenty-two. He reckons five double books, namely, Samuel, Kings, Chronicles, Ezra, and Jeremiah, as corresponding with the five letters in the Hebrew alphabet that have double forms —the so-called final letters, or as they are mnemonically termed, *Kamnephetz;* Ruth he connects with Judges; and the twelve minor prophets he ranges in one book, according to the well-known Jewish custom. Thus his list is precisely that of Josephus and of the Jews, as already seen. This array of testimony may be closed by referring to the councils, by which the decision of the Christian communities, long since come to under divine guidance, was registered, and the canon, already long in existence, was crystallised in the creed of the Church. For example, the list of canonical books authorised by the council of Laodicea is identical with the books in our Bibles at the present day, with a very slight deviation, and one easily accounted for. Baruch is mentioned along with Jeremiah, obviously from the circumstance that a portion of the prophet's words was written down by Baruch acting as his amanuensis, and, no doubt, in a separate roll.

SEC. IV.—*The Exclusion of the Apocrypha.*

This topic claims a brief discussion. (*a*) The Greek version of the Old Testament, called the Septuagint, dating— most of it—from upwards of two centuries and a half before Christ, and containing all the books in our ordinary Bibles, affords a powerful support to the canonicity of those books.

But this support is to some extent counterbalanced by an acknowledged difficulty and consequent objection. If we admit that the argument from the Septuagint is valid, and no one can question its admissibility, then, it has been urged, the argument proves too much, and constrains us to accept the apocryphal books as of equal authority with the canonical Scriptures. This version undoubtedly is chargeable, as already intimated, with redundancy, but not, there is good reason to believe, in its original condition; while the true history of this redundancy goes far to meet the objection which it occasions. It was among the sacred books of the Egyptian Jews that the admission, or rather intrusion, of the apocryphal books took place. Many special circumstances contributed to this disastrous result. (*a*) The Jews of Egypt were not so scrupulously conservative of their sacred writings, neither were they so punctiliously exact in their treatment of them, as their brethren in Palestine. Into the causes of this difference it is not necessary to enter. (β) Besides this difference, the form in which they possessed their books of Scripture had a good deal to do with their too facile introduction of apocryphal books into the canon. They were familiar with their books of Scripture only in the Greek version, made not by one person nor at one time, but by different translators and in successive parts. The production of this translation in such a piecemeal manner helped to weaken the notion of close connection and unity among its several portions as they were successively issued. (γ) The apocryphal books, moreover, would, as a matter of course, attain a high rank in their religious literature; and by and by they stealthily insinuated themselves among their sacred books. And yet we are firmly persuaded that they formed no part of the authoritative canon even of Alexandrian or Egyptian Jews. (*b*) (*a*) Sirachides, the translator of the Book of Wisdom, in a passage already referred to, when contrasting his own biblical studies in Egypt with those of his venerable grandfather, the author of the book, in Palestine, appears to assume the Biblical canon of both as identical, specifying its three well-known divisions as "the Law and the Prophets and the other books," that is, the Hagiographa. (β) Philo in Egypt a little before, and (γ)

Josephus in Palestine a little after, the beginning of our era, ignore, each in his own way, the Apocrypha. The former, a man of priestly origin and literary habits, a man intimately acquainted with the religious rites and customs of his fathers, has never once quoted any of the apocryphal books as of Scriptural authority. This is all the more remarkable, as it is certain, from his style and incidental notices, that he was well acquainted with the Apocrypha, and that they might have been adduced by him in several instances as confirmatory of his views. What makes this still more conclusive is the circumstance of his quoting so many of the canonical books as divine in their origin and authoritative in their declarations. Josephus, moreover, so far from quoting an apocryphal book as of Scriptural authority, actually cuts them off from all connection therewith. After speaking of the twenty-two books of canonical Scripture being "deservedly regarded as divine" ($\tau\grave{a}$ $\delta\iota\kappa a\acute{\iota}\omega\varsigma$ $\theta\epsilon\acute{\iota}a$ $\pi\epsilon\pi\iota\sigma\tau\epsilon\upsilon\mu\acute{\epsilon}\nu a$), he pronounces the books written from the time of Artaxerxes till his own time as "not entitled to like credit with those which precede them," at the same time assigning an admittedly valid reason which will afterwards present itself for consideration. Are we not then justified in drawing the legitimate inference that the acknowledged canon of Hebrew Scripture, whether in Egypt or Palestine, was identical, and consisted of the very same books which all Protestants own as constituting the Old Testament Scriptures; while the apocryphal books were never admitted into that canon by that people whom Jehovah had constituted the conservators of His truth and the depositaries of His living oracles? (c) In the third place, the matter is put beyond dispute by the fact that no apocryphal book is quoted directly or authoritatively by our Lord or His apostles, while they have quoted upwards of 600 times from the Old Testament canon, and from every book of it, with the exception of *six*, that is to say, Judges, Ecclesiastes, Canticles, Esther, Ezra, and Nehemiah. (d) Another argument of considerable importance against the canonicity of the Apocrypha, is the language in which the apocryphal books were written. With two exceptions, they were all written in Greek, as we still have them. Now, a genuine Jew would shrink from uniting

Greek books with those written in his own holy Hebrew tongue (קָדוֹשׁ לָשׁוֹן), to which he was so devoutly attached; so that however they may have obtained admission among the Greek books of the Septuagint version, they never gained, nor were likely ever to gain, a position among the canonical Hebrew Scriptures. Farther, taking the lowest reasonable date for the close of the canon of the Old Testament, we shall find that the Greek language was not sufficiently known to the Jews to be employed by them for literary purposes till a much later period. But there will be occasion to return to this. Meantime, it is sufficient to observe that of the two books written in Hebrew, one admits distinctly and decidedly its own inferiority to the books of the canon; while the other, with equal explicitness, disclaims all pretension to canonical authority. (*c*) To all this must be added the fact that among the very copious and numerous quotations from the canonical Scriptures that abound in the early Christian writers, not one is taken from the apocryphal books—Tobit, Judith, Wisdom, Ecclesiasticus (= the Wisdom of the Son of Sirach), Baruch, and First and Second Maccabees. Even Justin Martyr has not a single quotation from them. In fact, the only Father during the first four centuries of Christianity that countenanced the introduction of the six apocryphal books into the canon was Augustine. But eminent as he was in the domain of theology and interpretation, he possessed little skill in historical criticism; while all the other Fathers, distinguished for critical discernment, give in their adhesion to the Hebrew canon. Among these Origen and Jerome may be specially referred to,—the former so pre-eminent for persevering devotion to critical studies as to justly earn the name of *Adamantine*, the latter superior to all the other Fathers in Hebraistic attainments. Even up till the famous Council of Trent the canonicity of the apocryphal books was left an open question. In 1546, at a session of that council, consisting of some 53 members, the decree was issued that all the books and all their parts found in the Latin Vulgate should be acknowledged as sacred and canonical. Since then, judicious and enlightened theologians of the Latin Church, as, for example, Du Pin and Jahn, have tried to evade the stringency of the decision by having recourse to the doubtful expedient of dividing the books of Scripture into proto-canonical and deutero-canonical; the former possessing dogmatic, the latter only ethical authority. But this compromise is inconsistent and equally objectionable with the Tridentine decision. The choice must lie between two courses. The alternative is canonical or uncanonical. The ground of that alternative, as we shall see by and by, is inspiration or non-inspiration—prophetical authorship or non-prophetical. Is any of these documents inspired? then it is fairly and properly entitled to a place in the canon. Is it an uninspired production? then must it without any hesitation be excluded from that rank. There is no halfway house in regard to this matter. There is no middle region. The history of the introduction of the Apocrypha is soon told. It made way gradually. The Septuagint, it must be owned, laid the foundation; Augustine helped to rear the structure; and the Tridentine Council laid the topstone on the work.

Sec. V.—*Principle of the Canon's Formation, and Period of its Close.*

(1) The time when and the *principle* on which the canon was formed must now engage attention for a little. We have somewhat anticipated in refusing the Apocrypha a place in the canon, and in stating the ground of that refusal. Here, however, it is necessary to examine the matter a little more in detail. The question propounded at the outset in regard to the grounds on which Jews and Christians admitted certain books into the canon, and whether or how far they were justified in doing so, now comes up in its proper order. In other words, On what principle did they proceed? It will also become apparent that the time at which the canon was completed, and the principle on which it was formed, are so interlaced that it would be at once inconvenient and inexpedient to dissociate them; for if the canon of the Old Testament was formed on the principle of prophetic authorship, its close would, as a matter of course, have a near relation to or connection with the cessation of the prophetic element. Here it

will be necessary to have in recollection that by a *prophet* the Jews understood not always or necessarily one who foretold future events, but in every case one who spoke, or wrote, or prophesied, *giving religious instruction by divine inspiration.* Hence it is that we find the books which are mainly historical classed with the strictly prophetical, because the former as well as the latter were attributed to prophetic authorship. The Book of Wisdom or Ecclesiasticus, already mentioned, and composed, on the lowest calculation, nearly two centuries, but according to other and better authorities, early in the 3rd century, before the Christian era, affords data from which it may with good reason be inferred that long prior to its composition the canon had been closed, the succession of prophets having concluded and the spirit of inspiration ceased. At the very time Sirachides speaks of translating it out of Hebrew, he admits candidly and clearly its inferiority to any part of the canonical Scriptures. This is not brought out with proper distinctness or made sufficiently apparent in the common rendering of the words as they stand in the Prologue of Sirachides. To this Pusey has properly called attention. The words referred to are the following: οὐ μόνον δὲ ταῦτα ἀλλὰ καὶ αὐτὸς ὁ νόμος καὶ αἱ προφητεῖαι καὶ τὰ λοιπὰ τῶν βιβλίων οὐ μικρὰν ἔχει τὴν διαφορὰν ἐν ἑαυτοῖς λεγόμενα, and the ordinary mode of rendering them is: "Not only so, but the Law itself, and the Prophets, and the remaining books, exhibit no small diversity among themselves as to the mode of expression." Now, let us bear in mind that Sirachides is speaking of bringing out fully and clearly the meaning of an author by means of a translation, and the disadvantage the translation of any book labours under as compared with the same book in its original and native style of expression; and on carefully examining the original Greek, we must conclude that the correct rendering of the words is not that which is given in the common English translation, but the following: ["The same things uttered in Hebrew, and translated into another tongue, have not the same force in them]; and not only these things, but the Law, and the Prophets, and the rest of the books *have no small difference when they are spoken in their own language.*" By "these things" he evidently meant his grandfather's book which he had been translating, and thus he contrasts directly and distinctly — expressly and explicitly, the book he had been employed translating with the books of the three classes of canonical Scripture. The latter he speaks of as possessing primary authority, the former as of only secondary importance; the latter such as, from their divine power, would be most likely to retain to a greater extent their proper force and native vigour in a version; the former, as what might be expected to lose more in a translation, and that manifestly from its mere human original. From this passage, then, we safely infer three things—(1) that the Scriptures of the Old Testament, distributed into the three well-known classes, formed a completed whole; (2) that they had existed in that completed state for long previously, thus carrying up the close of the canon to a very early period, say four centuries, or nearly so, before Christ; and (3) that a broad line of distinction was currently believed to separate and shut them off from ordinary writings even of high excellence and acknowledged worth. All this is confirmed by another statement in the 36th chapter of the book of the Wisdom of the son of Sirach by the author himself, who, after claiming a high degree of authority and putting forth lofty pretensions on behalf of his own work, is nevertheless forward to acknowledge both his great inferiority in merit and posteriority in point of time to the penmen of the canon: " I awaked up last of all ($\check{\epsilon}\sigma\chi\alpha\tau\sigma\varsigma\ \dot{\eta}\gamma\rho\acute{\upsilon}\pi\nu\eta\sigma\alpha$), as one that gathered after the grape-gatherers." He was thus, by his own admission, a great way behind the writers of canonical Scripture; he came *after* them, and was only a *gleaner* after them. Another book written in Hebrew was the first book of Maccabees, which, while uncanonical, is nevertheless historical. The author of this book, as we have intimated, disclaims all pretension to canonical authority; but in that very disclaimer we have an indication of the principle on which and the period at which the canon took shape. He admits the absence of the prophetical spirit, that is, of a divinely-qualified and commissioned teacher; for in the 4th chapter he speaks of a matter of some moment being deferred until some prophet should arise whose decision would be authoritative and binding, saying: "Until a prophet should arrive to decide concerning them" (μέχρι τοῦ παραγενηθῆναι προφήτην τοῦ ἀποκριθῆναι περὶ αὐτῶν). So also in another passage of the same book, at the 14th chapter, the absence of such a one is distinctly acknowledged, and an indefinite expectation entertained of the appearance of a prophet at some coming time. That expectation is expressed in the words: "Till some faithful prophet should arise" (ἕως τοῦ ἀναστῆναι προφήτην πιστόν). Not only so; in the 9th chapter he acknowledges that a considerable time had elapsed since the appearance of the last prophet among the Jewish people. His words are: "And there was great affliction in Israel, such as was not from the time that *no prophet made his appearance among them*" (οὐκ ὤφθη προφήτης ἐν αὐτοῖς).

When we come to Philo, we find him speaking of the Scriptures in the following terms:—*Sacred Scriptures* (ἱερὰς γραφός); *most holy writing* (ἱερώτατον γράμμα); *prophetic word* (προφητικὸν λόγον); *oracle of God* (λόγιον τοῦ Θεοῦ); while his idea of the prophetic inspiration, and consequently divine authority of the books of Scripture, was of the most exalted kind. "Prophets," he says, "are interpreters of God, inasmuch as He employs their organs for the disclosure of whatever He pleases." Again he says: "A prophet exhibits nothing at all which is his own, but is an interpreter, another suggesting whatever he utters." He then proceeds to explain that it is the Divine Spirit that enters in and takes possession of his soul for that purpose.

We have already had occasion to quote that most interesting as well as instructive statement of Josephus when identifying the books of the canon; we must now advert to it not only because it states so very decidedly the principle on which the canon was formed, but also fixes, at least helps us to fix, the period at which it was closed. Having his statement in recollection, we learn therefrom that Josephus regarded the close of the canon as synchronous with the reign of Artaxerxes, upwards of four centuries before Christ. "From Artaxerxes," he says, "down to our own times events have been recorded, but they have not been accounted worthy of the same credit as those before them." He then proceeds to explain the cause; and when doing so, distinctly points out the principle according to which the canon was commenced, completed, and closed; "because," he adds, "the exact succession of prophets existed no longer." Thus he draws the line of demarcation clear and broad between the books really canonical and those that were uncanonical or merely apocryphal. He affirms that the annals of Jewish national history were continued, that the great events continued to be duly chronicled, that historic narrative ceased not to run parallel with and accompany the stream of current events; but makes a wide distinction, for the books of this subsequent period he cuts off at once from all claim to canonicity. He denies their prophetic authorship, and so sets aside any pretension to divine origin that might be made for them by their advocates, assigning, as we have seen, the reason, and a very sufficient and conclusive one.

We might multiply quotations from the apocryphal books, from Philo, and from Josephus, to prove that in the estimation of the Jewish people all the books composing the canon were inspired. For example, in addition to what has been adduced from 1 Maccabees xii. 9: "Having the holy books that are in our hands" (ἔχοντες τὰ βιβλία τὰ ἅγια τὰ ἐν ταῖς χερσὶν ἡμῶν), and from 2 Maccabees vi. 23, which speaks of "the holy and God-founded (θεοκτίστον) legislation," we learn that, in the estimation of the Hebrew people, the canon was not a collection of ordinary writings, but consisted of holy books; while in Wisdom vii. 27 we are assured that the men of God and the prophets obtained the highest wisdom; and in Baruch iv. 1 we are assured that their writings are divine dictations (προστάγματα τοῦ Θεοῦ). Philo and Josephus both repeatedly term the biblical books *divine*. In addition to all this, let it be kept in mind how severely a false prophet or pretender to prophecy was punished according to divine direction: "Then his father and his mother that begat him shall say unto him, Thou shalt not live, for thou speakest lies in the name of the Lord; and his father and his mother shall thrust him through when he prophesieth." In connection with this must be taken the oft-repeated commands of Jehovah to commit to writing for preservation and perpetuation His oracles.

Whether the prophet held a commission to publish God's will orally, or to make it known by committing it to writing in the Scriptures, he was in his official capacity under the guiding energy of the Holy Spirit. It were superfluous to prove that the prophetical men, who were divinely commissioned to write the books of the Old Testament, claimed for themselves the privilege of that commission, as also the possession of the needful power through the aid of the Spirit for its execution. We have sufficient evidence of both in the oft-recurring "Thus saith the Lord," or in such a positive and unmistakable assertion as: "The Spirit of the Lord spake by me, and His word was in my tongue." And yet they must have been well aware of, and fully alive to the peril to which they were exposed, if they arrogated to themselves a prophetic privilege and power which did not truly belong to them. We have already shown from the highest Jewish authorities that the unanimous sentiment of the Hebrew nation willingly conceded the prophetic function or divine inspiration of the penmen of the Old Testament Scriptures; while the references to those Scriptures by our Lord and His apostles in the New Testament place the matter beyond the possibility of a doubt. Had they not been divine in their origin and sacred in their character as well as holy in their influences, they would not be entitled, nor could their admission be justified, to a place among the living oracles. What, then, need we ask, was the principle on which books were received into the canon? It was not the circumstance of their being written in *Hebrew*—a point much insisted on, and deservedly so, in arguing against the Apocrypha. Still, this by itself was not enough to secure such documents a place in the canon; for, had this been a sufficient qualification, Ecclesiasticus and First Maccabees would have claimed admission thereto. And, indeed, nothing can explain the fact of either of these books, but especially of the former, a book written in the holy tongue, written in Palestine, of much intrinsic worth, and of public repute, being left outside the canon, except that the canon had been already closed, and that there was no longer any one possessing adequate authority either to write it or receive it into the canon. Neither was it the *antiquity* of a book that obtained it a place in canonical Scripture, for otherwise books of great antiquity, such as *The Book of Jasher*, extant even in the time of Moses, *The Book of the Wars of the Lord*, *The Book of the Acts of Solomon*, and others, could not have been excluded. And what is more, it was not even *prophetic authorship* per se that entitled to admission; for books of undoubted prophetic authorship, such as *The Book of Nathan the Prophet*, *The Book of Gad the Seer*, and *The Life of Uzziah*, written by the prophet Isaiah, the son of Amoz, were not included. And here we must not omit an important distinction. A book admissible to the honour of a place in the canon must needs have been written by a prophet, but every such book was not thereby *ipso facto* entitled to admission. The principle on which the canon was formed was inspiration; but that one term comprehends two agencies, namely, composition and reception. Not only were those who composed the books of canonical Scripture commissioned and empowered by God for their composition; those who received them into the canon needed in like manner divine authorisation and divine wisdom for the right discharge of their function. In other words, if the writers stood in need of inspiration for their work, the receivers also needed it for their task. Inspiration, extending to both agencies, and indispensable to both, is the necessary inference from our Lord's ratification of Old Testament Scripture. For, when He so fully recognises it as the word of God, and so urgently recommends it for the perusal of His people, He shuts us up to the inevitable conclusion not only that those who penned the Scripture were inspired, that is, divinely instructed for that purpose, but also that those who collected and put together the different parts of the volume were gifted with the requisite discrimination and guided to the proper selection. Had a single mistake been made in the latter respect, our Lord would not have pledged His word or made Himself responsible for the perfect correctness and entire truthfulness, in other words, for the divine excellence, of the whole. One single weak link in a chain, however otherwise strong and long, will break it; one single flaw in the compilation, just as much as in the composition of the canon, would mar the whole. Our Lord's approval is surely a sufficient security for both, and against error in either. The Divine Spirit was as much needed in the selection of the books as in the composition of them; while that influence was no more withheld in the one case than in the other. And here in confirmation of this view a striking statement made by Hofmann in his work on Prophecy and Fulfilment (Weissagung und Erfüllung),—a statement all the more noticeable and deserving of attention because of the directly opposite opinions broached on this subject by so many of his countrymen. The statement is as follows:—" The agency of the Holy Spirit has *brought into existence* the books of the Bible; the agency of the Holy Spirit has also *brought them together*. The former agency alone is not sufficient to account for all that is peculiar to Scripture; under that influence, which we are accustomed to name Inspiration, we must comprehend both agencies."

(2) But we hasten to a more particular consideration of the *time* at which the canon was closed. Here we have somewhat anticipated, as indeed was unavoidable, in citing the testimony of Josephus, who, as we have seen, referred it to the time of a Persian king four centuries before Christ; and in discussing certain statements of Sirachides, made, according to the best authorities, near the beginning of the third century B.C.; and yet a considerable interval had elapsed from the closing of the canon. Various circumstances, which help us to determine the time when the canon was completed, point to the period of Ezra and Nehemiah. The events of Jewish history at that particular period were such as to render a collection of the sacred records of the Hebrew people not only desirable, but in some sort necessary. The days of disaster then at hand were beginning to cast their dark shadow before. The fast-coming calamities of the nation called loudly for some means of alleviation. And what was so likely to sustain under the sorrows of the present as the recorded glories of the past and the no less glorious prospects of the future? What could be better calculated to impart confidence and inspire hope than those sacred documents, in every page of which were emblazoned the great achievements of honoured ancestors and the gracious dealings of God towards them, as also bright

glimpses of a still greater prosperity in time to come? How much was to be found in the annals of their nation to instruct and comfort—to enlighten and enliven! If they went back to the call of Abraham, when their illustrious progenitor left the land of his birth for the better land, and traced their history from its origin till their own day; how many helps to faith and incentives to hope did their collected Scriptures furnish! Surely the divinely inspired records of such a history, when brought together and collected into one, would serve as a mighty leverage to elevate the fallen fortunes, and would help to brighten the clouded prospects of the nation. Nor was this all—far from it. The same collected records contemplated the future, while they chronicled the past. They contained the promises of a good time coming, when their national calamities would be overpast. They gave repeated assurances of the fulfilment of promises already hoary with the lapse of centuries. They foretold the advent of one who would correspond to the description of the desire of all nations; and that the glory of the latter house would be greater than that of the former. Nothing could have been more suitable, and nothing, we think, more seasonable for the people of the Jews, under their peculiar circumstances in the days of Ezra and Nehemiah, than a collection of those heaven-inspired documents, which placed them midway between the historic retrospects of a wondrous past and the prospects of a glorious future.

Further evidence in favour of the same view may be produced from Scripture itself. Ezra's description of himself plainly points to his work in copying, or, at all events, the part he took in collecting the books of the canon. Thus in two successive verses of the 7th chapter of his book he styles himself, "The scribe, even a scribe of the words of the commandments of the Lord and of His statutes to Israel;" and again, "A scribe of the law of the God of heaven." So also, in the 8th chapter of Nehemiah, he is called once and again "Ezra the scribe;" also "Ezra the priest the scribe." The relation of Nehemiah himself to the canon is gathered in part from Scripture and in part from the Apocrypha; or rather his position is indicated in Scripture and confirmed by the apocryphal book of Second Maccabees. In the 10th chapter he refers to "the *law* of God," and again to walking in "God's law;" then in the 9th he speaks of "Thy law," and in the next verse of the "*prophets*," saying, "By Thy Spirit in Thy prophets;" but he does not confine himself to these *two* prominent portions of the canon,—the Law and the Prophets,—he proceeds in the 12th chapter to make mention of the *third* division of Old Testament Scripture, while the nature of that mention leaves us to infer the equally authoritative and equally canonical character of that same third division. After informing us that "both the singers and the porters kept the ward of their God, and the ward of the purification, according to the commandment of David and of Solomon his son," he adds, "For in the days of David and Asaph of old there were chief of the singers, and *songs of praise and thanksgiving* unto God." Here we perceive a clear indication of the third part, as elsewhere in the same Book of Nehemiah of the first and second parts, of which the canon was composed. But the connection of Nehemiah with the canon is asserted by the author of Second Maccabees, who in the 2nd chapter of that book contrasts Jeremiah and Nehemiah, and draws a parallel between the services which they had respectively rendered to the sacred writings. The former, he alleges, had preserved the law, the latter had performed a similar good office to the other books of Scripture, combining them into one sacred collection. The words in the original are:—ὡς καταβαλλόμενος βιβλιοθήκην ἐπισυνήγαγε τὰ περὶ τῶν βασιλέων καὶ προφητῶν, καὶ τὰ τοῦ Δαυὶδ, καὶ ἐπιστολὰς βασιλέων περὶ ἀναθημάτων, *how when founding a library he gathered together the acts of the kings and the prophets, and the writings of David, and the letters of the kings concerning holy offerings.* Here we have the prophets in combination with the historical books forming together one portion of the canon, and the Hagiographa named from the two leading portions, and the two portions which were of special interest in Nehemiah's day, that is to say, the Psalms on account of their liturgical use, and the letters of heathen kings in reference to the consecration of offerings—the manifestations of favour so acceptable to the Jews of Alexandria and Egypt in general. Such was the time assigned by the Alexandrian Jews for the closing of the canon, and such the share allotted to Nehemiah in that work.

In summing up the argument for the time, we have indications tolerably distinct and definite in Scripture itself. Then from the oldest book we possess, written early in the period that succeeded, we mean the book of Ecclesiasticus, we learn that the son of Sirach not merely cites and refers to separate books of the canon, but views it as a completed whole, the translator in his prologue quoting the three well defined departments of the canon, and in particular the last of them, by the expressions: "The other patristic books," and "The rest of the books." It is also worthy of particular attention, that certain reverential allusions to the canon as a completed collection of sacred documents occur for the first time in the period subsequent to Ezra and Nehemiah, though frequently from that time forward. As a single example of many such, we may refer to 1 Maccabees xii. 5: "Albeit we need none of these things, for that we have the holy books of Scripture in our hands to comfort us." Passing on to Josephus, we find his testimony much later, but it compensates for lateness by distinctness. We have already quoted it in full, and instead of repeating it, would only remind the reader of it. A most learned and distinguished writer on the Book of Daniel makes the following comment on that statement of Josephus: "The date at which the Jews, in the time of Josephus, believed the canon of their Scripture to have been closed, was about four centuries before the birth of our Lord. Josephus probably fixed on the reign of Artaxerxes as being the period of Nehemiah's great work of restoration, although the actual closing of the canon probably took place during the second visit to his country, the probable date of the prophet Malachi, under the son and successor of Artaxerxes, Darius Nothus. The period which lay between was a long one; the time of Antiochus Epiphanes lay some 250 years nearer. Yet it was a period of the most active human intelligence. It reached back into no ages really or hypothetically 'dark.' Socrates was a contemporary of Malachi; the source of the two philosophies, which have influenced the world, was of the same date as the last of the Hebrew prophets. Better might we suppose the Greeks ignorant as to the date of *their* philosophers, than imagine the Jews, to whom the word of God was dearer than life, ignorant as to the date of *their* prophets. The term, moreover, was measured by something besides years. Josephus speaks of it as a period of mental activity in Judæa. 'From that time down to our own,' he says, 'events were recorded; but they have not been accounted worthy of the same credit as those before them.' This describes a portion of the so-called deutero-canonical books of the Old Testament; books held in estimation among the Jews as well as by Christians, but not received by the Jews into their canon, because 'Israel had no more prophets, who had authority to receive them.'"

The conclusions thus arrived at are confirmed in no inconsiderable degree by Jewish *tradition* as preserved to us in the Talmud. In one of the oldest portions of that wonderful work, called *Pirke Avoth*, or Sayings of the Fathers, and at the very commencement, the following statement occurs: "Moses received the Law at Sinai; he transmitted it to Joshua; Joshua to the Elders; the Elders to the Prophets; the Prophets to the men of the Great Synagogue." That synagogue was a sort of collegiate institution, or, perhaps, literary association, formed for the express purpose of faithfully preserving the religion of their fathers. It was composed of 120 Elders in the days of Ezra, and, according to Surenhusius, reckoned among its members such men as Zerubbabel and Seraiah, with the prophets Haggai, Zechariah, and Malachi. But a more direct and detailed tradition on the same subject is contained in the Babylonian Gemara, where the tract Baba Bathra communicates some interesting Rabbinical traditions in reference to the formation of the canon. Here, however, it must be observed in passing, that there are two Talmuds— the Jerusalem and Babylonian. The text called Mischna, *i.e.* repetition, consisting in traditions about the Law, is the same in both; but their Gemara, *i.e.* completion, or commentary thereon, is different. Again, in the Babylonian Gemara, which is the later but larger and more important of the two, there are certain chapters called gates—the first gate, the middle gate, and the latter gate, which is Baba Bathra, and to which the reference here is made. In regard, then, to the arrangement of the canon, it is stated in this tract that "the wise men say: All is one, and each part again stands for itself." Farther on it adds: "And they have left to us הביאו לפנינו, literally, *brought before us,* the Law, the Prophets, and the Hagiographa *combined into one whole.* But who wrote them? Moses wrote his book and the section of Balaam and Job; Joshua wrote his book and eight verses in the Law. Samuel wrote his book, Judges, and Ruth. David wrote the Book of Psalms, with the assistance of ten elders, by the aid of Adam the first man, of Melchizedek, of Abraham, of Moses, of Heman, of Jeduthun, of Asaph, and of the three sons of Korah. Jeremiah wrote his own book and the Book of Kings and Lamentations. Hezekiah and his assistants wrote Jamshak, the symbol of Isaiah, Proverbs (Meshalim), Canticles (Shir Hashirim), and Koheleth. The men of the Great Synagogue wrote Kandag, the memorial word for Ezekiel and the twelve, Daniel, and the roll of Esther. Ezra wrote his own book, and continued the genealogy of Chronicles down to his own time." This tradition requires a few words of comment. (*a*) By "each part standing for itself" is meant a complete whole. (*b*) The word כתב has been proved by Hävernick to mean not *wrote,* as usual; or *wrote out,* that is, *copied* (as some think); but *wrote in,* that is, *inserted, edited,* from the use of the same word in the Targum on Prov. xxv. 1, to represent עתק in the sense of *collect;* while the context before and after confirms this meaning, for it refers to *left us* (or, *brought before us*) in regard to the constitution of the canon, and it is only in the sense of *editing or collecting into the canon* that it can apply to Hezekiah's work in relation to Isaiah and the writings of Solomon. (*c*) This Talmudic passage, notwithstanding its enigmatical reference to Adam, Melchizedek, and Abraham, and other seeming improbabilities, contains undoubtedly a very ancient Jewish tradition about the completion of the canon. Though committed to writing in the 5th century, it is the echo of a remote record handed down by a people distinguished even among Orientals for their tenacity to such tradition. (*d*) According to this tradition, the collecting of the books of the canon commenced with Moses, and was concluded in the time of Ezra and Nehemiah by the efforts of these and other eminent men associated with them, so that the closing of the canon and the editing of its latest writings were, according to the tradition, accomplished by the Great Synagogue, by Ezra and Nehemiah. Here it may be added, with reference to Ezra writing the genealogies of Chronicles, that the Talmudists ascribe the writing of Chronicles to Ezra, and the completion of the genealogies to Nehemiah; while Rashi, the eminent Jewish commentator, says that Ezra wrote the genealogies by means of Haggai, Zechariah, and Malachi. (c) In reference to the importance attachable to such tradition, Vitringa says: "Traditionum talmudicarum et inter eas exoticarum *tanta apud me est auctoritas*, quantum pondus est rationis qua fulciuntur; quæ si ab ipsis detur vel aliunde appareat probabilis nulla est spernendi causa." Besides, we rather appeal to the antiquity and substantial truth of the tradition, than pledge ourselves to the correctness of it in its entirety. We may therefore safely concur in opinion with Hävernick, when he affirms it as the result of his inquiry that "the Jewish tradition, viewed in its fundamental truth, is in pleasing harmony with historical evidence, viz. that the collection of the sacred writings was completed by Ezra in company with other eminent men of his time." Similar was the belief of the early Christian Church about the part which Ezra performed in helping to complete the canon. That belief is expressed by Irenæus in the following manner: "God *inspired* Ezra the priest to arrange (ἀνατάξασθαι) all the words of the Prophets that preceded him, and to restore to the people the legislation of Moses." Here two of the points we have insisted on are plainly embodied: (1) The inspiration necessary to guide the collectors as well as the composers of the books of canonical Scripture; and (2) that Ezra in his day prepared the way at least for laying the topstone on the sacred edifice.

CHAPTER XIII.

SUMMARY OF THE DEUTERONOMIC DISCUSSION.

THE controversy about the date and authorship of the Book of Deuteronomy has, we need scarcely remark, drawn to it of late a large amount of attention and interest. In opposition to the traditional belief that Moses is the author of Deuteronomy (except, of course, the account of his death and burial) as well as of the preceding books of the Pentateuch, it is alleged by some modern critics that at least the legislative portion of the book belongs to a period several centuries later than the time of Moses, and must consequently be referred to other authorship. In favour of this view, it is urged that in the progressive development or necessarily varying circumstances of Hebrew national life, new laws were required; that Prophets of the Lord were authorised to incorporate those needed laws with the original Mosaic code; that, proceeding on the same lines, and imbued with the spirit of Moses' legislation, these supplementary enactments were a legitimate addition, sharing the same respect and entitled to equal observance with the original laws. This course of procedure, it is further affirmed, involved no deception, but was a form of literary composition peculiar to and practised by writers in that age and country. In this way the date of Deuteronomy, or a large portion of it, is brought down to the prophetic period in the 8th and 7th centuries B.C. Here, again, certain alleged difficulties or supposed discrepancies are thought to necessitate this theory. We shall advert to some of the most prominent of these, and consider whether those difficulties are as formidable as alleged, or those discrepancies as great as supposed; or whether the former may not be eliminated and the latter reconciled in accordance with the traditional belief about the authorship of the book, and without resorting to a method so violent in its nature, and having so much the appearance of fraud and literary imposture.

The analysis of this book of Scripture is easy. It falls naturally into three parts, each of them containing an address by Moses to the people in the fortieth year of the Exodus. The first of these addresses occupies the first four chapters of the book; the second extends from the 5th to the 26th; and the third is contained in the 27th and on to the 20th verse of the 30th. Then follow the appointment of his successor in the 31st chapter; his Song in the 32d; his Benediction in the 33d; and his death and burial in the last chapter, which is the 34th. One generation, composed of all from twenty years of age and upwards at the time of the Exodus, had passed away; another generation had been born and had grown up in the wilderness—these had not witnessed the mighty acts of the Lord at the giving of the Law; there were those, besides, who had been under twenty years of age at the time of the departure out of the land of bondage, and who survived those weary forty years of wandering—all, in fact, between forty-five and fifty-nine years of age, who still remained on the land of the living, may be regarded as having a recollection more or less distinct of the passage of the Red Sea and the promulgation of the Law at Horeb. When we reflect on the persons addressed, the many things that had happened in those years, the changes that had taken place, their present circumstances, and especially the new condition on which they were just about to enter, as they passed from their nomadic life in the desert to settled life in the land of promise, we shall more clearly comprehend the necessity that existed for rehearsing much of their past history, and reminding them of all the way in which God had led them, and the tokens of His favour they had received by the way, as also for revising previous enactments—augmenting some, amending some, and modifying others. The first part is mainly introductory, and recalls to mind God's goodness in their deliverance, His guidance of them in their journeyings, their want of gratitude as evinced by frequent murmurings and rebellions, with warnings from the past and exhortations for the future. Of the second address seven chapters are employed in the exposition and enforcement of the moral law; five chapters deal for the most part prospectively with the future religious life of the nation; while ten more are taken up with personal rights, legal enactments, and sundry regulations pertaining to their civil polity. The style of the whole is rhetorical and hortatory; life and death, good and evil, blessing and cursing, are set before the people with solemn pathos and deep impressiveness. The past is graphically pictured, and the future vividly portrayed. Some of the remarkable predictions in the closing chapters of the third part have been fulfilled, others are being fulfilled, and more await fulfilment. The theory of divided authorship, and consequently later date, is largely based on passages contained in the second address.

1. We shall advert to the alleged difference between Deuteronomy and Leviticus with respect to priests and Levites, which has been so much mooted, and in which so much is supposed to be involved. In that Bible article of the *Encyclopædia Britannica* that has become so famous, it is asserted that "the Levitical laws give a graduated hierarchy of priests and Levites; Deuteronomy regards all Levites as possible priests." In reference to this, it may be observed that a similar view was maintained long ago by De Wette and others. They were of opinion that the sharp distinction between priests and Levites was obscured or entirely obliterated in Deuteronomy; and that to the latter that book assigns a competency for the superior duties of the priesthood, and consequently greater consideration. It is undeniable that some texts in Deuteronomy *seem* to favour this view; but a careful examination of them will, we are persuaded, lead to the opposite conclusion. (*a*) One of the passages relied on as confounding the distinction is Deut. xviii. 1: "The priests the Levites, לַכֹּהֲנִים הַלְוִיִּם, (and) all the tribe of Levi, shall have no part nor inheritance with Israel." This designation does not necessarily imply that all Levites were actual priests, or even possible priests; it implies no more than that all priests were from among the sons of Levi. If it be proper to insert the copula, as is done in our version, there is an obvious distinction made between the Levites who were priests and the other members of the tribe of Levi, that is, the rest of the Levites

who were not priests. In favour of the insertion we might quote the Syriac, which inserts the conjunction *vau* between the words "priest and Levite," reading: "For the priest and the Levite there shall be no part," and the Vulgate: "Non habebunt sacerdotes et Levitæ, et omnes qui de eadem tribu sunt, partem." So, among Jewish commentators, Ibn Ezra distinguishes the priests and Levites in this verse; for after commenting somewhat fancifully on the priest's portion, to the effect that he received the shoulder as a recompense for slaying the victim, the cheeks for the benediction, and the maw for the examination of the knife, he proceeds to account for the separate mention of the Levites, saying, "For they also teach the law in the gates." But there is no necessity for insisting on this. We may accept the rendering: "The priests the Levites, the whole tribe of Levi;" and the meaning can scarcely be different; for, if all Levites were priests, the priests the Levites would comprehend the entire tribe of Levi, and the addition of "the whole tribe of Levi" would be nothing more or better than a meaningless tautology. If all Levites were on a par,—if Levites and priests were identical,—why repeat "the whole tribe of Levi"? But if a distinction is implied, if two classes belonging to the tribe be meant,—the one directly specified, the other understood by implication,—then it is easy to perceive why the writer employs an additional term to comprehend both. Thus we have the two constituent parts of which the whole is composed, viz. the priests of the tribe of Levi and the non-priestly Levites, and the word "all" to emphasise the totality of the tribe and prevent the idea of any being excluded. Besides, (*b*) in this very chapter the distinction of priest and Levite is clearly recognised, and their respective portions specified; for in the 3d and 4th verses we have a statement of the priest's due from the people: "They shall give unto the priest the shoulder, and the two cheeks, and the maw. The first-fruit also of thy corn, of thy wine, and of thine oil, and the first of the fleece of thy sheep, shalt thou give him." Then in the 8th verse there is a separate and distinct reference to the remuneration of the Levite; that remuneration is assumed as well known, and the reference to it is occasioned by an arrangement in favour of a Levite, who, leaving some city where he had sojourned, and coming to the sanctuary, engaged in its service. This new-comer, if he heartily desired it, was not only permitted to officiate, but was placed at once on an equal footing, in point of provision, with the rest of his Levitical brethren; while at the same time he did not forfeit whatever might accrue to him from the sale of his patrimony in the Levitical town or city he had left. The revenues of the sanctuary, from which the maintenance of the Levites was derived, are presumed to have been regulated by existing laws previously made and well known, so that, there being no need of rehearsing them, the only point necessary to make plain, was the position of perfect equality with his brethren so equitably conceded to the stranger. "Then he shall minister in the name of the Lord his God, as all his brethren the Levites do, which stand there before the Lord. They shall have like portions to eat (lit. portion like portion they shall eat), beside that which cometh of the sale of his patrimony (lit. beside his sales by the fathers)." Thus his ministerial rights and his civil rights were both secured to the Levite on his change of residence.

But passing to another chapter of this same section of the Book of Deuteronomy, we find an arrangement about priest and Levite of a somewhat similar sort, which, in our opinion, positively proves the writer's perfect acquaintance with and plain recognition of the distinction between them. (c) In chapter xxvi. there is an account of a ceremony connected with the first-fruits and the year of tithing. The presentation of the former was in a basket handed to the priest. "The priest," it is written, "shall take the basket out of thine hand, and set it down before the altar of the Lord thy God." The delivery of the tithes of the latter was to the Levite, as it is written: "When thou hast made an end of tithing all the tithes of thine increase the third year, which is the year of tithing, and hast given it unto the Levite, the stranger, the fatherless, and the widow." Here a difference is made between the priest and the Levite, and it is very appropriate—a distinction is drawn, and it is very significant. The special object served by this presentation of first-fruits (besides a consecration of the whole) was a practical confession by the Israelite of his indebtedness to God for the land of his possession, with perhaps a symbolic intimation of his duty to support the priest who ministered for him before God. This Deuteronomic, or second tithe, as some call it, is not necessarily identical with nor supplementary of the tithes enjoined in the 18th chapter of Numbers. As the Levites were substituted for the first-born, so their interest in the land was commuted for the tithes; the tithes were in lieu of landed property such as was held by the other tribes, and as a remuneration for their services at the sanctuary. The tithe here specified as delivered to or designed for the Levite was, according to Keil and Delitzsch, " appropriated everywhere throughout the land to festal meals." But while it expressed their satisfaction in God's service, it also hinted at least the source of their support. The revenues of the priests consisted largely of first-fruits and certain portions of the sacrifices; so those of the Levites consisted mainly of tithes (of which, however, they themselves paid a tithe to the priests) and some altar gifts. The suitability, then, of the arrangement by which, at the presentation of the basket of first-fruits, it was handed to the priest, whose support in part was derived from first-fruits; and according ing to which, at the delivery of the tithe, it was consigned to the Levite, whose maintenance depended mainly on tithes, and for whose comfort, as also for that of certain destitute members of the community, this special tithe was set apart, is at once apparent. By this difference of the gifts themselves, by the difference in the manner of their presentation, and by the difference of the persons who were constituted the recipients, a distinction of office or of order is suggested by the writer of Deuteronomy himself as the groundwork which underlies the whole. But (d) another circumstance, and one closely allied to this, which shows the writer's familiarity with the fact of this distinction, is his repeated commendation of the Levite to the consideration of the people, and his frequent call for sympathy on his behalf; while for the priest, on the contrary, no place is found in such appeals. Again and again the practical sympathy of the people is enlisted in favour of the Levite; thus, in Deuteronomy, chap. xii. 19, we read: " Take heed to thyself that thou forsake not the Levite as long as thou livest upon the earth;" again, chap. xiv. 27: "And the Levite that is within thy gates; thou shalt not forsake him; for he hath no part nor inheritance with thee;" once more in chap. xxvi. 11, it is written: "Thou shalt rejoice in every good thing which the Lord thy God hath given unto thee, and unto thine house, thou, and the Levite, and the stranger that is among you." But among these many appeals almost to commiseration, at least to consideration, for the Levite, there is no reference to or mention of the priest; why is this? Obviously because the priest's source of income was different, the provision made for him more liberal, and better secured. But this very difference of remuneration implies a difference of office, so that the writer of Deuteronomy, by these very appeals in the one case and not in the other, implying a difference in means and amount of support, proves his knowledge of the difference of the office held, and of the duties discharged respectively by these two different orders of ecclesiastical functionaries.

Another (*e*) argument employed by those who hold that the priestly office and the Levitical office are confounded in Deuteronomy, is drawn from the 18th chapter and 7th verse of that book, as compared with the 5th verse of the same chapter, where it is alleged the vocation of the Levites has the same terms applied to it as the service of the priests elsewhere. There is, we readily admit, one expression identical in the verses named and applied to the office of the priest in the 5th verse, and to the calling of the Levite in the 7th verse; that expression is "to minister in the name of the Lord" (לְשָׁרֵת בְּשֵׁם יְהוָה). But while this expression designates the office of both in common as ministering by the divine appointment and authority, as also for the praise and glory of the divine name, and above all for the exhibition of the attributes of the divine nature which the divine name implies; still there appears to be a distinction involved in the employment of other and different terms used in relation to the respective offices. In relation to that of Levite in the 7th verse, after the expression "he shall minister in the name of the Lord his God," it is added, "as all his brethren the Levites (do), which stand there before the Lord," that is, to minister before the Lord. Now the words שֵׁרֵת אֶת־יְהוָה are the proper and specific designation of priestly service, as appears from chap. xvii. 12: "Unto the priest that standeth to minister there before the Lord" (אֶל־הַכֹּהֵן הָעֹמֵד לְשָׁרֶת שָׁם אֶת־יְהוָה); and xxi. 5: "And the priests the sons of Levi shall come near; for them the Lord thy God hath chosen to minister unto Him" (לְשָׁרְתוֹ); and other Scriptures;—in other words, the construction of the verb when so applied is usually with the accusative; while שֵׁרֵת לִפְנֵי יְהוָה is an expression of a more general kind and of wider application, sometimes referring to prophetical and sometimes to priestly service: this latter expression, or part of it, לִפְנֵי יְהוָה, is that which occurs in the added clause of the 7th verse in relation to the service of the Levite. While both expressions relate to the service of God, one of them is more restricted, whether it is that it denotes a greater nearness of approach to the divine majesty and a closer relationship for the time or not, we cannot say; but whatever be the ground of distinction, the freer use of the other comports with the difference of application just indicated. This distinction, insisted on by Keil and Hävernick, is denied by Oehler and others, who notwithstanding advocate the distinction of priest and Levite as acknowledged in Deuteronomy, as well as in the middle books of the Pentateuch. Oehler's statement on this latter point is so very clear, concise, and, we believe, correct, that, instead of merely referring to it, we think it best to subjoin it, especially as it is contained in a few short sentences. "Emphatically as it is inculcated on the Levites," he says, "that the dedication of their tribe does not involve the priesthood proper, yet their relative share in the priestly mediatorship, in contrast to the other tribes, is imprinted very clearly in the regulations of encampment,—in the Levites having to encamp with the priests close round the sanctuary, 'that wrath come not on the congregation of the children of Israel.' What has been said explains further the difference which exists in reference to the Levites between the legislation in the middle books of the Pentateuch and Deuteronomy—that, namely, the former gives special emphasis to the difference between the priests and Levites, while Deuteronomy, on the contrary, takes priests and Levites together as a holy estate in contrast to the people. The two views do not contradict, but supplement each other mutually. That Deuteronomy, as has often been said, does not at all acknowledge the difference between the Levites who were priests and those who were not, is decidedly wrong; for in Deuteronomy, where simply לֵוִי or לְוִיִּם stands, it is just the common Levites who are meant; see especially xviii. 6–8 compared with verses 3–5. It is correct, however, that both are treated as essentially a single whole, as is manifest even from the fact that while the middle books of the Pentateuch are wont to denote the priests as sons of Aaron; in Deuteronomy, on the contrary, the Levitical character of the priesthood is made prominent by the priests being called 'sons of Levi,' or 'Levitical priests' (הַכֹּהֲנִים הַלְוִיִּם)." Still it may be fairly asked how or why is it that in the middle books of the Pentateuch the priests are called "sons of Aaron;" while in Deuteronomy that designation gives place to "the priests the Levites," or Levitical priests? A good reason can be rendered for this change of title. During Aaron's lifetime the priesthood was confined to himself and his sons—restricted, in fact, to a single family. During that time the priests were literally sons of Aaron. Subsequently their descendants succeeded to that office; and as the priests were no longer the sons of Aaron in any proper sense, but formed a tolerably numerous spiritual class, they are named no longer after the nearer, but after the more remote progenitor who was head of the tribe. But even in these middle books the priests have the name Levites applied to them. This, we are aware, has been controverted, but it is confirmed nevertheless by the following statements of Scripture:—"Is not Aaron the Levite thy brother?" Ex. iv. 14; "And Eleazar, Aaron's son, took to him one of the daughters of Putiel to wife; and she bare him Phinehas: these are the heads of the fathers of the Levites according to their families. These are that Aaron and Moses to whom the Lord said, Bring out the children of Israel," Ex. vi. 25, 26; "Then Moses stood in the gate of the camp, and said, Who is on the Lord's side? Let him come unto me. And all the sons of Levi (including, of course, the priests) gathered themselves together unto him;" again, "And the children of Levi (necessarily inclusive of the priests) did according to the word of Moses," Ex. xxxii. 26, 28. The children of Israel were commanded to give to the Levites forty-eight cities in all; of these forty-eight cities thirteen were set apart for the priests, as we know from 1 Chron. vii. 62. But in Num. xxxv. 7 we read: "So all the cities which ye shall give to the Levites shall be forty and eight cities." Thus the thirteen cities specially reserved for the priests, as well as the remaining thirty-five cities, are said to be given—all of them—to the Levites; clearly, then, the term Levites is applied to the priests as well as other members of the tribe in this passage of Numbers, one of the so-called middle books of the Pentateuch. Not only so; of the cities of refuge Hebron was one, and it was given to Aaron's sons, as we read in 1 Chron. vii. 57: "And to the sons of Aaron they gave the cities of Judah, namely, Hebron, the city of refuge," etc. But again, in Num. xxxv. 6, we read: "And among the cities which ye shall give unto the Levites there shall be six cities for refuge;" a city given as we know to the sons of Aaron is here affirmed to have been given to the Levites; consequently, the name Levites is thus applied to the priests the sons of Aaron. In like manner, in Num. xxvi. 57-60, we read: "And these are they that were numbered of the Levites after their families ... of Kohath, the family of the Kohathites. ... And Kohath begat Amram ... and she (Jochebed) bare unto Amram Aaron. ... And unto Aaron was born Nadab, and Abihu, Eleazar, and Ithamar," and so the name of Levites is here also extended to the priests the sons of Aaron.

We are justified, then, in concluding (*a*) that by "the priests the Levites" we are to understand the priests from among the sons of Levi. With this the comment both of Rashi and Ibn Ezra agrees; the former says: הכהנים שיצאו משבט לוי, *the priests that issued from the tribe of Levi;* the other has: כי יש כהני' שאינם מיחס לוי, *that there are priests who are not of the family of Levi;* (*b*) that by the term "Levites" by itself alone, are meant the other ordinary and non-priestly members of the tribe; and (*c*) that in the middle Pentateuchal books, as well as in Deuteronomy, the priests have the name

x

of Levites occasionally applied to them. "The most plausible passage for confounding priests and Levites," says Keil in his Introduction, "is chap. x. 8." It appears to us, on the contrary, that this verse, with a clause of the 6th verse which precedes, presents, or at least implies, that very "graduated hierarchy," the absence of which from Deuteronomy has been urged against the Mosaic authorship of the book. The portion of verse 6 to which we refer, together with verse 8, reads as follows:—"There Aaron died, and there he was buried; and Eleazar his son ministered in the priest's office in his stead. . . . At that time the Lord separated the tribe of Levi, to bear the ark of the covenant of the Lord, to stand before the Lord to minister unto Him, and to bless in His name, unto this day." Here we have first the priestly office, or rather the high-priesthood of Aaron, and of his son and successor Eleazar, as a distinct thing; then we have the whole tribe to which this priestly family belonged separated for the discharge of certain duties—some to bear the ark of the covenant of the Lord, others to stand before the Lord to minister unto Him, and to bless in His name. Though on special and solemn occasions the priests bore the ark, yet in the wilderness the Kohathites, a non-priestly section of the tribe, were told off for this business, as we learn from Num. iv. 4, 5, 15: "This shall be the service of the sons of Kohath in the tabernacle of the congregation, about the most holy things: And when the camp setteth forward, Aaron shall come, and his sons, and they shall take down the covering vail, and cover the ark of testimony with it. . . . And when Aaron and his sons have made an end of covering the sanctuary, and all the vessels of the sanctuary, as the camp is to set forward; after that, the sons of Kohath will come to bear it: but they shall not touch any holy thing, lest they die. These things are the burden of the sons of Kohath in the tabernacle of the congregation." But while it was incumbent on a non-priestly portion of the Levites "to bear the ark of the covenant of the Lord," it was the exclusive duty of the priests "to stand before the Lord to minister unto Him, and to bless in His name." Here, then, is a graduated hierarchy —high priest, priest, and Levite, or rather, high priest, Levite, and priest (the Levite intermediate, as his office required him to minister to both). But it may reasonably be asked, What ground is there for this division of duties among the members of the tribe, or for this distribution of its members according to those duties? Our answer is as follows:—(*a*) God is a God of order, not of confusion; and that all the members of a tribe numbering so many thousands should be competent to the selfsame duties, and employed therein, would seem to tend directly to disorder, and could not conduce to any orderly discharge of the required duties. (*b*) Immediately after the mention of the separation of the tribe of Levi in chap. x. 8, reference is made to their support in these words: "Wherefore Levi hath no part nor inheritance with his brethren;" in chap. xviii. we have a similar, virtually the same, assertion in regard to them—they "shall have no part nor inheritance with Israel;" and then follows a statement (already glanced at) specifying as separate and distinct the priest's due on the one hand, and the Levite's portion on the other; so that, as it appears to us, while the distinction of office or service, in connection with support, is pointed out with tolerable plainness in the 18th chapter, a similar distinction of service is assumed in the 10th chapter as a matter of common notoriety. (*c*) Our understanding of chap. x. 8 is confirmed by the commentary of Rashi on that verse; thus לש׳ א׳ הלוים, to bear the ark—*the Levites;* לש׳ ב׳ הכהנים והוא נשיאות כפים ל׳ ול׳, to stand to minister unto Him, and to bless in His name—*the priests, and this is the lifting up of the hands.* The comment of Ibn Ezra makes a like distribution, but is somewhat fuller; its literal rendering is as follows:—*At the time of the worship of the calf the Lord separated the tribe of Levi to bear the ark to stand before the Lord;* to minister unto Him—*the sons of Levi with the sons of Aaron* (*i.e.* the priests assisted by the Levites); and to bless in His name—*for Eleazar lifted up his hands.* (*d*) We need not be in the least surprised if the line of distinction be not so sharply drawn in this book between the different orders in the tribe of Levi; for (*a*) the writer's object was not to give prominence to distinctions among the members of the tribe, but to place the tribe itself in its proper relative position with regard to the other tribes, to claim for it the prerogatives to which it had a right, to state plainly what was due to the tribe as such, and to enforce the consideration and treatment to which its members were entitled; (β) the style of the book is hortatory, rhetorical, and eminently popular—a sort of style which refuses to embarrass itself with and degenerate into wearisomeness by minute distinctions and details; (γ) such distinctions as those referred to, particularly that between priests and Levites, did not come within the writer's scope, and were not needed, as they could not be unknown to those who were addressed. The condign punishment with which Korah and his company were visited must have impressed the distinction in question with solemn awfulness on the heart of every Israelite. When Korah and his adherents, not satisfied with the honour of service in the courts of the tabernacle, aspired to the dignity of ministering at the altar, their destruction made the distinction between priestly and non-priestly Levite for ever memorable.

But surprise has been expressed that, when in Deut. xi. 6 the punishment of Dathan and Abiram is adduced as a warning, there is no mention made of the sin or punishment of Korah and his company; while the omission is urged as telling against the distinction for which we plead. Thus it is said: "His example could not serve as a warning in Deuteronomy, which concedes altar privileges to any Levite." No doubt Korah and his company made common cause with Dathan and Abiram and their abettors; they were all alike malcontents and fellow-rebels. But the cause of the rebellion in the one case was very different from that which operated in the other. Dathan and Abiram rebelled against the civil jurisdiction and authority of Moses; Korah and his company aspired to the sacred office of the priesthood hitherto vested in Aaron and his sons. Each party had a colourable pretence to allege in support of its claim. Dathan and Abiram were the sons of Eliab, the son of Reuben, Jacob's first-born; they had never forgotten nor lost sight of the rights of primogeniture though forfeited by the sin of their forefather. Those rights which Reuben forfeited were threefold, viz. that of pre-eminence transferred thenceforth to Judah; the double portion given to Joseph, so that the one tribe became two, and that of Joseph was represented by Ephraim and Manasseh; the priesthood bestowed on Levi. Accordingly, these chiefs of the house of Reuben opposed the civil power of Moses, and refused to acknowledge his right to rule; hence, when he summoned them to his presence they refused obedience, and declined to come, saying: "We will not come up: Is it a small thing that thou hast brought us up out of a land that floweth with milk and honey, to kill us in the wilderness, except thou make thyself altogether a prince over us?" Consequently when, in the 11th chapter of Deuteronomy, obedience is enjoined, and the observance of the divine charge, statutes, judgments, and commandments is inculcated, and the chastisements incurred by disobedience pointed to as warnings, the affair of Dathan and Abiram was just a case in point. They had resisted the divine administration of which Moses was merely the instrument; they had rebelled at once against the legislative power of the Most High and the executive authority of man, for God was their lawgiver and Moses the administrator. But Korah's pretensions were of a quite different kind, though here also they were encouraged by his rank. He was one of the chiefs of the family of Kohath, being the son of Izhar, the son of Kohath, the son of Levi; and we have already had occasion to remark on the position and privileges of the Kohathites who were specially employed to carry the ark and holy of holies, though strictly enjoined not to look into them; and thus among the Levites they stood next in dignity to Aaron and his sons, and next to them ranked highest in the sacredness of the service which they rendered and of the functions they had to discharge. Thus elevated by the sacredness of their function in being employed about the ark and holy place, as also by near kinship to Aaron, he laid claim to the priestly office on behalf of all his tribe, as we may rightly infer from Moses' remonstrance, as contained in the following words: "And Moses said unto Korah, Hear, I pray you, ye sons of Levi: Seemeth it but a small thing unto you, that the God of Israel hath separated you from the congregation of Israel, to bring you near to Himself to do the service of the tabernacle of the Lord, and to stand before the congregation to minister unto them? And He hath brought thee near to Him, and all thy brethren the sons of Levi with thee: and seek ye the priesthood also? For which cause both thou and all thy company are gathered together against the Lord: and what is Aaron that ye murmur against him?" It is plain then, we think, that while Dathan and Abiram constituted themselves the champions of popular rights, professing a desire for elevating the whole congregation of Israel, and possessing, probably, as much disinterestedness as such leaders are often found to have, Korah claimed the priesthood for himself and tribesmen. Consequently, in Deut. xi., where there is no special reference to the priesthood, or to Levitical service, or to any differences whatever among the members of a single tribe, or to any single tribe as such, but where God deals with all Israel,—the whole congregation, without respect to tribe, or rank, or office,— urging all to loyal obedience, and warning all against the sin and danger of disobedience, the sad story of Korah's ambition would have been as much out of place as that of Dathan and Abiram's disaffection was in place in the passage. Still that history of fearfully blasted ambition, when Korah and his men (probably his servants or others who supported his cause—not his sons who survived) miserably perished, and "the 250 princes of the assembly, famous in the congregation, men of renown," were consumed by fire from the Lord, drew the line of demarcation with sufficient sharpness to make the distinction remembered ever after in all the succeeding centuries of Hebrew history, and to supersede entirely such repeated reference to the distinction as some would appear to desiderate. But (c) reverting to the difficulty involved, as is thought, in Deut. x. 8, and referring to the supposed want of distinction between priest and Levite, and the consequent competency of the latter to discharge all the duties pertaining to both, we shall be excused for quoting the following sensible observations from Keil, who says: "If so" (*i.e.* if all Levites were competent to all those functions referred to), "it only remains to say that this is affirmed, according to the technical language of the old logicians, in a divided and not in a compounded sense; not that each individual Levite was separated to do all these things, but that all who were separated to do them were Levites." Then, after denying that Deuteronomy slurred the distinction between the two orders in the sense hostile to the belief of the Mosaic authorship, he goes on to say that " the character of the book did not call for the discrimination of the two orders. This will surprise no one who considers how much they were alike; so that the Levites were the companions and assistants of the priests, competent to do everything at their bidding which they could do, except ministering at the altar; and let it be noted how the distinction remains in entire abeyance, for instance, in the argument in Heb. vii., though the writer will be acknowledged to be familiar therewith."

One other passage of the Book of Deuteronomy, which presents in a strain of poetic and beautiful language the " graduated hierarchy" of the middle books, deserves attention. Here, however, we must premise that in the language of poetry we cannot expect a minute specification of the different orders of functionaries, and a particular allotment of the duties discharged by each; for while this might be done in a prosaic detail, it would not and could not suit the genius of poetry. The passage to which we refer is Deut. xxxiii. 8–10, where in the blessings of the tribes we read: " And of Levi he said, Let thy Thummim and thy Urim be with thy holy one, whom thou didst prove at Massah, and with whom thou didst strive at the waters of Meribah; who said unto his father and unto his mother, I have not seen him; neither did he acknowledge his brethren, nor knew his own children: for they have observed Thy word, and kept Thy covenant. They shall teach Jacob Thy judgments, and Israel Thy law: they shall put incense before Thee, and whole burnt sacrifice upon Thine altar." There is undoubtedly an intimation here of the different orders in the tribe of Levi, for though not specifically named, the nature of their respective duties sufficiently defines them. The Thummim and the Urim were the distinguishing privilege of the high priest; the instruction of the people in the divine judgments and law, but especially the ministry of the altar, described here as putting incense before the Lord and whole burnt sacrifice upon His altar, were the ordinary functions of the common priest; while the historical allusion is to the occurrence in the wilderness in consequence of the worship of the golden calf, when the Levites at Moses' command turned their swords against their brethren indiscriminately, and slew of them in one day about three thousand men. The record of this event is found in Ex. xxxii. 26-29, and is as follows:—" Then Moses stood in the gate of the camp, and said, Who is on the Lord's side? let him come unto me. And all the sons of Levi gathered themselves together unto him. And he said unto them, Thus saith the Lord God of Israel, Put every man his sword by his side, and go in and out from gate to gate throughout the camp, and slay every man his brother, and every man his companion, and every man his neighbour. And the children of Levi did according to the word of Moses: and there fell of the people that day, about three thousand men. For Moses had said, Consecrate yourselves to-day to the Lord, even every man upon his son, and upon his brother; that He may bestow upon you a blessing this day." Thus the sons of Levi—all of them—executed divine vengeance on their idolatrous brethren without favour or affection, or any respect of persons whatever. The conduct of the whole tribe had been meritorious in the past; this is the background of the picture of the future blessings to be bestowed. But while there are blessings in store for the whole Levitical body, there is a plain intimation of special duties and of special privileges that can only fall to the lot of few; the parcelling out of such duties and privileges, with specific mention of those to whom they should pertain, would not harmonise with the poetic diction of this address, and could not reasonably be expected in this place. The knowledge of such allotment is presupposed or to be gained elsewhere. And yet these orders are shadowed forth, and a graduated hierarchy of high priest, priest, and Levite outlined on the surface of the passage.

2. The law of the kingdom is the next topic to which we shall advert, but with due regard to brevity. In the article " Bible " in the *Encyclopedia Britannica*, the following statement occurs:—" If the law of the kingdom in Deut. xvii. was known in the time of the Judges, it is impossible to comprehend Judg. viii. 23, and above all, 1 Sam. viii. 7." The law of the kingdom as contained in the chapter referred to (*i.e.* Deut. xvii.) extends through vers. 14–20, and is too long for citation

here. On carefully examining the whole, one cannot fail to perceive an undertone of remonstrance, if not of rebuke, along with the directions and warnings that are contained in it. God foresaw that a time would come when Israel would backslide from the Lord, and when, forgetful or neglectful of the fact that God Himself was their king, they would seek an earthly king to reign over them; that, unmindful of and ungrateful for the blessings of His benignant sway, they would ask for another sovereign to rule among them. Foreseeing what in course of time would come to pass, God directs His servant to make provision for such an eventuality. But even in the instructions which He gives in this regard there is an intermingling, half apparent, half concealed, of justly deserved reproof. Such is our reading of the passage in question. "When thou art come into the land which the Lord thy God giveth thee, and shalt possess it, and shalt dwell therein;" here is an enumeration of the blessings God had bestowed on them—the land was the Lord's, and He gave it to Israel; they were now settled in quiet and peaceful possession by the good hand of His providence upon them; they were dwelling in it prosperously under His special sovereignty. But lo! their base ingratitude—stupidly and sinfully they reject the King who had been author of all these benefits, and under whose reign they had enjoyed all these blessings, saying: "I will set a king over me;" this was as much as to say, We will not have God any longer to reign over us—under the circumstances it could not mean less. "*Like as all the nations that are about me*," they add; but this is the very thing that God forbade—He separated them from the nations, and meant them to be a witness and an example to them, and a peculiar people to Himself; but they longed for assimilation to the nations, and a sovereign like the rest. If with any skill or any sort of clearsightedness we read between the lines, we cannot fail to read the meaning thus. Farther, provoked by their folly and faithlessness, God lets them have their way so that their own rod may chastise them; His repentings, however, are kindled together, He does not cast them off by dealing with them as they have sinned, or requiting their iniquity. He says in effect, if they must have a king let them have him, still let him be such an one as the Lord their God shall choose: "Thou shalt in any wise set him king over thee, whom the Lord thy God shall choose: one from among thy brethren shalt thou set king over thee." He then proceeds in a similar strain to blend warning with thinly veiled reproof—your king is not to multiply horses to himself, nor cause his subjects to go back to Egypt, you had enough of its slavery and its sin; I redeemed you from the house of bondage, do not return thither, nor allow your king—the king you substitute for me—to lead you back. Neither is he to multiply wives to himself, that his heart turn not away; nor greatly multiply wealth to himself—as though there was some danger that self-indulgence, or self-aggrandisement, or self in one form or other, should engage his thoughts and affections much more than his subjects or their interests. Now, (*a*) viewing this passage of Deuteronomy in this light, which we believe to be the true light, and comparing it with 1 Sam. viii. 7, 9, 19, 20, where we read: "And the Lord said unto Samuel, Hearken unto the voice of the people in all that they say unto thee: for they have not rejected thee, but they have rejected me, that I should not reign over them . . . howbeit yet protest solemnly unto them, and show them the manner of the king that shall reign over them. . . . Nevertheless the people refused to obey the voice of Samuel; and they said, Nay; but we will have a king over us, that we also may be *like all the nations*," we come to the irresistible conclusion that the spirit of the two passages is identical; that the tone of both is the same; that what was foretold in the one is fulfilled, and fulfilled exactly, in the other. Nor is this all, the very words of Deuteronomy are repeated in Samuel, so that instead of the knowledge of the law of the kingdom, as stated in Deuteronomy, making Samuel incomprehensible, it is almost indispensable to our right comprehension thereof, the latter being perfectly compatible with and complementary of the former. The cherishing of the desire for a king when God was their king was sinful, the motive that prompted that desire was more so —they aspired to similarity with the surrounding nations. The kind of king that the law of the kingdom contemplated —a king from among their brethren—a king whom the people would choose, God guiding the choice and setting him on the throne, was after all not exactly the thing they aimed at—they wanted a king like those of the heathen nationalities around. Moreover, if we compare the directions in Deuteronomy to the king, to fear God and to keep all the words of the divine law, for the prolongation of his days and those of his children in the midst of Israel, with the like exhortations of Samuel to fear the Lord, and serve Him, and obey His voice, and not rebel against the commandment of the Lord, that they and their king might continue following the Lord God, we are strengthened in the belief that Samuel, instead of being ignorant of the law of the kingdom in Deuteronomy, had it before his mind, and had an eye to it throughout the whole transaction.

(*b*) With regard to Judges, the case is similar. Putting aside the difference between משׁל and מלך, namely, rule of any kind, and the reign of a king, we find that Gideon had been raised up at a particular emergency and for a particular work; that done and the crisis past, he is invited to rule over Israel; but Gideon declined to accept a longer term of office or a higher degree of dignity than had been necessary for their deliverance out of the hand of Midian. As a return for the safety he helped to bring them, they wished to make him their sovereign: "Rule thou over us, both thou and thy son and thy son's son also: for thou hast delivered us from the hand of Midian." He saw full well that, as was their wont, they were putting man in the place of God—the instrument instead of the author of their safety; he accordingly reminds them of Jehovah, their proper saviour and sovereign, and refuses to usurp the glory due to God, saying with greatest propriety: "I will not rule over you; and my son shall not rule over you: the Lord shall rule over you;" He who delivered you has the sole right of dominion over you. We fail entirely to see any contradiction between Judges and Deuteronomy in this matter; on the contrary, we have positive evidence of acquaintance with the law of the kingdom in Deuteronomy on the part of Gideon's son Abimelech, when he was eagerly grasping at what his father declined; his words to his kinsmen of Shechem on the occasion were, "Whether is better for you, either that all the sons of Jerubbaal, which are threescore and ten persons, reign over you, or that one reign over you? remember also that I am *your bone and your flesh.*" Surely we have here an echo, and one very distinct, of the Deuteronomic terms in the law of the kingdom, viz., "One from among thy brethren shalt thou set king over thee."

(c) The view here taken of this whole affair is confirmed by several ancient authorities. The appointment of a king was out of harmony with the Mosaic constitution, according to which Jehovah was Israel's king. The revolutionary movement that issued in monarchy was predicted by Moses in the passage we are considering; but the change from Theocracy to an earthly king has neither the sanction nor recommendation of the Most High. No approval of the measure is either expressed or implied in this Scripture; and when popular clamour had brought it about, the prophet Samuel gives utterance to the strongest disapproval. A reluctant permission, it is true, is granted—a concession is made to a stiff-necked wayward people, who were ignorant of their own mercies and unthankful to the author of them. Instead of collision, then, there is correspondence between the concession made anticipatively in Deuteronomy, and the permission grudgingly granted when the emergency that had been thus anticipated actually arose. Ibn Ezra speaks of the nomination of a king as a permission (רשות) empowering, not a precept enjoining. Such, too, is the opinion of Abarbanel. Similarly Josephus says: "Aristocracy, and the way of living under it, is the best constitution: and may you never have any inclination to any other form of government; and may you always love that form, and have the laws for your governors, and govern all your actions according to them; for you need no supreme governor but God. But if you shall desire a king, let him be one of your own nation," B. iv. ch. viii. 17, Whiston's *Josephus.* The opinion of some, who hold that the rules laid down for the king point to the time and circumstances of Solomon, is quite unfounded. One of these rules furnishes positive disproof of that opinion. When the king is forbidden to multiply horses to himself, the reason assigned for the prohibition is lest the people should return again to

Egypt; "nor cause the people," it is added, "to return to Egypt ... forasmuch as the Lord hath said unto you, Ye shall henceforth return no more that way." This would be quite in keeping with the recent departure from that land, and the known fickleness of the people in the days of Moses, when on any occasion of danger, or difficulty, or distress, "back to Egypt" was likely enough to become the general cry. From the sad experiences of this sort in the past, the lawgiver with good reason guards against any temptation to such a contingency in the future. But to imagine an allusion in connection with such an event to the reign of Solomon, when the time of any thought of a return to Egypt was long past, after the people had been long in possession of the land of promise and in the enjoyment of unexampled prosperity, when the constitution was firmly and well established, and the nation fully conscious of its independence, would be as absurd as to fancy the United States again taking their place among the colonies of Britain.

3. The central altar or national sanctuary is the next subject for consideration in connection with the Mosaic authorship of Deuteronomy. "The law of the high places," says the article already referred to, "given in this part of the Pentateuch (*i.e.* Deuteronomy) was not acknowledged till the time of Josiah, and was not dreamed of by Samuel and Elijah." That it was not always acted on would be nearer the true state of the case. But let us examine the law itself, the occasional exceptions to its operation, together with the cause of such exceptions. The law is stated in Deut. xii. 5, 11, and is as follows: "But unto the place which the Lord your God shall choose out of all your tribes to put His name there for His dwelling ye shall seek, and thither shalt thou come;" again: "Then there shall be a place which the Lord your God shall choose to cause His name to dwell there; thither shall ye bring all that I command you; your burnt-offerings, and your sacrifices, your tithes, and the heave-offering of your hand, and all your choice vows which ye vow unto the Lord." But before examining the nature of this law, and the circumstances that occasioned it, let us look at the law of Exodus xx. 24, to which, as is thought, it stands opposed. In the

verse of Exodus just cited we read: "An altar of earth thou shalt make unto me, and shalt sacrifice thereon thy burnt-offerings, and thy peace-offerings, thy sheep, and thine oxen; in all places where I record my name I will come unto thee, and I will bless thee." Now the allegation is that these statements—one in Deuteronomy and the other in Exodus—contradict or are inconsistent with each other; that the former refers to the temple; and that it was not fully acknowledged till the reign of Josiah, and that consequently the time of the composition of the book was in that king's reign, or at least subsequently to the reign of Hezekiah.

The verses of this chapter, Deut. xii., going before and introducing the command of this text (ver. 5) required the complete destruction of all the places of Canaanitish worship as well as the idols worshipped there—the high hills and mountain-tops, chosen by heathen nations in general from their fancied nearness to the heavenly habitations of their numerous deities, the gloomy groves with sombre shade, the green trees with thick foliage, as though tending to inspire awe or dispose to devotion. All these, and such like means and memorials of idolatry, were to be cleared away in preparation for the pure worship of the true God. Then comes the contrast, "Ye shall not do so unto the Lord your God;" He was not to be worshipped in all places of man's choosing, nor with a variety of different altars at man's option erected to Him, nor by offering sacrifices of human selection. But, on the contrary, "unto the place which the Lord your God shall choose out of all your tribes to put His name there for His dwelling shall ye seek, and thither thou shalt come." Thus, in the first place, the direction was levelled against places, modes, and objects of idolatrous worship. Neither the place nor the manner of Jehovah's worship was left to human arrangement, but to exclusively divine appointment. The choice of a place for the erection of an altar was indicated by a divine manifestation—wherever He put His name, that is, made known His special presence. Thus in patriarchal times we read: "And the Lord appeared unto Abram, and said, Unto thy seed will I give this land: and there builded he an altar unto the Lord who appeared unto him." But in the days of the patriarchs there was less restriction in this matter, for in places without such manifestation, as far as recorded, the tent was pitched and an altar erected. After the Sinaitic covenant, however, the rule became more stringent, in order, as it seems, to prevent any approach to or contact with idolatrous practices. Henceforth the direction in Ex. xx. 24 came into operation, and in no place was an altar to be erected except where God recorded His name; and to all such He attached the gracious promise, "In all places where I record my name I will come unto thee, and I will bless thee." Soon as the tabernacle was erected there was a place where God put His name—recording that glorious name, and manifesting His gracious presence. *There* was the appointed place of worship. But during the wanderings and journeyings of the Israelites in the wilderness the tabernacle could not be permanently localised, but was shifted about from place to place. In Deut. xii. 5, however, an intimation is given that, in time to come, when the wilderness pilgrimage would be over and the land of promise gained, God would be graciously pleased to make choice of a place in one of the tribes of Israel for the setting up of His sanctuary, whether tabernacle or temple, or for the manifestation of His name. Here commentators and scholars diverge—some holding that the law of Deuteronomy in this matter is "only an explanation and more emphatic repetition of the divine command in Exodus;" others, that the Deuteronomic law repeals or collides with that in Exodus. We confess our inability to acquiesce in either statement of the case. That there is a restriction in Deuteronomy as compared with Exodus must, we think, be acknowledged; but, on the other side, the restriction to the one place is not so rigid as to exclude every other, no matter what circumstances might emerge, while an exclusive reference to Jerusalem or Moriah or Zion may be justly pronounced "an arbitrary assumption." A French Rabbi of note, commenting on the difficulty of bringing the one central altar of Deuteronomy into harmony with the plurality of altars in Exodus, thinks that one way of solving the difficulty is to refer the one passage to the nomadic life in the desert, and the other to the settled life in Canaan. His words are: "Ces difficultés disparaissent, quand on songe qu'il s'agit ici d'une époque où la vie nomade avait cessé, voy. ci dessous, v. 8 et 9." This is true as far as it goes, for, though there was the one legitimate sanctuary for divine service, namely, the tabernacle where God manifested Himself, yet that was moved about from place to place, and in all these places worship, if rightly offered, was acceptable and accepted. When they reached their destination in the land of Canaan there was to be one place chosen by God for recording His name and receiving His worshippers. This, under ordinary circumstances, was the divinely appointed place. But while the law of worship was restricted in one direction, it was enlarged in another. In Lev. xvii. 3-5, the people were enjoined under a severe penalty not to kill ox, or lamb, or goat, in the camp, or out of the camp, without bringing it unto the door of the tabernacle of the congregation, to offer an offering unto the Lord before the tabernacle of the Lord. They were required to bring the animals intended for food unto the priest, and offer them for peace-offerings unto the Lord. But that restriction is here relaxed, or rather that law is repealed, for in Deut. xii. 15 it is written: "Notwithstanding thou mayest kill and eat flesh in all thy gates, whatsoever thy soul lusteth after, according to the blessing of the Lord thy God which He hath given thee: the unclean and the clean may eat thereof, as of the roebuck, and as of the hart." Animals slaughtered for human food could be eaten by clean and unclean alike, just like the animals here named which were not offered in sacrifice, and so required no ceremonial distinction on the part of the eaters. It has been argued, indeed, from the words, "a statute for ever unto them throughout their generations" (Lev. xvii. 7), that this Levitical law was meant to be permanent, and by consequence necessitated a plurality of contemporaneous altars, contrary to the law of a single central one. But a careful reading of the context shows that the essential principle of the law, which was the prohibition of demon-worship and of blood, alone was permanent, the temporary restriction of the wilderness giving way to a regulation more liberal and suitable to the people settled throughout the promised land.

And now we come to consider the operation of the Deuteronomic law of one national sanctuary. In the normal condition of things this was the law to be observed, and yet circumstances might, as we shall see, transpire when God for good and wise ends would record His name and manifest His presence elsewhere. After the passage of the Jordan the ark was first set up at Gilgal, and there for the time was the national sanctuary; there the rite of circumcision was administered; there the Passover was kept on the fourteenth day of the month at even in the plains of Jericho. The next place where the ark was set up was Shiloh, after the conquest and division of the land by Joshua, as we learn from Joshua xviii. 1 : "And the whole congregation of the children of Israel assembled together at Shiloh, and set up the tabernacle of the congregation there." Here it remained many years, and during all these years God's name was recorded in Shiloh, and Shiloh was the place of the national sanctuary. The story of the disastrous defeat of Israel in the time of Eli, and of the capture of the ark by the Philistines, needs not to be repeated here. For seven months it was lost to the Israelites, and for twenty years after that it seems to have lain neglected at Kirjath-jearim, in the house of Abinadab. This was a time of disorganization of both Church and State in Israel; the circumstances were exceptional; it was a period of great spiritual declension. What was said shortly before the beginning of this period was very probably true throughout it : "There was no open vision." In this state of things the law of Deut. xii. fell into abeyance; and now that the people began to repent of their sins, for we read that "all the house of Israel lamented after the Lord," Samuel, acting on his own responsibility, or perhaps directed by the Lord, undertook the work of a reformer, and fell back on the rule in Exodus, for we find him at Ramah when there was a sacrifice of the people in the high place (1 Sam. ix. 12); again we read in Samuel's direction to Saul (1 Sam. x. 3), of three men going up to God to Bethel; then (1 Sam. x. 17) we find Samuel calling the people together unto the Lord to Mizpeh; also (1 Sam. xi. 15) Samuel invites the people to Gilgal, where Saul was made king, "and there they sacrificed sacrifices of peace-offerings before the Lord." In all this, as we shall see reason to believe, there was neither collision between Deut. xii. and Ex. xx., nor impropriety of conduct on the part of Samuel. Shiloh had been the national sanctuary in Samuel's youth, and thither his pious mother brought him. Of that as a national sanctuary he must have been well aware, and so of the law against high places; but in a quarter of a century or so from that time the condition of things both civil and religious had become abnormal. And so, when he engaged in the arduous work of restoring the state from its condition of decadence and of reviving religion after a long period of declension, he acted with undoubted judiciousness in exerting his influence for good in different places, and not confining himself, as he might and probably would have done in a normal state of things, to one centre of operations. Further, if we revert to the time when Samuel commenced his work of reform, after the ark had been brought to Kirjath-jearim, and Eleazar, son of Abinadab, sanctified to keep it, we find Samuel stirring up the people to humiliation and repentance in a solemn address unto all the house of Israel, saying: "If ye do return unto the Lord with all your hearts, then put away the strange gods and Ashtaroth from among you, and prepare your hearts unto the Lord, and serve Him only" (1 Sam. vii. 3). After their compliance with this direction, Samuel announced an assembly of all Israel at Mizpeh; at this great convocation of the children of Israel at Mizpeh he engaged in solemn religious exercises, offering up a sucking lamb for a burnt-offering, and engaging in prayer. Now while, as we have seen, he chose different centres of operation, and while that choice was in all probability dictated by what appeared most conducive to the more rapid and thorough revival of religion, it does seem strange that he did not begin at least with Kirjath-jearim where the ark was, or that he did not have the ark transferred to those different centres of operation in turn. Why was this? Was there in this any needless neglect of "the ark of the covenant of the Lord of Hosts which dwelleth between the cherubim"? In the absence of any direct or positive information on the subject we may only conjecture. The reason of the preference he shows to Mizpeh above Kirjath-jearim, and his apparent neglect of a former observance by overlooking the ark, may have lain deep down in his purpose to wean the people from what was *visible*,—even from the ark, though the visible symbol of the divine presence,—to turn their thoughts to what was inward and spiritual, and to concentrate them on their own hearts as the seat and source of true repentance and real reformation, that rending their hearts and not their garments they might turn unto the Lord. Thus he meant to turn them from a superstitious reverence of the symbol, like that of their heathen neighbours for the images of their idols, to the living One Himself—from the ceremonial to a complete abjuration of their present corruption of morals and irreligion. Besides, the law against high places was levelled against idolatrous practices and against self-constituted religionists; not assuredly against the servants of the Most High or the prophets of the Lord, when influenced by His grace and authorised by His spirit they reared an altar when it was most needed, and where it was most likely to serve the purpose of true religion.

But even in the same Book of Deuteronomy, where the national sanctuary or central altar is sanctioned, we find one of these exceptional cases. In chap. xxvii. 5–8 we read, "And there (*i.e.* on Mount Ebal) shalt thou build an altar unto the Lord thy God, an altar of stones: thou shalt not lift up any iron tool upon them. Thou shalt build the altar of the Lord thy God of whole stones: and thou shalt offer burnt-offerings thereon unto the Lord thy God. And thou shalt offer peace-offerings. . . . And thou shalt write upon the stones all the words of this law very plainly." This was strictly complied with, and with a particular reference to this very passage. It was a special occasion as well as a most imposing scene. The Law was to be ratified with unusually solemn ceremonies. In that lovely valley, bounded by Gerizim on the south and Ebal on the north, and with its wonderful acoustic properties, priests and elders and officers and judges round the ark forming a central group, while half that multitude of people crowded up the slopes of the northern hill and the other half those of the southern, the Levites read the curses of the Law, responded to by the loud *Amen* from Ebal, and the blessings, with a like response from

Gerizim. There an altar had been erected "as it is written in the book of the law of Moses, and thereon they offered burnt-offerings unto the Lord and sacrificed peace-offerings" (Josh. viii. 31). On that grand and solemn occasion, though the letter of the law about the one national sanctuary was departed from, yet its spirit lived and energised when on that fresh spring morning, as has been beautifully said, "Israel did consecrate Palestine unto the Lord, and take sea and lake, mountain and valley,—the most hallowed spots in their history, —as witnesses of their covenant."

But while the letter of the law in Deuteronomy may thus have been departed from for exceptional purposes or on special occasions, when a servant of the Lord acted on his own spiritual instinct, or it may be, according to some unrecorded intimation from the Most High, or even by express divine command at the very time when that law was fully known and acknowledged, we can conceive another and a far different cause of such departure—a cause for which there can be neither excuse nor apology. At a time of abounding ungodliness men may shut their eyes to the law though well known, and to all the consequences of transgressing it. In the subsequent history of Israel this many a time took place. But we have not to advance beyond the desert wanderings for an example and proof of a law being well known and acknowledged by all, and yet not acted on. Who in all the Hebrew host could be ignorant of the rite of circumcision, or rather of the law that so positively enjoined that seal of the covenant? and yet for nearly forty years that law was disobeyed and departed from. Thus it is written in Josh. v. 5: "Now all the people that came out were circumcised; but all the people that were born in the wilderness by the way as they came forth out of Egypt, them they had not circumcised." And all this in direct violation of a command so positive and a law so absolute as that relating to circumcision, and recorded in Gen. xvii. 12-14: "He that is eight days old shall be circumcised among you, every man-child in your generations. . . . He that is born in thy house, and he that is bought with thy money, must needs be circumcised. And the uncircumcised man-child whose flesh of his foreskin is not circumcised, that soul shall be cut off from his people; he hath broken my covenant."

But the Deuteronomic law of the national or central sanctuary was known, and well known, even in the time of Joshua, as we learn from the august embassy and earnest expostulation from Israel to the two tribes and a half on the occasion and in consequence of the erection of the memorial altar called Ed (surviving as *'Ayd* to the present day) by those trans-Jordanic tribes. When Phinehas the priest and the ten princes that accompanied him came unto the land of Gilead, to the Reubenites and Gadites and half tribe of Manasseh, they addressed them in the name of all Israel: "Thus saith the whole congregation of the Lord, What trespass is this that ye have committed against the God of Israel, to turn away this day from following the Lord, in that ye have builded you an altar, that ye might rebel this day against the Lord? . . . but rebel not against the Lord, nor rebel against us, in building you *an altar beside the altar of the Lord our God.*" What was it that aroused the fears of the people, and called forth the zeal of priest and princes? Evidently the strong suspicion of, or perhaps, we should rather say, the holy jealousy against any infringement of this very law which forbids another altar. It was plain that such an altar would be in unholy rivalry to the one at the national sanctuary, as much as those at Dan and Bethel, which were expressly set up for that very purpose by Jeroboam. It was equally obvious that such a rival altar, even if it did not tend to idolatry, which it would be most likely to do, would be certain eventually to rupture the tribal union. The building of such an altar for sacrifice would be attended by the worst consequences; it would be necessarily antagonistic, as we have said, to the national altar; it would be rebellion against the Lord, who had appointed one national place of worship; it would be isolation for the present, and separation from the congregation of Israel in the end. But such apprehensions were groundless. This altar was not for sacrifice in opposition to the Deuteronomic law; neither was it for separation, but to testify their share in the sanctuary and service and commonwealth of Israel. "It is a witness (עֵד) between us and you.

God forbid that we should rebel against the Lord, and turn this day from following the Lord, to build an altar for burnt-offerings, for meat-offerings, or for sacrifices, *besides the altar of the Lord our God that is before His tabernacle.*" The last words of the Scripture just cited seem to put it beyond doubt or question that the Deuteronomic law was both acknowledged and acted on in ordinary circumstances in the time of Joshua. Even in David's day, and after the disorders and disasters of the preceding reign, though the tabernacle remained at Gibeon, yet that reforming monarch appears not to have lost sight of the one national sanctuary when he had the ark brought up to Zion, purposing in his heart and making preparation for the building of that beautiful house which Solomon his son and successor was privileged to erect. Circumstances over which he had no control prevented the full accomplishment of all he desired. The great-grandson of Solomon, Asa, in acknowledgment of, and acting on the principle of the Deuteronomic law, "took away the altars of the strange gods and the high places, and brake down the images and cut down the groves: and commanded Judah to seek the Lord God of their fathers, and to do the law and the commandment. Also he took away out of all the cities of Judah the high places and the images" (2 Chron. xiv. 3–5). In the time of Jehoash, who reigned well all the days of the priest Jehoiada, and who repaired the house of the Lord; as also in the good reign of Amaziah; it was a standing drawback and subject of complaint that "the high places were not taken away: the people still sacrificed and burnt incense in the high places." They did what they could, but the evil was beyond their power to remedy. They evidently knew the law of the case and respected it, but were unable to secure compliance with it; and all this long before the time of Josiah. Even Hezekiah, great-grandfather of Josiah, was well aware of it, and succeeded where his predecessors had failed, for "he removed the high places, and brake the images, and cut down the groves."

We hold, then, that the traditional belief in the Mosaic authorship of Deuteronomy remains unshaken by any argument derived from supposed anachronism or fancied discrepancy in relation to the law of a national sanctuary, or the law of the kingdom, or the alleged equality of priest and Levite in Deuteronomy, as compared with their relative position in the middle books of the Pentateuch.

There are several minor matters in connection with which discrepancies are supposed to exist, and to militate against the authorship of Moses. We can barely notice these.

(1) The mountain of the law is called Horeb in Deuteronomy, and Sinai in the other books of the Pentateuch. But Horeb is the entire mountain range, and Sinai the single mountain-top, as pointed out by Hengstenberg and approved of by Robinson. This is confirmed by the prepositions employed with these words respectively, as may be seen from one example; thus: "Behold, I will stand upon (עַל) the rock in (בְּ) Horeb" (Ex. xvii. 6), the one being the individual spot, the other the whole region; while the latter preposition is usual with Horeb, the former with Sinai. Besides, Sinai occurs once in Deuteronomy, and Horeb thrice in Exodus.

(2) It has been inferred from בעבר ה' in the first verse of Deuteronomy that it was written on one side, and that Moses spoke on the other. But this expression, as also other forms of it, denote simply *across the Jordan*, sometimes west of the river, oftener east of it, just according to the position, real or supposed, of the persons addressed, and easily discoverable from the context.

(3) In Ex. xxii. 31: "And ye shall be holy men unto me: neither shall ye eat any flesh that is torn of beasts in the field: ye shall cast it to the dogs;" in Lev. xvii. 15, such a contingency is anticipated and provision made for it: "Every soul that eateth that which died of itself, or that which was torn with beasts, whether it be one of your own country or a stranger, he shall both wash his clothes and bathe himself in water, and be unclean until the even;" he was thus cleansed, otherwise he remained unclean and bore his iniquity; but in Deut. xiv. 21, it may be given to the stranger within the gates or sold to an alien, for it is there stated: "Ye shall not eat of anything that dieth of itself: thou shalt give it unto the stranger that is in thy gates, that he may eat; or thou mayest sell it unto an alien." The

eating of such flesh is forbidden in the first passage; non-compliance with this prohibition defiled either native or stranger, as we are taught in the second; in the third it may not be eaten by an Israelite, but may be given to a stranger. The same thing that pollutes the stranger in the one passage is permitted in the other. How is this to be accounted for? Apparently thus: the stranger in the one instance is a proselyte, and occupies the same position with a native Hebrew in respect of defilement. Not so a stranger who, declining to become a proselyte, preferred to throw in his lot with the heathen rather than with the Hebrews, and was accordingly treated with only a trifle more consideration than the alien—to the one it was given, to the other it was sold. Neither came under the Jewish ceremonial, the conscience of neither was bound by Levitical law. Want of time and space obliges us to reserve the consideration of many other important topics in this connection.

CONCLUSION OF THE WHOLE.

As an offset to cavils might be adduced the many wonderful confirmations of the Bible, from ancient history, modern discoveries, long-buried inscriptions, human experience, topographical research, and numerous other sources. As the centuries roll these confirmations have been multiplying. Let us relate an anecdote with which Mr. Bardsley illustrated the valuable confirmations of Holy Scripture in connection with the Palestine Exploration still going on. "A cloth factor in Yorkshire," he proceeded to say, "had a piece of cloth stolen from him. After careful inquiry he came to the conclusion that a neighbour of his, also a dealer in cloth, had stolen it. He went and claimed the cloth, saying that he thought this must be his cloth. 'Prove it,' said the other. 'I think I can,' said the first. He had reflected that if the cloth were really his, the holes in the selvedge would exactly fit the distances of the posts and nails in his field along which the cloth had been stretched. These holes had, of course, been made by the nails at the time of stretching. The cloth was carried to the field and tried. Every hole fitted every nail, no more and no less, and the distances were exactly right. The proof was sufficient. The man confessed the theft. Now, this is what the Palestine Exploration Society have been doing with the Bible and the Holy Land. They take the Bible to the Holy Land, and everything fits. The incidental allusions, the places, manners, customs, products, climate, all correspond. The Bible fits the land, and the land fits the Bible."

In the Bible, if anywhere in all the universe, is found the truth of God; here, as nowhere else, is presented not the word of man, but in truth the word of the Lord. Over the surface of this troubled unresting sea of human life many a storm sweeps, while many a sunken rock and perilous quicksand and treacherous shoal lie hid beneath; but in this Word of God is the evershining, everlasting lighthouse of our world. Amid the many changing scenes of earthly existence, the vanities of time, the uncertainties of condition, and even the treacheries of human friendships, we have in this Word of God an unchanging and never-failing testimony to heaven's unintermitting love. Under the deep unspeakable sorrows that at times overwhelm us in our sojourn, there are truths here that can soothe us now, and not only prove our solace on earth, but form part of our joyful triumphant song in heaven. The mightiest works of man may perish, powerful empires be overthrown, and great cities vanish, but the Word of the Lord, through all the ages that lapse and the centuries that roll, liveth and abideth for ever. Human institutions may live their day and die, having served their purpose they may grow old and outlive their usefulness, becoming obsolete and antiquated; but this Word of God is animated by a living imperishable principle that makes it proof against all feebleness or decrepitude of age. In all the years that have been it has proved the rod and staff, the stay and support of the faithful; in all the years that shall be it will retain its strength unshorn, and its vigour shall neither know nor feel decay. The myriad angels that came down on Horeb at the giving of the law, and the angelic hosts that carolled the nativity on the plains of Bethlehem, returned to the light and splendour of their native heavens; but the voices left behind and caught up in Scripture will reverberate round the world, awaking echo after echo in ceaseless succession that shall never die away. And though no voice from heaven may sound down to us through the blue empyrean, and no vision be vouchsafed to us as to ancient patriarch or seer; yet are we privileged to hold uninterrupted converse with prophets, apostles, and evangelists, and not only with them, but through them with Almighty God Himself, as He speaks to us by His servants and addresses us in His Word. This Word of God may be attacked in the future as at the present and in the past—the ribaldry of Paine, the wit of Voltaire, the subtilty of Hume, the theories of scientists, and the plausibilities of criticism, all in succession or combination may be arrayed against it, but it shall never be shaken, and can never be overthrown. This Word of God, in its stateliness and stability, may be compared to that great pyramid that stands in the Nile valley, the evidence of man's mechanical power and a wonder of the world; it has borne the brunt of countless storms, the thunders of heaven have rolled over it, the lightnings have flashed against it, all the fierceness and fury of warring elements have spent themselves upon it, the desert sands have been dashed around it, still it stands a monument of imperishable greatness, unshaken and immovable on its solid foundation. The elements themselves shall melt with fervent heat, this earth and all the works thereof shall one day be burnt up: Scripture affirms it, science confirms it; but even then the truths of this Bible will only be entering on a higher and grander fulfilment.

"How precious is this book divine,
 By inspiration given!
Bright as a lamp its glories shine,
 To guide our souls to heaven.

"O may its lamp, through all the night
 Of life, make plain our way!
Till we behold the clearer light
 Of an eternal day."

APPENDIX A.

THE following is the calculation referred to on page 37. This line of argument employed by Babbage was wrought out and extended by J. R. Young, Esq., formerly Professor of Mathematics in the Royal College, Belfast. We have here made some important additions to it, and at the same time modified and simplified it considerably:—

(a) As usual in such cases, put certainty $= 1$.

(β) Let it be borne in mind that the probability of an uncertain event is represented by the number of chances favourable to an event divided by the total number of chances, $= \dfrac{\text{No. favouring}}{\text{No. for} + \text{No. ag.}}$

(I.) Put the number of persons who died without resurrection $= d$.
Put the number of all persons born into the world $= d+1$.
Accordingly death prevailed over $d+1$, or failed in 1.

(a) ∴ *Probability* of resurrection $= \dfrac{1}{d+1+1} = \dfrac{1}{d+2}$ . . . (1).

(b) *Improbability* of same, or *probability* of non-resurrection
$$= 1 - \dfrac{1}{d+2} = \dfrac{d+2-1}{d+2} = \dfrac{d+1}{d+2} \quad \ldots \ldots \quad (2).$$

(II.) *Probability of falsehood* in case of a person who is—

(a) Guilty of one false statement in every ten statements that he makes $= \dfrac{1}{10} = f$ . . . . (1).

(b) *Probability of veracity* in case of the same individual
$$= 1 - \dfrac{1}{10} = \dfrac{10-1}{10} = \dfrac{9}{10} = \cdot 9 = 1 - f. \quad \ldots \ldots \quad (2).$$

(c) Now, in a compound probability, the rule is to multiply the chances of the separate events together.

∴ Chances for $= \dfrac{1}{d+2} \times (1-f)$ . . . . . . (3).

∴ Chances against $= \dfrac{d+1}{d+2} \times f$ . . . . (4).

∴ *Probability of resurrection*

$$= \dfrac{\dfrac{1}{d+2}(1-f)^n}{\dfrac{1}{d+2}(1-f)^n + \dfrac{d+1}{d+2}f^n} = \dfrac{(1-f)^n}{(1-f)^n + (d+1)f^n} \quad \cdots \quad (A).$$

∴ *Improbability of resurrection*

$$= \frac{\frac{d+1}{d+2}f^n}{\frac{d+1}{d+2}f^n + \frac{1}{d+2}(1-f)^n} = \frac{(d+1)f^n}{(d+1)f^n + (1-f)^n} \qquad (B).$$

(III.) In order that A may exceed B, or the probability *for* be greater than the probability *against* resurrection, let

$$\frac{(1-f)^n}{(1-f)^n + (d+1)f^n} > \frac{(d+1)f^n}{(d+1)f^n + (1-f)^n};$$

or, as denominators are the same,

$$(1-f)^n > (d+1)f^n$$

Dividing by f^n

$$\therefore \left(\frac{1}{f} - 1\right)^n > (d+1).$$

Taking the logarithms,

$$\therefore n\, log.\left(\frac{1}{f} - 1\right) > log.(d+1)$$

$$\therefore n > \frac{l\,(d+1)}{l\left(\frac{1}{f} - 1\right)} \therefore n > \frac{l\,10^{12}}{l\,9}$$

$$\therefore n > \frac{12\, l\, 10}{l\, 9} \text{ or } n > \frac{12}{\cdot 954} \text{ or } n > 12.$$

Put creation = 6000 years (ago),
A generation = 30,
∴ $\frac{6000}{30}$ = 200 generations.
Again, put average population = 1,000,000,000,
∴ $d+1$ = 200,000,000,000.
Suppose it 5 times greater, that is, = 1,000,000,000,000 = 10^{12}.
If prob. of resurrection = $\frac{1}{d+1+1}$ = $\frac{1}{200,000,000,000+1}$
∴ chances against = (denom. *minus* num.) = 200,000,000,000 + 1 − 1 = 200,000,000,000.

(IV.) Multiply the chances against R. by 5 = 1,000,000,000,000.
(α) Thus the odds against its occurrence = a million millions to one.
(β) Yet the testimony of any number of witnesses above twelve, though the truthfulness of each is one falsehood for every nine truths, renders the occurrence of an event against which the chances are a million millions to one more probable than its non-occurrence.
(γ) But, as a million millions is five times the number of the human race from its origin till the present time, the probability of the occurrence becomes five times greater than of its non-occurrence, under the circumstances and according to the data already assumed.

APPENDIX B.

THE LXX. version of Isa. liii. 7, 8, referred to on page 132, is here compared with the original Hebrew.

(1)

1. ὡς πρόβατον ἐπὶ σφαγὴν ἤχθη καὶ ὡς ἀμνός.
שֶׂה = lamb . . . . . . רָחֵל = sheep.

2. ἐναντίον τοῦ κείροντος αὐτὸν ἄφωνος, οὕτως οὐκ ἀνοίγει τὸ στόμα αὐτοῦ.
גֹּזְזֶיהָ, pl. and fem. suff. = her shearers.

3. ἐν τῇ ταπεινώσει αὐτοῦ ἡ κρίσις αὐτοῦ ἤρθη· τὴν δὲ γενεὰν αὐτοῦ τίς διηγήσεται;

מֵעֹצֶר וּמִמִּשְׁפָּט לֻקָּח = { He was taken from prison and from judgment; or (marg. A. V.), He was taken away by distress and judgment.

4. ὅτι αἴρεται ἀπὸ τῆς γῆς ἡ ζωὴ αὐτοῦ.
נִגְזַר מֵאֶרֶץ חַיִּים = He was cut off out of the land of the living.

(2)

The difference will also appear by comparing the following:—

Ordinary version of Isa. liii. in A. V.	Rendering of LXX. version of same in Acts viii. A. V.
"He is brought as a *lamb* (α) to the slaughter, and as a sheep before *her shearers* (β) is dumb, so He openeth not His mouth. *He was taken from prison and from judgment* (γ): and who shall declare His generation? for *He was cut off out of the land of the living.* (δ)" Vv. 7, 8.	"He was led as a *sheep* (α) to the slaughter; and like a lamb dumb before *His shearer* (β), so opened He not His mouth: *in His humiliation His judgment was taken away* (γ): and who shall declare His generation? for *His life is taken from the earth.* (δ)" Vv. 32, 33.

APPENDIX C.

SOME CONSIDERATIONS IN RELATION TO THE GENUINENESS OF THE IGNATIAN EPISTLES (quoted p. 260).

IN this case the external evidence ranges itself on one side, and is decidedly in favour of the genuineness of the letters of Ignatius. So much is this the case, that it may be safely affirmed that the external evidence for their authorship is greatly superior to that of three-fourths of the works of the classical authors of Greece and Rome.

1. The first is the testimony of Polycarp (Epist. xiii.) to the following effect:—"Ye wrote to me, both ye (*i.e.* the Philippians) and also Ignatius, that if any one went from hence into Syria he should bring your letters with him." Again : " The Epistles of Ignatius which were sent us by him, together with what others of his have come to our hands (lit. we have by us), we sent to you according to your order, which are subjoined to this epistle, by which ye may be greatly profited; for they treat of faith and patience, and of all things that pertain to edification in the Lord Jesus." Once more: " What ye know certainly of Ignatius, and those that are with him, signify unto us." It follows from these references, that whoever calls in question the Epistles of Ignatius must also impugn the letter of Polycarp. Now it is scarcely supposable that any writer of spurious epistles would be so audacious as to forge letters not only in the name of Ignatius, but also a letter in the name of Polycarp during the lifetime of the latter. There remains the only possible supposition, that the forgery of those letters had been delayed till after the death of Polycarp; but the testimony of Irenæus is an insuperable obstacle in the

way of such a supposition. Already in the time of Irenæus those letters were ascribed to Ignatius and Polycarp respectively. In reference to that of Polycarp he says expressly, "There is also a letter of Polycarp written to the Philippians;" while he states the fact of the condemnation of Ignatius and the mode of his martyrdom, quoting at the same time Ignatius' own words, as still found in the 4th chapter of his letter to the Romans. "As a certain (Irenæus, *adv. hær.*) one of our brethren, being condemned to wild beasts on account of his testimony for God, said, 'I am the wheat of God, and I am ground by the teeth of wild beasts that I may be found to be pure bread.'"

2. The next testimony is (Origen, *Hom.* vi. *in Luc.*) that of Origen, who quotes a saying from the 19th chapter of Ignatius' Epistle to the Ephesians in the following words:—"It is well written in one of the epistles of a certain martyr, I mean Ignatius, who was second bishop of Antioch after the blessed Peter, who in the persecution fought with beasts in Rome: 'the virginity of Mary was unknown to the prince of this world.'" He also cites (*Prolog. in Cant. Cantic.*) another statement out of the 7th chapter of Ignatius' Epistle to the Romans: "I also remember that one of the saints, Ignatius by name, said of Christ: 'But my love is crucified.'"

3. Eusebius refers to the journey of Ignatius to Rome in these words: "Tradition says that he was sent away (Eusebius, *H. E.* 3. 36) from Syria to Rome to be devoured by wild beasts, for the testimony of Christ. And making his journey through Asia under a strong guard, he confirmed the Churches in every city by his discourses, and especially cautioned them against the heresies then springing up and gaining ground, and exhorted them to adhere to the tradition of the apostles. And for the greater security, he also put down his instructions in writing. Therefore when he came to Smyrna, where Polycarp was, he wrote an epistle to the Church at Ephesus, another to the Church in Magnesia upon the Meander . . . and another to the Church at Trallium, . . . and beside these, he wrote also to the Church at Rome." Eusebius, after giving an extract from the Epistle to the

Romans, then proceeds: "Afterwards removing from Smyrna he wrote to the Philippians from Troas, and to the Church of Smyrna, and in particular to their president Polycarp." Eusebius next refers to sentiments contained in the Epistle to Polycarp, and quotes a passage from the Epistle to Smyrna, and then concludes his reference by citing a passage from the 13th chapter of Polycarp's Epistle to the Philippians. Part of the passage in question is the same as that above cited in evidence from Polycarp.

4. *Athanasius*, in his account of the Synods of Ariminum and Seleucia (*De Synodis Arimini et Seleuciæ*), testifies to the letters of Ignatius, and quotes an expression from the 17th chapter of the Epistle to the Ephesians. His words are: "Therefore Ignatius, who was appointed bishop in Antioch after the apostles, and became a martyr of Christ, writing about the Lord, has said, 'There is one physician, of flesh and of spirit, made and unmade (γενητός and ἀγένητος, or begotten and unbegotten, according to the γεννητός and ἀγέννητος of the Medicean text), God in man, true life in death, both from Mary and from God.'"

5. Jerome, who largely repeats the sentiments of Eusebius on this subject, says: "Ignatius, the third bishop of the Church of Antioch after the Apostle Peter, in the persecution under Trajan was condemned to wild beasts. And when he came to Smyrna, where Polycarp the disciple of John was bishop, he wrote an Epistle to the Ephesians, another to the Magnesians, a third to the Trallians, a fourth to the Romans; and when he was gone thence, he wrote to the Philadelphians, the Smyrneans, and in particular to Polycarp." Such is a brief outline of the external evidence.

But exception has been taken to the contents of these epistles, and their genuineness has been vigorously impugned, and as vigorously defended in turn. Of the three forms of these epistles, viz. the longer Greek recension, the shorter Greek recension, and the shorter Syriac recension; the first is unquestionably interpolated, the last most probably abridged, while the shorter Greek recension alone comes to be considered. The Syriac comprises only three epistles, one to the Ephesians, one to the Romans, and a third to Polycarp; the shorter Greek recension includes these three, and four others additional. In connection with this last form of the Ignatian Epistles may here be noticed a few of the leading objections. (1) Baur affirms that the interviews of Ignatius with the brethren at Smyrna and Troas, and the circumstance of his writing letters there, are inconsistent with the cruelty of his guards, whom he compares to ten leopards in the 5th chapter of his Epistle to the Romans. To this it is replied that Roman captives bound to soldiers were permitted to receive and hold free converse with friends. Paul supplies a case in point. In Acts xxviii. 16, we read that he "was suffered to dwell by himself with a soldier that kept him;" and in the last verses of the same chapter we are informed that, though still under guard, "he dwelt two whole years in his own hired house, and received all that came in unto him, preaching the kingdom of God, and teaching those things which concern the Lord Jesus Christ with all confidence, no man forbidding him." Nor was it any uncommon thing for friends to gain permission to visit Christians in prison by means of gratuities to the soldiers that guarded, or to the gaolers that kept them. This is hinted at by Ignatius when he says that the soldiers became worse by benefactions, that is, more severe or cruel, and that for the purpose of renewed exactions or fresh extortions. Time for writing letters, of which the shortest would not occupy more than an hour, and the longest not more than three, could without much difficulty be secured. (2) The same author looks upon Ignatius writing from Smyrna to Rome as absurd, and the circuitous route by which he was conducted as extremely improbable. The answer is not far to seek. There were two routes from Smyrna to Rome—one by sea and the other by land. The latter, or Egnatian way, was more circuitous. The letter forwarded by sea or sent as a despatch overland would reach Rome long before the martyr. The circuitous route may have been preferred by the soldiers in consequence of engagements in Troas or Macedonia, or even perhaps, as Chrysostom has suspected, for the purpose of testing the martyr's constancy, or with the view of weakening the firmness of his resolve. (3) Baur repeats an objection often urged from the vehemence of Ignatius' desire for martyrdom, and his earnestness in dissuading the friends at Rome from using any influence to effect his release. Let it be kept in mind that the eyes of heathendom and Christendom were fixed on him. His case, it must be supposed, had attracted a large share of attention; the sentence passed by the emperor was to be executed at the seat of empire, and that publicly before thousands in the amphitheatre. All the circumstances had gained such notoriety, that had the friends at Rome, by bribing or interceding or using influence of any sort, obtained a reprieve or relaxation or remission of the sentence, it would have reflected injuriously on Christian firmness and constancy, sorely discouraged Christians, and proved detrimental to the Church at large. He was anxious therefore that his faith should be strengthened and not weakened, and that his firmness in the faith should be maintained to the end. In a person of such ardent and enthusiastic temperament as Ignatius, the anxiety for martyrdom in order to promote the interests of the Church was not so condemnable as some suppose, nor so sinful as others seem to think. The motive has to be taken into account, as well as the measure of submission to the divine will, by which the desire was regulated. Besides, like Paul, he was ready to be offered, and the time of his departure he felt to be at hand. "This," says Cureton, "which has been accounted as a defect by some, has, in the estimation of others, given a vigour and personality to this epistle," that is, the Epistle to the Romans, one of the Syriac recension which alone Cureton considers to be genuine. Bishop Lightfoot expresses a somewhat similar opinion when he speaks of them as "stamped with an individuality of character which is a strong testimony to their genuineness. The intensity of feeling and the ruggedness of expression seem to bespeak a real living man." (4) Though these letters touch on so many topics of a historical kind in regard to the journey of Ignatius to Rome, the two stages of his journey Smyrna and Troas, his intercourse with friends there, as well as the circumstances of the Church of Antioch, no incongruity has been discovered, nor contradiction detected. When Polycarp, in the 14th chapter of his Epistle to the Philippians, requests them to give him whatever information they could about Ignatius and those that were with him, it is entitled to be regarded as an undesigned coincidence of some importance. Had Ignatius remained at Antioch, and not set out on a journey westward, it would have been absurd for the pastor of Smyrna to apply to the Philippians for information about the minister of Antioch; but quite natural, on the other hand, for a Smyrnean to seek information from the inhabitants of Philippi about what had transpired at Rome, the relative positions of these places from east to west being Antioch, next Smyrna, then Philippi, on the high road to the Roman capital; thus, "Rome ٭ .... ٭ Philippi .... ٭ Smyrna ..... ٭ Antioch."

(5) A supposed anachronism was hunted up in the 8th chapter of the Epistle to the Magnesians, and urged by Daillé and others. In that passage, according to the common text, we read in reference to Jesus Christ the Son of God, that He is "His eternal word, not coming forth from Silence;" from which it has been confidently though improperly concluded that the epistle must have been written after the time of Valentinian the Gnostic (140–160 A.D.), and that the expression in question was intended as a refutation of Valentinian. But Hefele adduces positive proof that Simon Magus, the first Gnostic, whom Irenæus calls the magister and progenitor of all heretics, was the first to give $\Sigma\iota\gamma\eta$, or Silence, a place in his system of Gnosticism. In the recently discovered book of Hippolytus, entitled *Philosophumena*, there is preserved a fragment out of the $\text{'}A\pi\acute{o}\phi\alpha\sigma\iota\varsigma\ \mu\epsilon\gamma\acute{a}\lambda\eta$, or great Announcement of Simon, from which it is clearly seen that $\Sigma\iota\gamma\eta$, or Silence, held the first rank in Simon's system. Even Bunsen, who advocates the genuineness of the Syriac recension only, is of opinion that the allusion of Ignatius is to the $\Sigma\iota\gamma\eta$ of Simon; "Was folgt heraus?" says Bunsen, "dass Ignatius, der sicherlich die grosse Verkündigung ($\text{'}A\pi\acute{o}\phi\alpha\sigma\iota\varsigma\ \mu\epsilon\gamma\acute{a}\lambda\eta$ of Simon) gelesen haben kann, ebenso wie Johannes, in dem Briefe an die Magnesier ... wohl darauf angespielt werden kann." A correction of the text, sanctioned by Petermann's Armenian version, the citation by Severus, and the paraphrase of the long recension, which omits ἀΐδιος, οὐκ, and leaves the words "proceeding from Silence," entirely disproves the supposed refer-

ence to Valentinian as well as the fancied design of refuting him.

(6) A forger, in exalting and recommending his pseudo-Ignatius, would certainly not have failed to mention the intercourse of Ignatius with the Apostle John; nor would he, in writing to the Romans, have omitted all reference to the episcopate at Rome, though, strange to say, the Roman epistle which is one of the Syriac recension contains none of the extravagant expressions about the episcopal office that have tended so largely to bring the Ignatian letters into disrepute. Nor does it seem to be his chief or primary object to advocate episcopacy, and urge obedience to episcopal authority, so much as to protect the faithful from the heresy of the Judaising Docetæ; and as secondary and subsidiary to this, he recommends close ecclesiastical unity with the bishop as representing Christ and as the centre of union in the Christian congregation. It is thus apparent, at the same time, that Ignatius' notion of a bishop does not differ materially from the New Testament model, and does not necessarily imply diocesan jurisdiction.

(7) The heresies condemned by Ignatius were of recent growth; some of the Churches, as that of Ephesus, were still free from them, in others only individuals (τινές, ὀλίγοι) were yet infected. These heretics were of two classes, Judaisers and Docetæ; or perhaps of one class—Judaising Docetæ, thus combining the two elements in one. This kind of heresy which united Judaism with Docetism prevailed only in the beginning of the 2nd century in the time of Cerinthus, the founder of the sect of Christian Gnostics, who embraced that twofold error in his system. About the middle of the same century these two elements were separated; Judaism and Docetism became distinct, Basilides and Marcion among the Gnostic Docetæ setting themselves in opposition to Judaism. Accordingly the heretics met with in the Ignatian epistles stand midway between Cerinthus and Basilides, and in point of time this corresponds to the interval between A.D. 90–130. These letters could not have been written after the middle of the 2nd century, because a churchman so orthodox and a controversialist so keen as Ignatius could not have passed over

in silence the burning questions that troubled the Church in Asia during the second half of the 2nd century. And yet we have no mention of Montanism, no allusion to the Paschal controversy, and no reference to Gnosticism as taught by Marcion, Valentinus, or even Basilides, who flourished A.D. 125-140. Besides, had the author of them lived or written in the second half of the 2nd century, such a staunch churchman would never have compromised his orthodoxy by using expressions such as *pleroma* or *matter loving fire* of passion, which became the watchwords of heresy after Gnosticism had fully developed in the hands of Valentinus and others.

Before closing this note, the object of which is to suggest some points for reconsideration in favour of the genuineness of the Ignatian epistles, a mere reference to the supposed allusion of Lucian the satirist to Ignatius is all that our space allows. The witty Samosatian is thought, and with good reason, to refer to Ignatius under the name of Peregrinus. This Peregrinus he styles miserable ($\kappa\alpha\kappa o\delta\alpha\acute{\iota}\mu\omega\nu$), the epithet applied by Trajan to Ignatius; he designates him as $\dot{\epsilon}\pi\acute{\iota}\sigma\kappa o\pi o\varsigma$ = bishop, and speaks of his being bound with chains in Syria. He ridicules his $\kappa\epsilon\nu o\delta o\xi\acute{\iota}\alpha\nu$, or vainglorious eagerness for martyrdom, and relates the circumstance of his sending letters to nearly all the chief cities of Asia, as also the circumstance of his *electing* ($\dot{\epsilon}\chi\epsilon\iota\rho o\tau\acute{o}\nu\eta\sigma\epsilon$) certain of his friends as ambassadors for this purpose, calling them *messengers of the dead* and *couriers of the dead* ($\nu\epsilon\kappa\rho\alpha\gamma\gamma\acute{\epsilon}\lambda o\upsilon\varsigma$ and $\nu\epsilon\rho\tau\epsilon\rho o\delta\rho\acute{o}\mu o\upsilon\varsigma$). Here is a close verbal correspondence with expressions in the 11th chapter of the Epistle to the Smyrneans: "It is fitting that your Church *appoint* ($\chi\epsilon\iota\rho o\tau o\nu\widehat{\eta}\sigma\alpha\iota$) some *worthy delegate* ($\theta\epsilon o\pi\rho\epsilon\sigma\beta\acute{\upsilon}\tau\eta\nu$);" and in the 7th chapter of the letter to Polycarp: "And choose some one . . . that he may be the messenger of God ($\theta\epsilon\acute{o}\delta\rho o\mu o\varsigma$)." He also speaks of deputies sent and sums of money forwarded from the Christian communities of certain cities in Asia to Peregrinus. The period of time also corresponds. The career of Peregrinus was towards the end of the first half of the 2nd century, during the reign of Antoninus Pius; while Lucian wrote only a very few years later, having been born about A.D. 120 in Samosata, a town of Syria near the Euphrates, and having lived mostly in Asia Minor. From the time, the place, the circumstances, and the character of the allusions, there can be little doubt that Lucian refers to Ignatius under the name of Peregrinus, and to the Ignatian letters under the epistles sent to the different cities.

APPENDIX D.

CORROBORATIVE STATEMENTS IN RELATION TO THE EARLY AND WIDE DIFFUSION OF THE CANONICAL SCRIPTURES.

(1)

"THE apostles found neither leisure nor occasion to write till Christian societies were formed; and all their writings were suggested by particular circumstances which occurred in the progress of Christianity."—*Hill's Lectures in Divinity.*

The same author adds—

"Some of the Epistles to the Churches were the earliest of their writings. Every Epistle was received on unquestionable evidence by the Church to which it was sent, and in whose keeping the original manuscript remained. Copies were circulated first among the neighbouring Churches, and went from them to Christian societies at a greater distance, till by degrees the whole Christian world, considering the superscription of the Epistle, and the manner in which it came to them, as a token of its authenticity, and relying upon the original, which they knew where to find, gave entire credit to its being the work of him whose name it bore. This is the history of the thirteen Epistles of Paul, and of the first of Peter. Some of the other Epistles, which had not the same particular superscription, were not so easily authenticated to the whole Church, and were, upon that account, longer of being admitted into the canon.

"The hesitation which, for several ages, was entertained in some places of the Christian world with regard to these books, is satisfying to a candid mind, because this hesitation is of itself a strong presumption that the universal and cordial reception which was given to all the other books of the New Testament proceeded upon clear incontestable evidence of their authenticity."

(2)

"An ecclesiastical tradition (Photius) ascribes to John the work of collecting and sanctioning the writings which were worthy of a place in the canon."

"Each of the original Churches, especially those of larger size and greater ability, collected for itself a complete set of those writings, which could be proved, by competent testimony, to be the production of inspired men, and to have been communicated by them to any of the Churches as part of the written word of God; so that in this way a great many complete collections of the New Testament Scriptures came to be extant, the accordance of which with each other, as to the books admitted, furnishes irrefragable evidence of the correctness of the canon as we have it."

This opinion is rendered still more probable by "the scrupulous care which the early Churches took to discriminate spurious compositions from such as were authentic—the existence among some of doubt regarding certain of the New Testament books, indicating that each Church claimed the right of satisfying itself in this matter—their high veneration for the genuine apostolic writings—their anxious regard for each other's prosperity leading to the free communication from one to another of whatever could promote this, and, of course, among other things, of those writings that had been entrusted to any one of them, and by which, more than by any other means, the spiritual welfare of the whole would be promoted —the practice of the Fathers of arguing the canonicity of any book, from its reception by the Churches, a sufficient proof of this—and the reason assigned by Eusebius (iii. 25) for dividing the books of the New Testament into $\delta\mu o\lambda o\gamma o\acute{\upsilon}\mu\epsilon\nu o\iota$ and $\dot{\alpha}\nu\tau\iota\lambda\epsilon\gamma\acute{o}\mu\epsilon\nu o\iota$, viz. that the former class was composed of those which the universal tradition of the Churches authenticated, while the latter contained such as had been received by the majority, but not by all. . . . Thus by the natural process of each body of Christians seeking to procure for themselves and to convey to their brethren authentic copies of writings, in which all were deeply interested, the canon of the New Testament was formed."—*Cyclopædia of Biblical, Theological, and Ecclesiastical Literature.*

(3)

"If every copy of the New Testament had been destroyed at the end of the 3rd century (*i.e.* by Diocletian's nefarious attempt to extinguish the book), it was asked 'whether it could have been recovered from the extracts made from it in the works of the Fathers of the 2nd and 3rd centuries.' . . . Lord Hales said to Dr. Buchanan, 'You remember the strange question about the Fathers and the New Testament, which was put by one of the company at Mr. Abercrombie's two months ago. . . . As I possessed all the extant Fathers of the 2nd and 3rd centuries, I commenced the search; and up to this present time, I have found the entire New Testament, all but eleven verses.'"—*New Companion to the Bible.*

APPENDIX E.

THE CHARACTER AND DATE OF THE EPISTLE OF BARNABAS
(referred to p. 259).

IT is acknowledged on all sides that the external evidence is exceedingly strong in favour of Barnabas being the author of this epistle. Clemens Alexandrinus, in his *Stromata*, quotes it no less than seven times, and four of these times he attributes it to Barnabas, of whom he speaks as a fellow-labourer with Paul, one of the seventy, and an apostolic man; also as one who had preached along with Paul in the ministry of the Gentiles, and as the Apostle Barnabas. Origen embraced the same opinion; he cites the epistle as that of Barnabas, and speaks of it again as the Catholic Epistle of Barnabas. In like manner, Eusebius, though repudiating its canonicity, asserts its genuineness. The testimony of Jerome is still more explicit. He tells us that " Barnabas, a native of Cyprus, who is also called Joseph the Levite, being ordained along with Paul as an apostle of the Gentiles, composed one letter tending to the edification of the Church, which is read among the apocryphal Scriptures." Here, it will be observed, Jerome ascribes the letter to Barnabas, and admits its usefulness for edification; but while asserting its genuineness and orthodoxy, like Eusebius, he denies its canonicity.

The evidence urged against the authorship of Barnabas, the companion of Paul, is chiefly internal; and while we do not deny the weight to be attached to some of the arguments employed, we cannot help thinking that even these have been unduly pressed, and that sufficient allowance has not been made for the circumstances of the writer, and the character of his style. His want of sympathy with Judaism, and apparent misapprehension of some of its rites; his frequent and rather far-fetched allegorisings; and his supposed survival after the destruction of Jerusalem,—are the arguments mainly relied on by the opponents of its authorship by Barnabas, the companion of Paul. While noticing these arguments, it is not our intention to controvert them, or canvass them with much minuteness, though undoubtedly they are not so convincing as some seem to take for granted. His depreciation of Judaism, for example, would be quite in keeping with a design to divert the Jews from resting in the mere letter of the law, to which they are still so addicted, as also to dispose them to inquire after its spiritual meaning, that they might the more readily yield obedience to the Gospel. In a word, he meant, it would appear, to diminish that excessive veneration for the Jewish ritual that stood in the way of Christianity. The allegorisings, again, are perfectly consistent with the spirit of those times, and were possibly the kind of argument best suited to the allegorising habits and tendencies of those whom he addressed. At all events, they are a good deal like the allegorisings of Clemens Alexandrinus and Origen, and not altogether unlike Paul's allegorising in relation to Hagar and Sarah, Sinai and Jerusalem, in the 4th chapter of Galatians. Further, the denial of the authorship of Barnabas on the ground of his supposed death before the destruction of Jerusalem, is entirely gratuitous. In the absence of any historic reference to his death, or the time of its occurrence, we are at perfect liberty to assume that he survived that catastrophe.

Moreover, the assertion that this epistle, if written by Barnabas, would have been included in the canon, is unfounded. Though called an apostle by Clement, he was not an apostle in the strict sense of having received that office from our Lord Himself, or by direct divine appointment, as had been the case with Paul or the twelve. It is acknowledged that in Acts xiv. 14 he is spoken of as an apostle in conjunction with Paul. Nor are we warranted in supposing that all the writings of apostolic men were preserved, or intended to be preserved, or meant to be included in the canon, if they had been preserved. Nor are we to suppose that apostolic men always wrote or spoke under special divine inspiration.

Peter was not moved by inspiration, but acting in his own individual capacity, when blamed by Paul; at the same time, what they did speak or record by divine authority for permanent instruction, the Church was divinely guided to treat as divine, and treasure up accordingly. The same Providence that guarded an inspired writer from error, guided, we are fully persuaded, in the choice of those writings that, owing to their inspiration, were entitled to, and designed for, insertion in the canon. Nothing but the same gift of the Spirit that produced inspiration could account for that unerring tact and fine discriminating instinct of the early Church in accepting those writings, and those only, that, as there is every reason to believe, had been given by inspiration. The marked inferiority of this Epistle of Barnabas as compared with Hebrews, when both treat of Old Testament topics, is sufficient to convince us of the undoubted inspiration of the latter, and of its entire absence in the former. The canonicity of the Epistle of Barnabas, then, we repudiate; its apostolicity is generally questioned, and is certainly very questionable; but its antiquity cannot be reasonably doubted.

Yet, after all, the most important point in our present inquiry is the date of this letter, which is adduced not because of its intrinsic merits or demerits, be they what they may, but as a witness to the reception and estimation of Scripture at the time to which it belongs. Now there appear to be two limits within which the date of this letter must lie. The one is the destruction of Jerusalem, A.D. 70, mentioned by the writer in the 16th chapter, and mentioned as something recent; the other is the rebuilding of the city, under the name of Ælia Capitolina, by Hadrian, in A.D. 119. The reference to Jerusalem is as follows:—"Because of their warring, the temple is *now* destroyed by their enemies; and those very servants of their enemies shall build it up." Others connect the νῦν with the second clause, which they render accordingly: "Now also those very servants of their enemies shall build it up." From the statement about rebuilding the temple in a spiritual sense, and no mention about rebuilding the city, it is inferred that Ælia Capitolina had not yet been founded. Another note of time occurs in the 4th chapter, to the following effect: "Consider yet this also: since you have seen so great signs and wonders in the people of the Jews, and so the Lord hath forsaken them." These signs and prodigies are understood to refer to those that happened before, and at the destruction of Jerusalem, and so to be fresh in the memory of the persons addressed. It may be added that another reading of the Latin is *derelinquit*, that is, *forsakes* them, in the present tense. The lower limit of date is fixed by Hefele at 137 A.D., when the second Jewish war terminating, put an end to the strifes of Jewish Christians, and to all dangers from Judaisers; others, at a period considerably before the work of Clemens Alexandrinus, as the existence of the epistle must have preceded by several years the citation of it by that Father. But even some who impugn its genuineness, and try to bring down its date as low as possible, acknowledge that all indications point to a time somewhere within the first quarter of the 2nd century. Thus, at the very latest, it must have been somewhere between 70 and 120 A.D.

INDEX.

	PAGE
ABARBANEL,	332
Antilegomena or Disputed Books,	233
Apocrypha—	
Not quoted by our Lord and His apostles,	296
Not quoted by early Christian writers,	297
Not regarded as canonical by Josephus,	296
Written in Greek with two exceptions,	296
History of admission into the canon,	298
Aquinas, Thomas,	17
Aristotle—	
His ethical system,	85
Its defects,	86
Relation to Socrates,	67
Athanasius,	352
Augustine—	
His definition of miracle,	17
His explanation of miracle,	17
Helped the introduction of the Apocrypha into the canon,	297
BABA BATHRA,	309
Babbage,	37
Bardsley on the Palestine Exploration,	344
Barnabas,	258
Baur,	353
Brown,	19
Bunsen,	355
Butler—	
Relation of miracle to a course of nature,	17

	PAGE
Answer to objection from false miracles,	34
CAMPBELL,	29
Canon—	
Explanation of the term,	204
Theories of canonicity,	205
Claim to divine direction by N. T. penmen,	225
Admission of the same by their contemporaries and successors,	257
Testimony to, and citation of, N. T. Books by Barnabas,	259
—— by Clemens Rom.,	258
—— by Polycarp,	259
—— by Ignatius,	260
Detailed account of certain books of N. T. canon,	234–257
Of Marcion,	264
Of Muratori,	265
Testimony to the canonical books of N. T. by Irenæus,	265
—— by Clemens Alex.,	271
—— by Tertullian,	273
—— by Origen,	272
Principle of the formation of O. T. canon,	299
Testimony of Apocrypha, Philo, and Josephus to inspiration of O. T. canon,	302
Period of the close of O. T. canon,	305
Books of O. T. canon according to Melito,	293
—— according to Jerome,	294

368　INDEX.

	PAGE
Chalmers—	
On testimony,	29
On verbal inspiration,	124
Chrysostom,	354
Cicero—	
On immortality of the soul,	13
His ethical treatise,	87
Comte,	31
Conder, Lieutenant,	64
Cureton,	354
DELITZSCH,	65, 177, 196
Delphic response,	44
Demosthenes,	117
Dionysius of Corinth,	278
Discrepancies, Reconcilement of—	
Between N. T. writers,	139–145
Between sacred and secular writers,	145, 149
Between O. and N.T. writers,	146, 154
ECCLESIASTES—	
Objections to the Solomonic authorship of, stated and answered,	187–199
Relation of the book of, to Job and Proverbs,	200
Its linguistic peculiarities accounted for,	198
Analogous case,	199
Why *Elohim* is the name of God in this book,	198
Egypt, Prophecies concerning—	
By Ezekiel,	51
By Jeremiah,	51
Encyclopædia Britannica,	328
Epictetus,	88
Epicurus—	
His system of morals,	90
Its principle embodied in certain modern systems,	91
Its practical side,	95
Eusebius, *H. E.* iii. 36,	351
Ewald,	187
Experimental evidence,	102
FATHERS in relation to the canon—	
The apostolic,	258–260
The most eminent of, in the second century,	264

	PAGE
Florinus,	270
French Rabbi,	335
GALLIO,	153
Gesenius,	187
Gibbon,	41
HAMILTON, Sir William,	21
Hävernick,	310
Hebrews, Epistle to the—	
Pauline authorship of,	244
Canonicity of,	245
Omission of superscription,	251
Hug's opinion in reference to its Pauline authorship,	252
Hefele,	365
Hippolytus (*Philosophumena*),	278, 355
Hitzig,	48
Hofmann,	305
Homer—	
Reference to his works,	288
His statement on influence of slavery,	52
His evidence on the extent of Thebes,	54
IBN EZRA,	321, 323
Inspiration—	
Not mechanical,	106
Includes both matter and manner,	110
Not omniscience,	115
Supposed degrees of,	118
Claimed by sacred penmen,	119
Verbal, Proof of,	121
Objections thereto stated and answered,	125–129
The possession of, by N. T. writers acknowledged by their contemporaries and immediate successors,	257
Irenæus—	
His connection with the apostles by a single yet twofold link,	265
His relation to three Churches,	267
Importance of his testimony,	268
JAMES, Epistle of,	256
Jerome,	362

INDEX.

	PAGE
John the Evangelist—	
Johannean authorship of the fourth Gospel proved by external and internal evidence,	60
His minute acquaintance with Palestine,	61
His Gospel contrasted with the synoptic Gospels,	69
Difference of style between his Gospel and Revelation accounted for,	76
Character of our Lord's discourses in his Gospel and in the Synoptists,	66
A parallel case,	67
Difference in the course of events in his Gospel and in the Synoptists,	71
Reconcilement,	72–75
Josephus—	
The weight to be attached to his testimony,	287
His important statement in relation to the canon,	288
Jude, Epistle of,	257
KANT,	16
Kaye,	35
Keil and Delitzsch, Commentary,	317
Keil, Introduction,	326
Koheleth, Various explanations of the term,	187
LAW of Nature—	
What is it?	21
It does not explain the origin of phenomenal succession,	21
It does not create it,	21
Agent lost sight of in the law according to which he acts,	21
Lightfoot, Bishop,	238, 354
Lucian of Samosata,	357
MACCABEES II.,	307
Mill,	19, 21
Miracle—	
Names of, in Scripture,	25
Various definitions of,	17
Is it a violation or suspension of a law of nature?	19
A superadded factor,	19
How is the new force introduced?	20
Withdrawal of miraculous powers from the Christian Church,	35
Differences between true miracles and false,	34
Objection from false miracles answered,	34
Mosheim,	42
Mozley,	31
NAHUM, Prophecy of,	46, 48
Nineveh, City of—	
Its position and wealth,	46
Its destruction,	47
Its entire disappearance,	46
Prophecies concerning,	47
OEHLER,	319
Oracles, Heathen,	44
Origen—	
His works,	272
His quotations of Scripture,	272
His strong assertion of the inspiration and divine authority of Scripture,	273
His Hom. vi. in Luc.,	351
His Prolog. in Cant. Cantic.,	351
PALEY, Horæ Paulinæ,	161
Papias, References to the Gospels,	236
Paulus,	56
Plato—	
Asserts man's need of revelation,	11
His account of the teaching of Socrates,	68
His ethical system,	86
His cardinal virtues,	87
His allegory of a chariot,	87
Polycarp,	350
Prophecy—	
Nature of it,	43
Conditions,	43
Predictions in secular history,	45
Oracles of the heathen,	44
Minute fulfilment of,	47
Continued fulfilment,	49

Three notable examples of fulfilment,	45-55
Pusey,	196
QUESTIONES Naturales,	45
Questions, Tusculan,	13
RASHI,	321
Renan—	
His legendary theory,	57
His admissions with respect to the Gospels,	236
SENECA—	
His supposed prediction,	45
His Stoicism,	88
Smith, J., Esq., Jordanhill,	178
Socrates,	11, 67
Stoics,	87
Strauss—	
His *Leben Jesu*,	79
His mythical system,	57
TAYLOR,	211
Tertullian—	
His apology to the governor of proconsular Africa,	40
His other works,	273
His citations of Scripture,	274-276
Testimony—	
Belief in,	29
Corrected by experience,	29
UTILITARIAN system,	101
VALENTINIAN, the Gnostic,	355
Vandevelde,	83
Verbanus, Lake,	257
Vitringa,	311
WESTCOTT,	272
Wordsworth,	231
Wouvermans,	83
Wunderbar,	177
XENOPHON—	
The retreat of the ten thousand,	46
His memoirs,	92
YOUNG, Professor,	37
ZENO,	87
Zumpt,	149

THE END.

www.ingramcontent.com/pod-product-compliance
Lightning Source LLC
Chambersburg PA
CBHW031420230426
43668CB00007B/379